A SHORT HISTORY OF
THE CATHOLIC CHURCH

Books by J. Derek Holmes

MORE ROMAN THAN ROME: English Catholicism in the nineteenth century

THE TRIUMPH OF THE HOLY SEE: A Short History of the Papacy in the nineteenth century

THE PAPACY IN THE MODERN WORLD, 1914–78

A SHORT HISTORY
OF THE
CATHOLIC CHURCH

J. DEREK HOLMES
and
BERNARD W. BICKERS

BURNS & OATES

First published 1983

by Burns & Oates
Wellwood, North Farm Road
Tunbridge Wells, Kent TN2 3DR

ISBN (UK) 0 86012 126 7 (hardback)
ISBN (UK) 0 86012 133 X (paperback)

Typeset by Inforum Ltd, Portsmouth
Printed and bound in Great Britain by Biddles Ltd, Guildford, Surrey

Contents

Authors' preface

It can be argued that the history of the Church began with the Descent of the Holy Spirit at Pentecost and will end with the Second Coming of Christ, in other words, with events of theological significance beyond the scope of mere historical description. But the historical character of the Church ultimately rests on the fact of the Incarnation and the implications of the Sacramental Principle, the belief that the historically human can also be doctrinally divine. The Church is an institution or society made up of human beings, is dependent on the human condition; in its growth and development, in its attempt to penetrate and influence human civilization, the Church has used historical circumstances and adapted itself to them. Whatever understanding of the Church, or interpretation of its past, historians might wish to adopt, they must always respect the academic demands of their discipline in spite of possible tensions between theological and historical opinions and claims.

Ecclesiastical history is limited by its sources, their content, accuracy and authenticity. It is in fact only as a result of the accessibility and critical study of the source material that the subject of Church history has been able to advance to the extent that is has since the seventeenth century. Church historians must also respect the findings of ancillary subjects such as chronology or palaeography, geography or sociology, economics and politics. Too often in the past historians have adopted unduly apologetic approaches to particular problems or have even imposed a 'non-historical orthodoxy' on earlier developments, whereas the great benefit of history is that, in the words of Professor Sir Owen Chadwick, it 'does more than any other discipline to free the mind from the tyranny of present opinion.' It is hoped, therefore, that this *Short History of the Catholic Church* will not only provide an up-to-date, reliable account of Church history, based on the latest historical research, but also contribute the necessary historical background to the deeper ecclesiastical, ecumenical and theological reflection which is still widespread even in this 'post-Christian' age.

Authors' acknowledgments

As lecturers in Church history we have long felt the need for a more updated short history than the immensely successful one first published in 1939 by the distinguished historian Philip Hughes, who was incidentally a former student of the college where we teach. We are therefore extremely grateful to Burns & Oates for giving us the opportunity of attempting to fill this need.

We are obviously greatly indebted to all those historians whose works we have consulted and used over the years, particularly those listed in 'Notes on further reading', and apologise if anywhere we appear to have been guilty of unconscious plagiarism.

Our colleagues and many of our students have also made valuable contributions, perhaps more than they themselves might sometimes imagine.

Finally we must express our deep thanks to Miss Teresa Mulhall who not only generously and conscientiously but willingly and eagerly deciphered and typed out various manuscripts.

The Feast of St Cuthbert   J.D.H. and B.W.B.
20 March 1983   Ushaw College, Durham

A SHORT HISTORY OF
THE CATHOLIC CHURCH

CHAPTER 1

The origins and early history of the Christian Church to 461

Christianity was born in one of the more remote outposts of the Roman Empire. Palestine, the birthplace of this new religion, lay at the eastern edge of the empire and had already taxed the Romans to an extent which belied its size and importance. Despite the politically stable but alien rule of Herod the Great (37BC–4BC), the Jews had never accepted him, and his decision on his death to divide the territory between his three sons plunged the country into a period of civil disturbance. By 6BC a Roman Procurator, with a garrison of 3,000 men, was resident in the coastal town of Caesarea. The Procurator was responsible for external affairs and financial matters, while the Sanhedrin, presided over by the High Priest, conducted internal and religious affairs. This division of power reflected the special status of the Jews within the empire.

Judaism was unique in that the Jews believed themselves to be in possession of a revelation by God which marked them out as the Chosen People. Their history, as detailed in the sacred writings, was dominated by a belief in the providence of God who would send the Messiah in the fullness of time. The precise nature of this messiah was coloured by the experiences of the people, and, by the time of Christ, their great desire for freedom from political oppression led many to look for a political figure who would bring about such freedom. During the Occupation, the Jews, both in Palestine and those who had settled in other cities, known as the Jews of the Diaspora, won concessions which safeguarded their freedom of worship, gave them exemption from the Cult of the Emperor and allowed them to be judged by their own law, a law which assumed enormous importance in their lives. As long as Christianity was regarded as part of Judaism it enjoyed the same rights, but once the differences between the two became manifest, the Christians found

themselves vulnerable in an empire which would willingly acknowledge another religion but which resisted, with hostility, their claim
to religious exclusiveness.

The Roman policy of allowing people freedom of worship had led
to a great number of religions. The ancient Greek and Roman gods
were now in decline, but there was a marked interest in the Eastern
mystery cults, which offered the initiated the answers to man's most
basic questions and held out the promise of life after death. From
Egypt, Asia Minor, Syria and Iran gods and goddesses of morality,
civilisation, fertility and agriculture made their impact within the
empire. The lower classes were more likely to be affected by such
popular manifestations of religion as astrology, magic, the interpretation of dreams and miracles. Neither the mystery cults nor the
popular religions were in any sense universal throughout the empire.
The only cult which could claim anything approximating a State
Religion was the Cult of the Emperor. This practice had been
brought from the East by Augustus (Emperor, 27BC–14AD) and
gradually, after him, emperors on their death were enrolled among
the ever increasing list of gods. In the first century AD some emperors,
Nero among them, grew impatient of delay and demanded divine
status during their lives. Since this particular cult was closely linked
with the power of the state, refusal to take part in it could be, and
sometimes indeed was, construed as treason, and the Christians soon
discovered that their abhorrence of emperor worship led to the
suspicion that it was impossible to be both a loyal citizen and a
Christian.

The historical sources for the initial birth and early life of the
Church are meagre and detailed evidence almost non-existent. However it is possible to reconstruct a basic outline which indicates both
the growth of the Church's mission and its conflict with orthodox
Judaism. The increase in numbers, due to the vigorous and effective
preaching of the apostle Peter, led to the necessity of appointing
others to free the Twelve from domestic duties to continue their
ministry of evangelising. The first recorded helpers were the seven
deacons, all of whom had Greek names – which raised the question
of the relationship between the Greek and Hebrew Christians in
Jerusalem. One of them, Stephen, was the first to be killed by the
Jews, probably about 37AD, and this open hostility was heightened
during the reign of Herod Aggrippa (42–4AD) who harrassed the
Christians in a blatant attempt to win the support of the Jews.
During his reign James the Elder was martyred and the leadership of
the Jerusalem Church passed to the other James who survived until
his own martyrdom, c.62AD. Jewish hostility towards Christianity

reached a climax in Jerusalem between 66–70AD. During this period of the Jewish revolt against the Romans, the Jewish Christians emigrated to Pella in northern Greece, an act which was regarded as treachery by those Orthodox Jews who remained to fight until the destruction of the city in 70AD.

Of all those responsible for taking the Christian gospel to the Gentiles, none compared in stature or significance with Paul. His initial distrust and persecution of the Church was matched only by his future acceptance and missionary endeavours. In three great missionary journeys between 46–58AD, Paul was responsible for founding Christian communities in modern-day Syria, Turkey, Yugoslavia, the Greek mainland and islands, and Cyprus. Wherever he went he preached initially in the synagogues and only after being rebuffed did he turn to the gentiles. With them he concentrated on the basic Christian message of Jesus' resurrection, aiming to create a group capable of existing on its own, thus freeing him to establish new communities. He kept in touch with his foundations both by return visits and by letter, answering their difficulties, and helping them to build on the rudimentary instruction, basic liturgy and primitive organisation that he had left them. His most difficult and yet his most important task was to give these individual communities a sense of belonging to one Church. His success in creating this consciousness not only avoided a decisive split between Christians of Jewish and pagan backgrounds, but also created a solidarity which was to be enormously important in the struggles still to come.

In 49AD Paul went to Jerusalem to attend a meeting with Peter and James and other leaders to discuss the question of the necessity of circumcision for gentile converts to Christianity. The community at Antioch, divided on the question, had sent Paul to ask the advice of the Jerusalem Church. After both sides had put their case the decision went in favour of Paul, namely denying the necessity of circumcision. It is difficult to overstate the importance of this meeting, opening as it did the pagan world to the Christian Gospel, raising questions of authority in the Church, and demonstrating the growing awareness of the differences between Judaism and Christianity.

The sources are less forthcoming about the missionary activities of the other apostles. Paul himself acknowledged the existence of other Christian communities which he did not found, and much later apocryphal writings linked Mark, the disciple of Peter, with Alexandria and Andrew, the brother of Peter, with Constantinople. Such claims are not historically reliable but they demonstrate the importance which the early Christians placed on apostolic foundations. Even our knowledge of Peter is very limited. That he enjoyed a special place during the life of Christ is seen from the Gospels, and that he continued to enjoy a place of prominence after Pentecost is witnessed in the Acts of the Apostles. After the Council of Jerusalem and a visit to Antioch *c*. 50AD, little is known. The strongest tradition links Peter with Rome, and if he did not found the Christian community there, he assumed the leadership of it. It was in Rome that he was martyred during the persecution of Nero, probably between 64–8AD.

As the apostolic era drew to an end, those who succeeded the apostles remained conscious of their links with them. In the second century the Christians struggled for survival on several fronts. There was the threat of physical persecution by the Roman government; a growing literary attack, developing from an ill-informed slander to a highly informed and critical attempt to destroy, through argument and ridicule, the very credibility of Christianity; and, finally, the insidious threat from heretical tendencies within the Church itself. Despite, or rather, because of such difficulties, the Church continued to grow and develop both in terms of self-understanding and organisation, clarifying her teaching and consolidating her structures.

The Christian claim to religious exclusiveness inevitably came into conflict with the Roman policy of religious toleration, especially after orthodox Judaism had disowned Christianity as a terrible blasphemy. The earliest non-Christian evidence of state persecution is given by the Roman historian Tacitus (*c*. 55–120AD), whose *Annals*, completed *c*. 115AD, contained the following extract in which the Emperor Nero made Christians the scapegoats for the fire of Rome in 64AD:

> Nero fastened the guilt and inflicted the most exquisite tortures on a class hated for their abominations, called Christians by the populace . . . accordingly an arrest was made of all who confessed, then upon their information an immense multitude was convicted, not so much of the crime of arson, as of hatred of mankind.

Tacitus was writing some fifty years after the event, by which time Christianity had spread significantly throughout the empire, and it is possible that he exaggerated the numbers persecuted which he calls 'an immense multitude'. There can be no doubt about his own opinion of the Christians, whom he distrusted and despised, and although he does not think they were guilty of starting the fire, which destroyed all but four of the fourteen wards of the city, he does believe that the Christians deserved to be punished, and that such persecution was popular among the pagans. Later claims, especially by Lactantius (*c*. 240–320), that this Roman persecution spread throughout the empire, are no longer supported. What seems clear is that Nero's persecution was possible because of a general attitude of hostility towards the Christians among those who suspected them of heinous crimes including atheism, immorality, cannibalism and secrecy.

There is little evidence of any serious change of attitude during the long reign of Domitian (68–98AD). None of the sources suggests any widespread or state-controlled persecutions, although Christian writings like the *Book of the Apocalypse* and the *Letters of Clement of Rome*, and pagan authors like Epictetus and Dio Cassius, suggest that individuals were martyred during this time. Apparently by the close of the first century, Christianity was attracting converts from the highest echelons of Roman society. In 91AD no less an official than the Roman consul Glabrio was condemned and executed, at least in part, on suspicion of being a Christian. Dio Cassius mentions Domitilla, possibly Domitian's own sister, as another who suffered exile because of her Christian beliefs. Such incidents suggest that the Roman authorities were prepared to allow the lower classes to embrace Christianity without too much discouragement, but were adamant that such leniency would not be shown to the aristocracy and ruling classes. Domitian's own insistence on emperor worship, according himself the title 'Dominus et Deus', inevitably heightened the difficulty for those who refused to participate in such a cult.

The next major source of information comes from the surviving correspondence of Emperors Trajan and Hadrian – whose reigns spanned forty years from 98–138AD – with some of their local governors. About the year 112 Trajan sent Pliny the Younger to Bithinia, a Roman province in Asia Minor which had suffered greatly in the recent past due to bad administration. On his arrival Pliny was confronted by the Christian 'problem' of which, on his own admission, he had been previously ignorant.

It is my custom, Lord Emperor, to refer to you all questions whereof I am in doubt . . . In investigations of Christians I have never taken part; hence I do not know what is the crime usually punished or investigated, or what allowances are made. So I have had no little uncertainty whether there is any distinction of age, or whether the very weakest offenders are treated exactly like the stronger; whether pardon is given to those who repent, or whether a man who has once been a Christian gains nothing by having ceased to be such; whether punishment attaches to the mere name apart from secret crimes, or to the secret crimes connected with the name.

In this passage Pliny sums up the uncertainty under which the Christians lived. He then goes on to tell Trajan what he was actually doing:

> Meantime this is the course I have taken with those who were accused before me as Christians. I asked them whether they were Christians, and if they confessed, I asked them a second and a third time with threats of punishment. If they kept to it I ordered their execution; for I held no question that whatever it was that they admitted, in any case obstinacy and unbending perversity deserve to be punished. There were others of the like insanity; but as these were Roman citizens, I noted them down to be sent to Rome.

Pliny then mentions that Christians were being denounced to him by informers, of whom some remained anonymous. He mentions several people who claimed that they had, for a time, been Christian but had ceased to be such. He even gives an insight into the practice of Christianity:

> They maintained, however, that the amount of their fault or error had been this, that it was their habit on a fixed day to assemble before daylight and recite by turns a form of words to Christ as a god; and that they bound themselves with an oath, not for any crime, but not to commit theft or robbery or adultery, not to break their word, and not to deny a deposit when demanded. After this was done their custom was to depart, and to meet again to take food, but ordinary and harmless food; and even this (they said) they had given up doing after the issue of my edict, by which in accordance with your commands I had forbidden the existence of clubs.

Pliny interrogated two women 'called deaconesses' in an attempt to obtain more information but: 'I discovered nothing else than a perverse and extravagant superstition'. Not only does this letter demonstrate Pliny's confusion about the right course of action to take, but it also suggests the extent of Christianity by the beginning of the second century, especially in Asia Minor. 'The matter seemed to me worth deliberation especially on account of the number of those in danger; for many of all ages and every rank, and also of both sexes, are brought into present and future danger. The contagion of that superstition has penetrated not only the cities, but the villages and country; yet it seems possible to stop it and set it right.'

Trajan replied commending the course of action taken by his governor, reminding him that there was no universal law against Christianity, but suggesting that each case should be judged on its own merits. Though the emperor disapproved of actively seeking out Christians and positively condemned anonymous denunciation, he agreed that anyone accused, convicted and persisting in his faith, deserved punishment; but anyone denouncing his faith, sacrificing to the gods and cursing Christ, should be freed. No proof of any other crime was necessary. There was no attempt to justify this position or appeal to precedents; rather, under Trajan, the plight of Christians was dependent on the policy of individual governors. Tertullian in his *Apology, c.*197, wrote:

> What a decision, how inevitably entangled! He says they must not be sought out, implying they are innocent and he orders them to be punished, implying they are guilty. He spares them and rages against them, he pretends not to see and he punishes.
>
> (*Apology* 2.8)

Despite this precarious position there are relatively few named martyrs from this reign, although Simeon, the aged leader of the Church of Jerusalem, and Ignatius of Antioch are two whom the sources do mention.

Emperor Hadrian went further in offering guidelines to Fundanus, the Proconsul of Asia. In a letter written *c.*125 he again condemned anonymous denunciations, adding that anyone found guilty of wrongful denunciation must suffer the punishment that would have befallen the accused. Further, he wanted positive proof that a Christian was guilty of 'offending against the existing laws' after which he was to be punished according 'to the gravity of the offence'. At first sight this appeared to bring considerable relief to the Christians, and the Apologist Justin Martyr suggested that this did improve conditions for the Christians of Asia. However this was a directive to one individual governor and there was no guarantee that such apparent leniency was practised elsewhere in the empire. The overall situation during the reign of Antoninus Pius (138–61) remained very similar. There is evidence of several individual martyrdoms, the most famous and best documented being that of Polycarp of Smyrna, but there is no evidence of any widespread attempt to rid the empire of Christianity.

Against such a background of uncertainty, the Church had not only to survive but to grow and develop. Insights into this development are given in the writings of the so-called Apostolic Fathers. The more important members of this group included Clement of Rome (*fl.*96), Ignatius of Antioch (d.*c.*117), and Polycarp of Smyrna (d.156). Other anonymous or compiled works include the *Didache* (*c.*100) and the *Shepherd of Hermas* (*c.*150). From a study of such writings certain conclusions emerge about the life of the Church. As well as the conflict with the Roman State there was still a major controversy with Judaism. The Christian authors answered charges made against them by the Jews by claiming that the latter had lost their right to be called the 'Chosen People'. Their rejection and killing of Jesus, the Messiah, meant that the Christians now enjoyed the favour once given to the Jews. With such a stress on the crucial significance of Jesus, the Apostolic Fathers constantly mention his death and resurrection as the central act of redemption.

The Christians were beginning to add new prayers to those they had inherited from the Jews, prayers characterised by their emphasis on hope and thanksgiving. They were conscious of the importance of baptism and of the Eucharist, although their writings reflect the slow development of the sacramental life of the Church. One discussion centred on the possibility of forgiveness for serious sin after baptism, and the division between the rigorists, who denied such a possibility, and the realists, who were prepared to countenance it, proved to be prophetic of a much keener debate in the third century; for the widespread apostasies then, during the Decian persecution, forced the Church to develop her understanding of penance.

Theological development did not, on the whole, keep pace with developments in the Church's organisation. The apostles had enjoyed supreme authority in the Church, but even during the apostolic period other offices had emerged, firstly the office of deacon and secondly an office which was named both presbyter (priest) and overseer (bishop), the two terms being originally interchangeable for the same office. With the deaths of the apostles the question of leadership and authority became increasingly important. Within a town or city there would be one Christian community and, within that community, authority was shared by two major offices. Clement of Rome, the *Didache*, and the *Shepherd of Hermas*, all witnessed to this situation. There was one major exception, however, which is the earliest written evidence of a further separation of office into a threefold ministry. Writing to the Christians at Smyrna, Ignatius of Antioch (d.110AD) refers to the situation in Antioch where the overseer (bishop) enjoyed ultimate authority and was helped in his ministry by the presbyters (priests) and the deacons, the latter two groups sharing in the bishop's authority to the extent they were invited, or delegated, to do so by him. This Ignatian model was known as the monarchical episcopate, and by the late second century, and certainly no later than 250, it was to be the pattern throughout the Church. Such a development, which gave to one person, the bishop, ultimate authority in the community, became an essential pre-requisite for the claims made by the Bishop of Rome for a position of primacy within the Church as a whole.

The Church needed a strong organisation and a sense of unity to survive further persecution under Emperor Marcus Aurelius (161–80). Originally he was regarded as friendly towards the Christians, but during his reign there was an increase in the number of martyr-doms, and evidence of whole groups, as well as individuals, being executed. At Lyons in Gaul in the summer of 177, following a rise in popular feeling against the Christians, trials were held in which Christians from the town, and from neighbouring Vienne, were tried and found guilty of persisting in their belief. A group, later tradition mentions 48 people, was then martyred. Three years later in 180 a group of twelve Christians, all named, were condemned at Scilli in North Africa by the governor Saturninus. According to Tertullian he was the first governor to persecute Christians in North Africa. Martyrdom was the ultimate punishment, but writers also mention fines, forced labour, confiscation of property and exile.

One of the reasons for this increased persecution under Marcus Aurelius was a growth in the literary polemic against the Church, a polemic which attempted to discredit Christianity by ridicule, invective and logical argument. In response to this attack there arose within the Church literature known as the 'Apology', and writers known as 'Apologists'. Literary attacks on Christianity were not new. The first century had witnessed several examples, but such writings were united by their lack of knowledge and understanding of the Christian faith rather than by any serious discussion or dialogue with Christianity. What was new in the second century was precisely a desire to understand this new religion, which had survived persecution, and seemed to be growing both in numbers and importance. Such writers as Crescens, Fronto and Lucian of Samosata accused the Christians of everything from atheism to incredulity. Of greatest importance, and the writer who posed the direst threat to the Church, was Celsus with the publication of his *True Discourse*, c.180. Although this book is no longer extant, Origen's reply some seventy years later in eight volumes, testifies to the enormous impact which Celsus had, both on his contemporaries and in the third century.

With the apparent attitude of the detached observer, Celsus made strenuous efforts to understand Christianity both by reading the scriptures and by having long discussions with Christians. The result of his research was the *True Discourse* in which he aggressively attacked Christianity at the level both of doctrine and of practice. Besides denying the Christian doctrines of revelation, creation and

incarnation, he presented a deeply offensive picture of Christ, por-
traying him as a charlatan who had attracted followers through
deception and witchcraft. Those who now called themselves Christian, he said, were drawn from the lowest dregs of society, little more
than criminals, and, like the one they followed, were proving themselves to be subversive by their constant refusal to obey the laws of
the state and by their desire to undermine the 'Old Religion'. The
State should therefore do everything in its power to crush Christianity once and for all.

Answering such accusations was the major task of the Apologists.
They gave a reasoned defence of the Christian position, attempting
to persuade the authorities of the right of Christianity to exist in
peace, and to dispel popular misunderstanding. Several people are
numbered among the Apologists: Quadratus and Aristides who
addressed their works to the emperor Trajan; Justin Martyr (d.165);
Tatian, famous for his 'Diatesseron' which was an attempt to create
a single gospel narrative out of the different ones available, and who,
because of his extremism, was forced out of the Church and became
the founder of the Enchratites; Athenagoras and Theophilus who
lived towards the end of the century; and finally Melito of Sardis of
whose writings only fragments remain.

Of these Justin Martyr is the most famous. He was born of pagan
parents in Samaria c.100 and came to Christianity through various
philosophical schools and systems, being baptised c.130. Sometime
after this he moved to Rome, where he opened a school through
which he exerted great influence on his own students and future
Christian writers, the most famous being Irenaeus (c.130–200). He
addressed his 'First Apology' (c.155) to the emperor Antoninus Pius
and his 'Second Apology' (c.162) to the Roman Senate. In between
he published his 'Dialogue with Trypho the Jew' which he claimed
was a record of the conversations between himself, the representative of Christianity, and Trypho, the representative of Judaism. In
165 he and some of his colleagues were denounced as Christians and,
under the changed atmosphere of Marcus Aurelius, were found
guilty of persisting in their beliefs and were executed.

Justin represents a significant advance both in theology and
apologetics. He is firmly monotheistic, and yet, with him, there are
the beginnings of a trinitarian formula. Against Jewish claims to the
contrary, Justin maintained that Jesus was the Messiah who fulfilled
the Old Testament, and whose death and resurrection were the
means of salvation for all who believed in him. Christians are initiated into the life of Christ by baptism and sustained by the Eucharist.
In all this Justin was claiming that Christianity was not only viable

but was 'the only certain and adequate philosophy'. He also refuted claims that Christians were guilty of immorality, incredulity and sub-version. Christians were exemplary citizens, displaying qualities of truthfulness and charity. Given the chance, they would add greatly to the Roman way of life and the state would gain from an active and flourishing Christian presence.

Taken as a group, the writings of the Apologists mark a develop-ment in theological expression from the Apostolic Fathers who preceded them. At the level of apologetic they failed in their main objective of placing Christianity on an equal footing with other religions so as to allow the Christians the opportunity of showing their value; but they did help to bolster the Church against an extremely hostile and dangerous attack, and they marked an impor-tant stage in Christian literature.

A further threat to the Church in this period came from within. Almost from the very beginning of its existence the Church had to cope with ideas which were somehow inconsistent with her basic teaching. Paul had warned against elitism on the one hand and syncretism on the other, and both of these ideas were found in a religious system which modern scholars have labelled Gnosticism, the various origins of which, despite the discovery in 1944–5 of an extensive Gnostic library in Upper Egypt, are still debated. There were traces of Gnosticism in milieux other than Christianity, notably among the Syrians, Iranians and the Jews. As the name suggests, the basic teaching of this system is that redemption comes through knowledge; and Gnosticism has been described as 'a system which taught cosmic redemption through knowledge'. This knowledge explained man's fundamental questions about his existence, purpose and future. Also central to Gnosticism is a tenet borrowed from the dualistic systems prevalent in the East, namely the division between the spiritual, which was good, and the material, which was evil.

Gnosticism appeared in several different forms normally associ-ated with, and named after, the founder or leader of a particular group; among them Saturninus in Syria, Basilides in Egypt, and Valentinus in Rome. Added to these there were also fringe groups, including the Barbello-Gnostics, the Naaseens, the Sethians and the Ophites. The Gnostics taught that the created world was the work, not of the Supreme God, but of a lesser god whom they called the Demiurge. This created world was the world of matter in which man was trapped. Some men possessed within them a divine spark or seed, a spiritual element, which, through knowledge, could be returned to a spiritual union with the Supreme God. This elitist group was known as the 'Spirituals' and they were distinct from the vast majority of humanity which had no hope of salvation. The purpose of Christ was to bring this knowledge, gnosis, as the messenger of the Supreme Being, and thus to effect a reunion. Since such a messenger must not be tainted with evil, Christ could not have been human, but only appeared to be so.

Though the different groups differed in detail, even this brief account highlights several points of dispute with orthodox Christianity. Against the Gnostic division of God, the Christians insisted on faith in one God. Against the dualistic division of spirit and matter, the Christians proclaimed the goodness of creation and material things. Against the notion of an apparent, or docetic,* Christ, whose sufferings were apparent rather than real, the Christians professed Jesus to be fully human and that he underwent bodily death and resurrection.

Included under the umbrella of Gnosticism, though arguably not strictly a Gnostic, and certainly highly critical of the more speculative aspects of the system, was Marcion (born c. 110). The number of Christian authors who wrote against Marcion indicates the impact he made. A native of Asia Minor, he was well educated and prosperous. After a conflict with the Christian community of his home town, Marcion travelled to Rome c. 140 where he quickly became a member of the Christian community. While in Rome he probably came into contact with the Gnostic Cerdon, from Syria, and during discussions with him, Marcion began to formulate his own doctrine. In 144 Marcion bowed out of orthodox Christianity to organise his own communities. In many places where Christianity flourished, a Marcionite community also flourished, vying, often successfully, with the orthodox for converts. After his death c. 160 his followers continued to pose a threat to the Church, but with the turn of the century many of them were absorbed into Manichaeism, though some continued in their own right to a later date.

Marcion was convinced of a distinction between the God of Law, as represented in the Septuagint – the Old Testament writings which had been adopted in their entirety by the Christian Church – and the God of Love revealed by Jesus. This contrast had only been fully grasped by the apostle Paul, and, because of this, Marcion took Paul's writings, at least the ones known to him, as the basis of his scriptures, adding selected parts of Luke's gospel. To demonstrate the differences between law and love he wrote his *Antitheses* which were, according to him, a series of contradictions between the Sep-

---

* Docetism – the belief that the humanity of Christ, his sufferings and his death were apparent rather than real.

tuagint and Paul's writings, proving beyond doubt the unbridgeable gulf between the God of Law and the God of Love. His dualism had theological and practical consequences. He divided God, denied the goodness of creation, the possibility of incarnation and presented a docetic Christ; and he imposed on his followers a strict moral code, rejecting marriage and championing personal austerity. His clearly defined canon of scripture, his extremely well organised communities and his obvious similarities with orthodox Christianity, forced the Church to respond to him in particular, and to the Gnostics in general.

This response came in the first instance from individual Church leaders, Justin, Irenaeus, Dionysius of Carthage, Tertullian and others who pointed out the dangers and excesses of Marcion. However, by formulating his own canon of scripture, he forced the Church to examine her own understanding of the scriptures. The starting point of any discussion was the Septuagint. With the passing of time and the deaths of the last eye-witnesses of the life of Christ, with the geographical distances between the communities and the catechetical needs of the missionary Church, certain works and letters had been written, which had already achieved a certain importance, but which as yet had not been officially approved. By 170 Melito of Sardis referred to the Septuagint as 'The Old Testament', and, even though he does not speak of a New Testament, it would seem that by this time certain other writings were now on a par with the Septuagint. Twenty years later a document known as 'The Muratorian Fragment' gave a list of writings acknowledged by the Roman Church, a list which bears a striking resemblance to the New Testament as we know it, although the first recorded use of the term came with Tertullian c.200.

The question of selection was enormously important and here the Church invoked the principle of tradition. Only those books which were of apostolic origin, that is, either written or commissioned by an apostle, were to be considered. Those responsible for judging a book in this way were the leaders of the communities who could trace their unbroken succession back to the apostolic period. Positively this assured the place of tradition as an essential element in the Church's life, and negatively it stripped Marcion's collection, or any other such collection, of any authority. Finally in terms of selection, a work must conform to the so-called 'Rule of Faith', a primitive credal formula used at the solemn initiation rite of baptism. Marcion had galvanised the Church into creating its canon of scripture.

Within a decade of Marcion's death another heresy emerged which took its name from Montanus who, c.170, proclaimed himself the New Prophet, the mouthpiece of the Holy Spirit. Montanism started in Phrygia and Montanus was quickly joined by two women, Priscilla and Maximilla. Together they created a wave of enthusiasm and popular support by insisting on the imminence of the second coming of Christ, even giving details of time and place. Pepuza, a town in Phrygia, was to be the location for this event and to prepare for the second coming Montanus at first demanded perpetual fasting, later relaxed to two full days a week, together with other ascetical practices. The aspect which attracted most attention was his teaching on martyrdom. The Montanists were not to avoid martyrdom, rather they should actively seek it out. This, at least in part, caused the promulgation of an edict in 177 by Emperor Marcus Aurelius banning fanatical sects.

Montanism spread quickly both eastwards towards and into Syria, and westwards as far as Gaul. Zephyrinus, the Bishop of Rome (199–217), initially welcomed the Montanists until he realised the true nature of their belief and practice after which he condemned the movement. By this time it was likely that Montanism would have died a natural death but for the fact that it was championed by one of the greatest Latin writers of all time, Quintus Septimus Florens Tertullian.

Tertullian was born c.160 in Carthage, where he was brought up by pagan parents who gave him a good education and encouraged him in a professional career. Towards the end of the second century he was converted to Christianity. Early in the third century he left orthodox Christianity and joined the Montanists, attracted both by their rigorous asceticism, which was in marked contrast to the lukewarmness of the Christians, and by their direct appeal to the Holy Spirit. However he did not accept Montanism uncritically, rather he changed the character to such an extent that some people question whether the heresy should still have been called Montanism after this time. He denied that Montanus and the two women had enjoyed ultimate authority; he reduced the role and importance of women and he made no reference to details of time and place surrounding the second coming. Instead he insisted on a state of preparedness best fulfilled by an ascetic life. This rigorism was demonstrated most obviously in his severity towards those guilty of grave sin, refusing them the possibility of reconciliation. In this he can be seen as a forerunner of Donatism, the heresy which was to split the North African Church in the fourth and fifth centuries. Despite his enormous literary powers – he has been called 'the father of Latin theology' – Tertullian failed to attract the great number of adherents who had followed Montanus, and, after his death in 225, the movement collapsed almost as quickly as it had arisen.

In its opposition to Montanism the Church again demonstrated the depth of her growing self-awareness. She refused to demand an unreasonable asceticism but presented a balanced attitude to Christian living which was in stark contrast to those groups who wanted to create a separatist Church of the 'Holy'. Similarly, while still struggling with the formulation of the doctrine of the Holy Spirit, she refused to recognise a subjective appeal to the Spirit as the final source of authority. Rather, she maintained that the Christian received objective guidance from the bishops as successors of the apostles. Finally, by refusing to rely on an immediate second coming, she taught Christians to face the future with realism and optimism.

By the end of the second century, despite the internal problems and external pressures, the Church had not only survived but had advanced both numerically and geographically. The missionary spirit, so marked in the apostolic period, had been maintained and new areas especially in the west, including North Africa and Gaul, had been added to those where Christianity had originally taken root. As yet there was neither a centralised nor a co-ordinated plan of campaign, but by preaching, writing and bearing witness in life, and in death, the early Church gained converts whose quality was to prove decisive in the century which still separated the Church from the peace of Constantine.

The third century opened with a feeling of optimism. In 196 the bishops had met in local synods to discuss the date of Easter, and such public meetings must have enjoyed at least the tacit approval of the State. In 202 however there was a dramatic change with the publication of an edict forbidding conversion to Christianity. The seriousness of this new situation was seen in 203 when a group of catechumens – men undergoing instruction prior to baptism – was arrested and executed. The motive for this change of heart by the Emperor Septimius Severus remains a matter of conjecture, though the increased numbers and influence of the Christians could well have unnerved him. From his death in 211 until the accession of Decius in 249 the emperors were mostly concerned with national security, safeguarding the borders of the empire and halting the numbers of invasions. During these years the evidence suggests that Christianity continued to grow. The only major setback came when Maximus Thrax (235–8) initiated a short burst of persecution against Church leaders. Though some suffered, his overall aim was unsuccessful and his own death brought a swift end to his policy. The reign of Philip the Arab (244–9) was so favourable towards

Christianity that there was a real possibility of reconciliation between the Church and the State, but this possibility was rudely shattered by the Emperor Decius who, despite a reign of only two years (249–51) posed the single greatest threat that the Church had, as yet, had to face.

Decius had won the support of the army, now an essential prerequisite for the imperial office, with his successful campaigns against the Goths. Even before the death of Philip the Arab, the army had proclaimed him emperor. When Philip died in 249 the Senate added their approval and Decius was officially recognised as emperor at a time of great emergency. The borders were too vast to control effectively, law and order was in danger of breaking down completely and the Old Religion had lost much of its influence with the re-emergence of the Eastern mystery cults and the continued advance of Christianity. For Decius the time had come to take stock, to prevent further decline and to make the empire great again. He used religion as his rallying call. There was to be a symbolic revival of the Old Religion and on a given day all the inhabitants of the empire had to offer sacrifice to the gods. This sacrifice was to be supervised by local magistrates who would issue a certificate, or libellus, to the person completing the sacrifice. This certificate was a person's guarantee against any future harrassment, while failure to produce a certificate was a treasonable offence punishable by fines, imprisonment, forced labour and death. This was the first State-controlled persecution of the Church. In January 250 Fabian, the Bishop of Rome, was executed and his death signalled a period of extreme difficulty for the Church. Though many Christians suffered, many others apostatised and, in doing so, forced the Church to develop her thinking about penance and reconciliation. The persecution ended with the death of Decius in 251, killed by the invading Goths whom he had previously repulsed with great success. Even before his death it was doubtful whether such a systematic attack on Christianity could have been sustained given the strain it had placed on resources through the need for supervision and constant surveillance.

In 257–8 there was a further outburst of persecution, first against Church leaders, but in the following year extended to the laity. The aim of this was to provide finance for the State through fines and confiscation of property. Several high ranking churchmen died including Cyprian, one of the great figures of the North African Church. Following the accession of Gallienus 260–8, a lengthy period of peace was inaugurated by his edict of toleration in 261. In writing to the bishops, Gallienus said: 'I have given my order that the benefit of my bounty should be published throughout the world, to the intent that the places of worship should be given up, and therefore you also may use the ordinance contained in my rescript, so that none may molest you'. According to the edict, all social classes were now free to profess their faith publicly, all had unrestricted access to places of worship, and all were allowed to preach openly and seek converts. Such freedom paved the way for forty years of peace before the final outburst of persecution under Diocletian at the beginning of the fourth century.

It was against this background that the theology, organisation and the sacramental life of the Church developed. The major theological discussions took place in the East linked, at least in part, with the theological centres associated with Alexandria and Antioch. Alexandria ranked, in size and importance, as the second city of the empire and c. 180 Pantainus was named as the first Christian teacher in the city. He was succeeded by Clement who converted to Christianity in adult life and reached Alexandria by the end of the second century. Whether he ran a theological school in the strict sense of the term is questioned, but his influence among the Alexandrians was immense. There is no such controversy about his successor, Origen, who c. 215 was commissioned by Bishop Demetrius to become the head of an ecclesiastically appointed school. He remained as Principal for fifteen years before a dispute with the bishop caused his resignation, after which he went to Caesarea where he continued his studies. Later he was tortured during the Decian persecution and died in 253 at Tyre.

Both Clement and Origen significantly influenced their contemporaries and successors. Both were agreed in drawing on philosophy in the service of theology, and both had a preference for the allegorical method of scriptural exegesis, by which each word was given a contemporary meaning. Of the two Origen's influence was the greater. Much of his writing was on the Bible in an effort to make it better known and understood. To this end he produced the *Hexapla*, a parallel text of the Bible in six languages. While in Alexandria he wrote his most famous theological work *De Principiis* which has been described as the first dogmatic text book. In this he covered a whole range of theological questions claiming that scripture and tradition were the two sources of theology and doctrine, and that the Church was, not only the guardian of scripture, but also its interpreter. His theological starting point was the Unity of God, and while he affirmed the threefold nature of the Godhead, future theologians were to accuse him of a form of subordinationism.* Whatever his

---

*An interpretation of the doctrine of the Trinity according to which the Son is subordinate to the Father and the Holy Spirit to both.

shortcomings he must be measured against the third century, and while future scholars, with their improved philosophical knowledge, point out these defects, Origen, nevertheless, represents an important advance in the Church's search for theological understanding and expression.

The other theological school was at Antioch. Throughout the Church's history Antioch had enjoyed a significant position and by the fourth century it was regarded as one of the three great patriarchates. The origins of the school are unclear, although Lucian is traditionally named as the founder. Antioch preferred the literal interpretation of scripture and its theological starting point was the Divinity of Christ. In both these areas Antioch differed from Alexandria, and this tension and rivalry was seen in the great conciliar period of doctrinal formulation.

Much of the theological interest centred on the Trinity. By defending the unity of God and promoting the so-called 'logos' christology, Origen and others had been charged with subordinationism. The opposite starting point, stressing the difference between the Father, Son and Holy Spirit, led to a charge of tritheism. One of the more important stages in trying to express the Trinity came with the theory known as Monarchianism. There were two main groups of Monarchian theologians, the Dynamic or Adoptionist group – who safeguarded the unity of God but failed to express adequately the full divinity of Christ – and the Modalist group. Modalism or Sabellianism, as it was also known, argued that in the one Godhead the only differentiation was the succession of modes. The Father was the essence of Godhead who expressed himself in the Son and the Spirit, one God revealing himself in three different ways. Their opponents accused the modalists of making the Father suffer on the cross under the mode of the Son, a theory known technically as Patripassianism. Such theological speculation demonstrated the importance of the point from which a start was made, and the terminology employed, both of which were to assume enormous significance in the fourth and fifth centuries.

Some of the writing of this period reflected the growing understanding of the sacramental life of the Church. Baptism was the official initiation into the life of the Church prepared for by a lengthy and demanding period called the catechumenate. This was controlled by the bishop and justified on the grounds of the necessity of a convert to be able to differentiate between the Christian and pagan worlds. By baptism a person received forgiveness and was freed from the powers of evil. This new life must prosper within the individual who had to strive to preserve his baptismal purity by resisting temptation and practising genuine Christian charity. Baptism allowed a person to take a full part in the Eucharist which was by now the central act of the Church's worship. The origins of the Eucharist are to be found in two originally distinct services, the service of the Word and the Fellowship Meal. Gradually certain features of the Fellowship Meal were dropped and, what was left, was joined to the service of the Word. Justin Martyr, writing c. 150, gives the following account:

> And on the day named after the sun there is a meeting in the same place of all those who live in the towns or the country. The records of the Apostles and the writings of the Prophets are read publicly, as much as time will permit. When the reader is finished, the president in his speech admonishes and exhorts to the imitation of these beautiful examples. Then we all stand up and pray together aloud. Whereupon, as we have already said, when the prayer is finished, bread is brought along with wine and water. The president sends up prayers together with thanksgiving to the best of his powers, and the people applaud saying 'amen'. Then takes place the distribution and sharing of these eucharistic foods, and they are brought to the absent by the deacons.

This celebration underwent certain developments and by 220 Hippolytus, a priest of Rome, recorded and preserved a text of a eucharistic prayer which he called the 'Apostolic Tradition', and although this certainly did not go back as far as the apostolic period, it was probably composed sometime during the middle of the second century. Though Hippolytus was at pains to stress that this prayer was a model rather than an obligatory text, it represents an essential clue in the history of this most central act of worship. The 'Apostolic Tradition' formed the basis of the Second Eucharistic prayer now in use in the Roman Church.

A further discussion centred on reconciliation after baptism. After the Decian persecution many of those who had apostatised rather than face punishment wanted to be reconciled with the Church. Until this time baptism was generally regarded as the sacrament of forgiveness and, once baptised, a person would remain free from serious sin. The realists had recognised that such absence from sin on the part of everyone was highly unlikely, and the *Shepherd of Hermas* had admitted the possibility of one opportunity for repentance and reconciliation after baptism. This so-called single penance theory had been accepted theoretically by others, but the numbers involved in the Decian persecution meant that the Church had to tackle the question urgently.

In 248 Cyprian had been appointed Bishop of Carthage just two years after his conversion. Within a year, at the outbreak of persecution, he had quit Carthage and gone into hiding, a decision he maintained was necessary for the good administration of the diocese, but which his enemies attributed to cowardice. With the cessation of persecution Cyprian returned to find an opposition party led by Felicissimus, and the thorny problem of the reconciliation of the lapsed. In practice several of the lapsed had received 'letters of peace' which supposedly came from the martyrs and confessors, whose merits in suffering were, by these letters, transferred to the lapsed, to compensate for their weakness and effect their reconciliation and re-admittance into full communion. Cyprian replied to this situation in a work called *On the Lapsed* in which he praised the martyrs and confessors for their patience and steadfastness, but denied them the right to reconcile those guilty of serious sin. Such reconciliation could only be affected by the competent ecclesiastical authority, namely the bishop.

In Rome around the same time a different problem highlighted the same question of penance. After the death of Bishop Fabian in 250, the Roman see had remained vacant during which time Novatian had assumed a position of importance without being elected bishop. When circumstance allowed an election Novatian was rejected and Cornelius appointed bishop. Novatian immediately set himself up as a rival, preaching a very rigorist doctrine, which denied in principle the possibility of reconciliation for the lapsed. Despite being condemned by a Roman synod, presided over by Cornelius, the rigorist doctrine of Novatian enjoyed considerable success among those who wanted the Church to be the Church of the 'Holy'. It was in the face of such practical difficulties that the theology and practice of penance developed and it is to the credit of the Church in the third century that the more compassionate and realistic attitude prevailed.

The Carthage incident also illustrated the importance by this time of the role of the bishop. He had become the pivot of ecclesiastical life in liturgy, theology and discipline. As representative between the communities he was not only spokesman but regarded as the guardian of unity. With such importance attached to the office, great care was taken in the choice of candidates. In his task the bishop still used the deacons as his personal aids. They were called the 'ear, mouth, heart and soul' of the bishop. The priests, on the other hand, were delegated on more and more occasions to look after smaller congregations, presiding at the Eucharist when the bishop was unavailable. By the middle of the third century other grades of clergy had become common. In the Church of Rome *c.*250 as well as the bishop 'there

are forty-six presbyters, seven deacons, seven sub-deacons, forty-two
acolytes, fifty-two exorcists, readers and door keepers', all of which
suggests a rapid growth in organisation aimed at meeting the needs
of the Church, which was to be tested yet again by a severe persecution.

In 284 Diocletian was proclaimed emperor by the army. After
ridding himself of potential rivals he set about a thorough reorganisation of the empire which involved the creation of a co-
emperor, Maximian, responsible for the East. In 292 he extended
this organisation by creating two subordinates to himself and
Maximian. Once he had achieved this stability he turned his attention to every facet of life including religion. Since his accession the
Christian Church had enjoyed a steady growth and expansion and,
by the end of the third century, the Christians numbered some
twenty per cent of the population of the empire. But the situation
changed dramatically towards the end of his reign. In 300, as part of
his general reorganisation, all members of the army were ordered to
offer sacrifice. Failure to comply led to loss of rank, expulsion from
military service and ultimately death. In 303 a further three edicts
were issued ordering the destruction of Christian places of worship,
the surrendering of Christian books and the arrest of the clergy.
Finally, a fourth edict in 304 obliged all citizens to worship the gods
of the empire by offering sacrifice. There is evidence of great blood-
shed, particularly in the East, and even the joint resignations of
Diocletian and Maximian in 305 did not put an immediate end to the
persecution, although Constantius in the West was more tolerant
than Gallerius, his co-emperor. In the East it was only with the
publication of Gallerius' edict of Toleration in 311 which stated that
'Christians may exist again and may establish their meeting houses,
so long as they do nothing contrary to public order', that persecution
ended with the first legal document, from the highest authority of the
Roman State, expressly recognising Christianity.

However, it was in the West that events were taking place which
were to shape the future of the empire and the Church. In July 306
Constantius died just a year after succeeding Diocletian as emperor.
The army in York acclaimed Constantius' son, Constantine, as
emperor. He had been the child of Constantius and Helena and had
been held in protective custody in the court of Diocletian where he
had inbibed the theory of absolute monarchy, a theory he was to
translate into practice. Now, with the support of the army in the
North-West, his first objective was to gain control of the whole of the
western part of the empire. His major threat came from Maxentius
who controlled Italy and North Africa. A successful and decisive

battle on the outskirts of Rome at the Milvian Bridge in 312 secured Constantine's first objective, making him undisputed Western emperor. In negotiations with his eastern counterpart, Licinius, an edict of religious toleration was promulgated in 313, the so-called 'Edict of Milan'. In this the co-emperors claim 'Our purpose is to grant both to the Christians and to all others full authority to follow whatever worship each man has desired'. Despite the all-embracing nature of this document a series of special ordinances for the Christian Church, which went far beyond Gallerius' grudging toleration of 311, together with later legislation favourable to the Church, pointed to a future where Christianity would not be one among many religions, but would be the sole religion of the empire. The historian Eusebius called the edict 'a very perfect and comprehensive law in favour of Christianity'.

In 324 Constantine achieved his second major objective, namely the defeat of Licinius and the uniting of the empire under himself as sole ruler. He chose not to appoint a co-emperor. The theory of the absolute monarch had now become a reality. Constantine's father had rejected any suggestion of religious compulsion and it seems likely that Constantine followed this policy, but as to his own personal commitment to Christianity the sources are at best doubtful. Those who favour the view that he turned to Christianity at an early date point to the vision of the cross recorded by Eusebius and others, under which sign he won the decisive battle against Maxentius in 312. They add the fact that coins struck in 315 carried the symbol of the cross and that later years saw a series of measures of pro-Christian legislation. Finally they appeal to his interest in Christian orthodoxy referring to his intervention in both the Donatist and Arian controversies.

Those people who question Constantine's commitment to Christianity point to the fact that the Triumphal Arch erected in 315 has pagan symbols on it, the fact that he kept the title 'Pontifex Maximus' which had pagan rather than Christian connotations, and finally, that his interest in orthodoxy stemmed from a desire for uniformity rather than desire for the truth. Any attempt to evaluate the personal faith of another is dangerous and clearly the evidence available can be read from opposite points of view. What seems irrefutable, however, was the rapid spread of Christianity during his reign, and the fact that imperial legislation approved of such growth. Under Constantine the Church emerged from being persecuted, and passed through a period of toleration to a position of supremacy. It is at least arguable that it was only because of this promotion of Christianity by Constantine that the Christians were able to enter a century of theological debate and doctrinal formulation that became the business of the first four General Councils.

After defeating Licinius in 324, Constantine began to move the seat of government to Byzantium, renamed Constantinople. It was from this position that he was able to gain first-hand knowledge of the theological questions which threatened to divide the Church. The immediate problem originated in Alexandria where a priest named Arius claimed that the Son was a creature, and, therefore not God, as the Father is God. His bishop, Alexander, condemned Arius who then went to Caesarea where he was befriended by Bishop Eusebius. This division within the Church was precisely the situation Constantine wanted to avoid. Using Hosius of Cordoba as his adviser and emissary, the emperor tried first to silence both parties and then to arbitrate between them. Neither course was successful and so he summoned a General Council, inviting the bishops as follows: 'Wherefore I signify to you my beloved brethren, that all of you promptly assemble at the said city, that is Nicaea'. This was to be the first formal meeting of the bishops, representing the whole Church, convened for the purpose of formulating doctrine.

In opening the council in 325, Constantine left the bishops, possibly as many as three hundred and mostly from Asia Minor, in no doubt that their task was to reach unanimity in their theological formulation. Under the presidency of Hosius and the two Roman legates, sent by Bishop Sylvester, they heard Arius repeat his denial of the Son's divinity. They quickly recognised that condemning Arius was a simple matter, but agreeing to a formula, which would satisfactorily state the truth of the relationship between the Father and the Son, was less easy. Eventually they produced the Nicene Creed which stated that the Son was 'of the essence of the Father', 'begotten not made' and 'consubstantial with the Father'. Only two bishops dissented, and they, with Arius, were exiled. The bishops then fixed the date of Easter, added some twenty disciplinary canons and returned to their dioceses. However, almost immediately, it became clear that, although the bishops had given their assent to the creed of Nicaea, there was no unanimity in their understanding of the formula. The major difficulty concerned the word 'homoousios', translated 'consubstantial', which was not a scriptural word but had its origins in gnostic literature, and was disliked by many of the bishops.

The opposition to the Nicene creed was led by Eusebius of Nicomedia and as early as 328, by skilful argument, he effected the return of the exiled Arian bishops. He then attacked the key orthodox figures, among them Eustathius of Antioch, Marcellus of Ancyra and the most famous of all, Athanasius of Alexandria. The Arian position gained popularity and Arius himself was recalled, but he died in 336, before a formal reconciliation could be achieved. In 337 Constantine himself also died, ending a reign of enormous importance in the history of the Church.

The empire was now divided between Constantine's three sons. Constantius ruled in the East from 337–61 and was sole emperor from 350–61. He favoured the Arian position and allowed Arianism to grow during these years. Constantine II survived barely three years from 337–40 and his portion of the empire passed to Constans who ruled the West from 337–50. Constans, in opposition to his brother, favoured the Nicene position and, under him, the West remained loyal to the Council. The Arian bishop Eusebius of Nicomedia was translated to Constantinople in 337 from where he could conduct affairs. Athanasius, who had returned to Alexandria on the death of Constantine, was again sent into exile, during which he journeyed to Rome where he was exonerated at a Roman synod in 341. In that same year a synod at Antioch drew up a new credal statement which excluded the term 'homoousios' but which otherwise was noted only for its vagueness. At this point the imperial brothers determined to convoke a council of the whole Church, East and West, in an attempt to reach a settlement between the two sides. This Council met at Sardica in 343, but the two groups failed to agree, antagonised each other even further, and retreated behind more intransigent language. A glimmer of hope flickered when in 346 the East reinstated Athanasius, who was widely regarded as the champion of Nicene orthodoxy, but the death of Constans in 350, which left Constantius (after a brief and successful skirmish against the usurper Magnentius) the sole ruler of the whole empire, heralded a new wave of persecution for the orthodox Christians and signalled the emergence of extreme Arianism.

The bishops of the West, at two synods at Arles and Milan, were constrained to deny the validity of Nicaea, accept a vague formula drawn up at Sirmium in 351 and agree to the deposition of Athanasius. At the same time the Arians themselves were showing signs of disunity. At one extreme were the radicals led by George in Alexandria and Eudoxius in Antioch. These were known as the Anomaens and they stressed the differences between the Father and the Son. The centre party was called the Homoeans who were satisfied with the statement 'according to the scriptures there is a similarity between the Father and the Son'. On the right were the Semi-Arians who used the term 'homoiousios' which avoided the idea of consubstantiality but stressed the likeness between Father and Son. This third group were the ones who initially entered negotiations with the orthodox which eventually paved the way for unity.

In 359 Constantius ordered councils to be held at Seleucia in the East and Rimini in the West. At Rimini the bishops initially upheld the Nicene Creed but, under imperial pressure, recanted and accepted a pro-Arian formula, which was regarded by some contemporaries as the sign of the complete victory of Arianism. However, the death of Constantius in 361 left the Arians bereft of their greatest champion and opened the way for the re-emergence of orthodoxy. The brief reign (361–3) of Julian the Apostate, so-called because he was said to have been brought up as a Christian, was notable for his attempt to preside over the collapse of Christianity and the revival of paganism. In order to cause schism in the Church he encouraged the exiled bishops to return to their sees without expelling the present incumbents. The shortness of his reign and his own personal unpopularity prevented any major return to paganism but it served as a reminder to the Church of the influence of the imperial government. Athanasius had been one of the bishops to return to his see and, in 362, he held a council at Alexandria which helped to facilitate the eventual reconciliation between the Semi-Arians and the pro-Nicene party, despite the activities of the Eastern emperor Valens (364–78), who was a strict Arian. In the West the emperor Valentinian was favourable towards the Nicene position and with the help of Damasus, Bishop of Rome from 366–84, orthodoxy flourished.

In the 370s there was a change in personnel. In 373 Athanasius died having survived several periods of exile and half a century of hardship. With his death the leadership of the Nicene party in the East passed to the Cappadocian Fathers, Basil of Caesarea (d.379), his brother Gregory of Nyssa (d.394) and Gregory Nazianzus (d.390). Together they prepared the ground for the final victory of orthodox Nicene theology under the Emperor Theodosius the Great at the Council of Constantinople.

This council, which met from May to July of 381 with about 150 bishops present, reaffirmed the decisions of Nicaea, and added the following carefully worded statement about the Holy Spirit: 'and [we believe] in the Holy Spirit, the Lord the Giver of life, who proceeds from the Father, who together with the Father and the Son is to be adored and glorified, who spoke by the prophets'. It also condemned other heresies and added various disciplinary canons. The Roman Church, at a synod in 382 presided over by Damasus, added its agreement to the creed and in so doing effectively ended the Arian attempt to take over the Church. Arianism did gain a foothold among some of the Germanic tribes, but the conversion of the Franks at the end of the fifth century signalled its death-knell.

Arianism was not the only heresy dealt with at Constantinople; Canon 1 had condemned as heretical the theology of Appolinarius (310–95) who taught that in Christ the human spirit had been replaced by the divine logos, thus questioning the full humanity of Christ. He stressed Christ's divinity and to this end had championed the Marian title of 'Theotokos' – the God Bearer. Among those who had already opposed Appolinarius was Theodore of Mopsuestia (d.428) who stressed both the humanity and the divinity of Christ and who also championed the title 'Theotokos' but who failed to answer how Christ could be both God and Man. These christological questions were taken up in the fifth century by Nestorius (d.451) and Cyril of Alexandria (d.444). In 428 Nestorius was appointed to Constantinople by Emperor Theodosius II despite the claims of more local candidates. Nestorius made it known that his policy would be the expulsion of heretical ideas and the preaching of orthodoxy, and to this end he supported his chaplain's criticism of the use of the title 'Theotokos' because of its links with Appolinarianism. However the term had by now been used by many orthodox theologians and was gaining in popularity because of the growing devotion to Mary. Any attack therefore on the title could be construed as attacking, rather than defending, orthodoxy.

On his appointment to Constantinople, Nestorius was faced with the necessity of passing judgement on Cyril of Alexandria for alleged ill-treatment of 'a pack of bankrupt failures from the dung heaps of Alexandria', as Cyril had described them. Cyril had then gone on to attack Nestorius, accusing him of heresy because of his rejection of the title 'Theotokos' which, Cyril claimed, proved that Nestorius denied the divinity of Christ and offended against the dignity of Mary. With this charge the disciplinary case against Cyril was forgotten and the Christological controversy burst open. The case was referred to Rome where a synod in 430 condemned Nestorius and instructed Cyril to serve an injunction on him to recant within ten days or face the possibility of excommunication. Not content with this, Cyril added twelve anathemas of his own.

Meanwhile the emperor determined on a General Council to be held at Ephesus to settle these christological questions. Pope Celestine reluctantly agreed to send legates who had been instructed to support Cyril and uphold the decision of the Roman synod. On 22 June 431 the council was opened by Cyril with the support of Memnon of Ephesus, this despite the fact that neither the Syrian bishops, led by John of Antioch, nor the Roman legates, had yet arrived. Nestorius refused to attend and was deposed in his absence, his doctrines condemned and he himself excommunicated. The creed of Nicaea was upheld and the term 'Theotokos' declared orthodox. On 26 June John of Antioch arrived with the Syrian bishops. They held a rival meeting in which Cyril and Memnon were declared deposed and Nestorius exonerated. Finally, in July, the Roman legates arrived to cast their vote in favour of Cyril. Despite the political overtones of the whole council, Cyril's position was recognised as orthodox and Nestorius was banished to a monastery. Rome was delighted with the outcome and sent congratulatory letters to Cyril on achieving this unity. The reality however was different. The gap between Antioch and Alexandria was wider now than ever before, and it was only under pressure from the emperor that a 'Formula of Union' was accepted by John and Cyril in 433.

In 446 the controversy broke out again, although this time with different characters. Eutyches, the leader of a large monastery in Constantinople and influential at court through his friendship with Chrysaphius, a court official, effectively denied the two natures of Christ after the Incarnation, thus giving rise to a heresy which later is known as Monophysitism. Flavian, the Patriarch of Constantinople, denounced Eutyches but, because of the latter's influence at court, was persuaded to summon a council at Ephesus in 449 under the presidency of Dioscorus of Alexandria. Dioscorus saw this as an opportunity of ridding Constantinople of Flavian, thus paving the way for his own appointment, and of crushing the Antiochene school once and for all by advocating an extreme form of Cyril's theology. Accordingly he refused to admit the legates of Pope Leo the Great, declared Eutyches orthodox and denounced the doctrine of the two natures after the Incarnation as an heretical innovation. The strenuous efforts of Flavian in the East and Leo in the West to have these decisions of the so-called 'Robber Council' reversed were rewarded when, in 451, the new Emperor Marcian summoned a General Council at Chalcedon, in Asia Minor.

On 25 October, after some 600 bishops had deliberated for just over a fortnight, the following decisions were made. The councils of Nicaea, Constantinople and Ephesus (431) were declared to be ecumenical, the Nicene and Constantinopolitan creeds affirmed, the 'Robber Council' condemned, and Eutyches and Dioscorus deposed, and the following statement of faith proclaimed:

We believe and we teach one and the same Christ in two natures, unmixed and unchanged, undivided and unseparated, since the distinction of the natures is by no means destroyed in the union, but rather the qualities of each nature are preserved and both are united in one person and one hypostasis.

This Chalcedonian definition formally set before the Church the official teaching on the Person of Christ. Even so it did not prove to be universally acceptable and was rejected by the Monophysites who, in one form or another, caused controversy and schism in the Church for the next two hundred years.

In reaching this definitive statement the bishops at Chalcedon had relied greatly on a letter written by Pope Leo the Great in which he outlined his teaching on the person of Christ. Whether the bishops on hearing this letter actually said: 'Peter has spoken through Leo' is disputed; but clearly by the middle of the fifth century the position of the Bishop of Rome had become both prestigious and powerful. From the outset the Christian community in Rome had naturally enjoyed some of the importance belonging to the capital city of the empire, but of far greater significance was the dual apostolic witness of Peter and Paul, martyred during the reign of Nero. Accolades from non-Romans had added weight to the prestige of the Roman Church. Ignatius of Antioch spoke of Rome 'presiding in love' and of the Roman Church as 'the bond of love'. Irenaeus c.185 had claimed that Rome enjoyed 'a plenitude of power'. Both honour and jurisdiction are mentioned in these two witnesses, and there were examples of Rome using this jurisdiction, or at least her honoured position in the Church. In the year 96 the Roman Church wrote to the Church at Corinth giving guidelines on how to deal with a division caused by the dismissal of some ministers. A century later Victor of Rome (189–98) threatened to excommunicate the churches of Asia Minor if they refused to agree to his dating of Easter. In the middle of the third century Stephen intervened in the Churches of Spain and Gaul. Not everyone was agreed on this presumption and practice by the Bishop of Rome, and Cyprian of Carthage was vehement in his denunciation:

> For no-one of us sets himself up as a bishop of bishops, or by tyrannical terror forces his colleagues to the necessity of obeying, in as much as every bishop in the free use of his liberty and power has the right of forming his own judgement and can no more be judged by another than he can himself judge another.

When Constantine moved to Constantinople in 324 he effectively shifted the centre of gravity of the empire eastwards and emphasised the growing separation between East and West. This divorce, highlighted during the Arian controversy, was enormously important in the development of the Roman Church and the primatial claims of the pope. The Roman bishop Damasus (366–84) pushed these claims considerably, referring to the other bishops as 'sons', using the plural 'we' and, most important, coining the term 'Apostolic See' for Rome itself, thereby underlining the immense importance of Peter and Paul. The Roman synod of 382 accepted the credal formula of Constantinople but rejected the renaming of Constantinople as the New Rome and the disciplinary canon which forbade a bishop the right to intervene in another diocese. Damasus claimed that Rome enjoyed her status, now referred to as primacy, not because of a decision of a council, however important, but by divine will! Siricius (384–99) was the first to use the title 'pope', in itself simply meaning 'father', but highly significant when taken in conjunction with the practice of calling the other bishops 'sons'. He began the system of decretals – decisions given by the pope in a particular dispute, but which soon assumed a much wider validity and importance. Innocent I (402–17) maintained that all major claims must be brought to Rome for judgement and that no bishop had the authority to set aside a papal decision. Boniface I (418–22) claimed that the Roman Church was the highest seat of judgement from which there could be no appeal.

The pontificate of Leo the Great (440–61) was the climax of the growing number of papal claims. He assumed the leadership of the city of Rome and its immediate environs, safeguarding food supplies and negotiating successfully with Attila the Hun and the barbarian invaders. He skilfully wove together a digestible theory of primacy, arguing that all bishops shared equally in the pastoral care of the Church, but that the Bishop of Rome, as successor of Peter, enjoyed Peter's authority and pre-eminence. Most important of all he successfully separated the objective office of the papacy from the subject who filled that office. Authority belonged to the office thereby allowing for bad office holders without fundamentally compromising the office itself. The acceptance of Leo's letter at Chalcedon was regarded as the formal acknowledgement of the special status of the pope in the Church. Historically the difference between theory and practice in papal history has been immense, but the special position of Peter and the claim to his succession has already assumed enormous importance in papal theory. In practice the separation between East and West, already hinted at, and soon to become clearly visible, was of greater significance, because it was precisely in the East that primatial claims were never really accepted. The absence of any significant rival to Rome in the West aided the popes who made full use of precedents to prove the antiquity of their claims.

While the christological controversies were consuming time and energy in the East, other problems were surfacing in North Africa which became particularly divided during the life of Augustine (354–

430). Augustine exerted an enormous influence on his contemporaries and has continued to influence theology right down to our own time. Born of a pagan father and a Christian mother, St Monica, in 354, and well educated at the university of Carthage, he decided, early in life, to pursue his interest in literature. During this period he gave up Christian practices and delved into various philosophical schools and systems, being attracted particularly to Manichaeism. His fascination ended with the realisation that Manichaeism could not solve some of the problems with which he had struggled. In 383 he arrived in Rome but was quickly disillusioned by the behaviour of the students under his charge, and in 384, he accepted a teaching post in Milan which at this time was under the influence of one of its greatest bishops, Ambrose (339–97). Ambrose had become bishop in 374 at the insistence of the people and despite the fact that he was only a catechuman. He was baptized and ordained in quick succession and then devoted himself to the study of the theology. As bishop he won fame for his preaching, his orthodoxy, his defence of the independence of the Church against civil authority and his high moral demands. He was responsible for opening Milan to some of the riches of eastern theology and for welcoming and supporting some of the first monastic settlements. His writings, especially on the sacraments and morals, have secured him a place among the Doctors of the Church.

Augustine was deeply affected by the preaching and example of Ambrose and, despite dallying for a while with Neoplatonism and questioning his own ability to live the moral demands of the Christian life, he was eventually baptised by the bishop on the eve of Easter 387. His first years as a Christian were tragic. His mother died soon after his conversion and his son, Adeodatus, born of a mistress to whom Augustine had been faithful for fifteen years, died in 390. Back in North Africa, where he had returned shortly after his baptism, he established a semi-monastic community at Thagaste which was modelled on his own understanding of the ascetic movement and which would inspire vast numbers of Christians in the future. In 391 he was ordained and quickly became co-adjutor bishop of Hippo in North Africa. In 396 on the death of the elderly bishop Valerius, Augustine was promoted to the see and for the next thirty-four years was sole bishop of Hippo until his own death in 430.

As bishop, Augustine soon encountered serious problems, the most pressing being that posed by the Donatists whose origins stretched back to the beginning of the fourth century. In 311 Caecilian was appointed Bishop of Carthage and duly consecrated by his fellow bishops. One of these was accused of cooperating with the persecutors during the reign of Emperor Diocletian by handing over the sacred books rather than face punishment. Such a person was known as a Traditor. Because of his involvement in the consecration, the opponents of Caecilian claimed that his consecration was invalid since an unworthy bishop had taken part. In 313 a commission in Rome had supported Caecilian and the synod of Arles in 314 upheld the Roman decision and stated that consecration even by a Traditor was valid. Undaunted, the opponents continued to support their rival candidate and, when he died in 315, they elected Donatus from whom the heresy took its name. Under his leadership the Donatists grew both in numbers and influence despite Catholic argument and State interference. Theologically the Donatists were rigorist, claiming that the Church must remain holy and that the validity of the sacraments depended on the worthiness of the minister. In practice they lived and demanded the highest moral code of conduct. They believed that they alone were the true Church and they demanded rebaptism for converts to Donatism.

In defending the Catholic position, Augustine stressed that the Church contained both good and bad and that God alone knew the difference. The validity of the sacraments did not depend on the worthiness of the minister, 'ex opere operantis', but on the fact that the sacraments enjoyed their own validity, 'ex opere operato', and depended on the correct celebration by the Church. Despite repeated attempts at discussion, the most elaborate being a three-day conference of African bishops in 411, the split between Donatists and Catholics widened and harsh legislation was introduced against the Donatists. Ironically both were thrown together during the Vandal invasions after which the Donatists never again posed a major threat to the unity of the Church and their final extinction came with the rise of Islam.

Augustine's later years saw him writing against another heresy called Pelagianism which taught that a person could take the first step towards salvation by his own efforts apart from divine grace. This was to have serious repercussions in several areas of theology notably over the questions of original sin and predestination. The origins, though, are to be found in the desire of Pelagius, from Britain, and others to defend the increasingly popular ascetic movement by emphasising the ability of a person to chose good rather than evil. Pelagius, though giving his name to the heresy, dropped out of the limelight and the others who succeeded him were condemned both by Church councils and by Augustine in his copious writings in which he developed the theology of free will, sin, grace and justification.

Augustine was one of the key figures not only of the African Church but of the whole western tradition. Much of his writing came out of controversy and he took theological argument and expression further than earlier writers. His *Confessions*, written *c.*400, and his *City of God*, completed *c.*426, are still regarded as classics, the latter greatly influencing the medieval concept of Church-State relations. Without Augustine's massive intellect and his deep spiritual perception, western theology would surely not have taken the shape in which it is now familiar to us.

Augustine wrote: 'The man who lets himself do everything that is allowed will very soon become slack and do what is not allowed'. Some historians have seen this idea as underlying Augustine's desire to live a semi-monastic style of life as a support to those who found the demands of the Christian life difficult, and the attractions of the world tempting. The monastic ideal did not originate with Augustine, rather its origins are to be found in the deserts of Egypt towards the end of the third century where first individuals, and then groups, practised great asceticism as an alternative witness to the Christian faith. According to Athanasius, the man responsible for all subsequent ascetical and monastic growth was Anthony of Egypt, who lived to the huge age of 106, dying in 356. In 271 Anthony withdrew into the Egyptian desert in an attempt, not merely to withdraw from the world, but to reach perfection through a successful struggle with evil. By prayer, reading and learning the scriptures by heart, by penance, self-denial and fasting, Anthony began a style of life which became known as the eremitical tradition of asceticism, where the accent was on a solitary, hermit style of life. The hermit waged a spiritual war against the evil spirits and a physical war against temptation by subjecting his body to the most rigorous testing. The motivation for such witness came partly from those sayings in the Gospel which invited a person to give up everything in the following of Christ, and partly from the increasing acceptance of Christianity by the state which had reduced the opportunity of witness by martyrdom, and induced a certain lukewarmness.

The second major form of asceticism was inspired by Pachomius (290–346), who encouraged like-minded people to live together sharing some kind of common life. This community style of monastic witness was known as the cenobitical tradition and it embraced far greater numbers than its eremitical counterpart. In *c.*320, in Upper Egypt, Pachomius founded his first monastic community living under obedience to the superior. Though not as ascetical as the hermits, these monks were still inspired to follow Christ through penance and self-denial. They joined together for community prayer, chanting the psalms and reading the scriptures, and, when a visiting priest was present, for the celebration of the Eucharist. At this stage monasticism was a lay movement in the Church and it is only at a relatively late date that most monks were ordained. As well as community prayer there was the support of the community and, in a short time, such communities became self-sufficient, attracting large numbers by their ordered and regular way of life.

From these beginnings in Egypt the monastic ideal spread throughout the Church. Hilarion of Gaza (291–371), was responsible for introducing the ideas and the ideals of Anthony into his native Palestine. Ephraem (306–73) introduced the cenobitical tradition into Syria, founding the first monastic school at Eddessa where the students lived under obedience. It was in Syria that some of the more bizarre and extreme forms of asceticism showed themselves: some monks lived on the top of pillars and others in tubs chained between trees. However the man who was to have the most profound and lasting effect on Eastern monasticism was Basil the Great (329–79). He took what he regarded as the most beneficial aspects of the Egyptian monastic traditions and returned to his native Caesarea. There he limited the size of his communities, this in contrast to Pachomius who had encouraged huge numbers, and introduced two important innovations. He demanded that the monastery be outward-looking, sharing in the life of the local Church by helping to run schools, teach employment through workshops, and aid the homeless by opening orphanages. Secondly he regulated the monks' day to an unprecedented degree, giving set time to liturgical prayer, meditative reading and manual labour. Between 358–64 Basil formalised this division of the day into a Rule which has come down in two forms, the 'Shorter' consisting of 55 items and the 'Longer' with 313 items. Most of the contents of the Rule were taken from the Scriptures or the writings of the Early Fathers, and though asceticism was still demanded, Basil was keen to avoid the eccentricities of some of the Syrian monks as well as unhealthy competition among those under obedience to him. The fact that some eastern monks today are known as Basilians attests to his lasting influence in the monastic tradition in the Eastern Church.

The West was slower to embrace monasticism and when it did, both the western climate and temperament were more suited to the cenobitical tradition. Athanasius informed the West, through his biography, of Anthony of Egypt. Martin of Tours founded the first monastery in Gaul c.360 and, after becoming Bishop of Tours in 372, was able to encourage the expansion of monasticism throughout that region. Augustine at the beginning of the fifth century organised the Church in Hippo on monastic or semi-monastic lines and his so-called 'Rule' was taken up and adapted by many future generations.

But arguably the most important contact between Egyptian monastic spirituality and the West was John Cassian (*c.*362–435). He had imbibed the monastic spirit in Egypt before being sent on a mission to Rome after which he settled in Marseilles. In 415 he established two monasteries at Marseilles and Lerins at which he wrote his two major works, the *Institutes* which set out the ordinary rules for monastic life and which mention the chief obstacles to Christian perfection, and the *Conferences* which were written as conversations with the great leaders of Egyptian monasticism in which they stress the positive ways of Christian perfection. Even before the emergence of Benedict, regarded by most people as the 'Father of Western monasticism', there were many examples of monastic life in the West and, although numbers were smaller than in the East, in both parts of the empire the birth and early development of ascetical and monastic practices proved to be of lasting significance throughout the history of the Church.

The development of the Western Church and its final separation from the East, 461–1198

In 476 the last Western emperor, Romulus, was deposed by the Barbarians and his deposition symbolised the different preoccupations of the West and the East in the early Middle Ages.

In the West the Church was concerned with meeting the needs of new peoples with different languages, cultures and backgrounds. In the absence of an emperor the Bishop of Rome was regarded by many as the natural leader in every sphere of life. In the East the main concern was theological, in particular with a growing reaction to the Council of Chalcedon which had defined the dyophysite doctrine that taught two natures, divine and human, in the incarnate person of Christ. Opposition to this definition came mainly from the Alexandrian theologians who suspected that Chalcedon had not only favoured the rival Antiochene school, but had also done less than justice to Cyril whose memory they revered. The opponents to the dyophysite definition were called the Monophysites who maintained that in the incarnate person of Christ there was only one nature 'and that divine'. This heresy spready so quickly into Palestine, Syria and Egypt that Emperor Zeno (474–91), together with the Patriarch of Constantinople, Acacius, determined to restore unity to the empire by publishing the so-called 'Henotikon'. This was written in the form of a letter addressed to the bishops, clergy and laity of the empire in 482, and was intended to replace the Chalcedonian definition. The 'Henotikon' contained the following statement – 'Christ is consubstantial with the Father in respect to Godhead and consubstantial with man in respect to manhood'. In this way it effectively by-passed Chalcedon, calling on Christians to accept Nicaea and Constantinople but omitting any reference to the natures of Christ and so avoiding the point at issue. The 'Henotikon' was accepted by all the major sees in the East and, in Antioch, a monophysite bishop was installed. Only Rome refused to accept it; this resulted in the so-called Acacian schism between Rome and Constantinople, a schism which lasted from 484 until 519.

In 527 Justinian became emperor with the clear aim of reuniting East and West in both politics and religion. His military achievements included the reconquering of North Africa and Italy from the Vandals and the Goths respectively; his judicial skill was seen in the collection of laws known as the Justinian Code, and his aesthetic taste was most clearly evidenced in the magnificent basilica of 'Santa Sophia' in Constantinople. In religious matters he was less successful. Justinian desired the restoration of orthodoxy and he enjoyed some success against ageing groups of Montanists and Donatists, but his handling of the monophysite problem highlighted, rather than eradicated, the difficulties and complexities of the heresy. Having failed to reconcile the monophysite and orthodox parties, he began, under the influence of his wife Theodora, to favour Monophysitism. In this he alienated and humiliated the pope and, after the Second Council of Constantinople in 553, he even caused two Western sees, Milan and Aquilaea, to break off communion with Rome.

After Justinian, the Eastern empire was threatened by the Persians and the need to survive became more important than theological questions. A reversal of fortune came with Emperor Heraclius (610–41) who, by 628, had restored peace and stability. Heraclius, a realist, recognised that Egypt and Syria were now almost lost to him and that to prevent any further losses he must reopen the theological question which had caused such severe division. Engaging Sergius, the Patriarch of Constantinople, he first proposed a solution to the christological question called 'Monoenergism' which he hoped would satisfy both orthodox and monophysite alike. Monoenergism maintained that in Christ there were indeed two natures but only one energy or active force. In the event, theologians from both sides derided such a theory with the result that a further solution called 'Monotheletism' was proposed. This theory maintained that in Christ there were two natures but only one will. This was promulgated in a document caled the 'Ekthesis' and was made binding on the whole empire. A similar pattern emerged as with the 'Henotikon': the East accepted it, Rome refused. In 648 the Emperor Constans II withdrew the 'Ekthesis' and replaced it with yet another document called the 'Typos' which was intended to end any further discussion. In 649 Pope Martin I summoned a Lateran synod and condemned all new teaching in the East and demanded a return to Chalcedon. His courage was rewarded by torture, exile and ultimately death. In 680 the Third Council of Constantinople officially condemned Monotheletism and reaffirmed the Chalcedonian definition, but the very fact that this proved necessary acknowledged two centuries of theological struggle which had preoccupied the East and strained relations with the West.

Theological debate had been far distant from the minds of those groups of Barbarians who had repopulated the western part of the Old Roman Empire. Central and Western Europe had witnessed the arrival of the Germanic tribes of whom the Franks had earned a claim to leadership. By 480 Clovis had emerged as the leader of the Franks but he recognised that his position rested almost solely on physical power and he began to search for another basis for his authority. In doing this he came to see the possibilities of Christianity where the faith shared by different people was the bond of unity between them. In 496 Clovis was baptised and many of his people followed his example. In 507 he moved his capital to Paris which was intimately connected with St Denis, one of the great patronal figures of the time. In this way he reaffirmed his commitment to Christianity. In 511 he summoned a council to meet at Orleans where he made it clear that he intended to use bishops as an integral part of his administration. Had circumstances been different, Clovis might well have laid the foundations for a fruitful alliance between Church and State, but the instability of the West and the weakness of the Church militated against such a development.

At the close of the sixth century the papacy received enormous encouragement from the pontificate of Gregory the Great (590–604). His pontificate was a watershed, the end of the fiction of one Church in one united empire, the beginning of an attempt to understand the differences between East and West, and of a willingness to build on the qualities specific to the West. Gregory was born the son of a senator, c.540, and was assured a career either in politics or administration when he was made City Prefect of Rome in 573. However, he sold his property, distributed his wealth for the relief of the poor and devoted himself to promoting monasticism, founding monasteries in Sicily and Rome. His retirement from public life was cut short because he was created one of the seven deacons responsible for the administration of the Roman Church and then, in 578, was sent as legate to the Imperial Court of Constantinople. During this period he was able to imbibe something of the Eastern mentality which was greatly to affect his relations with the East during his own pontificate. On his return to the West he again attempted to live within his own monastery in Rome, but in 590 was elected pope and thereby thrust once more into public life.

Gregory recognised the necessity of balancing the needs of the

Church in the West with the very real claims of the emperor in Constantinople. The emperor's representative in the West, known as the exarch, was stationed in Ravenna and, as the Civil Governor, was responsible for upholding law and order. In theory all important matters should have been referred to him but Gregory short-circuited the system by dealing directly with problems at hand without any reference to the exarch, the most notable example being his peace treaty concluded in 592–3 with the Lombards who had settled in Northern Italy some twenty years previously and who from that time constantly threatened the stability of Rome. This was followed by further independent action which helped to create a picture of the papacy's involvement in temporal as well as in spiritual affairs. Gregory was able to assert his own authority in the West due to his own strength of character and to the weakness of imperial Constantinople. He also promoted loyalty to the papacy by a vigorous and fruitful missionary policy.

Arguably his greatest success was in sending Augustine to England in 596. The exact date of the arrival of Christianity in the British Isles is disputed but Tertullian's cryptic remark, written c.200, that 'parts of Britain inaccessible to the Romans were indeed conquered by Christ' suggests a date, if not in the first, then at least in the second century. In 314 at the Council of Arles, there were three British bishops present and Athanasius reports that the British bishops, though not present at Nicaea in 325, accepted the Council. The first named Christian in Britain was Alban, whom Bede, one of the greatest English historians, maintained was martyred c.305, at the end of the Diocletian persecution. Early in the fifth century Germanus, the Bishop of Auxerre in Gaul, was sent to Britain to try and stamp out any ideas which may have been perpetrated by Pelagius, the only famous and named British heretic of this time. In the fifth century Britain became a missionary centre with men like Ninian (c.360–432) working in Cumbria and Southern Scotland, and Patrick (c.390–461) spending much of his life in Ireland – he became Bishop of Ireland in 432 and Bishop of Armagh in 444. Mainland Britain then suffered a succession of invasions from Jutes, Angles and Saxons and the Christians, such as they were, fled to Wales and the West Country.

In the sixth century Northern Britain came under the influence of Celtic Christianity with the arrival of Columba (521–97). Columba left his native Ireland c.560 after a tribal feud had left hundreds dead, and with twelve companions eventually settled on the island of Iona off north-west Scotland c.563. There he built a monastery and with his monks lived a life of extreme asceticism. However, he was

convinced also of the need to be missionary, and Iona became the
centre from which Celtic Christianity spread throughout Scotland
and Northern England. By the time Augustine landed on the Kent
coast in 597 the Celtic Church, with its accent on asceticism and its
centre of authority in Iona, was firmly established, and the Roman
missionaries found themselves not only converting the pagans but
also negotiating with the Celts. Augustine himself remained firmly in
the south but Paulinus, who joined him in 601, recognised the needs
and problems of the Church on a much wider scale. After his consecration as bishop in 625, Paulinus accompanied the Queen of Kent
on a journey to York for her marriage to Edwin, King of Northumbria. In 627 Edwin was baptised along with many of his people and
in 633 Paulinus was named the first Archbishop of York, hence
second to Canterbury in importance. However, before Paulinus was
officially instated he was retreating southwards in face of a persecution instigated by Cadwallon who had defeated Edwin in battle.
Only James the Deacon remained in the north during this bleak
period.

Cadwallon's own reign was brief. His defeat by Oswald at a battle
near Hexham allowed Oswald to be crowned King of Northumbria.
As a Christian Oswald looked for help to reorganise the Church;
however unlike Edwin, Oswald did not engage Roman missionaries
but sent to Iona, and it was to be Aidan who organised the Church in
Northumbria, working from Lindisfarne, a small island off the
north-east coast which, after Aidan's arrival in 635, was to become
the centre of the Celtic Church. Aidan was solidly within the Celtic
tradition. He had been brought up on Iona and, from his new centre
on Lindisfarne, he travelled the whole length and breadth of Northumbria preaching, and establishing churches and monasteries, the
most famous at Whitby where Hilda was abbess from 657–80. By
the time of his death in 651 Aidan had achieved so much that he is
regarded as the greatest figure in the Northumbrian Church.

The retreat by Paulinus in 633 had served only to highlight the
differences between the Celtic Church in the north and the Roman
Church in the south. There were liturgical differences, for example
the cut of the tonsure and the date of Easter, but the major difference
concerned authority. Where did people look for authority? The
south looked to Rome, the north to Iona and latterly to Lindisfarne.
This split was particularly noticeable to those who had been brought
up in the Northern Church and then studied abroad. Their main
concern on their return was a fear that the Celtic Church was in
danger of being isolated from the rest of the Western Church. Eventually, in 664, representatives from both the Celtic and Roman

traditions met in Synod at Whitby under the presidency of Abbess Hilda to try and work through the differences and reach agreement. In the event, the result of these discussions was a victory for the Roman tradition and those who adhered to the Celtic Church tended to return to Scotland which had been the first great centre of Celtic Christianity. The Roman practices were to take years to take root in Scotland and indeed there developed a certain national consciousness among Christians north of the border. It was not until the end of the eleventh century that the Church in Scotland could be said to be thoroughly Roman. Meanwhile in England it was to the credit of Theodore, Archbishop of Canterbury from 668–90, that the differences between the north and the south were bridged and that the Church in Britain recognised its links with the wider Christian Church by now spread through most of Europe. In the next century Britain was to provide both scholars and missionaries who had a lasting effect on the Church throughout the whole of the West.

The decision of Gregory the Great to send Augustine to Britain was part of a more general policy by which he aimed to evangelise those parts of the West which would attract little or no interest in Constantinople, thus helping to create whole new peoples whose primary loyalty was to the pope in Rome. His political awareness was matched by his pastoral zeal and exemplified in his *Book of Pastoral Care* in which he stressed the duties and responsibilities of the bishop whom he regarded as central and crucial to the life of the Church. Similarly important was his encouragement of monasticism. He himself had established several monastic foundations and throughout his pontificate he continued to promote the monastic life, building on the strong foundations of the most famous Western monastic figure, Benedict of Nursia (480-548).

Benedict lived at a time of great change and chaos. Italy was threatened by Theoderic, the king of the Ostrogoths who by 500 had become the accepted ruler of Italy, and many of the ecclesiastical institutions thought to be timeless were either discarded or already a distant memory. Against such a background Benedict had retired into his own personal desert at Subiaco, about fifty miles east of Rome, where he tried his vocation as a hermit. He was soon joined by other like-minded people and in time settled for the cenobitical tradition of monastic life which offered the help and encouragement of a community. His attracting so many followers caused jealousy among others in the Subiaco district and c.525 Benedict, with a handful of followers, moved to Monte Cassino some eighty miles south of Rome. It was here that he remained until his death in 548 and it was during his time at Monte Cassino that he composed his

Rule which ensured him a lasting place in monastic history in particular and the history of the Church in general. Pope Gregory in his *Dialogues* wrote the following tribute about Benedict's Rule: 'He wrote a rule for monks which is remarkable both for its discretion and for the lucidity of its style. If anyone wishes to know his character and life more precisely he may find in the ordinances of that Rule a complete account of the Abbot's practice; for the holy man cannot have taught otherwise than he lived'.

Benedict would never have claimed that his Rule was original, rather he would have readily acknowledged drawing on various sources, notably Basil, John Cassian and an anonymous work known as the *Rule of the Master*. The greatness of Benedict's Rule lies in its simplicity, moderation and completeness, catering as it did for every hour of the monk's day. He saw the monastic community as a family with the abbot as Father, elected for life and enjoying total authority – 'Everything is done by the abbot's will'. He holds the place of Christ in the community and obedience to the abbot is likened to obedience to Christ himself. The monks are to submit immediately and without question to the abbot. The notion of family determined a second aspect of the Rule, namely that of stability by which Benedict meant far more than perseverance in monastic life. He demanded a local stability whereby a monk remained with the same community from his profession to his burial. Bishop Ullathorne expressed this idea succinctly when he wrote: 'St Benedict binds his monks by the vow of stability to an irrevocable life in community, and in the community that has witnessed his training and profession'. Such local stability was essential for the family atmosphere that he wished to promote as was the moderate code of conduct he demanded. Within the Rule there was no place for any acetical extremism, no institutional harshness, rather the ordinances about food and drink, clothing and sleeping, all left open the possibility of personal abstinence without making such abstinence binding on all.

In the prologue Benedict wrote: 'We are going to establish a school of the Service of God, in which we hope we will establish nothing harsh, nothing burdensome'. This Service of God included self-discipline which demanded a renunciation of the monk's own will and a growth in humility; prayer which included both common prayer where the monks came together and, among other things, recited the whole of the psalter on a weekly cycle, and private prayer for which Benedict gave no scheme other than to say 'If anyone wishes to pray let him simply go into the oratory and pray'; and finally work, which meant both manual work and spiritual reading –

'Idleness is the enemy of the soul and therefore at fixed times the brothers ought to be occupied in manual labour, and again at fixed times, in sacred reading'. In Chapter 73 Benedict sums up the reasons for his Rule: 'We have written this Rule in order that by observing it in monasteries we may show we have in some measure at any rate integrity of morals and the beginning of the monastic life'.

In Western Europe the Rule of Benedict survived despite the serious threat posed by the rise of the Lombards who were particularly hostile to monasteries and monastic life. Just before his death in 548 Benedict, in a despondent mood, wrote: 'All this monastery that I have built and all things I have provided for the brethren are . . . delivered to the Barbarians, and I scarce was able to obtain the lives of the monks'. And yet despite this picture the Rule, due to its internal qualities, its suitability to the Western temperament and its popularisation by various important leaders, both clerical and lay, became the norm for religious life. It superseded the Celtic rules and remained observed throughout the history of the Church. Not until the emergence of the 'White Monks' in the eleventh century was there any serious alternative to Benedictinism, and even the White Monks looked to the primitive Benedictine Rule for their inspiration.

In the history of the Church the pontificate of Gregory the Great was of immense importance; but after him the papacy enjoyed little popularity and exerted little influence, which illustrated the need for a strong personality in an office which was not of itself capable of commanding obedience and respect. There were twenty popes in the century from 604 to 701 and few lived long enough to have any lasting effect. By the turn of the century Gregory's pontificate was a distant memory and the popes were struggling to keep control even of Rome itself; yet it was at this time of apparent weakness that a series of events occurred which together helped to change the future both of the papacy and of Western Europe.

Until this time the balance of power in the West was divided three ways. The emperor maintained a presence in the West through his exarch in Ravenna. He was theoretically responsible for all major decisions and changes of policy, although Gregory the Great had little difficulty in by-passing such procedures. the pope controlled the city of Rome, being responsible for such things as revenues, grain supplies and general administration. This area had grown as families living in the vicinity of Rome had contributed gifts of land and revenue in exchange for papal protection. Such gifts of land, together with the city, made up what was called the 'Patrimony of St Peter' and this in turn encouraged the idea of the pope as a temporal ruler in his own right responsible for certain territory. The third power in the

West was the various tribal groups which had settled inside the Old Roman Empire and now enjoyed autonomy within their own borders. The imperial presence, the papacy and the various tribes in this way made up a delicate balance of power. It was when this balance was upset that a new and crucial situation arose.

The first signs of a change came from Emperor Leo III (717–41), when he ordered the exarch to increase taxation on the West and to tighten up the methods of collecting such taxes. This brought to the surface much of the latent enmity between East and West and the situation deteriorated when Pope Gregory II led the refusal to comply.

Leo's second attack was potentially even more dangerous. In 726 he had ordered the destruction of a huge icon called the 'Antiphonites' which stood over the gates of the palace in Constantinople. This proved to be the beginning of the 'Iconoclast' controversy which plagued the Eastern Church for over a century. Iconoclasm concerned the veneration of icons which had been an accepted practice in the Eastern Church. However, during the seventh century there had grown up a reaction to such veneration due mainly to people who stressed the divinity of Christ to the exclusion of his humanity and who did not want to be associated with matters which they regarded as evil. The Iconoclasts, those who wanted the destruction of all icons and statues, claimed that the Old Testament had specifically forbidden images and therefore the making and use of statues and icons was wrong. This was reinforced by their philosophical belief that an image was consubstantial with its type and therefore any respect shown to images could, and did, lead to idolatry. Their opponents, the Icondules – those who respected icons and statues – accepted the Old Testament prohibition of images, but they rejected the philosophical presupposition of consubstantiality, maintaining that an icon or a statue was essentially different from its type, and that therefore, far from being objects of worship, such icons were 'silent sermons, books of the illiterate and memorials of the mysteries of God'. This controversy in the East lasted from 726 until 843 and for two long periods, 726–75 and 813–43, the Iconoclasts were firmly in control. Throughout the course of the controversy the position of the emperor was crucial since his support determined the official teaching of the Eastern Church. The one group who remained consistently opposed to the Iconoclasts and therefore loyal to the use of icons, were the monks led at different times by John of Damascus and Theodore the Studite. They provided the theological defence of icons and were at the forefront of discussion and argument. They also suffered the most during this whole period but in the end they emerged with the greatest credit and success.

Once Leo had initiated this controversy in the East he then tried to enforce the destruction of all icons and statues in the West. As with the heavier taxation, the papacy again led the refusal to bend under this second attack. In retaliation Leo confiscated some property in Sicily and ordered the reorganisation of the Church in Southern Italy making it more immediately dependent on him and less dependent on the papacy. Such measures heightened the tension between East and West and rendered any serious dialogue between pope and emperor impossible. A further consequence of this estrangement between East and West was the fact that it was now very unlikely that the pope would seek help from the emperor should a need arise. Such a need did arise with the growing influence of the Lombards who had by now formed a physical barrier between the papacy and the Franks, the pope's traditional allies since the time of Clovis in the late fifth century.

In the eighth century the Lombards were led by Liutprand (712–44) who was unashamedly expansionist. In 734 he captured Ravenna, the seat of imperial power in the West. If the pope was secretly satisfied with this offence to the emperor he became quickly more concerned with his own safety since it became clear that Liutprand's intention was to launch an attack on Rome itself. Pope Gregory III (731–41) recognised the seriousness of the situation and, being unable to turn to the East for help, approached Charles Martel, the leader of the Franks, in order to form a treaty against the Lombard aggression. Unfortunately for Gregory, Charles could see no benefit for himself or the Franks in such a pact and consequently he refused to become involved. In 751 the situation became even more desperate when the Lombards expelled the exarch from Ravenna and destroyed all the other imperial garrisons in Northern Italy. Again the pope, Stephen III (752–7), appealed to the Franks, now under the leadership of Pepin. This time the appeal found favour and resulted in the Franco-Papal alliance, an alliance which was to have such great effects on the future of Western Europe.

Unlike his predecessor, Pepin realised that a treaty with the papacy could be beneficial to himself, his family and to the Franks as a whole. Pepin needed to be recognised as the Christian ruler in the West and he wanted some guarantee that his sons would succeed him. He believed that the pope could supply both needs. In return Pepin would defend the papacy against the Lombards and return the lands the pope claimed as his own. In 754 at Ponthion the bargain was struck; Pepin and his sons were anointed as a solemn sign of Pepin's position as the Christian Ruler and of his sons' right of succession. In

756 Pepin defeated the Lombards and returned the territory claimed by the pope. This new alliance marked a significant step on the way to creating a Western Empire which would be independent of the East.

The wider historical question concerned authority. From where did the pope enjoy the authority to make Pepin the undisputed Christian Ruler in the West, and on what basis did he make claims to various parts of Italy? The answer lies at least partly with the 'Donation of Constantine' which was thought to be a letter written by the Emperor Constantine to Pope Silvester on 30 March, 313, In it there is a record of Constantine's conversion to Christianity, his cure from leprosy and his subsequent baptism. There is also a list of the gifts made by the emperor to the pope, among them the Lateran Palace, the recognition of Rome's pre-eminence over all other sees, and the transfer of imperial power to the pope in the West. There is no doubt, however, that this document was an eighth-century forgery written to justify the break with the East and to ease the minds of the Franks by providing proof of the pope's right to anoint Pepin. The author wanted the two basic claims of the papacy, namely, universality and temporal authority, to enjoy documentary proof, and Constantine, the first great Christian Emperor, was the ideal source of authority for such proof.

Once the Franks had given the pope the lands he claimed, he was in possession of a substantial geographical area which drove an east-west wedge across the middle of Italy. This territory was known as the Papal States, and the popes were to exercise authority over these states until 1870. However Stephen and his successors still needed physical help and protection and clearly the Franks' cooperation was vital for the well-being of the papacy. If that cooperation were withdrawn or the balance destroyed, the pope could find himself in a difficult position. As long as Pepin lived the popes could relax, but events were to prove such relaxation impossible under Pepin's successor.

In 768 Pepin died, and according to the alliance treaty of 754 his two sons, Charles and Carloman, succeeded him. In 771 Carloman died and Charles, who was soon to receive the cognomen 'great' and so be known to posterity as Charlemagne, reigned for the next forty-three years until his death in 814. His earliest biographer, Einhard, has left us the following description:

The emperor was strong and well built. He was tall in stature though not excessively so, for his height was just seven times the length of his own foot. The top of his head was round and his eyes were piercing and unusually large. His nose was slightly longer than normal. He had a fine head of white hair, and his expression was gay and good-humoured. As a result whether he was seated or standing he always appeared masterful and dignified. His neck was short and rather thick and his stomach a trifle too heavy, but the proportions of the rest of his body prevented one from noticing these blemishes. His step was firm and he was manly in all his movements. He spoke distinctly but his voice was thin for a man of his physique. His health was good, except that he suffered from frequent attacks of fever during the last four years of his life, and towards the end he was lame in one foot.

For much of his reign Charles demonstrated his military skill in subduing his enemies and extending the boundaries of his kingdom. His first major victory was against the Lombards in 774 at Pavia. Charles had already been involved with the Lombards since he had married, and subsequently divorced, the daughter of Desiderius, the Lombard king. After Pavia he forced Desiderius to retire into a monastery and he himself assumed the Lombard crown as well as being rewarded by the pope with the title 'Protector of the Papacy'. This latter was to be of value in stressing the connection between Charles and the Roman Church. In 778 Bavaria was conquered and subjected to a feudal type relationship. The Saxons were less pliable and for much of his reign Charles was engaged in his longest and most cruel campaign against the Saxon peoples who, on several occasions, rose up against Frankish attempts to dominate them. His first expedition into Spain in 778 ended in near-disaster with a major defeat on the return journey, graphically described with a poet's licence in *La Chanson de Roland*. Despite this setback Charles was determined to conquer Northern Spain and create a buffer between his kingdom and the Muslims firmly established in the south. Although this too was an arduous campaign, by the turn of the century he had captured Barcelona which became the capital of the Spanish March. By the time of his death Charles had expanded the territory under his rule beyond all recognition and had created the greatest empire since the Roman Empire centuries earlier.

Pope Hadrian I had worked for twenty-four years in harmony with Charles and won both his respect and his affection. On Hadrian's death in 796, Leo III was unanimously elected his successor. However, he was of a different calibre to Hadrian and soon found himself at odds with Hadrian's supporters. Rumours were spread about Leo's personal morality, about the validity of his election and even his right to continue in office. He appealed to Charles for help, denouncing the rumours as lies and claiming to be innocent of the slanderous attacks on his name and character. In 800 Charles eventually came to Rome to preside over a court in which Leo was to profess his innocence. The *Liber Pontificalis* or 'The Papal Book' which is a collection of early papal biographies, records the event:

> On the next day in the same Church of St Peter the Apostle, there assembled together all the archbishops, the bishops and abbots and all the Franks who were in the service of the same mighty king, and all the Romans as well in the same Church of St Peter the Apostle, and in their presence the venerable pontiff, clasping the four holy gospels of Christ, went up to the pulpit in the sight of all and said in a clear voice under oath: 'Of all these false charges which have been laid against me by the Romans who maliciously persecuted me I have no knowledge, nor am I conscious of having done such things'. And when this was done a prayer was offered, and all the archbishops, bishops, abbots and all the clergy gave praise to God and to Our Lady Mary eternally virgin mother of God, and to St Peter the chief of the Apostles and all the saints of God.

The significance of this incident lies in the fact that the pope was not tried as such, but that his own personal confession of his innocence was regarded as sufficient. This safeguarded the principle, to which popes in the future would make appeal, that the pope could not be judged by anyone.

On Christmas Day 800 Charles, still in Rome, was crowned as Holy Roman Emperor by Pope Leo III. This has caused controversy right down to the present day. The main questions concern Charles' own knowledge of Leo's intentions, the right of the pope to perform such a ceremony, and the reaction of the East to the creation of a Western Empire which was no longer part of a single whole but independent of the East. The *Liber Pontificalis* records the event:

> After this, when the birthday of Our Lord Jesus Christ came round, they all assembled in the Church of St Peter the Apostle. And on this occasion the venerable and gentle pontiff crowned him with his own hands, with a most precious crown. Then all the loyal Romans, seeing the great love and care which he showed for the holy Church of Rome and for its Vicar, inspired by God and by St Peter who holds the keys of the kingdom of heaven, cried out aloud with one voice: 'To Charles, most pious Augustus crowned by God, mighty and peaceable Emperor, long life and victory!' Before the holy tomb of Peter the Apostle it was said three times

with the invocation of many saints and by all the company he was established as Emperor of the Romans.

This account from the papal archives stresses the role of the pope and in particular links that role with Peter the apostle. Einhard, in his account gives a different emphasis:

Charlemagne really came to Rome to restore the Church which was in a bad state, but in the end he spent the whole winter there. It was on this occasion that he received the title of Emperor Augustus. At first he was far from wanting this. He made it clear that he would not have entered the Cathedral that day at all, although it was the greatest of all the festivals of the Church, if he had known in advance what the pope was planning to do.

Whether Charles could have been taken so completely off guard by the pope's action is at least open to question, but what is certain is that the coronation marked the creation of a Western Empire which was understood as the Roman Empire and which stood as a threat and challenge to the East. The gradual erosion of Eastern imperial influence in the West, added to the massive internal problems facing the Empress Irene – who, on the death of her husband Emperor Leo IV in 780, had become regent until such time as her son was old enough to exercise authority in his own right – meant that any opposition to the creation of the Western empire would be token at best. Nevertheless Charles had to withstand a certain pressure from the East for the rest of his life. However, it was the papacy and the city of Rome which gained the most from this historic event. For the next four centuries the Holy Roman Emperor was crowned by the pope, usually in Rome. Such a practice could only enhance the prestige of the papacy and further stressed that the bond uniting the still disparate groups in the West was the Christian faith as authoritatively proclaimed by the Church of Rome.

Throughout his long career Charles demonstrated a number of interests and skills. He recognised the importance of education, particularly so in the case of the clergy. At his capital city of Aachen he brought together some of the greatest scholars of the day, among them Paul the Deacon, Dungal, Theodulf and, most famous of all, Alcuin of York. He was responsible for pioneering a new handwriting known as 'Carolingian miniscule' and he arranged for the copying of books in unprecedented numbers, recognising the importance of making libraries available for a wide readership. He encouraged the establishment of many new schools, mainly, though not exclusively, to help prepare men for the clerical life. The most famous of these schools was the Palace School at Aachen, run by Alcuin. His patronage of education and culture has led historians to label this period as the 'Carolingian Renaissance'.

His relations with the Church were largely cordial and respectful, though there were few who doubted the immense influence he had over the Church. He believed that 'to us God has confided the task of ruling the Church' and he put his belief into practice. His understanding of the respective role of king and pope can be seen from a letter he wrote to Leo:

> For the King's task was the effective strengthening, consolidating, propagating and preserving the faith, the pope's task was to support the king in this duty by praying for him like Moses with outstretched arms.

Charles also enhanced the Church materially with many gifts of property and money and by his insistence on the tithe system of upkeep. He tried to impose uniformity in several aspects of Church life by promulgating Hadrian's code of ecclesiastical law, the Roman Sacramentary for use in the liturgy, the Rule of Benedict as the sole rule for monastic life and 'Books of Homilies' for preachers. He used clerics in the administration of his kingdom appointing them along with lay people and sending them as his representatives throughout the empire. He supported the local bishops and left no one in any doubt as to their importance in the life of the Church. He entered into dogmatic debate, usually supporting the pope as in his condemnation of Adoptionism in Spain, but on one occasion finding himself at odds with him, when Charles refused to accept the orthodoxy of the Council of Nicaea in 787 which had restored the use of icons. The reason for this may well have been in the faulty translation that Charles received and a consequent misunderstanding. His interest in dogma was at least in part motivated by the realisation that heresy posed a political threat as well as raising religious problems. He respected the papal office and worked well with Hadrian, while his refusal to judge Leo III suggested that he even respected him whom so many had abused.

By his death in 814 the Western Empire was beginning to look like the Western Europe of our own day. The kingdom Charles had inherited from his father Pepin had expanded both in size and influence and the creation of the Western Empire in 800 was really no more than official recognition of three major power blocks, the East, and West and the Muslims. He left the Church sounder in numbers and organisation, and his promotion of education was to withstand the difficulties yet to come. But the future was also to prove how much the empire had depended on Charles himself.

On Charlemagne's death, his son Louis the Pious (814–40) assumed office and was crowned emperor. Within a short time Louis' inability to govern the vast Western empire became increasingly apparent. This disintegration accelerated after his death and the subsequent division between his sons. Norsemen, Saracens and Magyars settled within the empire, administration broke down and no single figure was able to exert control until the appearance of Otto the Great in 936. In a little under forty years Otto then brought back firm government and imposed strict control on every aspect of life, including the Church. In 964 he deposed Pope John XII and appointed Pope Leo VIII, thus bearing witness to the relative fortunes of pope and emperor. This led to thirty years of schism between the supporters of John and those of Leo. Despite the brief pontificate of Silvester (999–1003) the papacy not only failed to exert any real leadership, it also became increasingly dominated by the leading Roman families, one of which, the Tusculum, provided three popes between 1012 and 1044. It was to be one of Otto's successors, Henry III (1039–56), who was responsible for freeing the papacy from such control and allowing the popes to concentrate on the reform necessary for the Church at that time.

In the century between Charlemagne and Otto, with the failure of imperial leadership, the papacy had the opportunity of imposing its authority in the West, but in the event only Nicholas I (858–67) whom one contemporary described as 'The Lord of all the World', seized the opportunity. During his pontificate relations with the East worsened considerably, but the East's attempts to depose him proved unsuccessful. In the West he was conscious of the necessity of demonstrating his authority in practice – he was successful in confrontations with churchmen like Bishop John of Ravenna and Bishop Hincmar of Rheims; and with statesmen like King Lothair of Lorraine. Nicholas, though, was an exception in a period which saw various factors militating against papal leadership. The bishops themselves were beginning to question the idea of papal monarchy, and questioning too whether Christ had in fact intended his powers to be conferred through Peter to all the apostles and hence not simply to the pope but to all the bishops. When, in practice, the popes were weak, the bishops were able to strengthen their claims. The rise of the so-called 'proprietary system' further eroded ecclesiastical authority. According to this system the owner of a piece of land was at liberty to build a church on that land and then appoint an incumbent. The greater landowners were in this way able to exert influence both on religious and on diocesan life. Such a system had serious repercussions for relations between the Church and the State and in part was to give rise to the serious 'Investiture Controversy'. With the rise of the Roman aristocracy the popes found it increasingly difficult to retain their independence or effectively to rule the city of Rome which, from the earliest period of the Church's history, had assumed enormous importance. Finally the popes themselves lost control. John VIII (872–82) was the first pope to be murdered. The body of Formosus (891–96) was exhumed, tried, found guilty of heinous crimes and disposed of in the Tiber. Between 896–98 there were six popes, none of whom reigned long enough to reverse this negative and self-destructive trend.

So many factors weighed against the papacy that the question was not why the popes failed to assume leadership, but how did the papacy survive at all? Nonetheless there were still people loyal to the papacy. Many of these had been brought to Christianity by the missionaries of the seventh and eighth centuries – men like Willibrord (658–739) who left his native Northumbria in 675 to spend twelve years in Ireland before working for the rest of his life in the Netherlands. Perhaps the most famous was Wynfrith, from Devon, known to posterity as Boniface (680–754) and called 'The Apostle of Germany'. After an abortive mission in 716 Boniface set out again for Germany in 718 where he worked under papal approval until his martyrdom at Dokkum in 754. He and others like him brought many converts to the Christian faith and practice, part of which was a loyalty to the Bishop of Rome.

Even more important for the survival of the papacy, indeed for the survival of the Church, was the reform of the Religious Orders. Benedict of Nursia had feared for the survival of his monks, and yet despite this his Rule had not only survived but had flourished, and another Benedict, of Aniane, helped to secure its long-term success. Benedict of Aniane was born about 750 and converted to Christianity c.773. For some six years between 775–81 he lived in a Benedictine monastery at Dijon where he came to believe that many of his fellow monks had lost their appetite for the religious life, preferring a more comfortable existence. In 782 he founded a monastery at Aniane, west of Marseilles, where he imposed on his companions such a strict regime that eventually all of them deserted him. Realising that he had over-reacted to his Dijon experience, Benedict aimed for the scrupulous observance of the primitive Rule, a copy of which he had recently acquired. He set about restoring the balance that had been such a feature of Benedict of Nursia's thinking and practice. He struck out any accretions or abuses that had crept in over the centuries, he upheld the primacy of prayer and demanded manual work of all, while allowing those who were capable the time to pursue more intellectual interests. In 814 Louis the Pious brought Benedict to Aachen and instructed him to establish a monastery near Aachen at Inde which was to serve as a model for others. Louis guaranteed Inde total freedom from any lay control and appointed Benedict as superior of all the houses in France. In 817 there was a meeting of all the major abbots at Aachen where they produced the 'Capitulare Monasticum' which was to be the official and binding version of the Benedictine Rule, aimed at imposing uniformity. Inspectors were to supervise the implementation of this reform and each house was urged to send two representatives to Inde for a period of in-service training.

This constituted a courageous attempt to reform and revitalise monastic life, as a result of which Benedict has been called the 'Second Founder of Western Monasticism'. However his death, in 821, together with the general breakdown of administration and the gradual disintegration of the quality of life within the empire, meant that it was nearly a century before monastic reform flourished again. This time the centre was at Cluny, near Macon, in Southern Burgundy. In 910 Duke William of Aquitaine founded a monastery at Cluny with twelve Benedictine monks. The charter which he granted was unique in that it placed the monks under the special patronage of the papacy, thus preventing any lay or episcopal interference, and linking the reform of Cluny directly with the papacy. The monks were to follow the Rule of Benedict and they enjoyed control over their lands and revenues as well as the right to elect their abbot and to see to the daily running of the monastery. In 931 Pope John XI gave Cluny the right to control those monasteries that wished to join the reform movement. This decree was to have far-reaching effects on monastic life both in France and beyond.

Any house wishing to be subordinated to Cluny had to make certain concessions. The abbot was demoted to the rank of prior and was appointed by, and answerable to, the Abbot of Cluny. Individual monks made their vows to the Abbot of Cluny while each community agreed to pay a small tax to Cluny and obey its rules. In return for this loss of independence the houses shared in the rights and privileges of Cluny, notably freedom from lay and episcopal control. By 1100 over one thousand monasteries had joined the Cluniac reform and had made Cluny the most powerful monastery of all time. This reform, which benefitted both religious life and the papacy during a period of great difficulty for the Church, was helped by a factor which no one could either have foreseen or engineered, namely the immensely long lives of the abbots. Between 927 – 1109, a period of 182 years there were only four main abbots; Odo (927–42); Maieul (943–94); Odilo (994–1049) and Hugh the Great (1049–1109). They brought not only stability but also vision and competence, and helped to make Cluny a centre of reform for nearly two centuries.

Other places inspired by Cluny were also influential in reform throughout the Church. In England, during the reign of King Edgar (957–75), there were several examples of monastic reform and revival most notably at Glastonbury with Dunstan, Abingdon with Ethelwold, and Ramsey with Oswald. All enjoyed a similar direct link with the papacy. They were particularly important for the intellectual life of the country, for much time and effort was spent there in copying and illuminating manuscripts. In Normandy, between Rouen and Lisieux, a monastery was founded at Bec which again was to have an enormous impact since men of the stature of Lanfranc and Anselm were among their number.

This monastic reform within the Church, together with the political stabilization under the Ottonians, helped the West to recover from the difficult century following the death of Charlemagne. However, in one area there was neither recovery nor progress, namely in relations with the East. The ending of the Iconoclast controversy in the East, with the accession of the Emperor Michael III and the subsequent Council of Constantinople in 843, had restored orthodoxy but had also ensured a host of difficulties. The controversy which had lasted for more than a century had split the Eastern Church and caused such bitterness as to make any reconciliation between the different parties almost impossible. The victory of orthodoxy was celebrated with an unprecedented wave of enthusiasm for the use and veneration of icons. The monks who had consistently opposed the iconoclasts emerged as both national heroes and watchdogs of orthodoxy. Throughout the controversy relations between East and West had been strained, at times almost to breaking point, and most significantly a new Western empire had been created at the very time when the East was powerless to prevent it. Now relations between East and West were strained even further by new pressures.

In 858 Ignatius, the Patriarch of Constantinople, a man who had refused any compromise with those iconcoclast clergy who sought re-admittance into the Church, was deposed by the more moderate Photius. In 861 a synod at Constantinople, at which the papal legates were present, formally accepted Photius as Patriarch. Two years later Ignatius appealed to Pope Nicholas I against this decision, and

Nicholas, on hearsay evidence only, declared in favour of Ignatius, thus contradicting the synod at which his legates had been present. Photius and his supporters regarded this as a blatant intrusion by the pope into the internal affairs of the Eastern Church. Relations were then further strained by an incident in Bulgaria. In 865 the Bulgarian leader, Boris, together with thousands of his followers, were baptised by missionaries from the Eastern Church which had naturally expected Boris to invite Constantinople to help organise the Church in Bulgaria. However Boris turned not to Constantinople but to Rome; and in 866 he invited the Western Church to establish a hierarchy in Bulgaria. Pope Nicholas, seeing this as an opportunity for expansion, despatched missionaries to Bulgaria to investigate the situation. To the uncommitted this episode might seem little more or less than an honourable squabble between East and West over some new converts, but to the parties involved it was a question, not simply of honour, but of authority.

In 867 Photius summoned a synod at Constantinople which attacked the errors and ignorance of the Western Latin Church, and excommunicated and deposed the pope. This hostile position lasted for a decade until the death of Ignatius in 877. His death removed any rival claimant to the Patriarchate of Constantinople and allowed renewed discussions to take place between East and West. After concessions by both sides, relations were restored and Photius was accepted by Rome. In 879 a synod at Constantinople formally accepted Photius, annulled any former condemnations and, significantly, condemned any additions to the creed. This last point was specifically aimed at what had been boiling up into a major controversy over the 'filioque' clause which was now accepted generally in the West, but resisted in the East. The 'filioque' is an addition to the Constantinopolitan creed of 381 which had claimed that the Holy Spirit 'proceeds from the Father'. At sometime around the sixth century in Spain certain theologians added the clause that the Holy Spirit proceeds from the Father 'and the Son' (filioque) and this gradually became accepted throughout the Western Church, notably by Charlemagne, and was taught by missionaries from that time onwards. The West agreed that it was an addition to the creed as proclaimed at Constantinople but claimed that it was both a natural and necessary addition. The Eastern Church steadfastly rejected the 'filioque' both on the grounds of its being an addition and also of its being theologically unsound. But behind this whole controversy, again, was the question of authority, the root of the differences between the two sides.

The fact that there were no further clashes between East and West until the middle of the eleventh century was due both to the internal problems suffered by both and to a general drifting apart. By the eleventh century these were in effect, two churches. The pope was no longer informed of the election of the Patriarch of Constantinople and he was removed from the prayers of the Eastern rite. This situation might well have continued but for a series of events in Southern Italy: around 1040 the papacy decided to rid Southern Italy of all traces of Eastern influence and to impose the Latin rite on the Churches there. To achieve this the pope made an alliance with the Normans who promptly provided the necessary military force. Hardly had this been achieved when the papacy became nervous of the growing strength of their new allies and appealed to the East for help against the Normans! The Patriarch of Constantinople, Michael Cerularius, led the refusal to become involved in such power politics and added fuel to the controversy by imposing the Eastern rite on Latin Churches in Constantinople and condemning several western practices – including the use of unleavened bread, the demand of celibacy on the clergy, and the use of the 'filioque'.

Pope Leo IX (1049–54), one of the first reforming popes of this period, sent Cardinal Humbert and a small delegation to Constantinople in 1054 in an attempt to defuse the situation. Humbert and Cerularius never met and, far from pursuing peace, were responsible for the final separation of 1054. Humbert left a bull of excommunication dated 16 July 1054 which, after giving the reason for his presence in Constantinople and praising the emperor, clergy and laity of the city, continued 'But as for Michael, called by the title of Patriarch, and those who share his folly, they are in fact sowing an abundant crop of heresies each day in the bosom of the city'. The following heresies are then mentioned to which Michael's position is compared and likened: the Simoniacs, Valesians, Arians, Donatists, Nicolatians, Serverians, Pneumatoachi and the Nazarenes.

Michael, after having received the written admonitions of our master, Pope Leo, has refused to amend all these errors and many other culpable acts . . . Let Michael the neophyte . . . and with him Leo, who calls himself bishop of Achridia, and Michael's chancellor, Constantine . . . and all those who follow them in the above-mentioned errors and presumptuous temerities, let all those come under the anathema.

. . . Let everyone who persists in attacking the faith of the Holy Roman Church and its sacrifice be anathema, Maranatha, and not be considered as a Catholic Christian but as a prozymite heretic!

Humbert beat a hasty retreat from the city and it was 24 July before Michael made formal reference to that 'impious and execrable document'. Before this, though, he had already pronounced his anathema 'on all those who blasphemed against the orthodox faith'. His reply took the form of a circular letter which upheld the orthodoxy of the East and condemned the heresy of the West. Significantly this letter maintained that Rome and Constantinople had gone their separate ways for years and that reconciliation with Rome was neither necessary nor even desirable. These last two statements spell out the reality of the situation. 1054 was only the final act in a long drama of difference and dispute.

After the excommunications of that year relations between the two Churches were damaged further by the activities of the crusaders in the twelfth and thirteenth centuries, while the attempts at reconciliation, at Lyons in 1274 and Florence in 1438–9, proved to be futile. The fall of Constantinople in 1453 was symbolic of the destructive forces that had been in evidence for so much of that city's history. In Church discipline, theology and missionary practice the two sides have continued to develop separately and it is only in the present day that serious dialogue has begun again. There was an historic moment on 7 December 1965 with the joint declaration of Pope Paul VI and Patriarch Athenagoras I in which they

> Regret the offensive words, unfounded reproaches and unworthy actions which on both sides marked or accompanied the unfortunate events of the period. . . . Regret equally and efface from the memory and presence of the Church the Sentences of Excommunication that followed them, the memory of which acts to our own day are an obstacle to our drawing together in charity, and consign them to oblivion. . . . Deplore lastly the unfortunate precedents and later developments which, influenced by various factors such as misunderstanding and mutual distrust, led in the end to the actual breaking off of ecclesiastical communion.

The declaration ends with the hope that full communion will be restored.

Eight years before the final separation between East and West in 1054, the situation facing the Western Church was complicated by the existence of three claimants to the papacy and the absence of any effective machinery to decide between them. In 1046 Emperor Henry III solved the problem with ruthless simplicity when he dismissed all three claimants and appointed a German bishop who took the name of Clement II (1046–7). He was succeeded by a second imperial appointment, Damasus II (1048), before Bruno, Bishop of Toul, became Pope Leo IX (1049–54). Leo was born in 1002 and, when five years old, he had been placed into the care of the Bishop of Toul. In 1026 he was ordained deacon and on the death of the bishop was consecrated as his successor where he remained, governing the diocese with great success, for the next twenty years. When Henry III offered him the papacy he agreed on condition that the clergy and people of Rome accepted him as their choice. As if to reinforce this condition he entered Rome as a barefoot pilgrim only to be acclaimed 'a most strong pope whom the Lord has sent us to free us from our enemies'.

During his short reign Leo demonstrated the same powerful leadership over the Church as had been his hallmark in Toul. He broke the opposition of the major Roman families; he was ruthless with churchmen who had gained their position through simony or who were living immoral lives. A reform synod in Rome at Easter 1049 set the tone for the pontificate and was the first of many such synods throughout the Church. He surrounded himself with known reformers, Humbert who was later sent to Constantinople, Hildebrand who became Gregory VII, and Peter Damiani, the deepest thinker of them all. He extended papal prestige by travelling throughout the Church, personally presiding over the reform synods and spending less than six months of his reign in Rome. For all this his pontificate was not one of total success. His demands on both lay and clerical orders caused both suspicion and hatred and he himself was to die a prisoner of the Normans; but he is regarded as the instigator of reform in the Church, a reform which was to develop into a direct conflict between Church and State.

The intervention of the State in papal appointments continued with Victor II (1055–7) and although all four had been effective popes, this did not remove the taint of imperial interference. In 1056 Emperor Henry III died leaving his son to assume the crown as Henry IV. However he was only seven and unlikely to pose any threat to the Church for the immediate future. In 1059, Nicholas II (1059–61) made use of this weakness in the empire and summoned a Lateran Synod during which certain guidelines for papal elections were drawn up. The seven cardinal bishops* were to be the first group to confer about a candidate after which they would involve the rest of the cardinal clergy, the twenty-eight cardinal priests, those whose churches were within the walled city of Rome, and the eighteen

---

*The cardinal bishops originated in the eighth century, being first mentioned in 732. One possible reason is that they were used by the pope as his representatives on different occasions. They were the bishops of dioceses near Rome.

cardinal deacons, those who held special administrative posts within the Roman Church. When this larger group had settled on a candidate they would invite the rest of the Roman clergy and the people of Rome to accept their choice. Only then would the emperor be informed of the election. Effectively this decree created the College of Cardinals as the body responsible for the election of the pope, reduced the role of the laity and attempted to prevent interference by secular authorities. Theoretically the guidelines were clear, but in practice they still depended on the good will of the secular rulers, and their credibility was stretched when Henry IV appointed an anti-pope, Honorius II, in opposition to the cardinals' choice of Alexander II (1061–73). Alexander, in fact, enjoyed the support of the vast majority of the Church, was very much a part of the reform movement and, despite the shadow of Honorius until his death in 1072, increased the prestige of the papacy and prepared the way for the pontificate of Gregory VII (1073–85).

Gregory's chances of ecclesiastical preferment had seemed to vanish when he was exiled along with Gregory VI in 1046. However Leo IX recognised in this austere and disciplined cleric a man who was bent on reform in the Church, and he brought him to Rome along with other reformers in 1049. After this he began to exert great influence in Rome and beyond until his own election in 1073. He was quick to repeat his predecessor's reform decrees concerning simony, clerical marriage and especially lay investiture. In March 1075 he issued the *Dictatus Papae*, of which only twenty-seven chapter headings survive. These dictates contained nothing original but, taken together, they represented a considerable challenge to that secular ideology which claimed and practised authority in its own right.

This clash of ideologies turned into the 'investiture controversy' between Church and State, when in 1075 Henry IV, having successfully campaigned against the Saxons, turned his full attention to the Church. In that year the archdiocese of Milan fell vacant. According to the sixth canon of the Lateran Synod of 1049, and the subsequent insistence of the popes, only the Church had the right to fill that vacancy. However this represented a change in practice and deprived the secular ruler of a legitimate voice in a position which had secular as well as spiritual responsibilities. Henry, recognising both the political and ecclesiastical importance of Milan, decided to appoint his own candidate and test the strength and resolve of the pope. On hearing of Henry's action, Gregory threatened him with excommunication to which Henry replied in January 1076 by denouncing Gregory as a usurper and claiming that his election was invalid. In this Henry was supported by many of the German bishops who were loyal to him and who also feared the growth of papal centralisation. At the Lenten Synod of 1076 Gregory retaliated by excommunicating Henry, declaring him deposed and releasing all his subjects from their allegiance to him. He went on to excommunicate the Archbishop of Mainz and gave the other bishops until 1 August to submit to papal authority. This effectively legalised opposition to Henry and caused many of his supporters to defect. At Easter, Henry from the safety of Utrecht, declared Gregory deposed. This was a major political blunder because he could neither supervise nor enforce the deposition from such a distance. This naive outburst cost Henry even more support and, with many of the bishops submitting to papal authority, he recognised that his own position was becoming untenable. In October he agreed to seek papal pardon and rehabilitation and to refrain from government until this had been achieved. He further agreed to a meeting at Augsburg organised by the German princes and presided over by the pope for February 1077.

Henry then made his best political move. He realised that both the pope and the German princes would want to extract as many concessions from him as possible at Augsburg, so he determined to appeal personally to the pope for pardon at Canossa in January 1077. The politician in Gregory recognised the importance of Augsburg, the priest in him recognised his responsibilities, and the priest overcame the politician when Gregory absolved Henry and lifted the censures against him. The effects were immediate as Henry, now freed from the ban, took up the reins of government and received enthusiastic support from those who had previously wavered. The German princes, feeling betrayed by Gregory, elected an anti-king, Rudolf of Swabia, whom they asked Gregory to recognise. However he procrastinated to such an extent that Germany suffered three years of violent civil war. In 1080 Gregory again excommunicated Henry but this second censure had little effect other than to provoke Henry into appointing an anti-pope, Clement III. Gregory's fortunes continued to spiral downwards until he felt compelled to seek help from the Normans who responded by ravaging Rome and taking Gregory into protective custody. On 25 May 1085 Gregory died after reputedly saying: 'I have loved righteousness and hated iniquity therefore I die in exile'. Broken and defeated, deserted by many and blamed for the war in Germany and the destruction of Rome, Gregory's pontificate which had begun with such optimism ended in personal tragedy. Ultimately he had been unable to put theory into practice and his words had become increasingly hollow. However he remains firmly within the reform tradition of the Church and his successors continued his policy and strove to improve the condition of the Church.

The anti-pope, Clement III, was resident in Rome supported by imperial troops when Gregory died. Those cardinals who remained loyal to Gregory eventually elected Victor III (1086–87), and then Urban II (1088–99), during whose pontificate the papacy won back much of its credibility. Urban shared Gregory's desire for reform but he displayed a political realism which had been lacking in his predecessor. He dispelled many of the fears of the bishops by taking them more into his confidence and using them in administration. He was even prepared to allow those clerics who had received their positions from lay hands, to retain them if they were prepared to swear an oath of loyalty to the pope. Both measures helped greatly to restore papal prestige but arguably the greatest single reason for this upsurge in papal fortunes came with the preaching of the first crusade. In March 1095 an emissary from the East appealed to the pope for help against the Turkish invasion of the Holy Land. It was in response to this appeal that Urban made an impassioned plea at Clermont which set in motion the crusading movement, with all its consequences.

By 1094 when Urban was finally able to enter Rome, his leadership had enhanced the prestige of the papacy, and by a strong yet realistic policy he had insisted on the prohibition of lay investiture. Significantly at this same time there was a growth in propaganda with the writings of men like Guido of Ferrara, Ivo of Chartres and Hugh of Fleury. They were trying to see both sides of the controversy and make distinctions between the spiritual and temporal responsibilities of a bishop, the consequent rights and duties of the office, and the rights of those responsible for appointing to the office. They were to be instrumental in laying the foundations for a solution to the question with the agreement at Worms in 1122. Before this, Pope Paschal II (1099–1118) had proposed a radical solution which, if accepted, would have stripped the bishops of their wealth and influence in political life and would have made a bishop simply and solely a pastor of the Church, free to concentrate all his attention on spiritual and pastoral obligations. In this way the State would have no claim on them and the temporal authorities would cease to have any interest in appointments. Henry V, who had succeeded his father in 1106, agreed to such a proposal, seeing in it the possibility of accummulating vast amounts of land and revenue; but neither the bishops, who were opposed to losing their wealth and standing, nor the German princes, who feared the emperor's authority would be hugely improved, would sanction such a proposal and Paschal was obliged to withdraw his suggestion.

Eventually pressures, especially in Germany, made it imperative that some solution be found and a compromise was thrashed out and

promulgated first at Worms and later ratified by the First Lateran
Council in 1123. The solution owed much to the work of the
propagandists attempting, as it did, to consider the claims of both the
Church and the state. According to the terms of the agreement all
higher ecclesiastics were to be elected canonically and inducted by
the local metropolitan. The secular authority was permitted to be
present at the elections and retained the right to invest the new
bishop with his temporal possessions. In disputed cases the 'Stronger
Party' was to decide, though who exactly constituted the stronger
party was not clear. Though certain areas remained undefined, the
controversy was ended in that each side recognised the rights of the
other and, at least for the time being, good relations were restored
between pope and emperor.

It was not only in the empire that Church-State relations had been
severely tested; the problem was much evident in England, albeit on
a smaller scale. In 1066 the Church in England had come under the
influence of the Normans after the successful invasion of William the
Conqueror, an invasion which had been supported by Pope Alexander II. The Conqueror brought strong government and reform to
the Church, but he remained adamant about his right to appoint
bishops and refused Gregory's demand in 1080 that he should
refrain from this. William went even further in preventing papal
interference by demanding royal vetting of any papal letters, royal
consent for any papal excommunication and royal permission before
any English bishop could travel abroad. Despite this hard line with
Rome, William was concerned for the well-being and development
of the Church, in aid of which he imported several Norman bishops,
most notably Lanfranc who, in 1070, became Archbishop of Canterbury. This partnership between king and archbishop was of great
importance and value to the Church in England. Canterbury became
the undisputed seat of authority in England by simply subordinating
York to it. The only serious opposition came from Scotland where
there had been a constant claim of independence from both Canterbury and York since the end of the eighth century. The reforms that
had taken place in England during the reign of the Conqueror had
already been implemented in Scotland with a division of the dioceses
and an increase in the number of monasteries. In both Scotland and
England Church councils pushed through reforms and improved
organisations. By the time of William's death in 1087 and Lanfranc's
in 1089 the Church in England was on very firm foundations, a
firmness which was matched by the massive solidity of the Norman
architecture which radically affected the shape and look of churches.

Lanfranc's eventual successor at Canterbury was Anselm who,

like Lanfranc, had spent considerable time at Bec where he had gained a reputation as both a philosopher and a theologian, and produced works of the lasting quality of the *Monologion* and the *Proslogion* in which he attempted to prove the existence of God by reason. In 1078 Anselm had become abbot at Bec and in this capacity had visited Lanfranc in England during which time he had won many admirers. In 1093 the king, William Rufus, appointed Anselm to Canterbury where he was consecrated on 4 December. If Rufus hoped for a partnership such as the Conqueror and Lanfranc had enjoyed, however, he was soon disappointed. Anselm, while believing passionately in reform, wanted the power of the king over the Church to be curtailed and the authority of the pope extended. A council held at Rockingham in 1095 brought this dispute into the open but nothing was achieved since the king was determined to keep control of episcopal appointments and Anselm was bent on giving this right to the pope.

In 1100 Henry I succeeded William Rufus and from the outset of his reign was determined to retain control of the Church, especially of appointments. In 1102 he recalled Anselm, who had gone into exile in 1097, but he was unable to reach any sort of compromise with the archbishop. Eventually, in 1107, Henry made his own personal agreement with the pope, by-passing Anselm completely. In 1109 Anselm died having spent more than half his term of office in exile. He was undoubtedly more of a theologian than a politician and his time at Canterbury caused him a great deal of personal suffering and drove a wedge between Church and State in England.

The controversy outlived Anselm, and the see of Canterbury remained vacant until 1114 when Henry appointed Ralph D'Escures as archbishop, an appointment which apparently contravened the terms of the agreement made with the pope in 1107 because Paschal despatched a papal legate to England with authority over the new archbishop. In 1122 Ralph died and the pope sent John of Cremona to assume the duties of the archbishop without actually being consecrated. However this position proved most difficult and he was removed in 1125. Ten years later Henry himself died after thirty-five years of stable government and he was succeeded by Stephen (1135–54) whose ineffectual leadership led to civil unrest and a widening split between Church and State. In 1154 the strong and capable Henry II (1154–89), succeeded to the throne and set about restoring good government. However, in so doing he began to infringe the privileges of the Church and make demands on the clergy. In 1161 the Archbishop of Canterbury, Theobald, died and Henry decided to appoint his friend and Chancellor, Thomas Becket, to Canterbury, thinking that in this way he would be able to gain the complete submission of the Church. In insisting that Becket should accept the appointment, the king had failed to appreciate that Becket the archbishop would work for the Church as single-mindedly as Becket the chancellor had worked for the State. In June 1162 Becket was consecrated archbishop and immediately adopted an austere monastic life which was in stark contrast to his days as chancellor, a position he resigned. He came into direct conflict with the king over the latter's Church policy especially over taxation and the proposed transfer of the trial of clerics from ecclesiastical to secular courts. Few of his fellow bishops recognised the implications of the king's plan, and they failed to support their new archbishop whom many of them also mistrusted. In 1164 Becket fled to France where he lived in both Cistercian and Benedictine monasteries. By 1170 Becket and Henry were sufficiently reconciled to allow the archbishop to return to England where he received an enthusiastic reception from the majority, but hostility from some of the bishops. On 29 December 1170 Becket was murdered by four knights in Canterbury Cathedral, acting, as they believed, on the wishes of the king who is alleged to have said 'will no one rid me of this troublesome monk'. This murder was regarded as an outrage both within and beyond England and Henry was obliged to do public penance to purge himself of responsibility for the death of his archbishop. Within three years Becket was canonized and his tomb became a centre for pilgrims and a constant reminder of the tension between Church and State.

Throughout Western Europe the twelfth century was a century of growth and richness in many spheres of life and, with the advantage of hindsight, it is now regarded as one of great importance for the Church. The new religious orders, reacting against the centralisation of Cluny, gave new vitality to the Church as a whole. The growth of canon law highlighted the legal machinery of the Church, improved the effectiveness of the curia, gave rise to a new breed of popes known as the 'lawyer popes' and ultimately paved the way for Innocent III. Three general councils of the Lateran, all concerned with reform, helped to confirm this generally good picture of the Church. However, the century also saw three double elections to the papacy – in 1124, 1130 and 1159 – two of which led to years of schism. It also witnessed one of the most powerful political figures since Charlemagne in the person of Frederick I 'Barbarossa' who for nearly forty years (1152–90) was a constant threat to the independence of the Church in general and the pope in particular. Finally there was the growth in opposition to the institutional Church, specifically in terms of heresy with the Manichees in France, Arnold

Brescia who denied the clergy the right to own property, and Peter Waldo who inspired the 'Poor men of Lyons'.

The new religious orders of the eleventh and twelfth centuries were represented by both semi-eremitical and cenobitical groups. Among the former were the Camaldolese who owed their inspiration and origin to Romuald (950–1027) and who settled around Camaldi in Central Italy. In 1072 they received papal approval and have existed until the present day with an accent on austerity, learning and latterly, ecumenism. The Vallambrosians were founded by John Gualbert (c. 990–1073) who left the Camaldolese c. 1036 and settled near Florence at Vallambrosa. With them the emphasis was on silent meditation and contemplation. In 1056 they were granted papal approval and existed until their final suppression in 1866. Among their alumni the Vallambrosians number Galileo (1564–1642) who was for some time a novice of the order. Of this group of semi-hermits the Carthusians remain the most famous. They were inspired by Bruno (c. 1032–1101), a highly gifted man who was in charge of education in the diocese of Rheims before being made chancellor of the diocese in 1075. He resigned his position after a series of disagreements with his bishop and, although he returned to Rheims briefly in 1080, he felt himself drawn towards an eremitical vocation and in 1085 he settled at Chartreuse near Grenoble. There he built a small monastery for like-minded people where each monk would occupy his own cell and meet only occasionally for office and Sunday Eucharist. It was not until 1127 that Guigo, the Prior of Chartreuse, composed the first written Rule, and in 1133 the Carthusians were officially recognised by the pope. Of all the religious orders within the Church they are the only ones of whom it has been said 'nunquam reformata quia nunquam deformata' – 'never reformed because they have never failed'. The Carthusians have never had great numbers but they did expand a little – for example, they arrived in England in 1178 and settled in Somerset where Hugh of Lincoln (c. 1140–1200) became prior.

All three semi-eremitical groups were in some ways offshoots from the Benedictines in that they accepted part of the Rule to which they added a much more austere tradition, more akin to Egypt than Monte Cassino. In terms of numbers and influence the second, cenobitical, reaction to Cluny was far greater, and of these the Cistercians were the most famous, the initial founder of whom was Robert of Molesme (1028–1112). In 1075 Robert founded a monastery at Molesme where he hoped to live and impose the strict observance of the Rule. However over a period of time the monastery grew in numbers and was endowed with gifts and privileges to such an extent that it became indistinguishable from the other Benedictine houses of which Robert had been critical. In 1098 he and twenty others left Molesme for Citeaux where they hoped to establish a monastery which, because of its position in a remote and unpopulated place, would not become the object of gift and preferment. In 1099 Robert was recalled to Molesme but his ideal was carried on by the next two abbots, Alberic (1099–1109) and Stephen Harding (1109–33). In 1100 the new monastery received papal approval. The Cistercians, having taken the name from Citeaux, now began a career which was to make them the greatest religious order since the Benedictines. In 1118–19 they produced the 'Charter of Love' which was effectively the constitution of the order, a second version of which appeared in 1152 and both received papal approval. Their desire was to observe the Benedictine Rule in its primitive simplicity but there were sufficient differences between them and the Benedictines to allow historians to speak of a new order. One major difference concerned authority which, under Benedict, was invested in the abbot and during the Cluniac reform had made the Abbot of Cluny one of the most powerful men in the Church, with authority over vast numbers of monks living in many different houses, resulting in excessive centralisation. In an effort to avoid such centralisation the Cistercians invested authority in the Annual General Chapter presided over by the Abbot of Citeaux but at which all abbots had an equal vote. This chapter possessed and exercised full legislative, executive and judicial authority over the whole order but left financial and administrative autonomy to the individual houses. Further, any daughter houses were not subordinated but affiliated and the abbot of each retained his status and equal voting rights. Relations with the local bishop were encouraged, with the bishop being invited to inspect and even suggest ways of improving the quality of life. No monastery could make financial demands on another but rather agreed to help each other financially should that be necessary. They agreed on a uniform discipline, which was in stark contrast to Cluny, with the emphasis on a simplified liturgy, austerity in food, clothing and living conditions, the reintroduction of manual labour and the assiduous declining of gifts whether land or revenue. By 1115 there were four main houses other than Citeaux namely La Ferté, 1113, Pontigny, 1114, and Morimond and Clarivaux, 1115. By 1153 there were 339 houses and by 1300 more than seven hundred. Their numbers were vast and included, on a scale hitherto unknown, many lay brothers who took the same monastic promises and renunciations without entering the clerical state.

The Cistercians soon became both famous and distinguished in the service of the Church. Popes used them as legates, consecrated them as bishops and instructed them to preach the crusades. Many wanted them as spiritual directors or commissioned them as spiritual writers. Their dedication to work brought its own success and prosperity and they contributed particularly to the agricultural and sheep-farming life of Western Europe. Almost inevitably they received gifts and privileges from both lay and clerical sources and by the end of the twelfth century, their life-style would certainly have surprised and probably saddened their founder.

Of all the Cistercians of this period the most famous was Bernard of Clairvaux (c.1090–1154). He was born at Dijon one of seven children, and c.1111 he decided to enter Citeaux where he began his novitiate under Stephen Harding. In 1115 he was entrusted with the founding of Clairvaux for which he is known to posterity. Both within the order and beyond, Bernard's importance from 1120 until his death has caused some historians to call these years 'the Age of Bernard', and to see him as the most powerful ecclesiastical figure of his time. He played a major role in the papal history of the period, being involved in healing the schism that split the Church between 1130–8, preaching the second crusade, and helping to reorganise and motivate the curia. As a great traveller, despite almost constant ill-health, he was in touch with all the leading personalities of the West. He demonstrated his breadth of interest and expertise in a theological clash with Abelard and through his many writings which have earned him the title of 'the holy abbot' despite his human failings which he recognised and sought to overcome. His forceful personality underlined the massive contribution of the Cistercians to Church and society in this century.

Somewhat more quietly but of great importance for the Church was the growth of canon law. About 1100 Irnerius began to lecture on Roman law at Bologna, which subsequently became the accepted centre for legal studies and has certain claims to being the first university. This attention to Roman law stimulated interest in Church law and in 1140 Gratian, a Camaldolese monk, produced the *Decretum Gratiani* which was a systematic compilation of previous church law drawn from papal decretals, conciliar canons and the decisions of the early Fathers. This became the standard text book of Church law on which other people began to write commentaries and thus expand the whole study. But there were other important repercussions. Gratian was a papalist who believed that the pope enjoyed supreme legislative authority in the Church. He accepted papal supremacy and gave precedence to papal decretals above both the conciliar canons and the Fathers. Underlying all his work was the belief that ecclesiastical law was far more important than civil law. With such a bias in favour of the popes, Gratian helped both to heighten the importance and change the character of the papacy. From the middle of the twelfth century an expertise in law became a prerequisite for a pope who was to spend much of his time on legal matters. The first example of such a pope was Alexander III (1159–81), an outstanding jurist, who despite problems posed by Frederick I enjoyed great prestige and was responsible for summoning the Third Lateran Council.

The twelfth century saw three Lateran Councils. The first in 1123 ratified the solution of the investiture controversy worked out at Worms in 1122. It was the first General Council in the West summoned by Pope Calixtus and attended by more than five hundred bishops and abbots. This council has been seen as the beginning of the second phase of reform which had begun with Leo IX and taken its name from Gregory VII. The characteristic of the second phase, which lasted until the Fourth Lateran in 1215, was its formulation in conciliar rather than papal pronouncements. Much of the other business at this first Council concerned the clergy, both diocesan and religious, aimed at tightening conditions and qualifications for entry into the clerical life and at giving the local bishop more responsibility over monasteries in his diocese. It was now necessary for religious monks to receive permission from the local bishop before preaching, or administering the sacraments, or making appointments to churches within the diocese.

The first Lateran Council was a demonstration of the strength of the Church and the decrees were promulgated in local synods throughout the Church. Almost immediately after the Council Calixtus died in 1124 and two candidates emerged both with sufficient support to persuade them of their right to the papacy. This showed up a weakness in the election decree of 1049 which had not made any provision for such a contested election. Schism was only avoided when one of the candidates was persuaded to withdraw. In 1130 a similar situation arose with two candidates being elected, consecrated and then setting out to win the approval of the Church. This led to eight years of schism which was only finally ended after the intervention of men of the calibre of Bernard of Clairvaux. He it was who stamped his authority on the Second Lateran Council, 1139, summoned by Innocent II (1130–43) to stress the unity of the Church and to continue the work of reform after the schism. At this council there was a clear condemnation of heresy: the Manichees in Southern France who were denying such central Christian doctrines as the Eucharist, marriage and infant baptism; Arnold Brescia was

also censured because of his insistence on the sinfulness of clergy
owning any possession. Lay investiture at every level was condemned as were simony, concubinage and clerical marriage which was
now declared to be invalid as well as unlawful. The laity was banned
from attending the services of a married priest and the sons of such
priests were debarred from the clerical life. Anyone appropriating
goods on the death of a priest was automatically excommunicated.
Added to this there was a certain amount of social legislation covering such distinct matters as forbidding marriage of close relations or
rights of sanctuary in churches and cemeteries.

The ending of the schism and the Second Lateran Council helped
to improve the prestige of the papacy as did the preaching of the
second crusade undertaken by Bernard in 1147–8. He was also
important in papal history for a work called 'De Consideratione' in
which he reminded the Church that the pope possessed both spiritual
authority, which he exercised personally, and temporal authority,
which he mediated to temporal rulers, and further, that his authority
embraced the whole world. It was as a result of this strong statement
on papal authority that the popes began to refer to themselves from
this time as 'Vicar of Christ'.

The middle years of the twelfth century proved to be crucial. In
1152 Conrad III of Germany died to be succeeded by Frederick I
'Barbarossa' (1152–90). In 1153 Pope Eugenius died to be succeeded
first by Anastasius IV (1153–54) and then by Adrian IV (1154–59)
the only Englishman so far to become pope. Also in 1153 Bernard of
Clairvaux died. In England Stephen was succeeded by Henry II
(1154–89); and in Sicily, an island of increasing political importance, Roger died to be succeeded by William. The accession of
Frederick I was to be of vital importance, not only because of his
ideology which made Church and pope subservient to the emperor,
but also because of his strength and his ability to transform theory
into practice. By 1158 he had gained control over Lombardy and
Milan and clearly posed a threat to Rome and the independence of
the pope. In 1159 Adrian died and, although the majority of cardinals elected Alexander III (1159–81) a small but powerful minority
elected an anti-pope, Victor IV (1159–64). The schism was precisely
the opportunity Frederick Barbarossa needed to manipulate affairs
to his own advantage. In 1160 he summoned a synod at Pavia where
he intended to judge the relative claims of the two 'popes'. Alexander
not only refused to attend but excommunicated Frederick and released his subjects from obedience. Such a forthright condemnation
was met by Frederick's denunciation of Alexander and his expressed
support for Victor. This schism was to last for twenty years and

produce a total of four anti-popes. In 1167 Frederick occupied Rome and Paschal III, Victor's successor, was solemnly crowned as pope despite Alexander's refusal to abdicate. Paschal in turn crowned Frederick as emperor.

Soon after, the imperial troops withdrew from Rome because of an epidemic and twenty-two Italian cities took this as an opportunity to form the Lombard League which was committed to self-defence and the curtailment of Frederick's power. Alexander added his support to the league and when, in 1176, it won an important victory over imperial troops at Lugano, the way was open for negotiations which found expression in the Treaty of Venice (1177) according to which Frederick abandoned the anti-pope and recognised Alexander, agreed terms with the Lombard League and gave back all papal lands, in return for which Alexander lifted the excommunication and in general accepted the appointments to the German hierarchy made during the schism.

In 1178 Alexander returned to Rome and in the following year summoned and presided over the Third Lateran Council. As with its predecessor the Council condemned heresy in the strongest terms, especially the Albigensians, and called upon the civil authorities to fulfil their obligations to root out heresy and punish heretics. The various indulgences which had been granted to the Crusaders were now extended to apply to those who fought against heresy in Europe. Peter Waldo and 'The Poor Men of Lyons' were refused approval to live and preach a mendicant life of Gospel poverty and were eventually outlawed. Further legislation concerning papal elections was introduced which demanded a two-thirds majority for the successful candidate. The minimum age for a bishop was set at thirty and for a priest at twenty-five, and further demands were made for integrity and quality. Clerics were to be judged by ecclesiastical and not civil law, the very argument which Becket had fought in England, and there was a general appeal for a simpler way of living, for example bishops were told not to take their falcons and packs of hounds on visitation in case they might give scandal! Social legislation included making provision for lepers and an improvement in the general standard of education which both encouraged the scholastic revival of the twelfth century and helped the growth of the universities.

In 1181 Alexander died after a pontificate of twenty-two years of almost constant struggle in which he had upheld and eventually exercised the rights of the papacy. The next decade produced four popes all of whom had to prevent Frederick from reneging on the Treaty of Venice and trying to rule rather than protect the papacy. In 1190 Frederick himself died while taking part in the third crusade which had been preached earlier by Gregory VIII and in which the kings of both France and England were involved. Frederick's successor, Henry VI, was determined to continue his father's policy but when he died in 1197 he left a child of three, Frederick Roger, as his successor. He was to become the very powerful Frederick II and cause the Church great problems in the future, but at this time he proved no match for the most powerful pope of the Middle Ages, Innocent III.

CHAPTER 3

Papalism and Conciliarism,
1198–1455

The aged Celestine, who had been elected pope in 1191 at the age of 85, had surprised everyone, including himself, by living until 1198. His successor, Lothar Conti, born in 1160, had studied theology at Paris and law at Bologna. In 1190, at the age of thirty, he was created a cardinal and enjoyed increasing importance during the pontificate of Celestine. On his election he took the name of Innocent III and his eighteen years as pope mark a high point of papal authority.

The political situation at his accession favoured an aggressive papal policy. The heir to the German throne was only three years old,. leaving Germany, and the empire, without an effective leader, and creating a vacuum in which different factions began to squabble. Italy had by now become thoroughly weary of the intervention of imperial troops and welcomed a break from such interference, looking to Rome for a strong and purposeful lead. The increased competence in, and influence of, Church law tended to support a papal ideology which made the pope 'the lord of all the world' and Innocent, more than any of his predecessors or successors, came closest to putting this papal theory into practice.

With his keen political sense Innocent recognised that his priority was to put his own house in order by creating a strong Rome in a settled papal state. From this well organised base he was able to extend his political power and interest throughout the Church. In the recent past the main threat to the Church had come from the German emperors, Frederick I and Henry VI. When Henry died his wife, Constance, was unable to press her claims to the throne, and, fearing for the well-being of her son Frederick, she asked the pope to act as guardian, a position he accepted on her death, placing the young boy in Sicily. In his absence there was a contest for the German throne between Philip of Swabia and Otto of Brunswick, a contest which boiled over into civil war. Whoever succeeded to the German throne would then automatically claim the imperial crown from the pope. Both contestants appealed to Innocent for his support but he delayed any decision until he could clarify what their ecclesiastical policy would entail. There can be little doubt that such procrastination was more to Innocent's benefit than to either of the contestants or to the people of Germany. This confused situation lasted until 1208 when Philip was assassinated and Otto was unanimously elected as king by the German princes. In 1209 Otto was crowned emperor by Innocent after Otto had promised to guarantee the independence of the papal States and refrain from any attempt to annexe Southern Italy and Sicily to the empire.

No sooner had Otto been crowned Emperor than he began to show his true intentions by planning a campaign against Sicily in a bid to capture Frederick whom he regarded as his only serious rival. At this, Innocent began to provoke opposition to Otto in Germany which caused him to postpone his campaign against Sicily and return to Germany in an attempt to settle the growing unease. In 1210 Otto was excommunicated and the following year all his subjects were released from their allegiance to him. In 1212 Innocent led those who now supported the claims of the young Frederick who was crowned as King of Germany by the Archbishop of Mainz. Once again there were two claimants to the German throne and the pope had been instrumental in creating them both.

In broad terms the north of Germany favoured Otto, and his supporters, called Imperialists or Guelfs, found a friend in John of England. The south supported Frederick II and they were known as Papalists or Ghibellines and they in turn enjoyed the friendship of Philip of France. But key to the whole situation was Innocent, who managed to extract from Frederick II some remarkable concessions which were expressed in the 'Golden bull of Eger' in 1213. According to this Frederick recognised the papal claim to territory in Southern Italy, agreed to renounce any involvement in lay investiture, accepted the superiority of canon law by allowing appeals from civil to ecclesiastical courts, and gave a positive commitment to rooting out heresy. Such a treaty bore witness to the strength of the papacy and to Innocent's own aptitude for extracting the most benefit from a given situation. In 1214 Frederick gained a crushing victory over Otto and, although unable to take him prisoner, was from this time onwards recognised as the undisputed king of the Germans until his death in 1250.

Throughout the whole controversy, which virtually spanned his entire pontificate, Innocent had exploited the German situation to his own and, as he understood it, the Church's advantage. He had proved himself to be more powerful than either Philip or Otto, and when Otto threatened to pose a real problem, he had produced Frederick as a rival thus creating civil discord and retaining his overall control. As long as Innocent was alive Frederick kept his promises, but after the pope's death Frederick began to impose his own will and threaten the independence of the Church.

It was not only within the Empire that Innocent demonstrated his great authority and strength. In France he became involved in the marriage affairs of King Philip Augustus when he compelled the king to take back his wife, the Danish princess Ingeborg. In Scandinavia, the Balkans, the Spanish Peninsula and elsewhere his authority was felt, but probably his most important trial of strength, outside the German struggle, was with King John of England. Since the death of Henry II in 1189 England was ruled first by Richard I (1189–99), and then by his brother John (1199–1216). Richard's first and only real preoccupation had been the Crusades and during his ten years as king he had spent less than six months in England. For much of that time he had left the running of the country to Hubert Walter, who was Archbishop of Canterbury from 1193–1205. Walter had accompanied Richard on the third crusade in 1190 and been responsible for raising the ransom to free his king from a French prison in 1192. In 1194 Richard left England again after making Walter his Chief Justice as well as Archbishop of Canterbury, positions which made him the most powerful man in the land. He outlived Richard and remained archbishop, under King John, until his death in 1205, a death which not only robbed the king of his most capable adviser but also gave rise to a contested election at Canterbury.

On Walter's death the younger monks at Canterbury elected as his successor their sub-prior Richard. King John, however, overruled them and appointed his friend Bishop John of Norwich. Both parties then appealed to Rome presuming that the pope would support their candidate, but he surprised and angered them all by naming Stephen Langton as the new archbishop. King and monks were united in their opposition to Langton and John flatly refused him entry into the country. On 25 March 1208 Innocent placed England under Interdict, an ecclesiastical censure which virtually closed down the Church by suspending the celebration of all sacraments – except baptism in the danger of death, and the final rites of the Church to one who had died. John used this as an opportunity to fill the royal exchequer with the Church's wealth and revenue. In 1209 John himself was excommunicated and his opponents among the barons seized their chance to increase their criticism of his government. In

1212 Innocent threatened to depose John if he persisted in his obstinate refusal to allow Langton to take up his appointment and he even sounded out Philip of France as to his willingness to lead an invasion of England. Faced with such internal unrest and external threats John eventually capitulated and agreed, in 1213, to allow Stephen Langton to take up his position as archbishop, and to receive his own crown from the pope as a sign of his being a papal vassal. In 1214 the Interdict was lifted and in 1215 the barons, supported by Langton, pressed home their advantage by forcing John to sign Magna Carta which curtailed the royal power in favour of the barons. Despite the fact that Innocent supported John over Magna Carta much of the king's reign was spent in opposition to the papacy, and his refusal for more than five years to concede to papal pressure can be seen either as wilful defiance or as defence of a principle. What remains indisputable is his ultimate defeat at the hands of the most powerful man ever to fill the role of pope.

There were those in the Church, both individuals and small groups, who found such papal strength unattractive, and they condemned it and other aspects of late twelfth-century Church life as unchristian. Such people believed passionately in Christ and especially in his call to poverty and simplicity. Christ had preached poverty, monastic rules included the vow of poverty and yet so many of the higher ecclesiastics, both religious and diocesan, enjoyed a standard of living that bore no relation to Christ's teaching. Their luxurious life-style led first to criticism then to anti-clericalism and finally to a break with the institutional Church. Men and women who had begun by reacting against the double standards of clerical life ultimately found themselves denying some of the central teaching of the Church and were condemned as heretics. As one contemporary historian has written:

> The most dangerous menace to the institutional structure of the medieval Church came from ideas that were deeply rooted in the ideals and teachings of Christianity itself.

For example, Peter Waldo sold all his possessions c. 1170, gave the proceeds for the relief of the poor, and set out to preach the Gospel uncluttered by worldliness. He and his companions gained grudging permission from Pope Alexander III to continue to live as mendicants and preach the Gospel on condition that they received the agreement of the local bishop. In 1184 after some Waldensians had violated this condition, a synod at Verona condemned and excommunicated them. In face of such treatment by the Church the Waldensians began to organise themselves apart from the institution and they began to ignore both the teaching and discipline of Rome. For them, preaching was of paramount importance, and they maintained that everyone had the right not only to read but also to interpret scripture to which end they had previously produced vernacular translations of the Bible. They continued to grow despite a series of repressive measures aimed at their total suppression.

The Cathari were much more numerous than the Waldensians, and the name Cathar was something of a generic term covering several small sects or groups which held the same basic belief but differed in detail. Underlying the Cathari were Manichaean tendencies towards dualism which rejected the flesh and material things as evil. The group that emerged as the most problematic for the Church were the Albigensians who were centred in Southern France. They taught that the soul was imprisoned in the body and the purpose of redemption was to achieve its release. They rejected Catholic teaching on the sacraments, and such fundamental beliefs as the resurrection of the body, as well as imposing on their followers a strict asceticism which included the prohibition of marriage. They were divided between the 'Perfect' – who received the baptism of the Holy Spirit and who were obliged to live the strictest code of conduct – and the far more numerous 'Believers' – who would lead relatively normal lives but who would only receive the baptism of the Spirit when in danger of death. The way of life of the Albigensians was in stark contrast to that of many of the Catholic clergy and it began to appeal to those who had little confidence in a clergy who knew nothing of the struggles of the ordinary christian.

Innocent was sufficiently honest and realistic to recognise the force of some of the Albigensians' criticisms, especially of the way of life of some of his bishops, but he could not and would not accept their deviation from Church teaching. For him the test of orthodoxy was submission to the teaching of the Church and he set about achieving the submission of the Albigensians. The local bishops in Southern France had proved ineffective since they would not admit that a problem existed. The Cistercians, to whom Innocent then turned, were ridiculed by the Albigensians because of *their* life-style which had changed dramatically since the beginnings at Citeaux. In 1203 Innocent authorised Dominic Guzman, the future founder of the Dominicans, to undertake a preaching tour in Southern France and even though Dominic recognised the need to speak a language the people understood and to live a life similar to their own, his results arrived too slowly for a pope rapidly losing patience. In 1208 the papal legate was murdered. Innocent then appealed to the French Knights to avenge his death by forming a crusading army under the leadership of Almaric. By 1209 this army had reached Southern France and on 21 July Beziers was razed to the ground and its entire population slaughtered. This outrage was justified by the leader in the following way, 'Kill all, kill all, for God will know his own'. In 1210 the leadership of the army passed to Simon de Montfort the elder who spent the next five years in attempting to eradicate the heresy. In 1215 Toulouse finally surrendered, an event which marked the end of this bloody campaign. Innocent was again vic- torious but only at a very heavy cost. He had eventually turned to using force after preaching and persuasion had proved either ineffec- tive or too costly in time. Force had apparently achieved the desired results, namely the expurgation of heresy, but the cost was high, and the temporary nature of this victory over the heretics only served to raise doubts about its value.

Similarly doubtful was the value of the fourth crusade, which set out for the Holy Land in 1202. Ever since the preaching of the first crusade by Urban in 1095 there had been a desire among some people in the West to aid the East in its fight against the Turks and to open a way for pilgrims to travel in safety to the Holy Places. These ideals had become obscured by the possibility of securing wealth and influence for those who remained in the East, and throughout the twelfth century the main objective shifted away from defending Christianity to maintaining a Latin presence there. The second cru- sade preached by St Bernard and undertaken in 1147 failed in its attempt to stem the spread of Moslem power and in 1187 Saladin recaptured Jerusalem. This prompted the third crusade in 1189 which cost Frederick Barbarossa his life and involved the kings of England and France. Although some territory was recovered, the primary objective, of winning back Jerusalem for the Christians, failed. Innocent himself had a two-fold aim when promoting the fourth crusade, namely winning back Jerusalem and the Holy Places and, secondly, restoring unity between East and West. He had shown an interest in crusades from the beginning of his pontificate. In 1199 he imposed a crusader tax on all clerical incomes to finance the next venture. The following year he sent a circular letter to all the leaders of Western Europe offering them the opportunity of leading the crusade. In the event all found themselves otherwise engaged and the leadership passed to a group of lesser nobles.

In November 1202, after enormous organisational and admini- strative difficulties, the fourth crusade of some 30,000 men led by Duke Boniface of Montferrat left by sea from Venice. These difficul- ties proved to be an omen because, after capturing Zarar on the coast of Dalmatia, despite strict papal prohibition, the fleet eventually anchored outside Constantinople and in 1204 the city was sacked and a Latin empire with Latin ecclesiastical organisation was established. This empire was to last until 1261 and it technically gave the pope jurisdiction in the East but the cost proved to be enormous. The East bitterly resented this unwarranted intrusion into its affairs and all the worst fears about the Western Latin Church were now confirmed. Even if Innocent was at first unaware, and then opposed to what was happening, he was in fact, once the crusading armies had left, impotent to influence their actions. Primatial authority was technically extended but the damage to the relationship between Rome and Constantinople was incalculable.

Innocent had received an excellent legal training at Bologna and had enjoyed eight years under Celestine at the very heart of the Church's legislative and administrative centre, the curia. Here he had already begun to assess the strengths and weaknesses of the Church and had determined to reform those areas of Church life which were in need of such reform. He began with the curia which he systematically divided into departments under capable and trained leaders. He counteracted various abuses by standardizing the method of appeals and introducing an exact tariff for the various stipends. He simplified the living standards of the curia officials causing resentment among those who were thus deprived, and a sense of hope among those who had long been critical of such luxury and excess. Having settled matters in the curia he then tried to improve relations between Rome and the dioceses. He recognised and constantly spoke of the importance of bishops throughout the Church and made genuine attempts to raise the standard, both of the education and zeal of those thought suitable for such an office. He believed in a regular contact between the pope and the bishops and began the practice of summoning the bishops to Rome every four years. These 'ad limina' visits were intended to be an opportunity for the local bishop to keep the pope informed about affairs in his diocese. During such visits his constant appeal was that they should keep a close watch over both the training and pastoral application of their priests.

The climax of his legal and pastoral reform came with the Fourth Lateran Council in 1215 which has been described as both the crowning point and the summary of his pontificate. This council was the most important of all those held at the Lateran and arguably the most important in the West before Trent. The groundwork and preparations began early in his pontificate and in 1213 the invitations were sent to bishops, abbots and representatives of the secular powers in an attempt to assemble together a Council which would, as far as humanly possible, represent the whole Church. When it opened on 1 November 1215, the Council boasted the largest number of members ever to meet, with more than 70 patriarchs, 400 bishops, 800 religious superiors and representatives from every major European ruler. The bull of convocation listed among the aims of the Council: the reform of the Church by rooting out abuses and building up virtues; the suppression of heresy and the strengthening of the true faith; and the relief of the Holy Land by a great crusade. The results were promulgated in seventy decrees beginning with a dogmatic decree reiterating the Church's traditional teaching in the light of various contemporary heresies. There were then a great many decrees concerning the appointment, duties and responsibilities of metropolitans and bishops, the training, education and ministry of priests and the obligations and life-style of religious. Further, there were to be no new religious orders, a law which directly affected the Dominicans. Annual Confession and Communion were demanded and, for the first time, the term 'transubstantiation' was used in official pronouncements on the Eucharist. Other decrees demanded that Jews wear distinctive clothing and live in particular areas so that contact with Christians would be minimal. There was to be an immediate cessation of hostilities in Europe and a breathing space of four years to allow negotiations between enemies. Finally another crusade was to be summoned to relieve Jerusalem for which various taxes and indulgences were specified. Nothing of importance in the life of the Church was knowingly omitted from this Council and the aim was that its legislation should be passed through local synods into the general life of the Church.

Professor Walter Ullmann has written in *A Short History of the Papacy in the Middle Ages*:

> There can be no reasonable doubt that at the time of Innocent III the medieval papacy had reached its apogee. Indeed Innocent appears as the pope who with consummate skill would seem to have accomplished the programme of the papacy, the pope who realised after some seven centuries the innermost aspirations of the papacy to become the focal institution of Europe in religious, moral and governmental respects. The papacy was held to be the nerve centre of a singularly homogeneous society the ideological foundation of which rested on the papally fixed christian faith.

Innocent himself would probably have approved of such an assessment. He saw his office in almost semi-divine terms 'Set in the midst between God and man, below God but above man', and he left no one in any doubt as to the priority of spiritual authority over temporal: 'Princes have power in earth, priests over the soul; as much as the soul is worthier than the body, so much worthier is the priest-hood than the monarchy'. Few would doubt the enormous power and prestige of Innocent and yet there were signs that all was not well. His political policy had left Frederick II free to assume a leading and potentially crippling role in the West. His treatment of John of England had angered those in that country who resented the idea of a pope even contemplating asking the French King to lead an invasion. His papally inspired crusades – both against the Albigensians in Southern France and, at least in theory, the infidel in the East – had caused deep outrage; and his enormous personal authority and growing centralisation had given rise to fear and opposition among bishops throughout the Church. If Innocent represents the zenith in papal fortunes, then of necessity the years that follow track a decline which reaches its nadir less than a century later with the unfortunate Boniface VIII.

Innocent's very strong papacy tended to conceal problems in the Church and changes in society which were affecting the life of the Church. At the local level the Church was again being subjected to state interference, laxness was rife and pluralism evident in almost every country. The great monastic orders who had served the Church so well in the work of reform were themselves in need of reform as they continued to decline both in numbers and effectiveness. There were those who had great difficulty with the institutional Church and felt the need to dissociate themselves from it, preferring to follow Christ and his Gospel according to their own lights. Others criticized a Church which had become almost totally clerical and distant from the vast numbers of laity whom many of the clergy neither under-stood nor served. Added to these internal problems was a great urbanization programme which saw a migration away from the countryside into new towns. Within these towns universities were beginning to gain in importance, such as Bologna, Paris and Oxford. Within these universities were those both ready and equipped to debate the role of the pope, the rights of the secular rulers, the respective positions of Church and State, as well as students of philosophy and theology. It was against this varied and in some ways new background that the Mendicants appeared. As R.W. Southern summarises in *Western Society and the Church in the Middle Ages*, 'Without the towns the friars would never have come into existence; without the universities they would never have become great'.

In 1203 Innocent had given his blessing to a missionary venture undertaken by Dominic Guzman among the Albigensians in South-ern France. Dominic, born in Spain in 1170, had joined a reformed order of the Canons of St Augustine in the diocese of Osma in 1199.

During his travels in France he recognised the necessity of preaching the Gospel in a language that people could understand and of adopting a way of life they would accept. By 1214 his thoughts were turning towards forming an order which would have its aim the teaching of true religion and the refutation of heresy. In 1215 Dominic and a few companions were welcomed into Toulouse, where they toured the whole diocese and adopted a mendicant life-style with the accent on mobility. In 1216 the Dominicans were given papal approval on condition that they adopted an existing 'Rule'. This condition was necessary if the ban on new orders demanded by Fourth Lateran was to be upheld. The Dominicans accepted the Augustinian 'Rule' as their basis, adding their own particular emphases which indicated the charism of the order. They placed great stress on study and from the outset intellectual interests and pursuits were given top priority. They also determined on a practice of poverty which would be evident to those who witnessed it. They lived in small houses in the middle of towns and provided for their needs by begging. These ideas were given formal approval at the First General Chapter in 1220. The Dominicans later came to be known as the Order of Preachers, a nickname capturing the spirit of the Order, and their preaching undoubtedly filled a gap in the Church. They were staunch supporters of the papacy and the popes used them in many areas of Church life.

The other major mendicant order of friars to arise at this time took their name from Francis of Assisi (1182–1226), one of the most powerfully charismatic figures of this or any other century. Francis had enjoyed a comfortable upbringing which, on his own admission, had equipped him well for living in a world which paid little more than lip service to God. In 1202 he was taken prisoner after an inter-city fight and during his internment he began to think seriously about the purpose of life and the way he was going to live in the future. On 24 February 1206 he was struck by the reading of Matthew's Gospel in which the disciples are called to give up everything in the service of the Gospel. From this moment Francis changed radically, quite literally leaving aside everything, apart from a rough cloak to hide his nakedness. He began to serve in a leper community and to restore the fabric of churches in answer to a call he believed to be from God. Others, at first startled by, and then attracted to, this simple gospel poverty, joined him until the initial group numbered twelve. Francis provided some sort of guidelines for this new community based almost exclusively on Jesus' words as recorded in the Gospels. In 1209 he went to Rome seeking approval from Innocent III who was sceptical about this rather shabby band of men. In 1210 papal approval was granted although Innocent could have had no notion of how important this new order was to become. In 1212 Clare, who had been born in Assisi in 1194 and had recently been attracted by Francis's preaching, requested membership of the order. At first Francis asked her and her companions to stay in a Benedictine convent before transferring to San Damiano where she lived until her death in 1253. This was to be the beginning of the Poor Clares, an order for women who wanted to live an enclosed life of poverty and prayer. In 1221 Francis also catered for those who wanted to share something of the spirit of the new order by creating what came to be known as the Third Order or Tertiaries, who observe a rule of simplicity while retaining their status and occupation.

As early as 1217 the numbers had grown to such an extent that Europe was divided into five provinces. In 1219 Francis went on a preaching tour to the East intent on stopping the crusade and converting rather than crushing the Muslims. On his return in 1221 he found changes had occurred in his absence and there was the danger of a serious split developing over the question of poverty. Francis drew up a rule which, regarded as too strict, was revised before being approved in 1223 by Honorius III. The need for organising such vast numbers proved too much for Francis who retreated to Laverna. In 1224 he received the stigmata which caused him intense suffering until his death on 3 October 1226. Within two years he was canonized by Pope Gregory IX on 11 July 1228. After Francis the Franciscans were divided over the question of poverty, especially the corporate poverty which Francis had demanded. The rigorists, led by Leo, wanted to keep to the literal observance of the Rule and of their founder's understanding of it, whereas the laxists, under Elias, felt the priority to be their apostolic work in the world and therefore were prepared to compromise the strict understanding of the Rule. Eventually the rigorists came to be known as the Observants and the laxists as the Conventuals, but it is important to remember that, despite the titles, both groups had the future of the order very much in mind. The papacy entered the debate over poverty and by a series of decrees tended to favour the Conventuals. In 1269 Bonaventure attempted to heal the division by making a distinction between 'ownership' and 'use':

> Since there are two things to be considered with regard to the possession of temporal goods, ownership and use, and use is necessarily annexed to the present life; it is the nature of evangelical poverty to renounce earthly possessions in respect of ownership and not to reject use utterly, but to restrain it.

This became the basis for the future but it did not bring about the hoped-for reconciliation. This division over poverty lasted until the two sides were finally and officially separated in 1517, the Conventuals eventually adopting the black habit and the Observants the brown. During the Reformation a third group, known as the Capuchins, grew out of the Italian Observants and were eventually approved in their own right. Although this problem over poverty dominated the internal life and politics of the Franciscans, their influence on the Church remained immense. They quickly became involved in the universities where their rivalry with the Dominicans was sometimes less than friendly. They attracted those who were experiencing difficulties with the institutional church and they were extremely influential in popular piety promoting such visual aids as the crib, and such devotions as the Stations of the Cross. They were extremely active in missionary work, taking the Gospel as far as Peking in China. Together with the Carmelites founded by St Berthold in Palestine c. 1140 and the Augustinian Hermits recognised by Pope Alexander IV in 1256, the Friars had an enormous impact on the thirteenth-century Church, an impact which long outlived their founders and is still present in our own time.

The Friars were one of three factors which came together at this time ensuring great developments in many branches of study, not least in theology. The other two factors were the universities and the introduction into the West of translations of Aristotle's works. In previous centuries education had taken place normally in cathedral or monastic schools, but the late twelfth and early thirteenth centuries saw the emergence of new educational centres which came to be called universities. These were essentially educational co-operatives or guilds formed to protect both masters and students and to create centres where educational interests could be pursued. Bologna, Paris and Oxford are generally accepted as the first universities that can trace their origins to the twelfth century but receiving formal recognition in the thirteenth. Their early development was often interrupted by serious clashes with both ecclesiastical and lay authorities who wanted to control such new institutions. Gradually, through both royal and papal patronage, the universities were able to order their own lives and create the structures most suitable for their aims. In some places preparatory schools were established to educate a candidate, especially in his understanding of Latin, before he embarked on his studies. By the middle of the thirteenth century patrons were found willing to provide accommodation for those students unable to look after themselves or find other places to live. Among such patrons were Robert de Sorbon, who established a college named after him in 1258 and Walter Merton who founded Merton College, Oxford, in 1264. The course was long and a student would expect to take five or six years to qualify as Master of Arts. A doctorate in theology was even more gruelling, lasting some dozen years for those who already possessed a M.A. degree. Few students had such staying power and those who wanted to study further would very often opt for a shorter course in medicine or law. There were soon many new foundations in Italy, Germany, France and Spain to which both students and teachers would go to find an environment conducive to study and research.

If the universities provided the physical setting, the introduction of the Latin translation of Aristotle provided an unprecedented impetus to both philosophy and theology. This knowledge of Aristotle came together with commentaries by Jewish and Arabic scholars, notably, Avicebron (d.1070), Maimonides (d.1204), Avicenna (d.1037), and Averroes (d.1198). This introduction of Aristotle was not without its difficulties, not least being the comparison with Plato who was less materialistic than Aristotle and who had been the inspiration of the Early Fathers. Any acknowledgement of Aristotle could be construed as an attack on Plato and therefore indirectly as criticism of the Fathers. Added to this was the suspicion surrounding the role played by the Jews and Arabs in transmitting Aristotle. Both were regarded as traditional enemies of Christianity, and there were those who presumed they were now trying to have an adverse effect on Christian theology. Finally there was the actual teaching of Aristotle which, with its insistence on the eternity of the universe and the mortality of the soul, seemed to the educated onlooker to contradict some of the most central doctrines of the Christian Church. This last point served to highlight the question of the relationship between faith and reason, a question which was far from new in the Church. Anselm, at the end of the eleventh century, had maintained that reason had every right to inquire into revealed truth in a genuine effort to improve a person's knowledge and understanding of what he believes. He made a clear distinction between understanding and belief and his statement – 'I believe that I may understand' – became something of a catchphrase.

This relationship between faith and reason helped to give rise to the systematic arrangement of theological questions using arguments from reason, which in turn gave rise to the method of putting arguments for and against a particular statement, a method known as the 'Quaestio'. This methodology became an integral part of scholasticism which was to find its greatest exponent in Thomas Aquinas. One scholar who helped to improve the technique of the

'Quaestio', by introducing the dialectical method into his own theological investigations, was Abelard (1079–1142). He was born near Nantes and had been taught and tutored by several noted teachers who recognised his intellectual abilities. After finishing his studies he began lecturing in Paris, gaining a reputation for both his content and his style. However, Abelard's own personal difficulties brought about by his love affair with Heloïse cast a shadow over him and his methodology and it was left to Hugh of St Victor to restore confidence in the method which found its most important expression at this time in the *Sentences* of Peter Lombard (*c.*1100–*c.*1160). The *Sentences* had become the standard textbook of theology and was used throughout the West for many years. Now, however, in the thirteenth century, this new wave of interest in Aristotle would cause tremendous repercussions throughout the study of theology.

There seem to have been three major reactions to Aristotelianism, the first of which was known simply as the Augustinian because the members of this group refused to accept anything that contradicted Augustine. The Franciscans championed this cause, none more so than Bonaventure (1217–74) who emphasised the need for good will and intuitive knowledge in any attempt to arrive at the truth. He was sceptical of the ability of the human mind, unaided by God, to reach the truth. He maintained that any philosophical propositions which were contrary to faith must be dismissed, and he reminded people that, in his opinion, philosophy was very much at the service of theology.

A second group was known as the Averroists, named after Averroes, and led by Siger of Brabant (d.1284). Siger accepted Averroes' interpretation of Aristotle as the true interpretation, and he believed that Aristotle was correct in all things. When Aristotle contradicted Christian teaching the Averrosists tried to overcome the difficulty by what was called the 'theory of double truth'. According to this, as philosophers they accepted the teaching of Aristotle and as Christians the teaching of the Church. In other words they claimed that the conclusions of theology and philosophy could contradict each other while both remained valid.

The third group wanted to harmonise Aristotle's philosophy with traditional Christian teaching, and especially to demonstrate that Aristotle and Augustine were not diametrically opposed. The most famous member of this group was Thomas Aquinas (1225–74), one of the greatest intellects of the Middle Ages. He was born at Roccasecca in Southern Italy in 1225 into a family with Hohenstauffen connections, Thomas being a second cousin of Emperor Frederick II. He was soon placed under the care of the monks at

Monte Cassino, the birthplace of the Benedictine Rule, but in 1240 he went to Naples to study for his Arts degree. In 1244 he joined the Dominicans, despite the opposition of his family who had gone to the extraordinary lengths of keeping him under house arrest for more than a year. Between 1245–8 he came under the influence of Albert the Great at Paris who probably introduced Thomas to Aristotle's writings. In 1248 both went to Cologne where Albert undertook the foundation of a Dominican School of Study. Soon after this they parted company and Thomas returned to Paris in 1252 where he wrote a defence of the Mendicant orders – those orders who worked or begged for their living and, unlike the older orders, were not bound to a rule of stability but travelled freely – against the attacks of the secular Doctors. This work highlighted one of the many different struggles that were taking place within the universities at this time. The seculars felt, with some justification, that members of the Orders were enjoying too many privileges and advantages in furthering their careers. In the decade between 1259–69 Thomas, now a Master of Theology, travelled through Italy teaching in different places including Agnani, Orvieto, Rome and Viterbo. He returned to Paris in 1269 where he became involved in controversy with Siger of Brabant. His last years were spent in Naples before he died on 7 March 1274 on his way to the Second Council of Lyons.

Aquinas had lived for just less than fifty years which makes his literary output all the more remarkable. His writing covered a wide range of subjects including commentaries on philosophy, theology and scripture, devotional, liturgical and homiletic material and many other smaller studies. But he is best remembered for his *Summa Contra Gentiles*, a treatise on Natural Religion, and especially for his *Summa Theologica*, the greatest scholastic systematization of Christian teaching. This work, which stretched to several volumes and was unfinished when he died, was the finest example of the dialectical method which had become a hallmark of the scholasticism. Each topic was treated as a question which in turn was subdivided into articles, and each article had its own objections which Aquinas both put and then answered. Unlike the Aveorroists, Aquinas believed that revealed truth never contradicted natural knowledge but that it complemented and completed it. There were truths that man could know, not because of the power of his own reason, but because God had chosen to reveal them. If there were occasions when Aristotle contradicted Christian teaching then Aquinas argued against him using philosophical arguments. He also demonstrated that some of the ideas attributed to Aristotle were in fact those of later commentators and not of 'The Philosopher' himself.

Aquinas was canonised in 1323, declared a Doctor of the Church in 1567, and Patron of Catholic Universities in 1880; but in his own time he was an extremely controversial figure whom many regarded as too radical in his willingness to use philosophy and promote the use of reason. The Dominicans at their General Chapter in 1278 ordered his works to be taught throughout the order, whereas the Franciscans, at least for a time, forbade any of their members to read him. This suggested that the difference between the orders went much deeper than the colour of their habits. Aquinas remains an outstanding figure of the thirteenth century, a century where many others, both Friars and Seculars, were involved in scientific, philosophical and theological research, all of whom owed a great deal to, and enhanced the reputation of, the new universities.

From the death of Innocent in 1216 until 1250 Western Europe was dominated by Frederick II, the last great German emperor. Frederick possessed qualities of leadership which, coupled with deep political insight and awareness, made him a constant threat to the well-being of the Church and the papal ideal of authority. Honorius III (1216–27) succeeded Innocent and was charged with the task of putting the decrees of the Fourth Lateran into practice. He saw as his priority the summoning and despatch of the crusade called for in 1215, and this became the overriding obsession of his pontificate. He exerted pressure on Frederick to lead the crusade but the latter was far more adept in political matters than the pope and he managed to have his son Henry crowned King of the Romans, and himself crowned emperor in 1220 as a precondition to leading the crusade. His coronation should have been the signal for him to give up his claim to Sicily, but instead he began to make Sicily the most efficient and highly organised medieval state. Neither did he set off on crusade but consolidated his strength in Southern Italy before turning his attention to the Northern cities of Lombardy. When Honorius died in 1227 Frederick had still managed to avoid going on Crusade and had made himself and most powerful political figure in the West.

Pope Gregory IX (1227–41) excommunicated Frederick in August of 1227 precisely because of his refusal to sail with the crusade. This censure had the required effect and in June 1228 Frederick finally fulfilled his promise and left for the Holy Land. In 1229 he signed a treaty with the Sultan according to which Jerusalem – apart from the Mosque of Omar – Bethlehem, Nazareth and a passage way for pilgrims from Jaffa to Acre were to be returned to Christian control. On his return to the west he was released from ecclesiastical censure by the Treaty of San Germano in 1230. This peace between pope and emperor was severely tested several times over the next few years because Frederick constantly worked and schemed against the spirit of the treaty. In 1237 he won an important victory against the Lombard cities and in 1238 he angered the pope by intercepting and detaining the bishops passing through his territory on their way to a council summoned by Gregory. This caused Gregory to excommunicate Frederick for the second time on Palm Sunday 1239. Frederick's reaction was one of defiance; he marched south and encircled the city of Rome. This second excommunication was the signal for an outburst of propaganda, polemical writings stressing the rights and obligations of Church and State, pope and emperor, spiritual and temporal authorities. As with the investiture controversy of the eleventh century, these writings were helping to form and change opinion. In 1241 Gregory died and Frederick withdrew to await developments. The cardinals eventually elected Celestine IV, who died within a month, after whom there was a vacancy for two years because the cardinals refused to proceed with an election until such time as Frederick released two of their number whom he held in protective custody. Once released the cardinals elected Innocent IV (1243–54).

There were two options facing Innocent IV: either he could attempt to come to some agreement with Frederick or he could try and mobilise the rest of Europe against him. In fact Frederick initiated negotiations which looked like succeeding until Innocent's suspicions were so aroused that he opted out of further discussion. Soon after this the whole papal court left Rome and went to Lyons where Innocent summoned a General Council, the thirteenth council recognised by the Western Church. The list of subjects to be discussed was long and varied, including reform where the Council was mainly concerned with tightening up judicial and administrative loopholes and laying down clearer guidelines delineating the precise powers of papal legates. Other subjects discussed were another crusade, which the Council endorsed without giving any details, and the Mongol threat after their invasion of Russia and Hungary, against whom the council called upon the whole of Western Europe to defend itself. The most precise measures were enacted against Frederick who on 17 July was solemnly excommunicated, deposed as emperor, king of Germany, king of Sicily and stripped of all authority, honour and dignity. His subjects were released from allegiance to him and the German princes invited to proceed to an election. The breakdown of papal/imperial talks was one thing, this solemn excommunication was quite another, and Frederick reacted by resuming his offensive in

Northern Italy. His threat to the Church ended abruptly with his unexpected death in 1250. Although his sons succeeded him and were also an irritant to the papacy, Frederick's death, rather than the end of the Hohenstauffen line in 1268, marked the conclusion of the great papal-imperial conflicts of the thirteenth century.

From the Church's point of view this struggle with Frederick II had been both wearing and damaging, and Christians could have been forgiven for thinking that the papacy had become obsessed with its own well-being to the almost total exclusion of the wider needs of the Church. The use of 'spiritual' powers against the emperor was regarded by many as excessive and unedifying, and contributed, at least in part, to some of the anti-papal propaganda. The crusades, for so long a source of prestige for the papacy, seemed increasingly irrelevant as the Friars initiated a different approach with their emphasis on missionary conversion rather than crusading compulsion. Even the political situation which had occupied so much time and energy remained unresolved as the 'Sicilian Question' continued to be a source of acute embarrassment until the end of the century. But the most important and damaging development in the second half of the thirteenth century was the papacy's growing reliance on France and especially on the House of Anjou. From the death of Innocent IV in 1254 until the accession of Boniface in 1294 there were twelve popes several of whom were French and who tended to appoint Frenchmen as cardinals and members of the curia. Whenever Rome became politically hostile the papal court sought refuge in France and it is surely significant that two General Councils in the thirteenth century were held, not in Rome, but at Lyons.

Urban IV (1261–4) made the problem of Sicily the priority of his short pontificate. His predecessor Alexander IV (1254–61) had seen the question of Sicily become more involved without being able to find a solution. In 1263 Urban signed a treaty with Charles of Anjou according to which Charles would take control of Sicily and Southern Italy, which were to remain united, for a down payment, an annual tax and the guarantee of the freedom of the Church. Further, Charles also promised never to seek the imperial crown. As with many other treaties between Church and State, the secular leader reaped the benefits of the bargain. By 1268 Charles had control, not only of Sicily but also of Tuscany and he was enjoying a growing influence in Lombardy, all part of preparations to extend his authority over the whole of Italy. From 1268–71 the papacy was vacant and Charles used this opportunity to suppress all opposition and improve his own position. By the time Gregory X (1271–6) was elected, the Church was in need of strong and positive leadership to break the growing Angevin domination and initiate a programme of reform.

In 1274 Gregory opened the Second General Council of Lyons where three main aims were mentioned: reunion with the East, the recovery of the Holy Land and general reform. Reunion was in fact briefly achieved when legates of the Greek emperor Michael VIII Paleologus presented letters of obedience to the Roman Church and solemnly repeated the western form of the Creed which continued the 'filioque' clause. On their return to the East the legates were met with such hostility that it became clear that the vast majority in the East felt that this so-called reunion was in fact a sell-out. Even the measure of union achieved in 1274 was formally dismissed in 1289, to the extent that this episode at Lyons can scarcely be regarded as union at all. The European rulers agreed in principle to a crusade but by this time few were taking the details of such a venture with any degree of seriousness. The council attempted to continue the reform work of the previous two councils attacking pluralism, absenteeism, simony and concubinage. It also laid down tighter rules for papal elections. There was to be a maximum of ten days from the death of the pope to the beginning of proceedings and the election was to be held in the place where the pope had died. During the conclave the cardinals were to be denied all contact with the outside world and refused all sources of income, the general aim being to speed up the elections and to protect them from external interference.

The tragedy for the Church was the relatively short pontificate of Gregory. He at last was showing a willingness to take the needs of the Church seriously, but after him the reform decrees were seen to be neither sufficiently far-reaching nor systematically applied. The popes after Gregory continued to be dominated by pressures and interests which had little connection with, or concern for, the spiritual and pastoral needs of the Church. Indeed this period witnessed an acceleration in the decline of papal authority. The universities were producing growing numbers of people critical of the theory and practice of papal government. Papal concern with politics, especially with Sicily, the long vacancies in the papacy itself and the growing tendency to judge the usefulness of the office by the quality of the incumbent, all helped to militate against papal prestige.

When Nicholas IV died the cardinals, despite the legislation of the Second Council of Lyons, took two years and three months to elect a successor, the second time in twenty years that the papacy had remained vacant for a lengthy period. Eventually Peter Murrone, a saintly and ascetic Franciscan Observant, accepted the papacy in 1294 much against his better judgement, taking the name of Celestine V. Almost immediately Celestine's worst fears were confirmed as he found himself ill-equipped to deal with the pressures now being exerted on the papacy from all quarters. On 10 December 1294 a law was passed in consistory which permitted the pope to resign and three days later Celestine invoked that law and abdicated all papal responsibility. Ten days later elections began for a successor and the original choice fell on Cardinal Orsini who declined the invitation. The cardinals then unanimously elected Benedict Gaetani who took the name Boniface VIII (1294–1303). His pontificate demonstrated just how far the papacy had sunk since the days of Innocent III.

On 23 January 1295 Boniface returned to Rome which he quickly reorganised before gaining control of the papal states. At this stage the future looked bright but he soon began to act in a way which illustrated how much he was out of touch with reality. He seemed unaware of the profound changes that had occurred in the thirteenth century and he yearned for a style of autocratic papal government which was not only anachronistic but also unacceptable to the temporal powers who were beginning to appreciate their national identity and the strength that came with it. His first major blunder came in his papal bull of February 1296 called 'Clericos Laicos' in which he disapproved of secular governments taxing the clergy. Philip IV of France regarded this as a denial of his royal authority over his subjects and he retaliated by banning the export of all revenues to Rome. Despite his immediate declaration of his willingness to die rather than sacrifice the liberties of the Church, the harsh winter coupled with dangerously low reserves caused Boniface to withdraw and allow the king, in an emergency, to levy a tax on the clergy. Later he even allowed the king to determine what constituted an emergency.

At the same time as this depressing episode with France, Boniface found himself subject to intense internal pressures. The Franciscan Observants constantly criticised him for arrogance and worldliness. They further suspected he had been responsible for the abdication of Celestine who had been one of their number. More important and threatening was the problem within the curia, exacerbated by the treatment of the Colonna cardinals whom the pope had deposed and excommunicated. Those who supported the Colonnas looked for opportunities to attack Boniface, spreading rumours about the validity of his election, the morality of his life and appealing to a council to rid the Church of this ruthless and incompetent pope. When the Colonnas fled to France there was a clear possibility of an axis between them and the French throne.

The year 1300 brought something of a respite and change of fortune for the beleagured pope. He declared 1300 a Jubilee Year –

in order to stress the strength of the papacy and to boost his own flagging reputation – which effectively made Rome an enormously popular place of pilgrimage. As vast numbers of pilgrims poured into the city Boniface forgot his previous difficulties and began to cling to an unreal appreciation of his own popularity and authority. His authority was again tested when he denied the French civil courts the right to try Bishop Saisset who had been accused of treason, sedition, simony, heresy and the defamation of the king! Boniface was defending a right the Church had enjoyed, namely the right to judge clerics in ecclesiastical courts, and although the case against Saisset was apparently conclusive, Boniface rightly feared that his concurrence with the French civil court's action would jeopardize that right. However, he again went much further than was necessary not only demanding the release of the bishop but also revoking all recent privileges granted to France and ordering a full investigation into the state of the French Church.

In April 1302 Philip IV summoned representatives from the clergy, nobility and commoners to meet at Notre Dame; this was to be the first meeting of what came to be known as the Estates-General. The two lay groups demanded the immediate deposition of the pope while the clergy fought shy of such a demand but expressed disquiet at the rumours of papal behaviour. Philip put forward a list of twenty-nine accusations against Boniface, the most important of which, the king maintained, was the pope's claim to both spiritual and temporal superiority over the French king and people, a charge Boniface studiously denied, though he did warn Philip that popes had deposed kings in the past and might do so in the future. In November 1302 the council of French bishops, summoned by Boniface to investigate the state of the French Church, opened in Rome with 37 of the 78 bishops present. Little of any importance was achieved at the meeting itself but almost as soon as it was over the pope published the bull *Unam Sanctam* which was a very strong statement about the unity of the Church, the authority of the pope and the balance of power between Church and State. There was however only one formal dogmatic statement: 'We declare, state, define and pronounce that it is altogether necessary for salvation for every human creature to be subject to the Roman Pontiff'.

Philip responded by demanding that Boniface should now stand trial, a demand shared by the majority of the French nation, only a few of the Mendicants refusing to acquiesce. In June 1303 Philip despatched troops under Nogaret to bring Boniface to trial. The pope retired to his home of Agnani where he composed the final excommunication of the French king to be delivered on 8 September.

Boniface was momentarily taken prisoner by Nogaret only to be freed by the inhabitants of Agnani who were outraged by the Frenchman's actions. Boniface returned to Rome where he died on 12 October 1303.

Any assessment of Boniface must of necessity be critical. His treatment of people gained him few friends or admirers; his nepotism laid him open to charges of favouritism but his greatest failure was his lack of judgment and his inability to grasp the reality of the times in which he lived. At the end of his pontificate the Church was weaker than it had been for years and the prestige of the papacy had reached a new depth. The growing sense of nationalism, particularly in France and England, raised serious questions about the necessity or even the advisability of a pope with universal authority throughout the whole Church, and this same nationalism would, in the future, cause grave problems to those who sought to be loyal both to the Church and to their country.

The death of Boniface occasioned both suspicion and fear of the French. Although many would have shared Philip's dislike of the pope, few would have initiated military force against him. The cardinals duly met within the stipulated time and elected Benedict XI who had to face the enormously difficult question of how to treat the French. He tried to steer some sort of middle course: absolving Philip from all censures, but excommunicating Nogaret and those others who were responsible for imprisoning Boniface; and releasing the Colonna cardinals from excommunication without restoring them to their full rights and privileges. For a while it seemed as though such a policy might work but within eight months the pope was dead and the Church was left yet again with a very difficult situation. This problem was exacerbated by a split within the college of cardinals. Matthew Orsini wanted trial proceedings to be brought against all those responsible for the outrage perpetrated against Boniface even if this meant accusing Philip IV himself; while Napoleone Orsini felt that some sort of accommodation and reconciliation with France would not only be more realistic but ultimately the more favourable course to follow. Both parties agreed that, whoever be elected, should not be of the same headstrong independence as Boniface.

Eleven months after Benedict's death the cardinals, failing to agree on one of their own, chose a compromise candidate, the Archbishop of Bordeaux, Bertrand de Got. He was French by upbringing and inclination, but as Archbishop of Bordeaux was technically a subject of Edward I of England. He spent the summer planning his journey to Rome, but after being 'persuaded' by French troops he summoned six of the cardinals to attend his coronation at Lyons on 1 November when he took the name of Clement V. The following month he created nine cardinals, eight of whom were French and, with winter now set, he remained in France until such time as a journey to Rome could be undertaken without too much discomfort. He was in fact to remain on French soil for several years before finally taking up 'temporary' residence at Avignon in 1309, although the temporary nature of the residence was brought into question by the fact that, apart from a brief spell in 1367, the popes were to remain in that city, which became part of the papal estate, for nearly seventy years. Although Avignon was technically part of the empire rather than France it was nevertheless greatly influenced by France. As a contemporary of Clement wrote, the Church now had 'A French pope surrounded by French cardinals, living in a French-speaking city on the French border'. There was little doubt that France was maintaining a very tight control of the Church and that Pope Clement was no match for King Philip.

The French king maintained this control by constantly threatening to open court proceedings against Boniface, exhuming his body and putting him on trial for his abusive treatment of France during his pontificate. This macabre threat had a precedent with Formosus in the ninth century, and Clement wanted at all costs to avoid a repeat of that episode. The future was to prove that the costs were very high indeed. The pope agreed to cancel all the papal bulls that Boniface promulgated which were detrimental to France and to remove them from the official registers. Such a decision was regarded by other nations as a complete volte-face.

Perhaps even more damaging to papal credibility was the treatment of the Templars. The Knights Templars had been a product of the Crusades when a small group of soldiers decided to offer protection to pilgrims visiting the Holy Land. In 1128 Bernard of Clairvaux had given them a short Rule which assured both their immediate approval and their long-term future. Throughout the crusading epoch the Templars grew in influence and wealth as they continued to provide not only protection but also manpower to aid the troops who had made the journey from the West. As a result of their work they began to accumulate both land and revenues in the West to await their return from duty, wealth which was increasingly the envy of those who were not so fortunate. In 1274 the Second Council of Lyons had attempted to amalgamate the Templars with the other military order, whose name indicated their work, the Hospitallers, but without any real or lasting success. By the beginning of the fourteenth century Philip of France planned a concerted attack on the Templars in a fairly blatant attempt to avail himself of some of their vast revenue. He began his own investigation with the help of a discontented Templar and produced various damning charges against the order and called for its suppression. Clement insisted on carrying out his own investigations and instructed members of the Inquisition to act on his behalf. Despite the use of torture, the findings of the Inquisition differed substantially from the 'confessions' obtained by Philip. Even so, Clement agreed to discuss the matters more fully at a council which he summoned to meet at Vienne in 1311, and although he procrastinated for a little while, the Templars were officially suppressed on 3 April 1312.

There can be little doubt that the whole sorry affair, from which Clement emerged with very little credit, was initiated by Philip and he must bear great responsibility for the destruction and suppression of this military order. For the rest of Europe it was yet further evidence of the domination of the papacy by the French, even if Clement felt such was the price he had to pay to prevent the trial of his predecessor. The pope lost an enormous amount of support as people began to realise that his main policy was one of appeasing the French monarchy rather than guiding the Church through a very difficult period. By the time of his death in 1314 Clement had left a whole series of problems for his successor. The city of Rome had virtually been abandoned despite a brutal and unsuccessful attempt by troops loyal to the pope to restore order in a city where rival groups had fought pitched battles in the streets. Even the most ardent papalist was concerned by the extent of French influence on Church policy and papal decisions. The composition of the college of cardinals was clearly stacked in favour of the French after Clement had appointed 25 Frenchmen among his 28 new cardinals.

Further problems for the papacy came with a new wave of polemical literature which extolled the State at the expense of the Church. Among such writings was the *Defensor Pacis* of Marsiglio of Padua (*c.*1275–1342) in which the author maintained that the Church must be subordinate to the State because it was from the State that the Church derived her jurisdiction, whether spiritual or temporal. Since the State gave this jurisdiction it could at any time take it back; indeed it was the State which had given the papacy the prerogatives it now enjoyed and therefore the State not only could, but should remove an unworthy pope. According to Marsiglio the pope did not even enjoy supremacy in the Church, the highest authority resting with a General Council made up of both laity and clerics. This document was so obviously contrary to the whole understanding of the relations between the Church and State as taught by the Church that it came as no surprise that the author was excommunicated in 1327 by Pope John XXII. When the *Defensor Pacis* was published at the time of the Reformation it was one of the first books to be placed on the Index of Prohibited Books in 1559. Another to find himself excommunicated by John XXII was William of Ockham who, born in Surrey *c.*1285, had entered the Franciscan order and began teaching at Oxford. In 1327 he accused the pope of adopting an heretical position for which he was excommunicated in 1328 and then expelled from the Franciscans in 1331. The Master-General of the Franciscans was also excommunicated. After this William composed other anti-papal works, attacking John on his attitude towards Franciscan poverty and then writing in favour of the emperor's authority over the pope. His influence in theological circles was due in no small way to his reaction against 'Realism' and his attack on 'Thomism'. However, his political writings were of more immediate concern to the papacy which could do little to withstand such attacks apart from condemning the ideas, excommunicating the authors and proscribing their works.

When Clement V died in 1314 the Conclave spent two years arguing over his successor but eventually on 7 August 1316 the Bishop of Ostia received the necessary majority and took the name of John XXII (1316–34). John's pontificate was indeed full of controversy, not least over theological questions. His decision on Franciscan poverty, while receiving the agreement of the majority, won him only hostility and disdain from those who upheld the ideal of absolute poverty. His theological opinion on the Beatific Vision which he denied to the dead until the Last Judgement caused both disagreement and embarrassment and it was significant that his successor defined the more generally accepted view. Politically John was extremely acute and managed to accrue to himself even more power to an extent that alarmed the cardinals, some of whom began talking of the significance of a General Council. He remained in Avignon throughout his long pontificate and, although he did not completely dismiss the possibility of a return to Rome, the longer he delayed coupled with the worsening situation in Rome itself, where law and order had now almost completely broken down, made a return all the less likely. His main opposition came from Louis of Bavaria who, in 1314, had received five votes from the seven electors responsible for the German throne. John was angry that he had not been consulted about the election and began to speak of his rights as pope in these matters. Louis resented these remarks and he became the focal point for all those who were dissatisfied with John. In 1324 Louis was excommunicated but an indication of how weak such measures had become was seen in the fact that in 1328 he took possession of Rome and even installed an anti-pope, Nicholas V. However, the whole episode was merely a shadow of previous titanic struggles between popes and emperors which in itself testified to the poverty of their own positions in relation to the growing strength of France. By the end of his pontificate the ninety-year-old John had left the papacy with little credibility, having lived and acted in a way which was outdated and unrealistic. 'His pontificate was the climax of the hierocratic system. Whoever regards this as important can admire John XXII as one of the most important popes,' as one historian has written. The problem for the Church was that a different style of leadership was called for but had been manifestly absent in John.

The conclave met in 1334 and elected James Fourier who had entered a Cistercian monastery before being consecrated bishop in 1317 and made cardinal in 1327. He took the name of Benedict XII (1334–42). Benedict was a capable theologian who managed to dispel some of the confusion caused by his predecessor. He remained, though, very much under French influence with the result that the opinion of the papacy elsewhere, and especially in Germany, became increasingly hostile, a hostility fuelled by the polemicists. Despite a fairly comprehensive reform policy which included checking abuses in the curia, introducing controls over the granting of dispensations, and reminding the religious orders of their obligations, his decision to erect a papal palace at Avignon gave credence to those who maintained that the papacy had no intention of returning to Rome and had in fact become entirely dominated by the French.

The extent of this influence was attested to at the next conclave when the French king sent his son, the Duke of Normandy, to the election. The fact that yet another Frenchman was elected who took the name of Clement VI (1342–52), and that with him the Church endured the climax of French control, did little to dispel what was now the accepted image of the papacy throughout the rest of the Church. His purchase of Avignon in 1348 confirmed people's worst fears. The situation in Germany was allowed to drift, papal influence in Italy was almost non-existent and Clement VI threw aside any pretence of impartiality when he took the side of the French against the English. During his pontificate the living standards of the papal court reached unprecedented heights and there was some reason to think that the pope had become unaware of the Church beyond the city boundaries of Avignon. There were those who regarded the Black Death, which plagued Europe between 1347–52, as a divine judgement on his whole pontificate.

After him the popes began to take more seriously their obligations to the wider Church and particularly they recognised the need to return to Rome. Innocent VI (1352–62), despite building a whole series of fortifications around Avignon, despatched Cardinal Albornoz to Italy with the intention of restoring order to the Papal States. He was to spend the next thirteen years, 1353–66, on this mission, and though Innocent died before he could return, his successor Urban V (1362–70), who retained his monastic habit throughout his pontificate and curtailed the luxuries of the curia, actually entered Rome on 16 October 1367, the first pope to do so for sixty years. He began the work of restoration but in the summer of 1368 he retired to Viterbo where he remained until the following year when, despite the attempts of many including the saintly Catherine of Sienna, he eventually returned, not to Rome, but to Avignon in September 1370 where he died three months later. Gregory XI, a nephew of Clement VI, was elected his successor and from 1372 a return to Rome became official papal policy despite concerted efforts by both the papal and French courts to dissuade the pope. In September 1376 Gregory left Avignon for good and on 17 January 1378 he entered Rome and was almost immediately stunned by the extent of the damage caused by the 'Babylonian Captivity' at Avignon. He summoned a council for the summer of 1378 but before it could meet he too was dead, and the importance of the conclave to elect his successor was apparent to everyone.

The Avignon period of papal and church history reflected the growing strength and importance of secular and temporal authority as understood in national terms, and as seen particularly in France. Arguably the greatest loss to the papacy was in terms of neutrality since not even the most ardent papalist could dismiss the great influence of the French in conducting papal policy. Nor was it insignificant that all the seven popes at Avignon were French and the majority of cardinals were also from France. The absence of the popes from Rome for such a long unbroken period allowed propagandists to speculate about its crucial significance to the Church, and although the popes were still elected as bishops of Rome there was at least a case for accusing them of absenteeism. The papacy was severely compromised by this whole episode and, even if one accepts that living in Rome would have been difficult, not to say, dangerous, the situation in Avignon proved to be such a cause of scandal to many, that few remained either impartial to, or supportive of, the papacy.

The Rome to which Gregory returned was run down, administratively chaotic, subject to outbursts of violence and in no way able to claim its previous title of the Capital City of Europe. When leaving

Avignon Gregory had failed to persuade all the cardinals to return with him and six had remained, ostensibly to tie up the loose ends, but secretly hoping, even presuming, that the papal court would return as had been the case in 1370. If Gregory expected a warm reception from the citizens of Rome he was soon to be disappointed by the realisation that the Romans wanted a pope but not a French one. This potentially explosive situation blew up into another major crisis with the election of Gregory's successor in 1378.

Gregory died in March and the conclave opened on 7 April within the stipulated period, when the cardinals were sealed off in the Vatican palace. Of the sixteen cardinals present, eleven were French, four were Italian and one was from Spain, and all were aware of the importance of their deliberations. There was more than a suspicion of external pressure when some Roman magistrates arrived to warn the cardinals that they could not guarantee their safety if the wishes of the Roman crowd, that the next pope be a Roman or at the very least an Italian, were not met. On the first ballot the necessary majority was reached and the Archbishop of Bari, Bartholomeo Prignano, was elected. He was a Neopolitan by birth and therefore not strictly an Italian, but in the eyes of the Romans he was infinitely preferable to a Frenchman. On 9 April the election was officially confirmed and he took the name of Urban VI (1378–89). The French cardinals then left Rome only to return the following week to take part in the coronation of Urban on 18 April where they took the usual oaths of obedience and loyalty, after which the secular leaders were notified of the election. At this stage there was not the slightest suggestion of the future furore, and yet within three months the Church was in turmoil. Urban VI, who had proved himself a capable administrator of his diocese, became so obsessed with his position as pope that people began to accuse him of megalomania. He demonstrated a rudeness that bordered on the insane, he threatened to create so many new cardinals that the present college would be superfluous. As a result serious doubts arose about his ability to govern the Church. The problem was all the more acute because there was no obvious way of ridding the Church of a pope who proved himself incapable of filling the office.

On 21 June all the cardinals, except four Italians, fled Rome and settled in Agnani where they declared Urban's election to be invalid and invited him to stand down. When he refused, three of the four Italian cardinals joined the rest at Agnani. On 20 September fifteen of the sixteen cardinals who had elected Urban proceeded to elect a Frenchman, Robert of Geneva, as Clement VII (1378–94). On 31 October Clement was duly crowned as pope at Avignon and in

November the two popes mutually excommunicated each other. The Great Schism had begun.

At the heart of the schism was the cardinals' claim that the election of Urban was invalid. They claimed that the election was not a free election quoting the Roman magistrates' blunt statement about their inability to guarantee the cardinals' safety should they fail to meet the wishes of the people. Against such a claim was the fact that Urban VI did not meet the demands of the people since he was neither Roman, nor strictly speaking Italian. Further, the cardinals returned to Rome, confirmed the election, took oaths of obedience and took part in the coronation ceremony. At no time was there any serious complaint of undue pressure. The cardinals also claimed invalidity on the grounds of Urban's mental state, claiming that he did not have sufficient responsibility for him to be regarded as a valid candidate. Certainly after his election, and very quickly after his election, he acted in a manner which caused the utmost concern, and even those cardinals whom he created wanted him to have a guardian. However, the real point at issue concerns his mental state at the time of his election and there seems little doubt that the cardinals regarded him as a perfectly suitable candidate given his success in the diocese of Bari. Such evidence as there is suggests that a definitive judgement about the validity of Urban's election is unlikely. The historian who suggested that the election was neither absolutely valid nor absolutely invalid may be accused, by some, of dodging the issue, but he is probably as near to the truth as it is possible to be. If, however, there was doubt about Urban's election, then presumably there must also be doubt about that of Clement VII, but whatever doubts remain the historical fact was that the Church was now in schism and remained so until 1417.

The majority of the curia left Rome and joined forces with Clement at Avignon, causing Urban to attend to the problem of organising a new curia which he began by creating twenty-nine new cardinals. Both popes recognised the necessity of gaining the support of the Church which was now divided with Italy, the empire, Hungary and England supporting Urban; and France, Burgundy, Naples and Scotland supporting Clement. Other countries remained neutral until such time as the evidence could be thoroughly investigated. The schism was also keenly felt and reflected in religious orders, cathedral chapters and even among members of the same family. Perhaps the confusion is best summed up by the Archbishop of Toledo who, in the canon of the Mass, replaced the name of the pope by praying 'for him who is the rightful Pope'. Other indications as to the doubtfulness of both claimants came with the changing of obedience and allegiance by some, though admittedly at times such vacillation was inspired by less than noble motives. As the schism wore on there were various suggestions as to how it might be ended, suggestions which assumed more importance when, on the death of Urban VI in 1389, the Roman cardinals proceeded to the election of Boniface IX (1389–1404), and similarly when Clement died, the Avignon cardinals elected Benedict XIII (1394–1423). On both occasions there had been the possibility of a solution with one of the 'seats' being vacant, but neither group at the time was willing to compromise.

In the past schisms had been solved by the intervention of the emperor, by one candidate gaining the majority opinion, or by being championed by a great saint of the Church; but at this particular time the emperor was too weak and Europe, including the saints, was almost equally divided on nationalist lines. At the university of Paris in 1394 three possibilities for ending the schism were put forward: mutual abdication, the appointing of a tribunal to decide between the two or, finally, a General Council. Neither of the popes would agree to abdicate and the other two alternatives foundered on the question of who would appoint the tribunal or summon the council. A fourth possibility then gained in popularity which involved the cardinals on both sides withdrawing their support from their respective pope and meeting to elect a successor, acceptable to all. This idea, more popular in France than elsewhere, had the effect of producing the so-called Treaty of Marseilles in 1407 when both Benedict XIII and Gregory XII (1406–15), agreed to meet at Genoa in September. For a variety of reasons this meeting did not take place and eventually, in 1409, the cardinals of both popes met at the Council of Pisa. They had summoned others to attend the council and in terms of response they were extremely successful with over 400 bishops and abbots or their proxies, representatives from the Orders, the universities and most of the secular rulers. At the opening session a strong statement upholding the right of the cardinals to summon the council, given the failure of the papal rivals to do so, was read and the principal task of the council was declared to be the ending of the schism. A committee was set up with responsibility for sifting through the minutiae of the evidence and eventually on 5 June the judgement against Gregory XII and Benedict XIII was solemnly pronounced, condemning them both as 'notorious schismatics, promoters of schism, and notorious and obdurate heretics and perjurors'. They were forthwith declared deposed, all obedience withdrawn from them and the Roman see declared vacant.

On 15 June the conclave opened to elect a successor and on 26 June the Cardinal Archbishop of Milan was elected, taking the name of Alexander V (1409–10). This new pope promised a further council in 1412 to look into the grave question of reform and ordered local national synods to prepare for it. On 7 August the Council of Pisa closed and it should have ended the schism but neither Gregory nor Benedict accepted its authority and in a very real sense there were now three claimants to the papacy! Although Pisa is not recognised as one of the General Councils of the Church its importance should not be under-estimated. It reflected a growing body of opinion which found its fullest expression in the Conciliarism of Constance. In terms of numbers it far exceeded all the later medieval councils except the Fourth Lateran and, if it failed to end the schism, this was largely because of the complexity of the political situation. In 1410 Alexander died, to be succeeded by John XXIII (1410–15), although future suggestions of bribery and simony caused John's name to be deleted from the list of popes and significantly Cardinal Roncalli took the number XXIII in 1958. John, in 1410, enjoyed more support than either of the other two claimants but not sufficient to end the schism. King Sigismund of Germany now emerged as the leading political figure who wanted both to restore unity to the Church and to press forward with a whole series of reforms. When John realised that his own position was becoming increasingly precarious he appealed to Sigismund for help, the latter agreeing on condition that John summoned a General Council whose aims would be to restore unity and reform the Church. Eventually, after protracted negotiations, a council was summoned to meet at Constance in 1414.

Sigismund had recognised that John enjoyed the majority support and it made good political sense for the king to negotiate with him. Gregory XII became even more isolated and was on the point of offering his resignation but Benedict XIII was still receiving support from the Iberian peninsula. Equally important were Sigismund's negotiations with the temporal rulers, especially his attempts to soften hostilities between France and England. All these very different preparations had been an essential prerequisite to the Council which was solemnly opened by John on 5 November. There were relatively few members present for this opening but the arrival of Sigismund himself early in 1415 guaranteed a sharp increase in numbers. Of great significance was the representation from the universities and a very strong lay presence. Throughout its three-and-a-half years there was scarcely a question of importance which was not discussed in the forty-five solemn sessions or the hundreds of ad hoc meetings. It was finally agreed that the voting would be on a national basis, each nation having one vote, with the cardinals being nominated for this purpose as a nation.

Sigismund had felt from the outset that the only real solution to the schism was the radical one of all three claimants abdicating, thereby leaving the way clear for a new election which would be binding on the whole Church. John XXIII reluctantly agreed to resign but then reneged on his promise and escaped to his supporters, hoping by this drastic action to disrupt the council. It was during his absence that the council promulgated the decree *Haec Sancta* which claimed that the General Council was the highest authority in the Church. John was quickly recaptured and deposed on 29 March 1415, a sentence he accepted, although the council's lack of confidence in his word was seen by the fact that he remained in protective custody until 1419. Gregory XII also tendered his resignation and was appointed Cardinal Bishop of Porto, which left only Benedict XIII. His position depended on his retaining the support of Spain, but gradually even the most loyal recognised the signs of the times and were won over to the Council. On 26 July 1417 Benedict was again deposed, a sentence he stubbornly refused to accept, regarding himself as the only legitimate pope right up to his death in 1423. After 1417 he was virtually alone in this belief and he posed no serious threat to the Church.

The council then agreed on an electoral procedure which respected the rights of the cardinals while recognising the special circumstances of the time. Cardinal Colonna was elected with the requisite majority and crowned pope on 21 November 1417, taking the name Martin V (1417–31). He now assumed the presidency of the council which had achieved one of its major aims, namely the ending of the Great Schism.

When the council had been opened in 1414 two other aims were expressed, the condemnation of heresies and the reform of the Church. Throughout the course of the council both of these had taxed the members as much as their search for unity. The most famous person to be tried on a charge of heresy was John Huss (c.1372–1415), educated at Prague university and ordained priest in 1400. Huss had been deeply affected by the teaching of John Wycliffe – the English scholar-priest who wanted to rebuild Christianity on the basis of meditation of the scriptures – and had promulgated some of his ideas in his own preaching and writing. He was eventually denounced to Rome by some of his own clergy who had felt the strength of Huss's criticism of them. After being warned by Innocent VII, Huss was eventually excommunicated in 1411 and in the following year his supporters were placed under ecclesiastical censure. Huss, more isolated than ever, now wrote his major work *On the Church* in which the influence of Wycliffe was clearly evi-

dent. Part of his work defended the superiority of the General
Council over the pope and he appealed to the Council of Constance
against his excommunication by John. He travelled to Constance
under a safe conduct guaranteed by Sigismund, but once there it soon
became evident that he was very much on trial and the proceedings
against him lasted some six months. He was found guilty of heresy,
almost a foregone conclusion since the Council had already condemned a wide range of Wycliffe's writings, and on refusing to
retract, was executed at the stake on 6 July 1415. Some saw this as
the rightful punishment for a notorious heretic, others as a martyrdom for freedom of conscience, and still others, mainly the Czechs,
treated him as a national hero.

Reform was the broadest and most difficult task of the council
made more complicated by the variety of interests expressed by those
present. From this time onwards the very idea of reform became
inextricably linked with a Church Council, an idea which was to
have grave consequences in the future. One of the major demands of
the Council, proclaimed in a decree called *Frequens*, was the regular
summoning of councils to regulate and foster reform. This was
meant to safeguard the Church against popes who, claiming supremacy, refused to summon councils but allowed the Church to
continue unreformed. According to *Frequens* the next council must
meet in five years, the one after that seven years later and then every
ten years. If the pope failed to summon it within the given time then
the cardinals were empowered to do so. Much of the other reform
talk centred on the clergy and the performance of their responsibilities, mentioning many of the abuses which had become common-
place throughout the medieval period. There was also, however, at
least the embryo of something which was to become increasingly
popular after Constance, namely private agreements, known as concordats, between the pope and individual secular rulers. When
Martin V closed the Council in 1418 a great deal had been achieved
but it was clear to all but the blind that the future would depend very
largely on the attitude of the popes despite the very strong conciliar
theme as represented in *Frequens* and *Haec Sancta*.

This latter document contained the following statement: 'This
holy synod of Constance declares that, being lawfully assembled in
the Holy Spirit constituting a general council and representing the
Catholic Church militant, it has its power directly from Christ and
that all persons of whatever rank, state or dignity, even the papal, are
bound to obey it even in matters relating to faith, the ending of the
schism and the general reform of the Church in head and members'.
This represented the high point in a Conciliar Theory which had

been evident in certain writings for many years. In the thirteenth century the universities had provided those who were ready to deny supremacy to the pope and invest such authority in a general council. Hugh of Pisa had taught that a pope could err and he tried to maintain the inerrancy of the Church by distinguishing between the Roman Church and the Universal Church. Others claimed that an unworthy pope could be deposed by a general council, or by the cardinals acting on behalf of the whole Church. A more extreme view reduced the papacy to an executive office established by the Church and therefore liable to abolition by the Church. The major difference at Constance was that the Western Church had already suffered more than thirty years of schism and, since other methods of ending the schism had failed, a general council appeared as the only practical solution regardless of any theory of authority. If Constance was the high point of the Conciliar Theory it certainly did not end the discussion about the relationship between the pope and council, or the relative authority of pope and council. Indeed the question, which had been of major interest throughout the medieval period was going to tax the Church for many years after Constance itself had ended.

Once the Council of Constance had been officially closed in 1418, Martin V's first objective was to achieve a degree of independence in both political and ecclesiastical matters. He believed that by returning to Rome he would escape the close attention of Sigismund who was still intent on exerting pressure on the papacy, and he would physically distance himself from Constance with all its connotations of conciliarism. However actually getting back to Rome was not as easy as he had hoped. The long schism had allowed different families and groups to carve up the Papal States among them and the pope had very little authority throughout the area. Similarly Rome was run down and in the hands of different pressure groups. Eventually, in September 1420, Martin finally entered Rome, stamped his personal authority on the city and set about renovating roads, bridges and buildings. For the rest of his pontificate he was master of Rome, but it took a further four years, until 1424, before papal sovereignty was again recognised throughout the papal states. During these operations and within the general administration of the Church, Martin had used and continued to use members of his own family. This worked to his advantage, but such blatant nepotism angered many, especially the Orsini, traditional rivals of the Colonnas, and they were to seek reprisals after Martin's death.

According to *Frequens* a council was to be summoned within five years and Martin observed the letter of this decree by summoning a council to meet at Pavia but soon moved it to Siena. However, Martin dissolved the council before any major business was undertaken, maintaining that the paucity of numbers and the dangerous political situation made the dissolution necessary. During the rest of his life the pope continued to claw back some of the rights he believed to be his. He had certainly subdued the Papal States and begun the process of restoring Rome but when he died in 1431 the future was far from secure for his successor Eugene IV (1431–47). Indeed the controversy between pope and council once again became central to the life of the Church and the whole of his pontificate was lived under the shadow of the Council of Basel (1431–49). Martin V had already fixed the opening date for July 1431 and Eugene agreed to the council's opening thought he let it be known that he was adamantly against it. He dissolved it in November of 1431 and summoned a new one to meet in Bologna in 1433. The council refused to be dissolved and since only six cardinals supported Eugene, the pope had to withdraw his bull of dissolution in December 1433. Despite this the battle lines had been drawn and the damage done was largely the responsibility of Eugene himself.

The first signs that council and pope might try to work independently of each other came with the renewed relations with the Greek Church in the East. Eugene had already begun discussions with the East and Basel followed suit by sending ambassadors to Constantinople. The negotiations were long and arduous and both sides at different times felt they were winning the confidence of the Greeks. Eventually in 1436 Eugene managed to persuade the Greeks to send their team of experts to a Council at Ferrara and avoid going to Basel. In 1437 Eugene officially transferred the Council to Ferrara in Italy and, in January 1438, it opened without the Greeks being present. They arrived in March and then asked for a postponement until June hoping that more of the bishops and secular rulers would come over from Basel. Much of the work between the two Churches was done in small committees hoping to reach agreement fairly quickly. The main theological points between the two sides concerned the 'filioque' clause in the creed, the doctrine of purgatory, the matter and form used in the Eucharist and the question of papal primacy. In January 1439 Eugene moved the council to Florence and in July, after yet more discussions between the two sides, the Union Decree *Laetantur Coeli* was promulgated. However, the Greeks had not finished their journey home before some of them began revoking their consent and the Union was never really accepted in the East, although some smaller groups, the Armenians, Copts and Syrians remained in communion with Rome. This whole episode illustrated

how deep the political aims and pressures had become. Theologically
the gap between East and West was still as wide as ever but a union
between the two was politically important for both the pope and the
emperor. The pope wanted aid against the council which still stubbornly remained in Basel and recognition of papal primacy would
greatly help his cause. The emperor wanted military help against the
Turks and that help could only really come from the West and be
provided by the pope. Meanwhile the council fathers at Basel were
deeply hurt by the Greeks' refusal to meet them because they believed
that the Eastern practice of investing authority in the council was
similar to their own sense of conciliarism.

In the first period of the Council of Basel up to its transfer in 1437,
there had taken place some very important discussions with the
Hussites. The execution of John Huss at Constance had caused a
reaction in his favour and his followers had increased in numbers
and importance. Between 1433–6 negotiations took place first at
Basel and later at Prague which led to a consensus on the four articles
of Prague, namely the reception of the chalice by the laity, free
preaching, punishment for those guilty of serious sin and finally a
far-reaching renunciation of ecclesiastical property by the clergy. In
1437 these articles were accepted by the Council of Basel, but they
were never formally ratified and were finally annulled in 1462.
However, in 1437 the agreement marked a notable success for the
Council and at least for a while posed a threat to the papacy.

The most difficult task facing the Church at this time was probably
that of reform. Constance had left much undone and the abortive
council of Siena had achieved nothing. All those who saw the need
for a thorough-going reform in the Church now looked to the
Council to achieve some success. In the early stages of the Council a
reform commission of some twenty-four members had been given
the task of furthering reform. Throughout its existence it was dogged
by clashes between council and pope which continually obstructed
its attempts to enforce reform. The commission recommended
several immediate reforms including the abolition of bishoprics and
abbacies reserved to the pope, clarification of the payments made to
the curia which were known as annates, and restriction of appeals to
Rome from local dioceses. The papal elections were restored to the
cardinals as their exclusive right and the number of cardinals was
limited to twenty-four, all of whom had to be doctors of theology or
law. Finally, no nation could have more than a third of the total
number of cardinals at any one time. In 1438 the French, who had
supported Basel and continued to do so, accepted these reforms with
certain minor modifications in a treaty known as The Pragmatic

Sanction of Bourges. The council wanted the French to go even further by suspending the pope and cutting off all relations with the Roman curia, but they refused. In effect by 1438 the council at Basel and the council at Ferrara were two mutually hostile groups desparately wanting to gain the support of the secular rulers.

In June 1439 Basel deposed Eugene IV and in November elected an anti-pope, Felix V (1439–49), who has the distinction of being the last anti-pope in the history of the Church. This was his only claim to fame since he was recognised by very few people and after a decade of futility he agreed to retire in 1449. Throughout that period the Council still continued at Basel until its transfer to Lausanne in 1447. However, it was the pope who was now making most headway by entering into private treaties with various secular rules. Alfonso, King of Aragon, conquered Naples and could have posed a severe threat to the pope, but Eugene managed to win him over to his side in return for certain concessions. Frederick III, King of Germany, was similarly disposed to support Eugene after the latter had promised him the imperial crown. In fact Eugene died soon after securing the support of Frederick in February 1447, but his successor Nicholas V (1447–55), signed the Concordat of Vienna with Frederick according to which the reforms of the Council of Basel, already accepted by the German Church, were now agreed upon by both pope and king but in a greatly modified form.

Time was now running out for those who clung to the policies of Basel/Lausanne and after the anti-pope Felix agreed to resign in 1449, it was not long before the Council agreed to dissolve itself, though not before it had 'elected' Nicholas V. In real terms the schism was ended more by political than theological argument. By negotiating privately with different nations Eugene had effectively restored to the papacy a great deal of its lost credibility and prestige. In an age when national rulers were becoming more aware of their own importance, these same rulers recognised the sense, from their point of view, of negotiating with another head, namely the pope, rather than with a council. The curia too had managed throughout this period to regain much of its previous power and responsibility. But there was a price for this. The Church still remained largely unreformed and Eugene, for all that he may well have saved the papacy from being dominated by conciliarism, must bear great responsibility for preventing reform throughout the Church, and in preventing reform he paved the way for the Reformation.

CHAPTER 4

The Protestant Reformation and the progress of Catholic Reform, 1455–1648

The closing of the Council of Basel in 1449 brought to an end three decades of conciliar activity and recognised the reality of papal and curial ascendancy. It would be wrong, however, to suggest that the conciliar idea was now forgotten. On the contrary there were those who continued to stress the superiority of the General Council despite the papal bull of Pius II (1458–64) which prohibited appeal from the pope to a council. The theory of conciliarism was kept alive and the idea of the council as the medium of reform in the Church was to assume enormous importance during the Reformation; but in practice the papacy, together with the curia, had effectively regained control. The most obvious sign of this was the pope's ability to disregard the conciliar decree *Frequens* which had called upon him to summon a council every ten years. In fact more than half a century passed after Basel before the Fifth Lateran Council was summoned by Julius II. If in the past the popes had great difficulty in transforming theory into practice it was now the conciliarists who experienced similar problems.

Throughout the second half of the fifteenth century the popes were engaged more in secular than in religious affairs. In the distant background was the Turkish threat, highlighted by the fall of Constantinople in 1453. The popes appealed time and again to Western leaders to go to the aid of the East but such appeals fell on deaf ears. By this time the crusading spirit which had consumed a previous generation was now dead and the national rulers were more concerned with problems at home than in helping distant and almost unknown Christians abroad. Even when there was a real opportunity of achieving some success against the Turks in the 1470s all the Western leaders employed delaying tactics and any advantage that could have been gained was thereby forfeited.

In Italy the popes were more successful. Indeed the major factor which allowed them to disregard demands for a council was the strength they enjoyed within the papal states. In 1454 the Peace of Lodi had recognised five main principalities in Italy: Milan, Florence, Venice, the Papal States, and Naples which since 1435 had been reunited with Sicily. Much papal time and energy was spent in power politics in order to maintain this delicate balance in the face of aggression from larger nations, notably France. However, many people outside Italy began to resent this concentration of effort in the political sphere and there was a growing suspicion that the popes themselves were beginning to gauge success or failure in terms of their own political achievements.

The popes were also preoccupied with the movement known as the 'Renaissance', although it was not until the nineteenth century that the term itself became popularly used. The Italian word 'rinascuta' simply means rebirth and contemporaries used it especially when referring to the rebirth of the styles of ancient Rome and Greece in the spheres of literature and art. It was also used by some in a much wider sense covering developments in politics, economics and society at large. Indeed the Renaissance period is often regarded as a link period between the medieval and the modern world, and the relationship between renaissance and reformation has been the subject of great discussion. Rooted within the Renaissance was the growth of humanism which was to have such a formative influence on the Church. The beginnings of humanism are normally associated with Petrarch (1307–74), one of the foremost poets of the fourteenth century. With a poet's sensitivity Petrarch was able to express the beauty of nature and emphasise the dignity and uniqueness of each individual. He recognised the great importance of education and he himself was inspired by his reading of the ancient Greek and Roman authors. He taught himself Greek so as to facilitate this and he had the works of Homer translated into Latin for those unable to read him in the original. This interest in languages and particularly in Greek was fostered by the Greeks themselves who at the turn of the fourteenth century had come to the West seeking aid against the Turkish threat. Some Greeks decided to remain and became tutors making the Greek language available to those wishing to learn it. This fuelled a desire to find and read original texts which in turn began to pose serious questions about the accuracy of translation and the possibility of obscuring the truth by mistranslation or misunderstanding.

One of the most important pioneers in this study was Lorenzo Valla (c.1407–57), a Roman by birth and ordained priest in 1431.

After ordination he began teaching at Pavia but his teaching was interrupted by a series of disagreements with the university authorities. He found himself dismissed and displaced but he received help and patronage from King Alphonso I of Naples. During the pontificate of Nicholas V (1447–55), he returned to Rome knowing that he would be welcomed by a pope who was a known supporter of humanism. Nicholas has been regarded as the founder of the Vatican library because of his policy of encouraging scholars to come to Rome and undertake the task of translating and copying manuscripts. Valla's own contribution was greater than that of simple translation. He recognised the importance of a critical study of the texts for philological reasons, but he also wanted to draw from this study conclusions for theology. In 1440 his work *De falso credita et eminenta Constantini Donatione Declamatio* proved that the 'Donation of Constantine' was a forgery. However, he was not content simply to announce this discovery, he wanted to discuss the consequences for the papacy if the temporal claims of the popes were based on a forgery! He went so far as to suggest that the popes should renounce all temporal claims and acknowledge the rights of the State. When he became involved with the critical study of the New Testament his discoveries were even more informative. In 1444 he completed a critical comparison of the Latin Vulgate and Greek New Testaments. His findings were contained in a work called *Annotations on the New Testament* which was not generally known until half a century after his death, when it was discovered and published by Erasmus in 1505. In this work Valla claimed that the Vulgate contained many errors and inaccuracies and that the translators were responsible, knowingly or otherwise, for many mistakes. Once published in the sixteenth century *Annotations* went through several editions and exerted a great influence on scripture studies. In 1559 it was placed on the Index of Prohibited Books and in 1590 Valla's other writings were also condemned. One of his greatest contributions was in creating a spirit of critical judgement and of encouraging all those who were not prepared simply to accept statements at face value. Such an independent spirit was a threat to the authority both of the Church and the State, so it was not surprising that his works were condemned and he himself suspected of heresy.

The new interest in languages led others to look beyond the Greek Septuagint to the ancient Hebrew Scriptures, but those wishing to pursue hebraic studies had to overcome more than the difficulty of learning a foreign language. In the fifteenth century the Jews were despised by almost everyone in the West and various attempts were made either to isolate them, by forcing them live in ghettoes and wear distinctive clothing, or to expel them altogether, as was the case in Spain whence they were exiled in 1492. Anti-semitic propaganda was reminiscent of the difficulties experienced by the Christians in the first and second centuries when they themselves had been accused of immoral and anti-social behaviour. Against such a background of hatred and mistrust the desire to learn Hebrew and study the Hebrew scriptures was regarded as highly suspicious and it is a credit to the courage of a man like Johannes Reuchlin (1455–1522) that Hebrew was made available to others in the West. In 1506 Reuchlin published a rudimentary Hebrew grammar and lexicon which proved to be an enormous incentive to the study of the Old Testament. Other works followed but his later years were dogged by controversy. He was tried by the Inquisition and though found innocent of all charges was later condemned for heresy by Pope Leo X. Reuchlin and others like him were greatly admired by the reformers, although Reuchlin himself refused to break from Rome despite the personal troubles he had encountered.

The humanists did not confine their interest to literature and their interest in education was much broader than exegesis. They believed that education was the only really effective means of reform, and reform of both Church and State was one of the greatest priorities of the age. The educated person was able to learn the lessons of the past, appreciate the absolute futility of war and recognise the advantages of persuasion rather than compulsion. The educated person could view man in a totally different way from the depressingly corrupt medieval view. To the humanist the world was essentially good, a place to be admired for its beauty, the resources of which were to be enjoyed. Man himself was essentially or at least potentially good, separated from the rest of the world by his reason. This reason gave a person dignity, freeing him to develop all aspects of his life. People were essentially social not isolated beings, and naturally yearned for and valued true friendship. Though the humanists stressed reason they never reduced the person to being simply a mind but emphasised the feelings which could appreciate music, literature and art. This had a very real effect on the city of Rome under the influence of the Renaissance popes, and during this period Rome was transformed into the most splendid European capital city. Nicholas V began this task. His successors, however, carried on the work and a great deal of building and restoration was done during the reign of Sixtus IV (1471–84) including the Palace Chapel in the Vatican and the famous Sistine Chapel. Julius II (1503–13) was responsible for commissioning the building of the new St Peter's, the painting of the ceiling of the Sistine Chapel by Michaelangelo, and the frescoes in the Vatican by Raphael. These have withstood several changes in the fashion of art and been admired by countless numbers of people over the centuries, but such a preoccupation by the popes of the Renaissance tended to obscure their spiritual and pastoral vision and led to criticism of them by their contemporaries.

One of the most important discoveries of the fifteenth century, which helped the cause of the humanists and which was to become very important during the Reformation, was that of printing. The beginnings can be traced back to the middle of the century and are associated with Johann Gutenburg (c. 1396–1468) who by 1450 had invented a sort of typecasting machine. Between 1453–5 he was involved in printing the 'Gutenburg Bible', also known as the '42-line Bible' because it had forty-two lines to each column. William Caxton (1422–91) was another pioneer in the printing field. An Englishman, Caxton was both widely travelled and fluent in several languages. One result of this fluency was that he was often asked by friends and patrons to translate different works. On one occasion he promised the same translation to several different people and the thought of having slavishly to copy each translation prompted him to investigate the possibilities of printing. He travelled to Cologne where, in 1474, he printed the first book in English, an unlikely work called *The Histories of Troy*. On his return to England he set up a printing press in Westminster from which came the first book printed in England, namely *The Indulgence of Sixtus IV* in 1476. By 1500 there were nearly four hundred titles printed in English including Chaucer's *Canterbury Tales*, published by Caxton in 1484. The majority of the books were orthodox works of piety, but it was clear that the printing press could be used for any sort of literature and there were those who would make capital of this new invention. John Foxe, in the sixteenth century, left this assessment of printing:

Hereby tongues are known, knowledge groweth, judgement increaseth, books are dispersed, the Scripture is seen, times compared, truth discerned, falsehood detected. Through printing the world beginneth now to have eyes to see and hearts to judge.

The majority of the fifteenth-century humanists were not ordained and this fact helped to free scholarship from the strict control of a Church which had enjoyed a virtual monopoly in education for centuries. Since the majority were lay people they indirectly affected other lay activities, such as business and commerce, and they helped to give such occupations a new dignity and respect. Much of their work was critical study and in this climate the Church herself became an object of criticism. The humanists did not fear highlighting the weaknesses and shortcomings, the abuses and privileges, which were all too evident to the critical. In many ways this spirit of criticism was important in helping to shape future events by allowing people the confidence to express their opinion even when this disagreed with the authority of the Church. They were particularly aware of the gulf between the primitive Church which, with their love of antiquity, they regarded as the ideal Church, and the contemporary Church which had suffered so greatly during the Middle Ages being now only a pale of reflection of their ideal. They reacted against the clericalising of the Church and they stressed that everyone was called to live a fully Christian life albeit following different vocations, an example of such sentiments being found in Erasmus' book *Handbook of the Christian Soldier* published in 1505. However, for all their criticism of the Church the relationship between humanism and reformation is a complex one. Certainly many of the reformers were brought up as humanists and imbibed many of their methods and much of their spirit. On the other hand many humanists, among them Erasmus and Thomas More, refused to become part of a reform movement which separated itself from Rome. The very idea of breaking the unity of the Church was anathema to many of them and as a result they fought shy of doing so despite being convinced of the need for a reform 'in head and members'. However, they did provide a great deal of the material and ethos which allowed the break-up of the Roman Church and the establishment of several churches, which all claimed to be Christian but independent of Rome.

The humanists had been particularly scathing in denouncing the clergy who, they claimed, were largely ignorant and ill-suited to undertake the pastoral care of the people under their charge. They also attacked much of the popular piety of the age which they maintained bordered on the superstitious. There had been, however, some significant religious trends in the late medieval period which, although not numerically strong, had affected and continued to affect piety. One such trend was known as German Mysticism and is associated in its beginnings with Master Eckhart (1260–1327).

Eckhart was a Dominican who quickly rose to the position of Provincial in Saxony and was later entrusted with reforming the Dominican Houses in Bohemia. He was best known for his preaching in which he emphasised the possibility of becoming close to God through a mystical union of the soul with God. His enemies claimed that in so stressing this mystical union he denied the need for the Church or the sacraments since such a union could be achieved through personal prayer. He was accused of heresy and tried by the

Archbishop of Cologne before appealing to the pope, but he died before the pope could give a ruling. In the event Pope John XXII condemned several of his propositions and this condemnation prevented his writings from enjoying the wide circulation he might otherwise have expected. His cause was taken up by his disciples, among whom was Johann Tauler (*c.*1300–61), also a Dominican. Tauler was also famous for his preaching and, like Eckhart, he laid great stress on the mystical union of the soul with God, but he went on to stress that such closeness to God would be evidenced in practical Christian charity. For Tauler, contemplation was not done for its own sake but to lead to an increase in charity and virtue. He demonstrated this in his own life, particularly during the Black Death, the great plague in the middle of the fourteenth century, when he was unstinting in his service of the victims. A contemporary of Tauler and another disciple of Eckhart was Henry Suso (1295–1366). His defence of Eckhart brought him into conflict with the Dominican authorities and probably cost him a career in the universities, but he turned his considerable talents to preaching and spiritual direction. His main literary contribution was called *The little book of Eternal Wisdom* which was a practical way of meditation especially on the Passion, and which was widely read and greatly influenced both his contemporaries and later generations. Although these men were mainly concerned with Germany, their influence spread wider and included a group called 'The Friends of God' who were centred in Switzerland.

Another major religious trend found its inspiration from Gerard Groote (1340–84) who, after a successful career as a student in Paris, and a short period of teaching in Cologne, left an academic career and devoted himself to a simple Christian life. At first he spent some time in a monastery before receiving permission to become a missionary preacher. His preaching soon brought him into conflict with the diocesan clergy who were offended by his biting criticism of their way of life, and with the Mendicants who also objected to his criticisms of them. In 1383 he was banned from preaching after accusations of heresy had been made against him and, although he appealed against this ban, he died a victim of the plague before any decision had been given. Groote had gathered around him a group of people who adopted a semi-monastic way of life and who later became known as 'The Brethren of the Common Life'. Though described as semi-monastic, the members of the group did not take any solemn vows but supported each other in their attempt to fulfil their Christian vocations as perfectly as possible. They laid great emphasis on perseverance, seeing true Christian living not so much in scaling great mystical heights but in terms of a practical, daily routine. At the same time that the universities were gaining in popularity and importance the Brethren placed great emphasis on education and providing free schooling in both Germany and the Netherlands.

One of the more famous students at their school in Deventer in the Netherlands was Thomas à Kempis (c.1380–1471). Thomas did not remain as a member of the Brethren but in 1399 entered the Canons Regular, being professed in 1406. He spent the whole of his life preaching, copying manuscripts and writing and the most famous work ascribed to him, though he was probably only responsible for part of it or for its final presentation, was *The Imitation of Christ*. First circulated c.1420, this has been one of the most influential spiritual works of all time, translated into nearly a hundred languages and published in more than three thousand editions. As the title suggests, the book invites the reader to seek perfection through an assiduous following of Christ himself.

The Imitation of Christ is divided into four different sections or books, the first of which aims to create within the reader an inner peace of mind and soul by helping him to become more truly humble. It paints the world in such a way as to make it utterly contemptible and it stresses the need for self-control and true contrition for past sins. In keeping with the general tenor of the time the first book closes with a meditation on death and the judgement which must surely follow. Book Two concentrates on perseverance through suffering. Since the Christian seeks to imitate Christ he will often find himself at odds with the world and despised by people he thought were his friends. All of this should be accepted since friendship with Christ is the real goal, and taking up the cross is one sure way of remaining in such friendship. By this stage the reader could well have become thoroughly depressed with his own faults and lack of strength which is one of the reasons why Book Three stresses the power of God through his free gift of grace. It is precisely to the measure the Christian strips himself of his own self and reliance on himself that he will be filled with the grace of God. Book Four, which is mainly concerned with the sacrament of Holy Communion, gives three different exercises to help the Christian better appreciate the wonder of God's love for him.

In the fourteenth and fifteenth centuries English mystics and writers also made contributions to the spiritual heritage of later generations. Among the more important was Richard Rolle (c.1300–49), a Yorkshireman who became a hermit and as such exerted great influence during his lifetime. He was a prolific writer tending to express his experience of God in three distinct words: 'heat', 'sweetness' and 'song'. His writings included scripture commentaries, poems and mystical works of exhortation. After his death he became even more famous and was included in martyrologies as late as 1672. Very much within the tradition of Rolle but not attributed to him was *The Cloud of Unknowing* which has come down through the centuries anonymously. As the title suggests, the author reacts against the possibility of knowing God by reason but stresses that our knowledge of Him comes through His own self-revelation. The book stresses the need for contemplation and is meant to be an aid to those already practised in this form of prayer. Another example of the wealth of English mystical writing was Walter Hilton (d.1396) who, like Rolle, spent some time as a hermit although, unlike him, he abandoned this way of life and became an Augustinian Canon. His most famous work *The Scale of Perfection* was one of the first books to be printed in English. In this Hilton tried to marry the active and contemplative lives, claiming that perfection could only be achieved by both contemplation and the fulfilment of the routine of Christian life. Not all the English mystics were men: one of the most influential was Lady Julian of Norwich (*c*.1343–1413). According to her own writings she became ill at about the age of thirty and during her illness fell into a trance lasting some five hours during which she received fifteen revelations. A further vision was received the following day and she then spent several years meditating on these visions before writing *The Revelation of Divine Love*. In this she states her great belief in the value of the passion and cross of Christ and in the ultimate triumph of love which will see the final expulsion of all evil. Although most of the mystics lived in the fourteenth century their influence was felt more in the fifteenth century and beyond, while they all helped to provide a backcloth for the Reformation.

However, such spiritual classics were unlikely to affect the vast majority of people who were struggling to make sense of their religious belief and practice in a world that showed little of the love and mercy of God. Indeed the constant wars in Europe, for example the Hundred Years War from 1337–1453, the outbreaks of plague, culminating in the Great Plague of 1499–1502, and the harshness of life in general all militated against a picture of a God of Love. Fear was far more dominant than love, and fear was encouraged by many of those responsible for preaching the Gospel. Two major themes dominated the preaching manuals, the first of which was Death and Judgement. Death was a very public part of the late Middle Ages and it found expression in sermons, pictures and the morality plays. The

preacher was concerned with preparing people for death and particularly stressing those temptations most likely to affect one who
was about to die, including loss of faith, despair and impatience.
When besieged by such temptations the dying person was urged to
look at the crucifix and remind himself of the death of Jesus. He was
also reminded that judgement must surely follow death and the
pictures of hell for those who failed the Last Judgement were both
lurid and realistic. Some stressed hell as a place and others as a state,
but common to both was the absence of God. For many the daily
round of living must have seemed little more than hell on earth.

The second major theme was the Passion and Death of Jesus. Here
the preachers' words were reinforced in the strongest possible way
by pictorial images of the Passion found in every church in the West.
The crucifix was dominant in every church and with the introduction
of Rood Screens, the instruments of the passion, nails, thorns and
whips were painted on to the screens. Many churches would also
have group scenes of the Passion with Mary and John standing at the
foot of the cross. The Pieta – Mary holding the lifeless body of her
son – was also common. Reminders of the Passion were found
outside churches, wayside calvaries were evident in many places and
the Morality plays, now increasing in popularity, devoted a great
deal of time to the Passion. In this way Christ was presented in very
human terms and his sufferings were meant to shame people into
sorrow for their sins. As a result of this emphasis, the resurrection of
Christ was hardly ever mentioned and the scripture passages most
widely used were not the parable of the Prodigal Son nor the image of
the Good Shepherd, but the parable of the Sheep and the Goats and
the image of God as the Judge.

This preaching emphasised the distance between God and his
people, and even Christ, who was the mediator between the Father
and his people, seemed beyond the reach of most. Consequently
there developed the practice of seeking help in approaching God and
the first person to whom appeal was made was Mary. She was seen as
the one most likely to be able to avert the wrath and judgement of
God, and devotion to her, which had always played a significant part
in the Eastern Church, now increased in the West. Devotion to Mary
was advocated by the Dominicans, who were sponsoring the doctrine of the Immaculate Conception, and by the Franciscans, who
were recommending people to recite the rosary. The saints too were
seen as friends who might be persuaded to help and some of them
began to be associated with specific skills, such as Dennis for averting headaches, Vitus for averting epilepsy, Barbara for keeping
people safe from the effects of lightning, Christopher for ensuring a

safe journey, and Margaret for preserving a person from insanity.

This devotion to the saints increased the importance attached to relics – the material remains of a saint after death and those objects which were thought to have been in contact with the saints. The veneration of relics was neither peculiar to Christianity nor an invention of the Middle Ages. In the Christian Church from the earliest times the mortal remains of the martyrs had always been accorded the utmost respect and shortly after the persecutions ended, the Eucharist was often celebrated over the tombs of the martyrs. However, the increased demand for relics led to the transfer of them from place to place and to the division and dismembering of the saints' bodies. The West received a great influx of relics during the time of the crusades when people returning from the Holy Land brought great quantities of bones and other objects. The difficulties involved in objective verification were immense and the Reformers were quick to point out the anomalies of various Churches claiming to have the head of the same saint! John Calvin in his *Small Treatise on Relics* was bitterly scathing of the incredulity of those who believed in the authenticity or usefulness of relics.

Some saints were associated with particular shrines to which people would make pilgrimage. As with relics, the idea of pilgrimage was not exclusive to Christianity but was practised by many other religious people who believed that certain places or shrines were especially blessed by the Deity. For Christians in the West the whole idea of pilgrimage had received enormous encouragement from the Jubilee Year of 1300 after which places other than Rome became increasingly popular. Among the more famous were Compostela in Spain, St Michel in France, Aachen in Germany and Walsingham in England. Both relics and pilgrimages had one thing in common, namely their connection with indulgences, which were believed to release a person from the temporary punishment due to sins, and which therefore helped to relieve the terrible emphasis on judgement, and helped a Christian to face God with more confidence.

Central to the devotional life of the Church was the Mass, which had undergone tremendous changes in emphasis and celebration over the centuries. In the Early Church the Eucharist had been primarily a community prayer when the whole community gathered round the local bishop and different people had different roles to play. In the seventh and eighth centuries a notable deviation from this community activity took place with the rise of the so-called 'Private Mass', the origins of which are to be found in the monasteries and among the missionaries. In a private Mass a priest, either alone or with just one other person present, would celebrate Mass saying privately those parts which had previously been said by others. With the use of Latin in the liturgy, language became a barrier to understanding rather than a vehicle of communication and people became increasingly dependent on the priest for their understanding. At the same time the priest was now seen as offering Mass for the people rather than presiding at a liturgy in which all played a part. Theological controversies also affected the emphasis in celebration, for example the denial, by some, of the divinity of Christ, caused a reaction among the Catholics who began to stress the divine nature of Jesus in the sacrament. This in turn affected practice, with the introduction of genuflections after the consecration as a mark of respect and belief in the real presence of Christ. The laity were discouraged from receiving communion in case they did so un-worthily, the punishment for which was too horrible to contemplate. Since people received communion less there was no longer any need for a loaf of bread and this was replaced by a thin wafer. At a later stage priests stopped offering the chalice to the laity for fear of spilling the precious blood, and this denial was justified on the grounds that Christ was present 'under either kind alone'. The very architecture of the churches reflected these changes with altars being placed against the East Wall so that the priest now offered the Mass with his back to the people. Side altars were built to facilitate the private Mass, crucifixes were placed above the altar and statues became prominent throughout the church. The laity were physically separated by the erection of Rood Screens which increased their distance from the liturgical action and heightened the sense of mystery and awe. Communion rails were a further innovation and the laity were now expected to kneel in a physical posture of adora-tion and be fed the host by the priest directly on to the tongue. As one historian of the liturgy, Joseph Martos, has written:

> By the thirteenth century the liturgy which had once been a com-munal prayer was now a clerical ritual separated from the congre-gation by barriers of language and architecture, and the theology of the Middle Ages reflected that change. For the liturgy instead of revealing the Christian mysteries had itself become a mystery in need of explanation.

After this time the great emphasis shifted from receiving com-munion to 'seeing' the host. To accommodate this desire, elevations were multiplied and lasted longer, bells warned the congregation when the elevation was happening. In the larger churches people would rush from altar to altar in order to catch a glimpse of the host in the superstitious belief that their fortunes would change for the better, they would not grow older or any child born on the day the mother 'gazed' on the host, would be a son. The feast of Corpus Christi, which originated in France in the thirteenth century, spread throughout the whole Church and Eucharistic processions became so popular that legislation was necessary to limit them to the octave of the feast of Corpus Christi. To quote the same historian of the liturgy:

> By the end of the Middle Ages the Mass had been transformed from an act of public worship into a form of clerical prayer. Instead of being offered once a week as in Patristic times, it was offered many times a day. Instead of being concelebrated by the bishop and his assistant priests, it was said simultaneously in the same church by several priests. Instead of being a service of scripture reading followed by a communion service, it was a symbolic sacrifice in which the readings were not heard and communion was not distributed. Although Sunday Masses continued to be attended by the faithful, the vast majority of Masses were ones paid for by the laity and said by the priests on weekdays. By and large the Mass had become a Good Work performed by the priest for the spiritual benefit of the Church. This was the Mass the Reformers knew and this was the Mass they rejected.

Finally, to quote another historian of the liturgy, Josef Jungmann:

> The holiest of the Church's possessions remained, it is true, the centre of genuine piety. But alas the clouds and shadows surrounding this centre brought matters to such a pass, that the institution of Jesus, that well of life from which the Church had drawn for 1500 years, became an object of scorn and ridicule and was repudiated as a terrible idolatry by entire peoples.

Consequently although there were some positive aspects of popular piety and liturgy at the end of the Middle Ages, there was also a great deal of superstition and several practices were adopted which were open to criticism. The Reformers were quick to highlight such anomalies especially when the papacy continued to obstruct a reform movement which might have gone some way towards finding a remedy.

As well as the difficulties and changes, superstitions and abuses peculiar to the Church, the second half of the fifteenth century saw very significant social changes and upheavals. The population of Western Europe had increased markedly, rising from some 53 million in 1350 to around 70 million in 1500. As well as this increase in numbers, the distribution of the population had changed with more than ten per cent of the population in 1500 living in or around towns whereas less than one per cent lived in towns in 1350. Within the towns the wealth was held by relatively few people which caused envy among the rest while those still living in the country had seen a steady decline in their standard of living. Such social difficulties were potentially explosive.

A further important development was the expansion of Europe in the late fifteenth century, after years of near strangulation by the Turks. Spain and Portugal led the way in making several very important discoveries including India and the Far East, North and South America, by men like Diaz, Vasco de Gama and Cabral. The first circumnavigation of the world was achieved during this time by Columbus, and Cabot represented England in the new discoveries. In 1493 Pope Alexander VI issued a papal bull dividing these newly discovered lands between Spain and Portugal. Such expansion led to increased trade and commerce which in turn caused the creation of a new middle class which disturbed, if it did not actually destroy, the established social order. These people had achieved their status not by birth or by ordination but by money, and this relatively new commodity was to assume an enormous importance in the lives of everyone.

The national consciousness which had been evident towards the end of the Middle Ages, and which had received encouragement from the Consiliar movement was now being consolidated. France had received a very strong identity as a result of the Hundred Years War and was ruled by a king exercising control over a strong central government. In Spain the marriage between Ferdinand of Aragon and Isabella of Castile brought together the two most powerful families. In 1504 Ferdinand became the sole ruler on the death of his wife and in 1516 he left his heir the whole of the Iberian peninsula except for Portugal. England had developed constitutional government relatively early and royal power had been curtailed by Parliament, but the success of Henry Tudor in winning the Wars of the Roses in 1485 and his long reign of twenty-four years consolidated England's national consciousness. Significantly Germany did not share in this general trend but continued to be divided between several individual rulers who enjoyed sufficient autonomy within their boundaries to exert control over every aspect of life. It was from one such German territory that a man emerged into the Church and society of the late fifteenth century who was going to be responsible for instigating the greatest change ever experienced in the Western Church. This man was Martin Luther.

Martin Luther was born, in 1483, into a world which was changing socially, economically and politically and into a Church which was in need of reform. He belonged to a new generation which was prepared to be critical of abuse and less willing to accept the status quo simply on the orders of a pope. He grew up when national consciousness challenged the idea of Christendom and questioned the need for a central authority and a source of unity in Rome. The popes had successfully countered the threat of conciliarism by a series of concordats which had increased the State's control of the Church and highlighted the political role of the papacy at the expense of its pastoral responsibilities. Sixtus IV (1471–84), in office when Luther was born, exemplified the major traits of the Renaissance: an absorbing interest in Italian politics, a great patronage of humanism and the arts and the increasing worldliness of the curia. He was succeeded by the weak and indecisive Innocent VIII (1484–92), before the accession of Alexander VI (1492–1503) Borgia whose pontificate emphasised all that was wrong with the Renaissance popes. A Spaniard by birth he was made a cardinal by his uncle Pope Callixtus III who later appointed him as Chancellor of the Church of Rome. He was himself elected pope in 1492 but the suspicion of bribery to secure this election did not augur well for the Church. His whole pontificate was dogged by his immoral reputation, his unashamed nepotism and his determination to make international politics a priority. In Luther's most formative years the popes could hardly have given a worse example, in fact, of pastoral and spiritual care unappreciative of the seriousness of the problems facing the Church they claimed to rule.

Added to this was the dogmatic uncertainty created by the humanists in their desire to study the Church and her teaching in a critical way. They had already raised serious doubts about the reliability of the Vulgate text of the scriptures, and by their yearning for the past which they regarded as ideal, they debated whether the contemporary Church reflected or rejected the teaching of Christ. They disputed the nature of the Church, the necessity of the papacy and the source of authority. The nominalism of Ockham – a theory which denied reality to universal concepts – had challenged the scholasticism of the Thomists, and was being championed in the fifteenth century by men like Gabriel Biel (1420–95) who was to influence the reformers themselves. To some, the last decades of the fifteenth century were a time of suspicion and unnecessary questioning, to others they were a time of new discoveries and genuine excitement. To all they were a time when neutrality remained impossible and individuals were called upon to take their own particular stand.

Martin Luther was born at Eisleben in Saxony, into a working-class family of industry and integrity. Baptised the next day, 11 November he received the name of the saint of that day, Martin of Tours. Within a year the family had moved to Mansfeld and it was there that he first went to school before proceeding, at the age of fourteen, to Magdeburg to attend a school run by the Brethren of the Common Life. His religious upbringing was conservative, almost puritanical, and the discipline imposed was severe to the point of being cruel. Later in life he reflected on the image of God he had received as a child:

> From childhood I was so trained that I could not but turn pale and become terrified if I merely heard the name of Christ mentioned, for I was taught only to regard him as a stern and angry judge.

His ability and hard work enabled him to matriculate in the university of Erfurt in 1501 from which he obtained both his Bachelor and Master's degree by 1505. During his studies he came under the influence of Ockhamism especially on the question of universals – general concepts representing the common elements belonging to individuals of the same species – and in his understanding of God. He showed a willingness to argue from the Scriptures against the conclusions of the philosophers and some historians trace his future doctrine of 'Scripture Alone' back to this time. After completing his M.A. degree, he transferred to the faculty of Law at Erfurt but in July 1505 his life was transformed by an experience which so frightened him that he vowed to become a monk if he was saved from death. Accordingly he entered the Reformed Monastery of the Augustinian Canons at Erfurt despite the vigorous and aggressive objection of his father. His decision to take the monastic habit demonstrated his belief that the safest and surest means of salvation was to cooperate with the means offered by the Church, and the most effective means involved adopting religious life. It is not too simplistic to say that the major motive for his decision to become a monk was to save his soul. He was professed in 1506 and ordained priest in 1507. His profession assumed an enormous importance because it stressed his acceptance by his fellow monks and the approval of his superiors. His ordination convinced him of his own unworthiness and the utter transcendence and majesty of God and led him to question how the gulf between God and man could be bridged. He was soon to maintain that a man could do nothing to earn his salvation which was a free gift of God, but that a man was 'justified by faith alone'.

His spiritual director was Johann Staupitz, the Vicar-General of the Augustinians and Professor of Scripture at Wittenberg University, whom Luther acknowledged as one of the most formative influences on him especially in helping him to overcome his fears and scruples. The word Luther himself used to describe his spiritual state was 'Anfechtung' which includes such characteristics as doubt, fear, panic, despair and a sense of desolation, and his favourite prayer at this time was to repeat Jesus's cry from the Cross, 'My God, my God, why have you forsaken me'. His future liberated spirit was in marked contrast to this spirit of depression. Academically his career continued to progress. He became Professor of Moral Philosophy at Wittenberg in 1508 and pursued his own biblical studies, gaining his Bachelor's degree in Theology before studying the *Sentences* of Peter Lombard. In 1510 he was sent to Rome to represent Erfurt at a conference of Augustinians, and of this visit he later maintained: 'I would never have believed the papacy was such an abomination if I had not myself seen the Roman Court'.

In 1512 he received his doctorate in theology and succeeded Staupitz as Professor of Scripture. The next five years were of crucial importance both for Luther himself and the whole course of the Reformation, as Professor Rupp comments: 'It seems clear that in all essentials his theology was in existence before the opening of the Church struggle in 1517'. And again: 'The whole of the later Luther may be found in his lectures on the Psalms'. His study of the Bible, to which he brought a subjectivism in keeping with his personality, began to relieve the pessimism and melancholy which had previously gripped him. He became utterly convinced that faith alone justified a person and that nothing a man did could alter that fact. This led him to question the role of the Church, the sacramental system and the ministerial priesthood, and further, to stress the primacy of the Word of God as the only binding source of authority for the Christian. It changed his picture of God who, from his youth, he had feared as a judge; God was now the one who justified a man by his free gift of faith. This revelation came to him while he was studying in the tower of the monastery at Wittenberg and is often referred to as his 'Tower experience'. Both the dating, 1515 or 1518, and the nature, either a sudden flash of inspiration or a painful struggle for awareness, of this experience are disputed, but what remains clear was that the change that was taking place was of enormous significance. As yet his thinking and lecturing had been within the confines of a university atmosphere but in 1517 he felt constrained to make his views public after hearing of the teaching of the so-called 'Indulgence Preachers'.

As the sacrament of penance had developed in the life and history of the Church so other developments had taken place including the distinction between guilt and punishment, and the possibility of substituting one penance for another, known as commutation. In the

Middle Ages the Church began the practice of granting certain 'spiritual' benefits, or indulgences, on the completion of particular tasks, such as the building of a church or taking part in the crusade. The later Middle Ages saw an increase in the number of such indulgences and also the beginnings of a kind of financial exploitation. One major problem was that the practice of indulgences had outstripped the theology behind them and both unconscious error and genuine misunderstanding crept in. In 1505 Pope Julius II (1503–13), began to rebuild St Peter's basilica in Rome and according to now accepted custom he announced an indulgence to help finance this costly project. In 1514 Albert of Magdeburg became the Archbishop of Mainz but only after paying a huge sum of money to the curia to dispense him from his lack of years and the charge of pluralism. As part of the arrangement with the curia he allowed the St Peter's indulgence to be preached in his dioceses, and although Albert issued an instruction which technically came within the sketchy limits of the Church's teaching, the preachers largely ignored this, preferring to stress the value of big contributions. In this way the dominant theme was not contrition for past sins but the highest possible financial gain. The Dominican Tetzel was appointed to preach the indulgence in Mainz which was within twenty miles of Wittenberg, from where great numbers of people flocked in the mistaken belief that they could guarantee their salvation.

Luther became involved when these same people returned with their indulgence papers wanting him to reassure them that they were effective, but he was both psychologically and spiritually incapable of guaranteeing such certainty, fearing that such a practice offered only false security and militated against the ideal of a life of repentance. He did not reject indulgences completely but limited their effectiveness to the satisfaction imposed by confessors, denying that they could increase grace or guarantee a place in heaven. In October he wrote to Archbishop Albert criticising the way the indulgence was actually being preached and asking him to impose stricter sanctions to avoid misunderstanding. He enclosed a copy of the 95 Theses which he offered as a way of clarifying the teaching on indulgences and other theological questions he regarded as doubtful. These theses, written in a polemical and provocative way, touching on questions and grievances long felt, became the symbol, and Luther the spokesman, of all those who were disillusioned with the present state of the contemporary Church. The historical importance of this whole episode lies in the Church's failure to respond because of both an inability or unwillingness to accept the seriousness of Luther's complaint, and to recognise the numbers of those who supported him. Even Tetzel failed to grasp the situation, and dismissed Luther's views as heretical, defending his own as orthodox and even dogmatic.

On 7 August 1518 Luther was ordered to appear in Rome after efforts to silence him had failed and some younger theologians like Martin Bucer had given him their support. Eventually Pope Leo X allowed his case to be tried in Germany and sent Cardinal Cajetan, the General of the Dominicans, to interrogate and pass sentence on him. The two met at Augsburg but the difference in mentality, personality and philosophy meant that the meeting ended inconclusively as a discussion, although Cajetan wrote to the secular ruler of Saxony, Frederick the Wise, demanding Luther's extradition to Rome for further questioning. At this point international politics caused a delay in the proceedings with the failing health of the Emperor Maximilian I and the subsequent concern over his likely successor. Pope Leo X was especially keen to prevent Charles of Spain from succeeding as emperor but to achieve this he needed the support of Luther's secular ruler, Frederick the Wise. Consequently the case against Luther was shelved until June 1519 when Luther met John Eck at Leipzig. They debated a whole series of subjects including predestination, Divine Law, papal primacy and the authority of Councils. On this last point Luther maintained that Councils could make mistakes and he instanced Constance's condemnation of John Huss as an example. He again defended Scripture as the final source of authority, no longer accepting that the Church enjoyed the authority to give the binding interpretation of Scripture and refusing to accept any error unless proved wrong by Scripture. The meeting at Leipzig forced Luther to recognise that his condemnation of the Church of Rome was inevitably leading to his separation from it.

This separation came significantly closer with a whole series of writings in 1520 climaxed by three celebrated reformation works. In the summer Luther wrote *An Open Letter to the German Nobility* in which he caught the feeling of the German people in a style they could appreciate. The Roman Church had erected three 'walls' which had effectively blocked all attemps to reform, namely, the claim that spiritual jurisdiction was greater than secular, that the pope was the sole interpreter of scripture and that the pope alone could summon a council. Against such claims Luther argued in favour of the priesthood of all believers, the essential equality of everyone and the subservience of a corrupt Church to the reforming influence of the State. He then presented a twenty-eight point plan for reform in 'head and members'. The demand for this letter proved to be phenomenal, and the printing presses had to produce four thousand copies a week to meet the need.

In October he published *The Babylonian Captivity of the Church* which was a discussion of sacramental theology and practice in which Luther denied seven sacraments and maintained that the Roman Church had 'shackled' the Eucharist by refusing the chalice to the laity, maintaining the doctrine of transubstantiation and referring to the Mass as a sacrifice thus reducing it to a good work. In June 1520 in his bull *Exsurge Domine* Pope Leo X had condemned as heretical forty-one of Luther's theses and it was in response to this that Luther wrote the third of his Reformation manifestos *The Freedom of a Christian*. Addressed to Leo X and written in a conciliatory tone, this letter was a genuine attempt to state his own understanding of the Christian life and faith, stressing the three major doctrines of the primacy of scripture, justification by faith alone, and the priesthood of all believers. Despite this letter, on 3 January 1521 Luther was formally excommunicated and, according to custom, the State authorities should have taken him into custody. However, contrary to custom he was given a safe conduct to appear before the emperor at Worms in April where Luther acknowledged his writings and refused to recant. Frederick the Wise, fearing the worst, 'kidnapped' Luther and placed him in the relative safety of the Wartburg Castle where he was to remain for nearly a year cut off from the outside world and coping with his isolation by writing and by translating the Bible. On 26 May Charles V eventually signed the Edict of Worms which 'declared that the aforementioned Martin Luther is to be regarded by us and you, each and everyone, as a member severed from the Church of God, an obstinate schismatic and a manifest heretic'. Luther was now officially under the ban but the delay in publishing the ban and the fact that Charles was both absent from Germany for nine years and needed the military help of the German states who supported Luther, meant that politics and religion were once again confused and Luther escaped the effects of his excommunication.

During his exile in Wartburg Castle others were proceeding with the work of the Reformation. Despite the cautionary counsel of Philip Melancthon, the Professor of Greek at Wittenberg who frequently represented Luther, the first wave of popular support centred on Carlstadt (1480–1541) who celebrated the first protestant Eucharist in Wittenberg on Christmas Day 1521 without vestments, without any sacrificial language, without any elevation, and with communion under the form of both bread and wine. In January 1522 he openly defied the laws of celibacy by marrying, launched an increasingly aggressive attack on priests, nuns and religious, and called for the destruction of altars, images and pictures. Carlstadt proceeded too quickly, however, confusing the people he hoped to win over, and in February of 1522 Frederick the Wise ordered a restoration of the Old Mass, recognising the need for well-informed and realistic leadership. To this end he recalled Luther who, from March, assumed the leadership of the Reformation in Wittenberg and throughout Germany.

Luther recognised the need to persuade and educate rather than upset and coerce, the necessity of only making vital changes and avoiding the danger of change for its own sake, the need to allow the individual to decide on non-essentials, and the necessity of securing the agreement and cooperation of the secular authorities. In practice the Mass retained, for the present, the shape and feel of the Roman Mass and people were allowed to go to confession again, while in the churches pictures and statues were returned. By such means he gained people's confidence, a prerequisite for any further and more radical changes. His only opposition came from Carlstadt and his supporters who accused Luther of compromise; but their position was weak and Carlstadt was relieved of his teaching responsibilities before he left Wittenberg, at first temporarily and then in 1524 permanently, eventually settling in Basle. This early disagreement was to be prophetic of future disunity between the various reformers as they struggled to create churches in place of Rome.

In 1524 Luther finally threw off his monastic habit before marrying an ex-Cistercian nun, Catherine von Bura. His marriage was a source of great strength and happiness and it sustained him through one of the blackest periods of his life when he lost a great deal of popular support by his condemnation of the peasant's revolt between 1524–6. Since the 1490s the peasants had periodically resorted to violence to press their claims for better conditions and in the sixteenth century they were stimulated by the teaching of the Reformers which they applied to their own impoverished social conditions. In their 'Twelve Articles' they pressed home their various demands but negotiations gave way to violence and Luther wrote a pamphlet condemning the peasants and calling for their subjection by the authorities. The peasants felt themselves betrayed and no longer looked to Luther for leadership or inspiration while the Catholic authorities made capital out of the incident and warned people of the practical consequences of joining the reformers.

In 1529 there was an important meeting at Speyer which recognised the effect and rapid growth of the Lutheran Church and gave rise to the term 'Protestant'. The meeting was summoned by Charles V as part of the Catholic reaction to the increased influence of the

Lutherans in Germany especially under the vigorous leadership of Philip of Hesse. Three years previously a meeting, also at Speyer, had agreed in principle to allow individual princes to organise ecclesiastical matters within their own territories. Charles at this second meeting at Speyer, failed to get this decision reversed but managed to pass legislation forbidding toleration of Lutherans in Catholic areas. Later, in April 1529, six princes, including Philip of Hesse together with several cities, signed a formal 'protest' defending freedom of conscience and the rights of minorities. In that same year Philip organised a conference at Marburg in an attempt to heal what was becoming an embarrassing rift between Luther and the Swiss reformer Ulrych Zwingli.

Zwingli had been born in 1484, educated at Basle and Bern and ordained in 1506. His humanist and patriotic tendencies together with a period as military chaplain made him a strong critic of countries using his fellow men as mercenaries. By 1519 he was resident in Zurich where he was noted for his forthright preaching against abuses in Church and State. He soon came to possess some of Luther's writing, though his dependence on Luther is disputed, and in 1522 he preached a sermon against fasting in Lent, allegedly eating two pork sausages in the pulpit on Ash Wednesday as a visible sign of his rejection of Roman teaching. He demanded the free preaching of the Word, claiming it to be the sole rule of faith; he rejected the authority of the pope, clerical celibacy, the sacrifice of the Mass, invocation to the saints, the doctrine of purgatory and monasticism. By 1524 Zurich had become the centre of the Swiss reform and in 1525 the Roman Mass was abolished to be replaced by Zwingli's communion service. The great Minster was turned into a theological school and Zwingli began translating the whole of the Bible, finished this mammoth task in 1530 just a year before his death. During this time his eucharistic views were sharpening, moving away from any notion of real presence to an understanding of 'symbolic' presence. This became evident at Marburg where he met Melancthon who was representing Luther, and the two failed to reach any agreement over the nature of Christ's presence in the Eucharist.

Such differences between the reformers did not help their preparation for the Diet of Augsburg summoned by Charles V in June 1530 in an attempt to restore peace and unity between Catholics and Protestants. Luther was prevented from appearing personally and once again was represented by Melancthon (1497–1560). Melancthon was a distant relative of Reuchlin and like him showed a flair for languages which won him the Chair of Greek at Wittenberg.

Under Luther's influence he became more involved in reformation theology and his *Loci Communes* of 1521 was the first attempt to offer a systematic presentation of reformed doctrine. His own theology developed as the successive editions of the *Loci Communes* show. Among the reformers he remained one of the more conciliatory and as such he participated at Augsburg presenting the confession of faith which stressed the positive side of Luther's teaching together with practical remedies for the abuses in the Roman Church. This Confession became the authoritative doctrinal statement of the Lutherans and formed the basis for future statements, but it failed to win Catholic approval and the two sides remained in dispute. This failure at Augsburg was potentially of great danger to the Protestants who determined to join forces by forming the Schmalkadic League in 1531 in order to unite different protestant groups in Germany and beyond.

The spread of Lutheranism after this time was rapid, owing much to the sheer inspiration and charism of Luther himself. Enjoying the support of Frederick the Wise, and after him the Elector John, Luther transformed Wittenberg into the reformed city which became a model for so many others. As confidence in him increased so he brought in more changes, replacing daily Mass with a morning service which stressed the importance of the Word of God. The Eucharist was restricted to a Sunday celebrated in the vernacular, participated in by all who now received the chalice. His hymns, the first published in 1524, became famous both for their use in the liturgy and as an effective means of preaching the Reformed Gospel. The congregation now assumed responsibilities previously undertaken by the hierarchy and the ministers were made accountable to the whole church. Through his vigorous preaching, his writings, his inspirational hymns, he caught the imagination of the people and provided them with a liturgy which, in terms of participation, was closer to the early Church than the medieval practice they had been accustomed to attend. By providing catechisms he helped both ministers and people to come to a deeper understanding of his doctrine. In these ways he gave people hope, introducing them to a faith that was real, opening up for them the treasures of scripture, allaying their fears and giving them the confidence which would help them overcome their differences with other reformers in the future, and even most differences among themselves which occurred after his death. These difficulties were real and it was not until 1580 that the Book of Concord was signed by ninety representatives of Lutheran State Churches and over 8000 ministers and teachers. By this time much of the old Holy Roman Empire, Scandinavia and parts of

Poland were Lutheran, testifying to the enormous importance and popularity of a Church which took its name from the man who initiated the mass defections from the Roman Church but who would have preferred his followers to be called, not Lutherans, but, simply, Christians.

In 1509 – when Luther was 26, Julius II was pope, Henry VIII king of England, Louis XII king of France, Ferdinand king of Spain and Europe still to experience the destruction of Christendom – John Calvin was born at Noyon some sixty miles north-east of Paris. His father was a self-made man who had become manager of the properties of the Cathedral chapter, a position which was to lead to his excommunication in 1528 because of suspicions of financial and other irregularities. In 1531 he died, still under the ban, and his family had to pay a heavy fine to secure him a Christian burial. Such incidents affected John deeply. Some years earlier in 1520 a benefice had fallen vacant and Calvin senior had obtained it for John both as an investment, should he decide to follow a clerical career, and as a means of income to finance his studies. In 1523 he went to Paris to continue his schooling where his French name, Cauven, was latinised to the much more familiar Calvin. In Paris his abilities were quickly recognised and he received a special coaching in Latin from Mathurin Cordier, one of the leading latinists of the time. The following year he transferred to the Collège de Montaigu, to which Erasmus had been sent and had complained about the strictness and rigorism. By 1528 Calvin had successfully completed his arts course before spending some time at the Sorbonne, noted for its orthodoxy. However he soon left Paris and took up legal studies at Orleans where the famous d'Etoile lectured in law. Despite his father's death, he graduated in law in 1532 and wrote his first major work, a commentary on Seneca's *Treaty on Clemency* in the hope that someone would recognise his talents and give him employment.

The following two years proved to be a turning-point in his life. In 1533 Nicholas Cop, with whom Calvin had become friendly some years previously, was promoted to the Rectorship of the University of Paris and in his inaugural address entitled 'Blessed are the Poor In Spirit' he stressed the importance of faith, minimised the effectiveness of good works and criticised the Sorbonne theologians for their intolerant narrow-mindedness. These same theologians reacted by accusing Cop of heresy, forcing him to quit Paris and take up residence in Basle. Calvin also came under suspicion, not simply because of his friendship with Cop, but also because of his alleged involvement in the writing of the address. He too left Paris and went into hiding, finding support and friendship from the reformers and humanists. Under their influence Calvin concluded that Rome could no longer be defended, indeed that the Roman authorities were an obstacle to reform. Later he maintained how it was during this period that he underwent a conversion which made him commit himself unreservedly to the living God and leave the Church of Rome.

This decision forced Calvin to leave France and find safety in the reformed cities of Switzerland where he met several reformers including Bullinger, Capito and Martin Bucer. It was during this time that he was accused of being an Anabaptist, a charge he deeply resented because of their theological views which placed great emphasis on practical Christianity at the expense of binding confessional statements. The Anabaptists, of whom there were many different groups, were condemned by both the Roman Church and the majority of the reformers. Calvin was so incensed at this accusation that he responded by publishing the First Edition of *The Institutes of Christian Religion* in March 1536. This book assumed enormous importance as it passed through various editions and translations between 1536 and 1559, becoming the foremost systematic textbook of reformed theology and proving Calvin's talent as a theologian and writer. Indeed he looked set at this stage for a scholarly career until in July 1536 a chance stop in Geneva changed the course of his life. In Geneva he met William Farel (1489–1565) who, in the previous year, had been largely responsible for the success of the reformation in Geneva. However, Farel recognised his own limitations and saw in Calvin the ideal theologian and organiser who could turn Geneva into a truly reformed place. Despite Calvin's own reluctance he was presuaded by Farel's threat 'If you refuse to devote yourself to this work, God will condemn you'.

In September 1536 Calvin published his *Draft Articles concerning the Government of the Church in Geneva* which imposed a system of strict discipline on all citizens together with a credal confession binding on all. Both were to be accepted before admission to the Lord's Supper and in order to retain citizenship. In practice the 17,000 Genevans who had agreed in May 1536 'to live in this holy evangelical law and Word of God, to abandon all Masses and other papal ceremonies and abuses, images and idols' found their freedom curtailed. Grumbling gave way to resentment which was shown in the polls of 1538 which recorded a massive swing away from Calvin and Farel. The situation was exacerbated when, on Easter Sunday, both men refused to administer the Lord's supper, believing that such a service, given the amount of discord, would be sacriligeous. Three days after Easter both men had left Geneva, and Calvin eventually settled in Strasbourg which was at this time under the guidance of Martin Bucer, an ex-Dominican. He had been one of the first to declare his support for Martin Luther, leaving the order in 1521, marrying in 1522 and publicly preaching reformed doctrine from 1523. On the death of Zwingli in 1531 he assumed the leadership of the Reformation in Switzerland from where he participated in the various discussions between Catholics and Protestants, all of which proved unsuccessful because of the growing realization of the differences between them. However this desire for unity was evident at Strasbourg where Calvin experienced for the first time a city marked by charity and a lack of extremism. He remained there for three years during which he was responsible for the pastoral care of over 400 French refugees who soon became noted for their 'hearty singing' and the atmosphere of 'holiness and fraternal gladness'. He was involved in teaching from which came the first of his scripture commentaries beginning with his work on St Paul's letter to the Romans. Other writings included his *Small Treatise on the Lord's Supper* in which he stressed the symbolic presence of Christ, the spiritual reception of the communicant and the sinfulness of unworthy participation. He completed the second and enlarged edition of the *Institutes* which was translated into French in 1541, and he wrote his celebrated reply to Cardinal Sadaleto. Sadaleto had written to the Genevans on hearing of their expulsion of Calvin and Farel, inviting them to learn from this episode and return to communion with Rome. The Genevan magistrates had forwarded the letter to Calvin, since he was the one Sadaleto had particularly criticised, and asked him to reply. In responding, Calvin refuted all charges of schism, denounced the Roman Church and upheld the principles of the Reformation.

His 'Strasbourg period' was both successful and fulfilling. In August 1540 he married Idelette de Bure and although the beginnings were happy, the marriage was to be dogged by ill-fortune – their infant son, James, died in 1542 and Idelette in 1549. He took part in two meetings at Hagenau and Worms both of which sought to find some common ground between Catholics and Protestants. Though he was not present at the final meeting at Ratisbon he kept abreast of developments and remained in touch with other reformers, notably Melancthon. Perhaps surprisingly he never met Martin Luther.

While Calvin and Strasbourg were flourishing Geneva was declining since no effective leadership had been found to replace that of Calvin and Farel. In 1540 a party called the 'Guillermins' achieved a majority on the city council and they began to work for the return of Calvin. An initial approach left Calvin declaring 'I would submit to death a thousand times rather than to that cross on which I had daily to die a thousand deaths'. And again, of Geneva itself, 'There is no place under heaven I am more afraid of'. Added to his own personal doubts was the pressure exerted by Bucer who was loath to lose him but who finally agreed to release him on a temporary basis. It was perhaps a letter from Farel urging him to take up the challenge and, as previously, appealing to the will of God which finally persuaded Calvin to return, and, on 7 September 1541, he re-entered the city promising to be 'forever the servant of Geneva'.

Calvin remained in Geneva until his death in 1564, during which time he successfully overcame all opposition and transformed Geneva into the leading city of the Swiss reformation and the centre of Calvinism. At the heart of this theology was his doctrine of the Church, expounded in the *Institutes*, which is recognised by two signs, the Word and the Sacraments – 'Wherever we see the Word of God sincerely preached and heard, wherever we see the sacraments administered according to the institution of Christ, there we cannot have any doubt that the Church of God has some existence since his promise can never fail, "where two or three are gathered in my name, there I am in the midst of them".' The primary function of the Church is the forgiveness of sins: 'Let us sincerely hold that if we have been admitted and engrafted into the body of Christ and Church, the forgiveness of sins has been bestowed and is daily bestowed upon us'. Such a high doctrine of Church explains Calvin's meticulous and detailed organisation as given in the *Ecclesiastical Ordinances* of 1541. According to these there were four offices – Pastors, Doctors, which after 1543 were merged with the Pastors reducing the number of offices to three, Elders and Deacons. They were to be helped by a group of ministers and laymen known as the Consistory which met every week under the influence of Calvin, and was responsible for discipline. There followed detailed instruction concerning the rite of celebration for baptism and the Lord's Supper and a demand for clear and continuous instruction in the faith in order to lead the young to a state of preparedness for admittance to the Lord's Supper.

In practice this new regime had a great effect on people's lives where Church attendance was not only compulsory but scrupulously monitored, reception of the Lord's Supper, four times a year in the three major Churches, being regarded as a sign of loyalty and general discipline strictly imposed. One particular example concerned the taverns, which Calvin tried to turn into Christian meeting houses, where innkeepers were warned to report excessive drinking, betting or obscene songs. A bible was to be kept open on the bar and people who failed to pray before eating were to be refused a meal. Although such an experiment failed in the long run, it serves to illustrate the strictness of morals which Calvin regarded as essential for the Christian life. Absence from Church, criticism of sermons, attendance at theatres, dancing, embracing and playing cards were all offences punishable by the Consistory. Between 1542–6 over seventy people were excommunicated and banished from Geneva and nearly sixty were executed for heresy, adultery, blasphemy and witchcraft, all of which were capital offences throughout Europe. Among those who opposed Calvin was Sebastian Castellion (1515–63), who was refused entry into the ministry because Calvin disapproved of his theology. In 1544 he applied a second time only to be refused again, finally leaving Geneva for good. Ten years later Castellion wrote *Whether heretics ought to be persecuted or not* in which he criticised the regime at Geneva, appealing for religious toleration by claiming 'killing a man is not defending a doctrine, it is simply killing a man'. Unfortunately neither the Roman Church nor many of the Reformers accepted that proposition and many people were to lose their lives on charges of heresy or treason.

One man who met his death in Geneva was Michael Servetus, a Spaniard, who travelled extensively and met many of the Reformers including Bucer and Melancthon. Before this he had published a work entitled *On the Errors of the Trinity* which claimed that the doctrine of the Trinity 'could only be defended by sophistry'. In 1532 the Spanish Inquisition proscribed this book and invited anyone who knew the author to hand him over to the Catholic authorities. Servetus managed to avoid detection and began moving within reformed circles only to find that they too were hostile to his doctrinal views. Eventually Servetus contacted Calvin who responded by adding his condemnation. In 1552 Servetus was named by the Inquisition and sentenced to death by burning. The following year he arrived in Geneva and between April and September was interrogated by, among others, Calvin himself, whom Servetus criticised and condemned. On 26 October he was sentenced to death by slow fire, dying after some half an hour of acute agony. Calvin was criticised for his part in the proceedings against Servetus and was forced to write a defence of his position disclaiming all charges of cruelty.

The death of Servetus marked the end of opposition to Calvin within Geneva and the next decade, until his death, saw the city completely under his control. The physical personnel of the city had changed, with the expulsion and voluntary departure of those opposed to him, and the influx of refugees and like-minded people bringing, not only their support, but also their skills and occupations. The wider political outlook brightened considerably with the numerically large cities recognising Geneva as an equal, and this culminated in the Perpetual Alliance in 1558 between Bern and Geneva. This alliance reduced the chance of any opposition party calling on outside help or using the possibility of an invasion as a realistic threat. In this favourable atmosphere, Calvin was able to lay firm foundations for the future. Discipline remained strict but social conditions improved especially in the areas of hygiene, housing and medicine. Arguably of greatest importance for the future of Calvinism was the establishment of the Genevan Academy which had the twofold aim of training the young in the fundamentals of Reformed Doctrine and preparing men for ministry. Among the first and most outstanding teachers was Theodore Beza (1519–1605) who became the leader of the Swiss Calvinists on the death of Calvin. Calvinism spread rapidly both during Calvin's life and beyond, especially in his native France where the first Calvinist Church had been established in 1555 and where by 1561 there were over 2000 such congregations. The main reason for the rapid development in a predominantly Catholic country was the king's preoccupation with relations with Spain. It was only in 1559 that Henry II (1547–59) signed a peace treaty with Philip II of Spain, but no sooner had he turned his attention to the religious question than he was killed in an accident. The numbers of the Calvinists made the French wars of religion in the next generation almost inevitable. In Germany, the stronghold of the Lutherans, there were less obvious signs of success, and the differences, especially over the doctrine of the Eucharist, were a constant source of tension. However, some foundations were made although the numbers were never as great as in France.

Calvin died in 1564 without ever achieving the popularity of Luther and yet proving himself to be the far more methodical, organised and systematic. Geneva, described as 'a Church, a school and a fortress', became the model and inspiration for countless other reformed cities. Calvin's many writings – on a whole range of subjects including liturgy, exegesis, catechetics and systematic theology – made him the most influential writer among the reformers. The most important single work was *The Institutes of Christian Religion* which began as a single book of six chapters in 1536 and ended in a final edition of 1559 as four books with eighty chapters; and it was translated into French, Dutch, English, German and finally Spanish. The *Institutes* contain all of Calvin's major theology and became the authoritative theological text book for the non-Lutheran reformers. The book was written in a clear explanatory way and was meant to be taken in conjunction with his Scripture Commentaries which he wrote on the whole of the Bible except for the Second and Third Letters of John. The fact that he has been called the 'Protestant Aquinas' may not have pleased Calvin but clearly testifies to his immense importance as a systematic theologian. Many people link Calvin and the doctrine of predestination as though this was his major concern. He certainly regarded predestination as an important part of his theology but it should not be allowed to overshadow his writings on the Trinity, the Person and Work of Christ, the Word and Sacraments and the Church. He was undoubtedly largely responsible through his own example and through leaving such an impressive array of literature for the future spread and consolidation of Calvinism as a major force throughout the whole of Europe.

In England, during the brief reign of Edward VI (1547–53), Calvin had written to Somerset, the Protector, suggesting certain changes in the English Church, but far more influential was the period of Mary's reign, (1553–58), when reformers fled from England to the continent, spent time in Geneva and returned during the long reign of Elizabeth (1558–1603), providing then a very strong Calvinist lobby which was at least partly responsible for the rise of Puritanism. In Scotland Calvin's influence through John Knox was very much stronger. John Knox was born c.1513 and educated at Glasgow. He received minor orders as a cleric of the Church but by the middle of the 1540s he had become caught up with the ideas and principles of the Reformation. Instrumental in this change was George Wishard (1513–46) who had fled Scotland in 1538 after being charged with heresy but who had returned after a brief period abroad to campaign actively on behalf of the reformers. His death by burning at the hands of Cardinal Beaton in 1546 left a deep impression on Knox who from this time became the leader of the reformers in Scotland. His capture and subsequent release by the French preceded a couple of years in England where, as Chaplain to Edward VI, he came into contact with Thomas Cranmer and others. As with many of the English reformers, Knox fled to the Continent on the accession of Mary, and it was during this time that he met Calvin. In 1559 he returned to Scotland and, after the death of Mary of Guise in 1560, he was largely responsible for persuading the Scottish Parliament to reject papal authority, abolish the mass and accept his Confession of Faith. The following year he published the *First Book of Discipline* which, echoing the *Ecclesiastical Ordinances*, provided for the reorganisation of the Church, known as the Kirk, of Scotland. His relationship with Queen Mary was tempestuous and his vitriolic sermons against the queen made any reconciliation unlikely. Perhaps it was only after his death in 1572 that the true value of Knox to the Reformation in Scotland was recognised. In the years that followed the main issue concerned the fortunes of the Presbyterians as they struggled with those, including the Stuart Kings, who wanted to make the Scottish Church episcopalian.

The Reformation in England differed from that on the continent in as much as it was largely an Act of State carried out under the leadership of the King supported by Parliament. The Church in England at the end of the fifteenth century reflected many of the difficulties and abuses that existed throughout Europe, including absenteeism and pluralism among the higher clergy, lack of education and low moral standards among the lesser clergy, and ignorance and superstition among the laity. There were those who were willing both to acknowledge these abuses and to point to those responsible; for example John Colet (1466–1519) the Dean of St Paul's, could say of the Clergy in 1512:

> I wish that you would consider the reformation of ecclesiastical affairs, for never was it more necessary, and never did the State of the Church need your endeavour more . . . nothing has disfigured the face of the Church as the secular and worldly way of living on the part of the clergy . . . priests seek after sensual pleasures, eating and sports; they are covetous for more and better benefices and haggle over tithes and mortuaries; they are immersed in worldly occupations and concerns.

He appealed to the bishops to be signs of justice, to select candidates for the priesthood with great care and to appoint to positions on the grounds of ability. Humanist bishops like John Fisher, Richard Foxe and John Langland accepted Colet's analysis and tried hard within their own dioceses to improve matters. Other encouraging signs included a growing number of graduates offering themselves for the ministry, more and more priests taking their pastoral responsibilities seriously and genuine efforts among some of the religious orders to reform, notably the Franciscan Observants and the Bridgettines of Syon Abbey. Among the laity there were those supporting the Church both financially and by their active presence and participation in Church life just as there were those only too ready to voice their criticism in an unveiled anti-clerical attack. England had a Church which was in need of reform but which was also showing signs of reform at the beginning of the sixteenth century.

Those who were most vociferous in their demands for reform were descendants of the Lollards, a name which literally means a mumbler or a mutterer. Their origins can be traced back to John Wycliffe (1329–84), who had been critical of papal authority, pluralism, absenteeism and monasticism and certain doctrines including transubstantiation, the Thomistic theory to explain the Real Presence of Christ in the Eucharist. Wycliffe had believed in the right of every Christian to read and study the Bible rather than to depend on priests, many of whom knew very little. As time passed this insistence on the Bible as the sole authority in the Christian's life became associated with the desire for the scriptures to be translated into the vernacular language of the people. A synod at Oxford in 1408 had forbidden the translation of the Bible without the express permission of the local bishop and no diocesan bishop would grant such permission as long as the English Bible was associated with the Lollards who were regarded as heretics. However, despite this connection both the humanists and the continental reformers added their considerable voices to the growing demand for the vernacular scriptures and the first English translation was undertaken by William Tyndale (1493–1536) who, after his suggestion was rejected by Bishop Tunstall of London, travelled to Antwerp from where he sent the first translation of the New Testament in 1526, followed by the Pentateuch in 1530. The first English Bible printed in England was largely the work of Miles Coverdale (1488–1568), appearing in 1535 and being 'opened' in Churches from 1536 onwards. After him there were a number of translations including The Great Bible of 1539, the Genevan or Breaches Bible of 1560, the Rheims New Testament of 1582, the Douai Bible of 1609–10, these latter two being the work of Catholics, and the Authorised Version or King James Bible commissioned by James I and produced in 1611. As the name suggests, this last Bible became accepted as the norm.

A century before the Authorised Version was published, Henry VIII was crowned King of England on 29 June 1509, his eighteenth birthday. Born in 1491, the second son of Henry VII, the first Tudor monarch, he became heir to the throne in 1502 when his elder brother, Arthur, died leaving a childless widow, Catherine of Aragon. On his accession the country was stable and solvent and the new king was regarded by many as the ideal Renaissance monarch, educated, intelligent, artistic and theologically orthodox. The one cause for concern was his apparent impetuosity and determination to have his own way seen especially in his decision to marry Catherine of Aragon, six years his senior and, as the widow of his brother, related to Henry so that he needed a papal dispensation for the marriage. She bore Henry five children in seventeen years, three sons and two daughters, but only Mary survived infancy. By 1525 Henry had given up any hope of Catherine having more children and by 1527 he had become infatuated with Anne Boleyn. The fact that he had no male heir, coupled with his new love, prompted Henry to investigate the possibilities of having his marriage to Catherine declared invalid on the grounds that the papal dispensation had itself been invalid. The problems facing such a possibility were immense: not only was it unlikely that one pope would reverse the decision of his predecessor, but at this particular time Pope Clement was a prisoner of Charles V, the nephew of Catherine of Aragon, and as such was unlikely to do anything as provocative as declaring against the validity of Henry's marriage.

This refusal by Clement led Henry to question the legitimacy of papal jurisdiction in England and from this time he searched for ways of gaining an annulment and of transferring papal authority to the crown. In 1527 he ordered Thomas Wolsey (1474–1530) to gain the necessary dispensation which would free him to marry Anne but Wolsey despite his impressive career – which had seen him ordained in 1498, become royal chaplain in 1507, elected to the Privy Council in 1511, consecrated Bishop of Lincoln in 1514, translated to York in 1515, made Lord Chancellor in the same year and created papal legate with authority over all bishops including Canterbury in 1518 – failed to produce the freedom to enter a new marriage. Wolsey was charged in 1529 under a statute called Praemunire which forbade dealings with foreign powers; he resigned his chancellorship and though allowed to retire to his diocese was charged with treason, dying in 1530 before standing trial.

His fall from favour opened the way for the rise of Thomas Cromwell (1485–1540) who between 1529–34 guided through Parliament a whole series of legislation which effectively transferred ecclesiastical jurisdiction away from the pope into the hands of the king. Cromwell had returned to England about 1520 after seeking opportunity and adventure as a mercenary in the French army. His potential as a lawyer was appreciated by Wolsey, into whose service he was taken, but by 1529 he had appreciated the difficulties the Lord Chancellor was experiencing and transferred his loyalty to Henry, who promoted him throughout the 1530s before discarding him in 1540 for persuading the king to marry Anne of Cleves. During his time in power Cromwell proved himself a loyal servant of the king at the expense of the Church by preparing for and making the break with Rome, assuring Henry the title of Supreme Head of the Church of England, and supervising the dissolution of the monasteries between 1536–40.

There have been few more crucial times in the history of the Church of England than the five years from 1529 to 1534, and yet the importance of what was happening was appreciated by relatively few people. In 1529 the Commons reacted to Henry's growing pressure on Wolsey by passing a series of bills against him in particular and the Church in general. The following year the charge of Praemunire was brought against the whole clergy who could be absolved from the charge on payment of a huge fine of £200,000 and an acknowledgement of Henry as 'singular protector, only and supreme lord, and as far as the law of Christ allows, even Supreme Head' of the Church. Further legislation included the 'Supplication of the Commons against the Ordinaries' which laid down guidelines curtailing the power of ecclesiastical courts, 'The Submission of the Clergy' which effectively replaced the pope with the king as the supreme legislator in the Church, and 'The Conditional Restraint of Annates' which stopped all but a nominal payment of bishops' taxes to Rome.

In August of 1532 Thomas Cranmer became Archbishop of Canterbury on the death of William Wareham. He knew the priority of Henry's desire for a dispensation. In January 1533 Henry was secretly married to Anne who was expecting their first child in September. In May Cranmer, acting under the terms of The Restraint of Appeals, which prohibited ecclesiastical appeals being made to Rome and transferred that power to the king's court, declared Henry's marriage to Catherine null and void and presided over the official wedding of Henry and Anne who was crowned queen on 1 June. In July, Clement VII declared Cranmer's decision unlawful, condemned the second marriage and excommunicated Henry. The following year, 1534, further legislation strengthened the King's position, the Restraint of Appeals was made absolute, the Act of Dispensation transferred papal powers of dispensation to the crown, the Heresy Act made the denial of papal primacy no longer heretical, the Treason Act made it treason to deprive the monarch of any of his titles and the Act of Succession obliged all to recognise the validity of Henry's marriage to Anne Boleyn, and declared their children as the only rightful heirs to the Throne. Finally, the Act of Supremacy gave Henry the title 'Supreme Head of the Church of England' and the power to discipline the clergy, make visitations and define doctrine.

By 1534, in less than five years, this whole set of legislation effectively broke relations with the pope who was no longer recognised as having authority over the English Church. Those who opposed the changes were severely punished, among them Bishop

John Fisher of Rochester, thought to be instrumental in writing *The Assertion of the Seven Sacraments against Martin Luther* for which Henry had received the title of 'Defender of the Faith' from the pope in 1521, and Thomas More (1478–1535), one of the best known English humanists whom Henry had previously appointed as Chancellor. Both Fisher as bishop and More as statesman were passionately concerned for the reform of the Church but they would not accept the Act of Supremacy which severed relations with Rome. On the whole, however, there was little opposition to such a major change as people failed to appreciate the cumulative effect of the legislation and preferred to rely on the credibility that law enjoys. It was only after the Dissolution of the Monasteries – the lesser monasteries with incomes of less than £200 per annum or communities of less than twelve in 1536, and the greater monasteries between 1539–40 – that ordinary people were made aware of the consequences of the Reformation. It was these acts, together with inflation, food shortages and bad harvests which caused the Lincolnshire rebellion in 1536 and the more famous but equally ineffective Pilgrimage of Grace in 1536–7.

Once the legal position had been clarified, Henry turned his attention, through his advisers, to matters of doctrine. Discussing the writings and teachings of the continental reformers had begun in Cambridge at the White Horse Tavern where a group including Thomas Bilney, Hugh Latimer, Nicholas Ridley, John Frith and Thomas Cranmer had met secretly to plan ways of bringing the reformed ideas into England. Henry was to prove a great disappointment to these men because of his own theological conservatism and his desire to keep doctrinal changes to a minimum. The first statement was the so-called 'Ten Articles' of 1536 – which mentioned three sacraments of baptism, Eucharist and penance without denying the other four – allowed people to understand the Eucharist either in the Roman or Lutheran way, approved of prayers for the dead and encouraged the intercession of the saints. The *Bishop's Book* of the following year was even more conservative and the 'Six Articles' of 1539, described by the reformers as 'the bloody whip with six strings', maintained such Catholic doctrines and practices as transubstantiation, withholding the chalice from the laity, clerical celibacy, monastic vows, private Mass and auricular confession. There could hardly have been a more reactionary statement and its promulgation caused several bishops, including Latimer of Worcester, to resign their sees. After the fall of Cromwell in 1540 this conservative element became even more influential as the *King's Book* and 'Act for the advancement of true religion' in 1543 demonstrated. However, Henry's last marriage, to Catherine Parr in 1543, gave the reformers new hope and they managed to take control of the Regency Council formed to govern the country during the first years of Edward VI. Perhaps Edward's upbringing illustrates the enigma of Henry's whole reign. Personally conservative and successful in resisting all attempts to be more radical in doctrine or liturgy, he had nevertheless severed relations with Rome, taken the title of Supreme Head, and prepared the way for England to become more Protestant after his death by entrusting the education of his son, Edward, to the reformers.

Throughout the latter part of Henry's reign and the whole of Edward's, one man dominated doctrinal and liturgical life, namely Thomas Cranmer (1489–1556). In 1523 Cranmer had been ordained priest after a marriage which had ended with his wife's death in 1515. He came to the notice of the king who agreed to his suggestion of touring the universities of Europe in an attempt to ascertain their opinion of the validity of Henry's marriage. In 1532 Cranmer had secretly married the niece of Osiander, one of the leading Lutheran theologians, and in that same year became Archbishop of Canterbury with the blessing of the pope, in which office he annulled Henry's marriage to Catherine, a service he was to perform again with two of the king's other marriages. Such obedience to the will of the king was a hallmark of his whole life and explains his apparent willingness to support Henry's conservatism despite his own more Protestant views which became apparent during Edward's reign. He was imprisoned under Mary in 1553, spending two and a half years in custody before, finally overcoming his doubts and fears, protesting his faith, and being burnt to death on 21 March 1556.

When Henry died in 1547 his son Edward was a minor of only nine years and, on his accession, Edward Seymour, soon to be titled the Duke of Somerset, gained effective control of the Regency Council. As a convinced reformer Somerset began making England more protestant, supported by some of the continental reformers including Martin Bucer and Peter Martyr who had arrived in England and who encouraged men like Cranmer to pursue far-reaching changes. Within six months The Six Articles were repealed, all restrictions on the use of the English Bible were lifted, various royal injunctions, providing books of homilies and preventing 'practices' liable to lead to superstitution, were imposed and an Act dissolving the Chantries was passed. These measures provoked some opposition especially in Devon and Cornwall where there were repeated demands for the return of the Old Religion, but such opposition was more than balanced by the support of the continental reformers, some of whom were now promoted to places of importance in the Church.

The first Edwardian Act of Uniformity in 1549 established Cranmer's *First Book of Common Prayer* as the only form of worship now permissible in England. This was an attempt to standardize worship by presenting a strongly biblical yet simple ritual. Reactions varied, some were critical of the content because it was open to different interpretations and others because it offended their Catholic beliefs. This opposition led to the fall of Somerset and the emergence of Northumberland as the power in the Regency Council under whom even more Protestant measures were passed. Over the next four years conservatives including Gardiner, Bonner and Tunstall were deprived and replaced by more Protestant bishops including Ridley, Ponet and Hooper. In 1552 the Second Act of Uniformity, which enforced the *Second Book of Common Prayer*, clearly showed the influence of the continental reformers, denying among other things all Catholic teaching on the sacraments, the validity of praying for the dead and the adoration of the Sacrament. The following year the 42 Articles, originally 45 and eventually reduced to 39, were drawn up by Cranmer as a basis for the doctrinal *via media* of the Church of England. In the event these articles did more to divide than unite different opinions in the Church.

The six years of Edward VI's reign saw remarkable advances in protestantism in England as politicians like Somerset and Northumberland, encouraged by theologians and liturgists, had imposed, by law, a much more radical religion than ever envisaged by Henry VIII. What no-one could have easily foreseen or prevented was the death of Edward on 6 July 1553, leading to the accession of Mary and her attempt to provide a massive Catholic reaction. According to the Act of Succession of 1533 Mary had been made to share the disgrace of her mother, Catherine of Aragon, and was debarred from her title to the throne. In 1536 she had come back into favour after agreeing to sign a document accepting Henry's position as Supreme Head and in 1544, largely due to her excellent relations with Catherine Parr, she was made second heir to the throne after Edward but ahead of Elizabeth. When Edward died, Northumberland tried to secure the succession of Lady Jane Grey, but without success, and Mary was greeted with a mixture of sympathy, for the way she had been treated, and of genuine enthusiasm by those who had become disillusioned with the Regency Council. All were aware of her religious convictions, which she had staunchly maintained throughout Edward's reign despite the successive pressure of Somerset and

Northumberland, and at the beginning of her reign it was probable that the majority of the country would have accepted them. But when her religious policy became associated with her marriage to Philip II of Spain even her most ardent supporters found themselves severely compromised.

The Parliament of 1553 passed the first Statute of Repeal which removed all Edwardian ecclesiastical legislation and returned the country to its position during the last years of Henry. In that same year there took place the restoration of the conservative bishops and the demotion, imprisonment, exile, voluntary or enforced, of the more radical reformers. A series of royal injunctions, aimed at removing all traces of protestantism and reintroducing Catholic liturgy and practice, were also passed. The clergy were subjected to a thorough examination resulting in the deprivation of the married clergy and of some of those ordained during Edward's reign. Mary experienced her first real opposition when she announced in January 1554 her proposed marriage to Philip II which was to take place in July. This marriage proved to be a major disaster, both personally since it failed to bring her any happiness, and politically since it raised doubts and fears in the majority of people, Catholic and otherwise, crystallised opposition to her, and in turn led to stringent and repressive royal measures including the execution of Lady Jane Grey and her husband and the imprisonment of Elizabeth in the Tower. Later that year Reginald Pole (1500–58), appointed papal legate by Julius III in 1553, returned to his native England to negotiate the return of the country to full relations with Rome. The Heresy Act restored to the Church the power to try and punish heretics, powers that were quickly put into active use, and the Second Statute of Repeal, removed all the ecclesiastical legislation since 1529. The only exception concerned the monasteries where the practical problems of returning land and property proved too great, with the result that the property remained in the hands of the present owners. In November 1554 Pole, acting on papal instructions, absolved England from schism and formally restored the country to full communion with Rome. This Catholic restoration proved to be shallow because, instead of building on the good will she had been shown at the beginning of her reign, Mary failed to recognise the strength of Protestant and anti-Spanish feeling and concentrated on stamping out all opposition. This brutal policy, under which more than 300 persons died, served only to sharpen opposition to her, and leading reformers like Hooper, Saunders, Latimer, Ridley and Cranmer were regarded as martyrs and their lives and deaths were recorded in John Foxe's hugely influential *Acts and Monuments* published in English as early as 1563. Those Protestants who could fled abroad, finding safety and shelter on the continent and coming more deeply under the influence of Calvin. The majority stayed at home, went underground and carried on as best they could. When Mary and Pole died within twelve hours of each other in 1558, many regarded the coincidence as an act of divine providence and looked to Elizabeth to restore peace to the country.

On her accession Elizabeth was faced by a country increasingly dissatisfied with Mary's ecclesiastical and foreign policy and with a Church even more clearly divided between the Marian bishops in office and the Protestants soon to return from exile. These differences made the Settlement of Religion in 1559 both necessary, for the stability it brought, and remarkable for the speed with which it was carried through. As Francis Bacon was to remark, 'Within the compass of one year she did so settle and establish all matters belonging to the Church, as she departed not one hair's breadth from them to the end of her life'. She inherited a Church, in which attitudes had hardened considerably and she had to settle for a Church, which was more Protestant than she personally would have wanted, but one forced on her by the resignation of the Marian bishops and her need to turn to the committed Protestant clergy returning from exile.

In January 1559, aided by William Cecil, her principal secretary, and Matthew Parker, the future Archbishop of Canterbury consecrated in that year by four Edwardian bishops, she summoned the first Elizabethan Parliament which, by April, had passed two major Acts which together made up the Elizabethan Settlement of Religion. The Act of Supremacy broke relations with the papacy and made Elizabeth the Supreme Governor of the Church of England, returning the Church and the country to the position at the beginning of Edward's reign. Elizabeth seemed satisfied with this but she was persuaded to reopen Parliament in April which quickly passed the Act of Uniformity obliging Church attendance on a Sunday and enforcing the 1552 *Book of Common Prayer* with the provision for the use of vestments. After this a series of royal injunctions filled in the details of implementation, stressing the great importance of licensed preaching and instituting a graduated list of penalties for failing to submit to the terms of the Settlement.

Despite the great loyalty of Matthew Parker as her archbishop and the fact that as early as 1561 the majority of the dioceses had been filled, the Settlement did not find universal acceptance and, in 1565, the first major controversy erupted over the issue of wearing vestments. The Act of Uniformity had obliged the wearing of vestments but at a convocation in 1563 it became clear that many were against such a practice and in 1565 some clergy at Oxford openly defied the rule giving rise to the Vestiarian controversy. On hearing of this Elizabeth rebuked Parker over his laxness and ordered him to ensure the exact fulfilment of the Act. Having failed to persuade the clergy to back down he introduced the 'Advertisements' in 1566 which threatened deprivation for those refusing to wear vestments at liturgical celebrations. In the event thirty-seven London clergy were deprived and these became associated with the beginnings of the Puritan movement. Since the bishops had been charged with imposing uniformity the Puritans began to question the need for bishops and in 1570 Thomas Cartwright put forward an alternative form of government based on presbyterianism for which he was dismissed from his chair of Divinity at Cambridge. Others called for 'puritanizing of the English Church' demanding the abolition of the Prayer Book described as 'an imperfect book, culled and picked out of that popish dunghill the Mass book full of abominations'.* The Puritans received little support from Parliament and during the 1570s they changed their tactics with the introduction of 'prophesyings' which were meetings of clergy and laity for the study of the Bible.

In 1576 Matthew Parker died and was succeeded by Edmund Grindal, translated from York to Canterbury. It was a sensitive time with the growing influence of the Puritans and Grindal soon showed a sympathy towards them, even defending the 'prophesyings' which so displeased the queen that within the year she had Grindal suspended until his death in 1583. His successor, John Whitgift (1583–1604), was a staunch supporter of the episcopacy and his Articles of 1583, followed by an Act of 1593 against 'Seditious Sectaries', were aimed at those separatist Puritans, including Robert Harrison, John Perry and Robert Browne, who now faced severe penalties if caught. Those who stayed within the Established Church tried to make it more puritan by setting up 'classes' which were groups of local puritan clergy working independently of the bishop. In the following century the Puritans continued to press their claims, were hounded by Archbishop Laud (1573–1645), and became the forerunners of the Congregationalists. Since they had little interest in a national Church, Elizabeth and her immediate successors saw them as subversive and insisted on the bishops keeping a strict control over them.

The Catholics, on the accession of Elizabeth, had a great deal to fear not least a backlash against them after the brutality which had marked the latter part of Mary's reign. However, contrary to such

*quoted in J.R.H. Moorman, *A History of the Church of England.*

fears the first decade of the reign was relatively peaceful for the Catholic population who enjoyed what could be described as an official policy of turning a blind eye. There were no executions prior to 1570 and less than two hundred between 1570 and 1603 in marked contrast to more than three hundred protestants executed during Mary's five-year reign. But for all this optimism there were early signs of future difficulties mainly because of the lack of any real leadership. The Marian bishops had resigned and gone into exile and Pope Pius IV, hoping at this stage for reunification, was adopting a policy of non-interference. The result of this lack of leadership was a type of outward conformity on the part of many Catholics unsure of how they now stood with regard to their religious obligations. This situation changed dramatically as a result of three incidents at the turn of the decade.

In 1569 Mary Queen of Scots (1542–87) fled south and became the focal point for the Catholics in the North of England. Some even began to plan her marriage to the Duke of Norfolk and press her claims for succession to the English throne. In that same year there was an uprising also in the North led by the Earls of Northumberland and Westmorland. As with previous rebellions during the reigns of Henry and Edward, their motives were a mixture of religious, social and economic, but the Catholic Mass was celebrated in Durham Cathedral and the *Book of Common Prayer* and the English Bible were symbolically burnt. Their demands were equally uncompromising, including the restoration of traditional Catholic worship, the trial of Cecil, the release of the Duke of Norfolk and the recognition of Mary, Queen of Scots' title to the throne. The rebellion in fact came to nothing due to bad leadership, lack of support and the determined opposition of the government, but it served notice of the attitudes and demands of the largely Catholic North of the country.

The third event was the publication in 1570 of the papal bull 'Regnans in Excelsis' excommunicating Elizabeth and anyone who obeyed her laws. Pope Pius V had concluded that the likelihood of England submitting to papal supremacy was minimal and, acting on his own initiative and probably against the advice of those more politically aware, he brought matters to a head by issuing this bull. The effect on the Catholic population was immediate and daunting as the government reacted by carrying through a whole series of anti-Catholic legislation supported by those Protestant propagandists who saw the bull as a blatant attempt to cause sedition and overthrow the queen. Even worse, it left Catholics themselves confused, demanding of them an unwelcome choice between loyalty to their country and loyalty to their faith.

The Parliament of 1571 was composed entirely of non-Catholics since it was now obligatory on all members of parliament to swear the oath of supremacy. It was this Parliament which passed several Acts including the 'Treason Act' which made it a treasonable offence to write or say that Elizabeth was not the lawful queen or that she was guilty of heresy or schism. This was followed by an Act forbidding the Introduction of Papal Bulls which also banned devotional writings and articles, and an Act against Catholic exiles depriving them of their property if they failed to return to the country within one year. The anti-Catholic feeling within the Commons can be gauged from their desire to oblige everyone to receive the Anglican Communion annually, but such a move was blocked by Elizabeth herself who felt that such legislation would be a gross infringement of individual consciences. Despite the legislation against the exiles it was precisely these men and women who were important for maintaining traditional Catholic beliefs as they became caught up with the Catholic response to the Protestants throughout Europe. Throughout the 1570s the exiles who had most immediate effect on English Catholicism were the seminary priests and the Jesuits. In 1568 a seminary was founded in Douai by a Lancastrian, William Allen, and in that same year it accepted its first English students who returned as priests, the first arriving in 1574, and within a decade the number had risen above three hundred. Their fortunes were mixed, some remaining undetected for years, others were picked up by government officials as soon as they landed. By 1584 thirty-three priests had been executed, eight had died in prison, sixty had been exiled and more than fifty were still awaiting trial. In all, Douai sent 438 priests to England of whom 98 were put to death.

In 1580 the first two Jesuits, Edmund Campion and Robert Parsons, arrived in England, and they and those who followed them gained a reputation which far exceeded their numbers. Reginald Pole had refused an offer by the Jesuits to come to England during the reign of Mary, a decision which, in the light of their effectiveness after 1580, can be seen as a lost opportunity. Administering the sacraments, preaching, teaching, writing and even setting up their own printing press, the Jesuits and diocesan priests attempted, under the most trying circumstances, to encourage the Catholic population and maintain the Catholic Mass. Their own courage and conviction was beyond question as they zealously cooperated with the Catholic gentry who did much to provide safety and shelter.

Their success, together with worsening relations with Spain and the discovery of several plots against Elizabeth, led to even harsher anti-Catholic legislation. Fines were increased for saying or hearing

Mass and for failing to attend the Established Church. The Treason Act now prescribed the death penalty for anyone converting or helping another to convert to Catholicism. In 1584 the death penalty was extended to include those receiving or harbouring a priest. In 1587, the Recusants, those Catholics who refused to attend the Established Church, were obliged to pay their fines in a lump sum twice a year and later, in 1593, they were ordered to remain within five miles of their homes or risk forfeiting all their lands and property. The last decade, in marked contrast to the first decade of Elizabeth's long reign, saw a concerted attempt to rid the country of all traces of Catholicism, but the courage and resourcefulness of many helped to resist this increased pressure and was a sign of the general improvement in Catholic witness which became part of the Catholic response to the Protestant Reformation both in England and throughout Europe.

By the middle of the sixteenth century great numbers of people had deserted the Roman Church, now regarded by many as an abomination, and had joined forces with the major reformers in establishing and consolidating Protestantism. The Catholic Church responded by putting its own house in order, encouraging those who had remained loyal and attempting to win back some of those lost to Protestantism. Such a response was, at least in part, the fruit of reform which had been taking place from the end of the middle ages and was seen particularly in the new religious orders and congregations. Although such reforms seemed insignificant when compared with the lack of interest and downright obstructiveness of the papacy and curia, it was not irrelevant, but it would need papal recognition and support in order to flourish. When the popes eventually grasped the reality of the situation both within the Church and throughout Western Europe and supported the existing reform movements, then the Catholic reform, seen most obviously in the decisions of the Council of Trent and the subsequent implementation of the conciliar decrees, became both visible and forceful.

The new orders and congregations which emerged at the end of the fifteenth century were found in Latin rather than Germanic countries, and they were involved in active rather than contemplative apostolates, devoting their attention to such needs as teaching, preaching, nursing and providing for the poor. The religious congregations differed from the orders in that their members were only obliged to simple vows and were not obliged to enclosure within a monastery or abbey. Although there were various brotherhoods established in the late fifteenth century it was the 'Oratory of Divine Love', established c.1515 in Rome, which inspired further developments. The Oratory had relatively few members but among those enrolled in 1524 were six bishops, and several high ranking members of the curia. The demands made on the members included daily personal prayer and Mass, monthly Confession and Communion, and practical charitable works including the care of the sick. The motivation behind the Oratory was the realisation of the members' need to deepen their own spirituality in an attempt to bear witness to true Christian values. Others followed their example, forming prayer and study groups and organising various pastoral activities.

Two members of the Oratory were responsible for one of the first religious orders of this period, namely the Theatines, approved by Pope Clement VII in June 1524. Cajetan of Thiene (1480–1547) and Gian Caraffa, the future Pope Paul IV (d.1559), were the founders of the order which took the Augustinian Rule as its basis. All the members were priests who recognised their responsibility of fulfilling their priestly duties including praying the office, celebrating Mass, preaching and undertaking their pastoral work with real care and genuine zeal. Their numbers were never great and their influence was felt almost exclusively in Italy, and yet they raised the standard of their own clergy and after the Council of Trent they provided, from among their number, several bishops who were instrumental in implementing the decrees of the Council within their dioceses. About the same time as the Theatines, Anthony Mary Zacchary established a society of priests in 1533 known as the Barnabites, after the Church of St Barnabas in Milan. Their official title was the 'Clerics Regular of St Paul' and their taking of his name reflected their concern about mission. They were instrumental in deepening devotion to the Eucharist at a time when Christ's real presence was being questioned by the reformers and their introduction of the Forty Hours devotion of the Eucharist was formally approved in 1570. They themselves received papal approval in 1579 and, like the Theatines, exerted most influence within Italy. A third order of men were the Somaschi founded in Somascha, a town near Milan, by Jerome Emiliani. Their charism was specifically pastoral, caring especially for orphans, the poor and the sick. Their interest and work among boys and men was parallelled by that of the Ursulines founded by Angela Merici in 1535 and officially approved in 1544, who looked after the well-being and education of girls.

Alongside the establishment of these new congregations and orders was the reform of the older orders, especially the mendicants. Throughout the medieval period there had been members of the mendicant orders who looked for a stricter observance of the original Rule. These Observants gained ground in the late fifteenth century and several generals of the major mendicant orders emerged from their ranks. In 1525 Matthew de Bascio (1495–1552) undertook the strict reform of the Italian Observants calling, yet again, for the precise observance of the primitive rule and charism. In 1528 Pope Clement VII recognised this work and allowed them to live in smaller houses and to wear a habit with a long pointed hood called a capuche, from which they later became known as the Capuchins. They survived two serious blows when Louis of Fossombrone in 1536 and then Bernadino Ochino in 1542 left the Church and became Protestants In 1574 the Capuchins received papal permission to establish foundations outside Italy and in 1619 they were recognised as a separate order distinct from the other two Franciscan branches.

In 1563 the Council of Trent in its twenty-fifth and last session passed a very important decree concerning Religious in which it stressed the prohibition of personal property, receiving monasteries from lay people and admitting young children at an early age. Positively the decree stressed the relationship between religious and the diocese, giving the right of visitation to the local bishop even among those orders which were previously exempt. This was a bold attempt to build on reforms that had been taking place since the end of the previous century. In 1580 the French Cistercians were reformed as were the Benedictines. In 1618 the French Benedictine community at St Maur gave rise to the Maurists who became particularly influential in the field of history and education. In Spain John of the Cross (1542–91) and Teresa of Avila (1515–82) were responsible for the reform of the Carmelites which eventually led to a division in the order between the Calced and Discalced. Their main contribution was in their insistence on the value and practice of contemplative prayer, and both have left lasting testaments to the Church in their numerous writings.

However, of all the religious orders, both renewed and newly established, the most important and influential was the Society of Jesus founded by Ignatius Loyola and officially approved in 1540. As one historian has written 'The Society of Jesus became the most effective agent of Catholic recovery. In the person and work of its founder, the fundamental principles of Catholic Reform clearly emerge, obtain a new character valid for centuries, and become of great historical significance'. Ignatius came from Spain where the reform of the Church in the fifteenth and early sixteenth centuries was being taken very seriously. The Catholics were united in their desire to expel the last remnants of Muslim influence from their country, and the capture of Grenada in 1492 and the uniting of

Castile and Aragon by the marriage of Ferdinand and Isabella were seen as symbolic high points of Catholic reform. The monarchy and hierarchy worked closely in an attempt to reform and renew the Church by rooting out such abuses as absenteeism and pluralism and insisting, through a very careful selection of bishops, on the assiduous fulfilment of religious duties. Their cooperation was seen when Ferdinand summoned the bishops to discuss their preparations for the Lateran Council called for 1513. Although this council achieved little, the Spanish bishops had served notice that they would play an important role in any future reform of the Church.

Ignatius was born in 1491 into a noble family in the Basque region of Spain. He was seriously wounded fighting in the siege of Pamplona in 1521. During his convalescence he read a life of Christ and various biographies of the saints which eventually resulted in his determination 'to do great things in God's service'. After recovering from his injury he went first to Monserrat before spending a year at Manressa where he began his own writing, composing the first part of the *Spiritual Exercises* which became the central core of Jesuit spirituality. The next years were spent largely in study, first in Spain and latterly in Paris. On 15 August 1534 Ignatius and six friends, including Francis Xavier (1506–52), who was to be one of the greatest missionaries of the time, vowed to live poverty and chastity, to go on pilgrimage to the Holy Land and devote the rest of their lives to the pastoral needs of those with whom they lived and worked. Two years later this small group renewed their vows, were joined by two others and went in 1537 to Venice to put the final touches to their preparation for the pilgrimage. Various problems caused them first to delay, then to abandon their plans, and they travelled to Rome to put themselves at the direct service of the pope. It was about this time that Ignatius and some of his companions were ordained to the priesthood and although for some time in Rome 'the windows remained shut tight' he eventually presented his plans to Pope Paul III who formally recognised the Society of Jesus in the papal bull 'Regimini Militantis Ecclesiae' on 27 September 1540. The close relationship between the Jesuits, as they came to be known, and the papacy is illustrated in their desire 'to fight for God under the standard of the cross and to serve only the Lord and the Roman Pontiff, his vicar on earth'. When eventually the Constitutions were written and promulgated they contained a fourth solemn vow of 'obedience to the pope' which was to be taken only by the most capable members of the society.

The preparation of a candidate for the Society was long and arduous and marked a significant contrast to the ease with which people had entered priesthood and religious life in earlier ages. At the heart of Jesuit spirituality were the Ignatian Exercises which have been described as follows: 'It has long been established by history that the spirit and thought of Ignatius Loyola acquired their clearest expression in the book of the Spiritual Exercises and that his Order emanated from the deliberations of this book and continued to come forth from it'. Originally the Exercises were to be undertaken over a four-week period during which time the person would spend one week meditating in turn on sin and its consequences, the kingdom of Christ, the passion and death of Jesus, and finally his resurrection. The effectiveness of the Exercises was proved almost immediately and has since withstood the test of time. 'The work of Ignatius is unequalled in its ability to transform, in the spirit of its author, the men who came upon it'.

By the time of Ignatius' death the number of Jesuits was over one thousand, organised in twelve different provinces. From the very beginning certain members had recognised the need for missionary endeavour and Jesuit missionaries soon preached the Gospel in places as distant as India, Brazil, Japan and China. By 1625 there were more than 16,000 Jesuits in twenty-three provinces but this growth and expansion should not be allowed to hide the difficulties they experienced through suspicion and envy. Both factors also lay behind future difficulties which led to their expulsion from various countries and their temporary suppression in 1773. At the time of the reformation, though, they proved invaluable, and the popes used them as the 'shock troops' of the Catholic reform. They recognised the necessity of using the same methods as the Protestants and concentrated great time and energy on training clergy for which purpose they founded colleges in Rome in 1551 and France in 1556. Even earlier, in 1548, Pope Paul III recognised the quality of the Jesuits and, wishing to raise the general standard of the diocesan clergy, made the Jesuits responsible for the examination of all candidates for the priesthood. In preaching and teaching they gained a reputation for such clarity of thought and expression as to leave no room for theological doubt. In Germany, Peter Canisius (1521–97), produced both a large and short catechism on the lines introduced by Martin Luther several years earlier. As confessors to the Catholic monarchs and rulers they exerted enormous influence throughout the period and their reputation, as in England, belied their numbers.

Effective as they were, the Jesuits needed the support of the papacy and it was only when the popes recognised the seriousness of the Protestant Reformation and joined forces with all the separate reform movements in the Catholic Church that general reform became possible. The popes had first to overcome external pressures, especially from Emperor Charles V, and internal pressures from the curia which had a vested interest in preventing reform. Added to this was the difficult relationship between pope and council caused by the recent clash of ideologies witnessed in the debate between papalism and conciliarism which had left the popes suspicious of councils and jealous of their own rights. When Paul III made it papal policy soon after his election to summon a council then, and only then, did the reform movement within the Catholic Church enjoy support from the very office which had the authority to make such reform effective.

When Martin Luther criticised the Indulgence preachers Leo X (1513–21) was pope. Cultured, educated and beyond personal reproach he was nonetheless unsuitable to guide the Church through those extremely difficult times. His understanding and style were of an age now past and he was incapable of keeping pace with a world changing more rapidly than ever before. During his pontificate the Fifth Lateran Council (1512–17) conducted most of its business but, apart from some success in reforming the mendicant orders, other attempts at reform were cosmetic and this tended to exacerbate rather than improve matters. Leo's immediate successor was Adrian of Utrecht who had been educated by the Brethren of the Common Life at their school in Deventer. In 1507, at the age of forty-eight, he had been appointed tutor to the future Emperor Charles V, and within a few years had risen to a position of great power in Spain. When he was unanimously elected pope in 1522 he took the name of Adrian VI (1522–3) and from the outset made the reform of the Church his priority. He recognised the necessity of beginning with the curia but he soon found that this particular group was able to defend itself from any serious changes. He wanted to reconcile the various European powers and mobilise them against the Turkish threat but all his overtures proved fruitless. By his death, within little more than a year of his election, he had achieved little despite his own selfless service to the ideal of reform. The inscription on his tomb was a fitting summary, 'Alas that the work of even the best of men must be at the mercy of the age in which he lives'. Adrian was the last non-Italian to be elected pope until John Paul II over 450 years later.

Had Adrian lived longer or had Clement VII (1523–34) taken up some of his ideas the numbers of those who joined Luther and the other reformers might have been considerably less. In fact Clement's eleven-year reign proved to be of enormous cost and consequence to the Roman Church, mainly because of his refusal, either to recognise, or to tackle the abuses which had caused the Protestant reformers to take their stand. He was regarded as similar to Leo X and as a Renaissance figure became embroiled in Italian politics as well as harbouring vain thoughts about his own importance in international foreign policy. In fact his advisers were so poor that Clement ended up a prisoner of Charles V after the pope had agreed to an alliance with France against Spain. It was only in 1529 that Charles felt able to release the pope from protective custody, and even then, on condition that he would call a council to reform the Church. Clement managed to avoid a council by a blatant mixture of luck and procrastination but in doing so he left a terrible legacy to those who followed him. His failure to recognise the need for reform, or even to foster those signs of reform already evident, was greatly responsible for the rapid spread of Protestantism which could only have been checked by drastic action.

The first official mention of a General Council came in 1535 when Paul III (1534–49) summoned the bishops to meet at Mantua in the following year to 'condemn heresy, reform the Church and unite the Christian rulers against the Turks'. This council never met, neither did the one he summoned to meet at Vicenza, and within a short time he prorogued the council without fixing any firm date or place for the future. Although his plans for a council were meeting with difficulties he was piecing together an honest assessment of the state of the Church as a result of the findings of a Reform commission which produced its report in 1537. Among the root causes of the miserable state of the Church were the exaggerated growth of papal theory and the steadfast refusal of the curia to accept any changes or to promote any reforms in its own procedures. Absenteeism was also singled out as a dangerous cancer in the Church and there was another call to improve the general standard of the clergy. The findings were never made public because Paul recognised the damaging nature of the report but some of its contents were leaked to the Protestants who made capital of the criticisms. Paul accepted the findings and worked even harder for a council but the bad relations between France and Spain, which often broke out into open hostilities, caused endless delays and it was only after the Treaty of Crepy in 1544 that the Council of Trent eventually opened. Even before this further disagreements over the venue, the composition of the membership and the order of the business, together with the personal intervention of Charles V who attempted to set up meetings between Catholics and Protestants independent of the pope, added to the list of obstacles Paul III had to overcome.

In 1542 Paul issued a bull summoning a council to meet at Trent (Triento) in Northern Italy, only to be blocked by renewed hostilities

between France and Spain. On 30 November 1544 Paul again summoned a council to meet at Trent on 15 March 1545 and although
the months passed the first session of the Council was held in 1545
opening on 13 December. The Protestants refused to send any representatives and Luther wrote his most vitriolic attack on the papacy.
The numbers present at the opening session – the local bishop of
Trent, three papal legates, four archbishops, twenty-one bishops and
five leaders of religious orders – hardly suggested the future importance and significance of a council which was to meet in three major
periods over the next eighteen years. Indeed the numbers throughout
the whole course of the council, ranging from 27 to 197 bishops,
were never great and certainly fell far short of the numbers attending
previous general councils. Paul III must be congratulated for his
dogged determination to summon a council despite all the difficulties
he experienced. He also gave his full support to the religious orders
and congregations and his appointments to the College of Cardinals,
despite the occasional lapse into nepotism, brought the very best men
into the central government of the Church and changed the character
of the curia. By the time of Paul's death the Catholic reform had
begun in earnest and the Roman Church at the highest levels had
accepted the need for reform in 'head and members'.

The first period of the Council, between 1545–47, began with
disagreement and controversy over the order of business. There were
those who wanted to deal with doctrine first and those who thought
reform and discipline deserved prior attention. In the event the
members reached a compromise, agreeing to discuss both together,
although there can be little doubt, with the benefit of hindsight, that
doctrine received more thorough examination than discipline. The
bishops did not regard themselves as summoned to enter theological
debate but rather to express in clear, unambiguous language Catholic doctrine laid out positively in chapters and negatively in canons,
condemning various errors and contrary positions. In this first
period they dealt with the sources of revelation, the role of the
Church as the interpreter of scripture, the approval of the canon of
scripture and the continued acceptance of the biblical text of the
Latin Vulgate, original sin and justification and finally the seven
sacraments instituted by Christ. Taken against the teaching of the
reformers on all these subjects, the business concluded during this
first period assumed enormous significance. The disciplinary decrees
included a general demand for raising the standards of the clergy, a
reminder of the duty and importance of preaching, a renewed call for
episcopal residence and a condemnation of pluralism.

Despite the importance of the first period it became clear that the

Emperor Charles V was becoming increasingly unhappy with the way the Council of Trent was being conducted. He felt that the reforms were not sufficiently far-reaching while the doctrinal statements made reconciliation with the Protestants even more unlikely. Paul III recognised the emperor's unease and, fearful that the latter intended to control the council, he took the outbreak of plague in Trent as an excuse first to transfer the council to Bologna and later that year to suspend it until the situation returned to normal. Paul died within two months of his decision and the conclave that followed was long and stormy. Reginald Pole came within two votes of becoming only the second Englishman to become pope, but eventually his support evaporated and an Italian received the necessary majority taking the name Julius III (1550–55). He had been the first president of the Council and so it came as no surprise when he reconvened the Council for its second period from 1551–2.

The doctrinal statements at this time dealt with the Eucharist, penance and extreme unction. Again the insistence was on clear Catholic doctrine including the real presence, transubstantiation, the reservation of the sacrament and a repeated demand for annual confession and communion. The arrival of the Protestant envoys during this second period served only to highlight the divisions between Catholics and Protestants. Their demands, which included summoning a new council, the revocation of all the decisions already made, the denial of papal supremacy and the recognition of the superior authority of the council, were so unrealistic as to make their participation impossible. In 1552 war broke out in Germany and Julius III suspended the council, which did not reconvene for almost exactly ten years. The major reason for this was the pontificate of Paul IV (1555–9) who was determined to continue to reform the Church but equally determined to have nothing to do with the council.

His pontificate began in the same year as the Peace of Augsburg which officially recognised the rights of both Catholics and Protestants to worship freely. The pope, however, remained adamant that despite this treaty he would give no concessions to the Protestants; on the contrary he worked for the absolute annihilation of Protestanism. He had worked with the Catholic reform movement all his life and, having had experience within the curia, was determined to abolish all abuses and privileges, reducing living standards, passing strict measures against simony, prohibiting payment for dispensations and demanding greater devotion to duty. His pontificate was marked by a growth of repressive measures with a greater use being made of the Inquisition, which he himself had introduced and organised in Italy as early as 1542, and the introduction in 1559 of the Index of Prohibited Books which condemned certain authors and writings. Despite his own personal zeal for reform, Paul was unrealistic in his refusal to trust the curia which by now was largely staffed by like-minded reforming prelates, and in his obsessive disregard for the council which many regarded as an essential part of the Catholic reform programme. It was therefore not surprising when his successor, Pius IV (1559–65), reconvened the Council of Trent and, thanks to the diplomatic skill of Cardinal Morone, brought the council to a successful conclusion.

The third period of the council, 1562–3, was dogged in its beginning by an internal struggle between those who wanted to make some concessions to the Protestants, especially in the area of practice – for example giving the chalice to the laity – and those who were adamantly opposed to any such moves. This disagreement allowed the papal party to seize and maintain the initiative and defend itself against the spectacular, if somewhat unrealistic, reforms plans of the new Emperor Ferdinand II. The Eucharist was again the subject of two of the sessions when the denial of the chalice to the laity was reconfirmed on the grounds of the doctrine of concomitance. Other subjects decided by the council included the Cult of the Saints, the veneration of relics, the use of indulgences and the doctrine of purgatory. The bishops were again reminded of their duties and responsibilities but, arguably of greater significance in the long term, was the desire to provide seminaries specifically designed to train candidates for the priesthood. Despite the fact that many Catholics believed there was still a great deal to be done by the council, fears for the health of the pope proved to be the opportunity Morone needed to bring it to an end on 4 December 1563. All the decrees of the twenty-five sessions spanning the eighteen years of Trent were sent to the pope for his approval which was formally announced on 24 January 1564. Various works not completed by the council were also handed over to the pope which strengthened his own position and made the choice of future popes of great importance. It was more than three hundred years before the next General Council was summoned to meet at the Vatican in 1869–70.

The Council of Trent failed to satisfy the Protestants and they remained unconvinced by its teaching. However, it established a firm foundation for the renewal of Catholic life, and it should be regarded as both the fruit of a Catholic reform movement which was now a century old and the cause of that Catholic Reformation which now enjoyed papal support. This latter point was vital for the immediate future, namely that the popes remained loyal to that teaching and spirit of Trent. Pius V (1566–72) was responsible for carrying through to a successful conclusion much of the unfinished business including the revision of the Roman Catechism in 1566, the Roman Breviary in 1568 and the Roman Missal in 1570. During the pontificate of Gregory XIII (1572–85) the emphasis changed slightly as he turned his attention to completing a revision of canon law and the publication in 1582 of the Gregorian Calendar. He began the practice of having permanent papal nuncios resident in various Catholic countries as agents of papal authority and as a means of keeping in close touch with the situation outside Rome. He was a firm supporter of the Jesuits, and he promoted and accelerated the establishment of seminaries. By 1584 there were some twenty seminaries in Italy, by 1616 twenty-six in Spain, by 1620 eight in the Low Countries. When it proved impossible to establish a seminary in a particular country a national seminary would be opened in Rome, as for example the German College in 1575 and the English College in 1578. In 1622 the Propaganda College was opened to cater for all those priests coming from the mission countries.

In 1582 the Dome of St Peter's basilica was completed and it became the symbol of the great Catholic revival. Pope Sixtus V (1585–90) continued the work of reform and improved administration throughout the whole Church by establishing congregations headed by cardinals and entrusted with a particular aspect of Church business. The College of Cardinals was increased in numbers and this larger group of seventy members began to play an increasingly important role in the Church. The popes were greatly helped and supported by many of their bishops who not only imbibed the spirit of Trent but implemented the decrees of the council within their dioceses. Among the most famous was Charles Borromeo (1538–84), the hugely influential Archbishop of Milan. By giving his assistant Bishops real authority over small areas of the diocese, and by grouping parishes together into deaneries, he implemented the reforms of Trent most effectively and efficiently in Milan and became an example for others to follow. This work of the bishops was complemented by others like Philip Neri (1515–95) in Italy who began a confraternity for lay people in 1544 before establishing an Oratory for secular priests after his ordination in 1564. These Oratorians were approved in 1575 and gave great encouragement and mutual support to secular priests in their attempts to fulfil their priestly duties. In France, Francis de Sales (1567–1622), who was to inspire the future Salesian Order with their charism for the well-being and education of the young, and Vincent de Paul (1581–1660), whose influence is still felt among lay men and women to this day, helped the Catholic revival.

Europe after Trent could never be the same as Europe before the Protestant Reformation. The Peace of Augsburg had recognised the fact of division and the Council of Trent had formulated a clear body of Catholic doctrine expressed in various decrees, made known through catechisms, which if anything stressed the differences and divisions. The Reform programme depended on good bishops raising the standard of both clergy and laity and constantly referring to a Rome where centralizing policies were increasingly adopted. The popes themselves gave unstinting support to ecclesiastical reform after Trent and proved to be effective leaders, although the effectiveness of the Catholic reform movement differed from place to place while the early part of the seventeenth century witnessed a hardening of attitudes on both sides which found expression in various religious wars.

During the first decade of the seventeenth century several Catholic rulers in the Empire were forced to grant concessions to their Protestant subjects. However when a Catholic procession in the Free City of Donauwörth was disturbed by Protestants, Catholicism was imposed on the city which was annexed to Bavaria. This led to the formation in 1608 of a Protestant Union led by the Elector Frederick IV and then to the organisation of a Catholic League under the leadership of Duke Maximilian of Bavaria. The Emperor Matthias and his even more forceful successor Ferdinand II also attempted to restrict concessions previously granted to Protestants and a revolt of Protestant nobles in Bohemia inaugurated the religious war which had threatened for so long and led to an extensive restoration of Catholicism in Bohemia and Hungary, Silesia and Austria. But the attitudes of the popes as well as secular rulers were complicated by the confusion of their political and religious interests. In 1631 Urban VIII was prepared to collaborate with the alliance between Protestant Sweden and Catholic France on the basis of dubious Swedish reassurances and because of French threats of schism. Armand Jean du Plessis, Duc de Richelieu, hoped to use both the Hapsburgs and the Protestants in his efforts to weaken them both and was prepared to add the support of France to that of England and Holland in favour of the Union. Ferdinand II for his part secured the powerful help of Spain. However this confusion of interest damaged Catholic interests within the Empire where abbeys and monasteries, estates and prince-bishoprics were being restored to the Church. Catholics lost many of these gains as a result of the victorious advance of King Gustavus Adolphus of Sweden into southern Germany. By this time widening divisions, the repeated failure of various schemes to promote reunion and a growing awareness that civil governments might have to tolerate the existence of other Christians coupled with a heightened sense of secularization, were forcing Church leaders to court the support of secular rulers who, in the event, were not always successful in achieving their religious aims.

Meanwhile in England, for example, the 'Gunpowder Plot' of 1605 had simply succeeded in intensifying the persecution of Catholics and in widening divisions among them; those Catholics who were prepared to swear that James I was their legitimate king whom the pope could not depose were bitterly criticised by those who accepted the papal condemnation of the oath. Although Charles I sympathised with his Catholic subjects, and in spite of the fact that his wife was a Catholic, parliamentary pressure prevented him from helping them in any substantial way. Nevertheless Catholics in England and Ireland tended to support the Royalist cause during the Civil War which broke out in 1642 and, as a result, paid the penalty under the harsh rule of the Lord Protector, Oliver Cromwell, who as an Independent believed in a religious toleration that did not embrace Roman Catholics. Charles II was also well disposed towards Catholics and his brother James II was actually received into the Church but, by then, the strength of English prejudice against 'Popery' was such that, when James imprudently attempted to help his co-religionists, he was deposed and replaced by the Protestant William of Orange.

CHAPTER 5

The Age of Rationalism and Absolutism, 1648–1789

In 1648 the Peace of Westphalia finally brought to an end a century of bitter strife and the wars of religion in Europe. The provisions of the treaties were largely based on the principle *Cuius regio, eius religio* and gave to secular governments the right of reforming the Church which flatly contradicted claims made by the Fathers at the Council of Trent. At the same time the religious status of territories and subjects was not automatically expected to change following any future 'conversions' of their rulers. The treaties guaranteed the freedom of private or public worship where this had existed on the 1 January 1624 and determined that ecclesiastical property should belong to the organisation which was in possession at the same time. Although the treaties were condemned by Protestants as well as Catholics and failed to end intolerance or even persecutions, they marked a crucial stage in the acceptance of religious diversity and inaugurated a new political order in which Catholics and Protestants would finally be forced to accept the fact of Christian or religious pluralism. The reformed and centralized Roman curia continued the fight against Protestantism strengthened by the new maritime powers, but neither Catholic nor Protestant forces could hope in future to destroy the other and the religious divisions in Europe which had been a reality since 1609 were finally confirmed, leaving the northern and north-western areas of Europe as almost solidly Protestant territories.

When Pope Innocent X in the much delayed bull *Zelus domus meae* castigated the treaties as 'perpetually null, worthless, invalid, iniquitous, condemned, frivolous and without authority' he was simply ignored. In fact papal representatives had been excluded from the negotiations leading up to the Peace of Westphalia and the pope would not be represented at the Peace of the Pyrenees in 1659, or the

Treaty of Ryswick in 1697 or the Treaty of Utrecht in 1713. Furthermore the Treaty of Vienna in 1735 completely ignored the feudal
rights of the pope and gave Naples and Sicily to the Spanish Bourbons. Papal feudal rights were again ignored in the disposition of
Parma and Piacenza at the Peace of Aachen in 1748. In 1787 the king
of the Two Sicilies refused to pay tribute to the pope – the customary
sign of vassalage. The point was that the popes, who continued to
claim to be arbiters among and above the other European rulers,
were being forced to accept that in practice the papacy was but one
power – and that a very minor one – among many, while the papal
territories were economically weak and militarily helpless.

During the fifteenth and the first half of the sixteenth century,
Rome and Italy had been centres of European thought and culture,
but during the seventeenth and eighteenth centuries the position and
prestige of the papacy dramatically declined. Furthermore the
pattern of events in Spain and the empire had tended to influence the
history of the Church in the century before 1648, whereas events in
France subsequently tended to dominate ecclesiastical developments. At the beginning of the period France was the leading political
and cultural force in Europe, but the Catholic powers of France,
Austria and Spain later declined during the eighteenth century as
the Protestant powers of Britain and Prussia became increasingly
important.

Meanwhile the spread of nationalism and political absolutism in
Catholic as well as Protestant countries was a further threat to the
exercise of authority in the Catholic Church. The policy of 'one king,
one law, one faith' and the principles of absolutism spread throughout Europe and were widely accepted as the best means of maintaining order and preserving national unity. Kings were described as 'the
living image of God' by whom they were chosen and from whom
they held their authority. Bishop Jacques-Bénigne Bossuet of
Meaux, one of the most powerful Christian writers of his day,
declared that obedience to princes was an obligation of religion and
in conscience: 'One should not consider how princely authority was
established; it is sufficient that it exists and governs'. 'The Most
Christian Sun King' of France, Louis XIV, disregarded the claims and
rights of the papacy at the very time that he was persecuting the
Huguenots. He not only regarded religious diversity as a threat to
law, order and national unity but he also resented the independent
attitudes of French Protestants towards himself and his position as
king. Consequently they were subjected to increasing pressures and
even persecution in an attempt to force them to conform to the
Church of Rome and in 1685 the king signed the Revocation of the

Edict of Nantes which had given some legal protection to the
Huguenots. They were now compelled to go into exile, suffer persecution or engage in violent resistance.

In the context of the time many ecclesiological theories such as
Gallicanism, Febronianism or Josephinism were simply used, in spite
of their medieval antecedents, to disguise the erastian determination
of contemporary secular rulers to control the Church or treat it as a
department of State. Ecclesiastical or episcopal Gallicanism, political or royal Gallicanism could be used by churchmen desiring to
preserve the independence of a local church against undue interference from Roman authorities or by politicians intent on keeping the
Church under the control of the State. Of course the doctrine of
papal primacy, universal authority and the position of the pope as
the centre of Christian unity, which were hardly new in the teachings
of the Church, were consciously and explicitly acknowledged by
French theologians, for example, in the famous *Declaration of the
Gallican Clergy*. But there were few or no signs of the dramatic
extension of Ultramontane or centralised notions of papal primacy,
at least in countries north of the Alps and especially in France, until
the beginning of the nineteenth century.

In 1662, during a controversy over the extent of French diplomatic
immunity in Rome, Corsican troops serving with the papal forces
killed a French page. The pope offered immediate satisfaction, the
soldiers involved were tried and two of them were executed. Louis
XIV, however, seized the opportunity to humiliate the papacy. The
nuncio was expelled, the papal city of Avignon was occupied, Cor-
sicans were banned from ever again serving with the papal forces and
a monument commemorating the event was erected in front of the
Corsican barracks; it was only removed four years later. Louis also
threatened to invade the Papal States and unilaterally imposed the
Peace of Pisa in 1664.

In 1673 the French Government extended two royal privileges
known as the *régale*: the collection and administration of the finances of vacant dioceses and the nomination to benefices during
episcopal vacancies. Two bishops appealed to the pope and Innocent
XI repeatedly demanded the repeal of the decree. The king, however,
had the support of the French clergy who in due course issued the
Gallican Declaration drawn up by Bossuet, though his *Defence of
the Gallican Declaration* was only published after his death. The
Four Articles of Gallicanism (1682) defended the independence of
the king in the temporal sphere, maintained the superiority of
General Councils over the popes, upheld the traditional prerogatives
of the Gallican Church and claimed that papal definitions in matters

of faith were only irrevocable after receiving the consent of the Church. Louis XIV demanded that all candidates for theological degrees should subscribe to the articles, and the pope retaliated by refusing to accept as episcopal candidates those who signed the Four Articles. By 1688 thirty-five dioceses were without bishops and the king himself was excommunicated. However in September 1693 the king needed to strengthen his position both at home and abroad and he therefore decided to come to terms with the new pope Innocent XII. He withdrew the articles, though without the publicity that had accompanied their publication, and ordered that those ecclesiastics who had signed them should send letters of apology to the pope. The issue of the régale was simply ignored. Nevertheless French rulers continued to apply Gallican principles, which also enjoyed wide support among French Catholics, until the outbreak of revolution in 1789.

According to Claud-Henri Saint, even communicating with the papacy during the reign of Louis XIV was regarded as an unpardonable crime against the state and the practice ceased. The few expressions of support there were for Ultramontane views were bitterly criticised and quickly condemned by French authorities. In 1663 the Parlement of Paris had forced the faculty of theology to deny papal infallibility and to acknowledge that a General Council was superior to the pope. The same Parlement would refuse to allow the celebration of the office of St Gregory VII, the pope who had ostensibly humiliated the emperor at Canossa in 1077, on the grounds that it was prejudicial to royal authority, and the Austrian government took a similar line. The French Government was also able to delay the canonizations of Robert Bellarmine, the Catholic and papal apologist, and Innocent XI who were only proclaimed to be saints as late as 1930 and 1956.

At one stage the Church in France was subordinated to the State to such an extent that Archbishop François de Salignac de la Mothe Fénelon of Cambrai protested: 'Abuse of our rights and usurpations no longer orginates in Rome. The king rather than the pope is the master of the Gallican Church, and the king's power over the Church has passed into the hands of laymen who lord it over the bishops!' Meanwhile Louis XIV conducted his foreign policy with scant regard for the interests of the Church. He strengthened the alliance between France and Turkey at a time when the Turks were still a serious threat to Christians in Hungary and Austria. Although French troops had helped to win the victory of St Gothard in 1664, they did not take part in the campaign to drive the Turkish forces out of Hungary which began some twenty years later, after John Sobieski had raised the seige of Vienna and won the battle of Kahlenberg in 1683.

Austrian monarchs came into conflict with the Church and the pope long before the reign of Maria Theresa (1740–80) and her son Joseph II. In 1708 the occupation of part of the Papal States by Joseph I resulted in the last armed conflict between pope and emperor; papal threats to impose an interdict on Austria had no effect whatsoever. But it was not only the Hapsburgs and the Bourbons who were able to dominate the life of the Church and even demand papal approval for their policies. In almost every Catholic country contacts with the Vatican were reduced to the minimum as secular governments freely interfered in Church affairs, confiscated ecclesiastical property and reorganised dioceses and religious orders. Catholic rulers had on the whole raised no difficulties over the dogmatic and disciplinary reforms of the Council of Trent. But they were not willing to accept the legislation governing relations between the Roman authorities and diocesan bishops, and had no intention of surrendering their 'Spanish' or 'Gallican' liberties.

Similar erastian policies were also pursued by the non-Catholic and Protestant rulers of Europe. Frederick William I of Prussia declared that princes should be regarded as popes in their own dominions and his successors strictly controlled the Church through the privy council and the Ministry of Spiritual Affairs. Frederick the Great was an unbeliever but he appreciated the social utility of the churches which he closely supervised. The erastianism of the Hanoverians in England ensured that the Anglican Church was subordinated to the interests and authority of the government and the State. Peter the Great in Russia ruthlessly ruled and reformed Church as well as State. He confiscated monastic property to finance his army and suspended the building of new churches during the construction of St Petersburg. For twenty years he left the Patriarchate of Moscow vacant before abolishing the office and establishing the Holy Governing Synod whose members were appointed by and subject to himself and his successors. The empress Anne despised the Orthodox Church, treated its clergy with contempt and conscripted ecclesiastical officials into the army. Catherine the Great was a deist who respected the Church but without allowing it to exercise any influence over her political interests. In 1764 for example she confiscated many monastic estates and used two-thirds of the proceeds for secular purposes. Her son Paul I was declared 'Head of the Church' and ruthlessly used it in support of his fight against the forces of the French Revolution. Churchmen of the Orthodox Churches and Christian communities in the Turkish empire were used as agents of the brutal regime of their Moslem masters who, for example, received bribes in return for investing the patriarchs of Constantinople. Churches everywhere were regarded as useful instruments of the secular powers and valuable means of promoting the social and political virtues of loyalty and obedience to local rulers.

Empress Maria Theresa was one of the most pious and genuinely Catholic rulers of the century but she had no scruples about reorganising the Church within her dominions. She reduced the number of monasteries and holy days, restricted the use of processions and exorcisms, ended some judicial privileges of the Church and clerical exemption from taxation, censored the publication of pontifical decrees and controlled the education of seminarians. Joseph II (1765–90) went much further in asserting his authority over the Church, as part of his determination to reform and control the political and economic structures of the empire. He restricted appeals to Rome, while authorising the publication of works condemned by Rome. He introduced the principle of religious toleration, civil marriage and divorce, nationalised Church property, suppressed 600 religious houses, appointed 1500 priests to new parishes and reorganised dioceses and seminaries. He also attempted to abolish superstitious practices and the sale of Indulgences, and restricted the number of Masses, processions and even candles. Frederick the Great referred to him as 'My brother, the sacristan of Europe' and Voltaire remarked that the Holy Roman Empire was now neither Holy nor Roman. In 1782 Pius VI personally visited Vienna in a futile attempt to persuade Joseph to moderate his religious policies. The emperor received the pope with formal courtesy but the crowds greeted him with enthusiasm – a contrast and portent the significance of which was not immediately recognised at the time. It was only when Joseph began to reform popular devotions, to change burial practices and religious services, that popular hostility forced him to give way. Incidentally, the secularization of church property by Catholic rulers on economic or utilitarian grounds and to finance ecclesiastical reforms was to reach its culmination in the radical measures later adopted during the French Revolution.

Joseph's brother Leopold, as Duke of Tuscany, had encouraged Bishop Scipione de Ricci of Pistoia and Prato to hold the Synod of Pistoia which promoted radical as well as moderate reforms, endorsed the Four Gallican Articles and recommended *Réflexions morales sur le Nouveau Testament* by the Jansenist Pasquier Quesnel. Leopold and Ricci reformed liturgical and pastoral practices, clerical education, parochial boundaries and ecclesiastical finances. They encouraged the reading of scripture but disparaged hagiographical legends and ordered the police to extinguish any lighted candles in front of an altar in excess of the statutory fourteen. Their attacks on 'superstition' provoked the uneducated in ways in which their other reforms could never do and was the chief reason for the failure of their policies. In May 1787 there was a civil riot when it was rumoured that an altar dedicated to the girdle of the Virgin was about to be demolished. In the same year a synod at Florence rejected the reforms of Pistoia and in 1794 Pius VI, who succeeded in obtaining the resignation of Ricci, condemned 85 of its propositions in the bull *Auctorem fidei*. However, support for Jansenist and conciliarist theories in Italy as elsewhere would only finally seem to have been brought to an end with the rapid growth of Ultramontanism in the revolutionary era of the nineteenth century.

What has too often been ignored is the fact that by this time some Catholics were already beginning to face up to the issues raised by the growth of religious pluralism, political secularisation and philosophical empiricism. Groups of Catholics attempted to reconcile their religious faith with the realities of contemporary culture though the majority of Catholics and most Roman authorities including, to some extent, Benedict XIV simply continued to reject or react against what they regarded as transitory and dangerous trends. As a result many genuine attempts to secure ecclesiastical reforms were rejected as being unduly influenced by Jansenism or Gallicanism, Febronianism or Josephinism. Of course such theories were influential, at least in part, but they were not always as significant as was sometimes suggested. Furthermore recent commentators on the history of the Church in the eighteenth century have identified a sort of 'Third Party' of moderate Catholics, neither conservative nor radical, who adopted a middle position between the 'Romans' and the Jansenists. Members of this reforming group supported a Catholic Enlightenment and a moderate approach towards the ideology of Ultramontanism or the condemnations of Febronianism and Jansenism. They tended to be hostile to scholasticism and in favour of ecumenism or liturgical reform. They distinguished the accidental from the essential elements of the faith and were prepared to support some of the reforming policies of a Joseph II or even of a Joseph de Varcalho e Melho, Marquis de Pombal.

In 1763 Bishop John Nicholas von Hontheim of Trier published, under a pseudonym, *Justini Febronii De statu Ecclesiae et legitima potestate Romani Pontificis liber singularis ad reuniendos dissidentes in religione christianos compositus*. He reasserted the claims of conciliarism, defended the rights of bishops and secular rulers, and closely distinguished the essential and accidental prerogatives of the pope. The book was clearly based on the works of earlier canonists such as Zeger Bernard Van Espen. 'Febronius', who dedicated his book to Pope Clement XIII, argued that the restoration of the ecclesiastical organisation and ecclesiology of the early Church would help to promote the reunion of Christians. Bishops in General Council, he claimed, were the highest authority in the Church. Rome was the centre of unity and the pope enjoyed a primacy of honour but he was not infallible. Hontheim believed that any abuse of authority by the Roman curia should be resisted and he advocated that secular princes acting on the advice of their local bishops should promote ecclesiastical reform. Although Hontheim himself was later to issue an ambiguous retraction, and in spite of the fact that the Roman authorities repeatedly condemned his book, Catholic governments translated and distributed his work in an effort to spread his ideas which, incidentally, were most immediately applicable in Germany where some bishops were also the temporal rulers of their prince-bishoprics.

In an effort to control subjects who came under the jurisdiction of foreign bishops, the Duke of Bavaria established a nunciature in Munich. Papal nuncios, directly subject to the pope, replaced the medieval system of using local archbishops as papal representatives. The nuncios increasingly became not only papal ambassadors to courts or governments, but agents of the papacy who ensured that papal policies would be pursued. The Archbishops of Cologne, Salzburg, Mainz, Freising and Trier protested against the appointment of the nuncio and justified themselves by appealing to Hontheim. In 1786 their suffragan bishops issued the 'Punctation of Ems' in which they demanded that the Roman authorities should recognise the rights of the bishops and denounced the unjustified extension of papal authority. However secular rulers as well as other bishops began to suspect that the ambitions of the metropolitan bishops might conflict with their own interests and when the civil jurisdiction of the prince-bishops came to an end with the secularisations of 1803, bishops, secular rulers and Roman authorities were quite content to allow them to disappear into the mists of history.

It was then inevitable that, as a result of ecclesiological differences and the erastianism of the time, the popes in the seventeenth and eighteenth centuries should have been on the whole weak and powerless. Popes were the temporal rulers of the Papal States as well as the spiritual leaders of the Church, but with the exception of the Turkish empire and the Kingdom of the Two Sicilies, the papal territories were widely regarded as the worst governed in Europe.

There were several reasons for this including the concentration of power in the hands of the elderly, financial problems and a weak economic base, clerical administration, inequity and even corruption. The apparent splendour and majesty of the city of Rome camouflaged an administration dominated by ambition, etiquette and crude trading in relics or sacred objects. In the Papal States, it was said, one man in three was a priest, one worked very little and one did nothing at all.

The popes at the time were not wicked or evil men. They were respectable and sometimes energetic but they were usually old, unimaginative and unenthusiastic, often out of touch with the realities of their situation and apparently incapable of taking the measures needed to reform it. Neither the secular nor the ecclesiastical authorities, including the cardinals, wanted young, efficient or powerful popes. Furthermore the popes tended to be elected for political rather than religious reasons and sometimes as a direct result of political pressures. The election of Innocent XIII owed much to the influence of France and Austria, while Cardinal François-Joachim de Pierre de Bernis, the French ambassador in Rome, was largely responsible for the elections of Clement XIV and Pius VI. The Catholic powers could also veto the election of particular candidates and although this weapon was used cautiously, it is said to have been used informally in the case of twenty-three candidates during the Conclave of 1769.

Not all papal appointments were either successful or happy ones. The College of Cardinals was dominated by Italians and even children were given the red hat. 'Nepotism' was almost traditional and 'cardinal nephews' were appointed who were not priests but close relatives in whom the pope had confidence and of whom he was expected to take care. Inevitably there were scandals. Innocent X allowed power to fall into the hands of his sister-in-law who was happy to receive presents in return for favours. Clement X appointed a greedy inefficient uncle of his niece's husband; but there was such a hostile reaction that his successor, Innocent XI, refused to appoint any of his own relations and Innocent XII succeeded in abolishing the system altogether at least until the election of Pius VI.

Benedict XIV (1740–58) was regarded as being the most enlightened pope of the age. David Hume and Charles Louis de Secondat de Montesquieu both spoke highly of him, Frederick II corresponded with him and Robert Walpole described him as 'a sovereign without favourites, a pope without nephews, a censor without severity, a scholar without pride'. Benedict was conscious of the limited extent of his power and authority. He was cautious in dealing with international affairs and moderate in his application of the condemnation of Jansenism. But although he was willing to make concessions in negotiating concordats with secular governments, he always put religious interests above political concerns and was unwilling to compromise over essentials. He condemned an edition of Voltaire in spite of the fact that the latter's *Mahomet* had been dedicated to him. Benedict surrounded himself with good advisers and the Secretary of State even more clearly adopted the position and carried out the work with which he is now associated. The pope reduced the number of feast days, removed some legends from the Breviary, relaxed the laws on usury, ended the ban on Copernicanism, defended the rights of South American Indians, modernised the Index and the work of that office. As a distinguished canon lawyer, he devoted himself to the promotion of learning and research, the preservation of the artistic treasures of Rome, the preparation of a catalogue of Vatican manuscripts. He also initiated a programme of economic developments and reforms. Charitable and charming as well as intelligent, Benedict revived the Mandatum – the rite of washing the feet on Maundy Thursday – and personally visited the sick and the poor.

On the whole, however, 'The pope was more often regarded as a petty Italian prince than as a spiritual leader with world-wide responsibilities'. And, as Charles de Brosses remarked in 1740, the year in which Benedict XIV was elected pope, 'If in Europe the credit of the Holy See is shrinking daily, this loss stems from an unawareness by the papacy of its antiquated modes of expression'. The popes were forced to make significant concessions to secular rulers in concordats signed with Piedmont and Austria, Spain and Portugal whose king, incidentally, was given the title 'Rex fidelissimus'! Clement XIV (1769–74) was too weak even to protest against the partition of Poland, preoccupied as he was with the threat to the Society of Jesus which dramatically illustrated the inability of the papacy to defend even its most important interests. A society, established to provide the popes with a body of men dedicated to their service, was to be destroyed by the Holy See itself as a direct result of the pressures of secular governments.

Catholic powers had frequently attempted to influence the elections of Jesuit generals as well as the elections of Roman pontiffs. When in 1682 a new General had called on the Spanish before the French ambassador, Louis XIV had ordered Jesuit Provincials in France to prostrate themselves before him in order to avoid being subjected to the control of the civil authorities. Enemies of the Jesuits included secular priests and other religious orders, bishops and freethinkers, Jansenists and Gallicans as well as political and economic rivals. The attitudes adopted by Jesuits on the issue of Chinese Rites (see below, pages 197–9) aroused hostility among other Catholic missionaries and in Europe where the members of the Society were accused of acting in their own selfish interests. Jesuit support for Indians in Paraguay angered those colonists who were more interested in exploiting the local natives.

The Marquis of Pombal, who regarded Jesuits as enemies of progress, was confirmed in his hostility by the military resistance of Indians in South America to Portuguese colonial expansion, by reports of the Jesuits from government officials in Brazil, and by the preaching of an old Italian Jesuit missionary who claimed that the Lisbon earthquake had been a divine judgement on a wicked and tyrannical atheist. Pombal expelled the Jesuits after suggesting that they had been responsible for an attempt on the life of King Joseph Emmanuel I of Portugal and many of them died during transportation. Portuguese Jesuits were imprisoned, some for twenty years. The eighty-year-old missionary, Gabriele de Malagrida, well-known for his defence of the Indians, was ordered to be garrotted and burned at the stake.

The trading activities of French Jesuits were being adversely affected by economic setbacks and the rising supremacy of British naval power and influence. A Parlement influenced by Jansenists and Gallicans forced the Society to make good losses incurred and, although this was done, in November 1764 Louis XV reluctantly signed a decree abolishing the Society and subjecting its former members to the jurisdictions of local bishops. On 3 April 1767 the Jesuits in the Spanish Empire were arrested and forcibly exiled to the Papal States. The King of Naples and the Duke of Parma, son and nephew of the Spanish King, followed his example in 1768. France, Spain and Naples then demanded that the pope should suppress the Society, but Clement XIII, who was at the end of his pontificate, refused.

During the subsequent Conclave the Cardinals were subjected to various pressures in an attempt to secure the election of a pope who would be more hostile to the Jesuits. Nevertheless the new pope, Clement XIV, issued a letter in July 1769 encouraging the missionary activities of the Society and the French and Spanish Governments retaliated by demanding the suppression of the Jesuits. When the King of Spain questioned fifty-six Spanish bishops about his policies forty-two positively approved of his measure against the Jesuits and only eight explicitly opposed them; the rest abstained. At first the pope tried to play for time but in July 1773 he finally suppressed the Society in the Brief *Dominus ac Redemptor* which listed many of the accusations made against the Society since its foundation without actually endorsing them. Ironically it was two non-Catholic rulers who enabled the Jesuits to survive: the Empress of Russia and the King of Prussia refused to allow the pope's letter to be published within their dominions.

The comparative weakness of the papacy and the strength of rival ecclesiologies were again evident in the long struggle against Jansenism and the fact that the help of the secular authorities was needed in order to contain it. Jansenism, which must be seen not as a simple monolithic movement but from several different points of view, began in 1640 as a theological debate on the burning question of the relationship between the free will of man and the gift of God's grace. But these controversies also raised subsidiary issues such as the use of the Sacraments of Penance and Holy Communion or the respective rights of popes and bishops. The Fathers at Trent had said nothing on the main point at stake because they were unable to show how free will was compatible with the grace of God, at least in the way in which St Augustine spoke about grace as the free gift of God constraining the will to do good. Bishop Cornelius Otto Jansen of Ypres sharply formulated his position and apparently denied universal redemption because he claimed that, after original sin, man needed efficient or all-powerful grace in order to do good or to obey God's commands, but he also argued that such grace was not always given even to those who asked for it. Following original sin man was essentially perverted and free only to commit evil. Jansen's teaching on grace and the emphasis on man's total dependence on God also seemed to imply the doctrine of predestination, and Jansenism itself has in fact been described as a sort of 'Calvinised' Catholicism.

Jansen's book *Augustinus*, which originally was to have been dedicated to Urban III, was first published in 1640 two years after the death of its author. In the following year *Augustinus* and publications of both rival parties were put on the Index following bitter controversies in Paris and Louvain. In 1643, following further fierce arguments, the Roman authorities again condemned *Augustinus* in the bull *In eminenti* and in 1653 Innocent X condemned five propositions ascribed to Jansen in the bull *Cum occasione*. These five propositions gave the impression that Christ had not died for all men, that efficacious grace was necessary for salvation but that God did not give sufficient grace to everyone. The Jansenists accepted that the five propositions were indeed heretical but denied that they were the teaching of Jansen. They therefore distinguished between the infallibility of the Church in matters of faith or doctrine and matters of fact such as whether a particular theologian actually taught a particular doctrine; in matters of fact the Church could only demand respectable silence. Alexander VII retaliated by declaring that the propositions had indeed been taken from Jansen's work, that they were part of his teaching, and that they had been condemned in the sense in which he had understood them.

Jansen had several influential supporters including Antoine Arnauld, theologian at the Sorbonne and author of *De la Communion fréquente*, Mother Jacqueline Marie Angélique, Arnauld's sister and abbess of the Cistercian convent of Port-Royal, and Jean Duvergier de Hauranne, Abbot of Saint-Cyran, head of a reforming party and political opponent of Cardinal Armand-Jean du Plessis Duc de Richelieu; Arnauld succeeded Saint-Cyran as chaplain of Port-Royal. In 1630 Port-Royal was a model reformed convent governed by a saintly abbess with a devout community which was already exerting a powerful influence for good among the Catholic laity as well as religious in the world outside. It was at Port-Royal that the Jansenist doctrines of grace and free-will were transformed into those severe and austere moral attitudes which could be contrasted so strongly with the lukewarm and even corrupt attitudes of hostile Catholics. There was at the time a strong reaction in progress against lax moral views, accompanied with positive aspirations towards a life of perfection and, as a result, Jansen's strict interpretation of the thought of St Augustine was welcomed and supported by many sincere and religious Catholics.

Jansenism then was developing into a rigorist morality, reflected in the attitudes of Jansenists towards frequent communion and the need for contrition: sorrow for sin because of love of God – as opposed to attrition: sorrow for sin because of fear of hell. For Jansenists the reception of the Eucharist was a sign rather than a means of perfection. The Jesuits, on the other hand, were thought to have adopted a lenient or even lax approach to Confession. They were accused of lengthening the creed and shortening the commandments and of allowing their penitents to dance on the same day on which they had received Holy Communion. Blaise Pascal, whose sister was at Port-Royal and whose niece had been cured there, bitterly condemned the laxity of the Jesuits in his *Provincial Letters* which went through three editions between 1657 and 1659 in spite of being put on the Index and banned by the French king.

Pascal accused the Jesuits of putting 'cushions under the elbows of sinners' and condemned those casuists who allowed priests to take several stipends for one Mass or religious to disobey their superiors, who permitted children to desire the deaths of their parents or servants to take part in the orgies of their masters, and who agreed that creditors could practise usury or debtors escape by fraudulent bankruptcies. There did seem to be a striking contrast between the Jansenists, who were prepared to suffer much for their beliefs, and the lukewarmness of their opponents. Saint-Cyran spent five years in prison and Arnauld was in hiding for twelve. But although Pascal respected the spiritual fervour of his Jansenist friends, his own theological views reflected a more passionate understanding of the love of God than was typical of them. Furthermore not all the advocates of frequent communion, for example, were members of the Society of Jesus. St Vincent de Paul and several French bishops expressed their fears that Jansenist teachings might have an adverse effect on the spiritual lives of many Catholics.

When Archbishop Fénelon and Bishop Bossuet became involved in the Jansenist controversy they had already been at bitter odds over the question of Quietism and the theories of Jeanne-Marie Bouvier de la Motte, although the pope's condemnation of Fenelon was only done reluctantly as a result of pressure from the French government and was by no means as categorical as Bossuet would have wished. If Jansenist claims seemed to bring the ascetic tradition of the Church into disrepute, the Quietists apparently compromised the mystical tradition of the Church. The Quietists seemed to overemphasise that doctrine of indifference, renunciation or abandonment to God which was part of the long and respected tradition of Christian spirituality. Quietism advocated the adoption of a passive rather than an active approach to the spiritual life, not only in the case of devotional exercises, but also in resisting temptations. The major theological objection to Quietism resulted from the extreme claim that if human wills were lost in God and individuals committed sin, they did so without offence. In effect Quietism seemed to result in indifference towards religious obligations rather than in abandonment into the hands of God.

Meanwhile the French king began to suspect that the Jansenists were becoming part of the political opposition to his absolutist claims and both Church and State united in an effort to put pressure on them. But Catholics were still divided over the issues in question and at least four bishops instructed their priests simply to maintain an attitude of respectful silence. A compromise was reached in 1669 which allowed the bishops to maintain their belief in the purity of Jansen's intentions in private while officially accepting a formula negotiated between Clement IX and Louis XIV. After this 'Clementine Peace' the influence of Jansenism began to spread widely both within France and abroad through publications and personal contacts. Jansenists could be found in parishes and religious houses, colleges and universities while several bishops in the Low Countries, including two Archbishops of Mechlin, were known to have Jansenist sympathies.

In 1671 Pasquier Quesnel published *Réflexions morales sur le Nouveau Testament*, a combination of Jansenist, Gallican and Richerist* theories which became increasingly and more explicitly Jansenist with every new edition and which received the approval of Bishop Louis-Antoine de Noailles. In 1701 forty doctors from the Sorbonne claimed that absolution could be given to a penitent – Louis Périer, Pascal's nephew, in fact – who maintained that the five propositions were not in *Augustinus* and who, while maintaining a respectful silence, had signed the formula of Alexander VII with that mental reservation. Louis XIV, increasingly irritated and bored by the whole business, asked his grandson, the king of Spain, to seize Quesnel, who was jailed in Mechelin, and then asked Pope Clement XI to condemn the Jansenists again. In 1703 the pope published 'Vineam Domini' in which he declared that respectful silence was not enough and demanded denial in word and conscience of the five propositions which, he maintained, were part of Jansen's teachings. The Assembly of clergy and nuns of Port-Royal only gave qualified assents to the papal condemnations and so in 1707 the king secured an interdict against them. The nuns were dispersed to other convents, bodies in the cemetery were disinterred and the convent itself destroyed.

In 1708 Clement XI condemned *Réflexions morales* and Noailles, by then Cardinal Archbishop of Paris, was ordered to withdraw his approval. The Cardinal hesitated and Quesnel himself tried to win the support of Gallican sympathisers. As a result of the subsequent controversy the king asked the pope again formally to condemn Quesnel's book and in September 1713 the pope issued the bull *Unigenitus Dei Filius* condemning Gallicanism as well as Jansenism. During 1781 'Unigenitus' would be annulled in Austria on the grounds that it was an illegal extension of papal power and there is no doubt that its publication occasioned further discussion of papal infallibility and Gallicanism as well as Jansenism. Clement XI and his theological advisers were agreed on the need to distinguish Catholic teaching from that of Protestants who at the time were emphasising the need for good works rather than justification by faith alone. The result was that the Bull of 1713 would condemn

---

*Edmond Richer, the conciliarist and political Gallican, who wrote *De ecclesiastica et politica potestate libellus*, argued that authority in the Church was first given to the faithful who, in turn, entrusted sacerdotal power to the clergy and sovereign jurisdiction to the bishops.

Augustine and Aquinas as well as Luther and Jansen if it were to be taken at its face value. Claims that the grace of Christ was necessary for every good work, that biblical reading was for all, that Sunday should be kept holy by devotional reading were also condemned, though not necessarily as heresy. Noailles and other bishops therefore refused to accept the Bull without qualifications and appeals were made to a General Council, but the pope retaliated by excommunicating those who appealed to a future council.

The resistance of the Jansenists strengthened after the death of Louis XIV, although the death of Quesnel in 1719 also widened divisions amongst them. In 1720 the French Government accepted 'Unigenitus' and some eight years later Noailles himself, by then sick and old, finally submitted. Meanwhile in 1723 the chapter of Utrecht had elected a bishop and begun the Old Catholic schism of Jansenist Catholics separated from Rome. In 1730 Louis XV threatened that those churchmen who refused to accept the condemnation of Jansenism would lose their positions and dying Jansenists were refused the sacraments unless they explicitly accepted 'Unigenitus'. Nevertheless Jansenists continued to be influential, especially in the Parlements and among the lower clergy, and to trouble the Church in France for the next fifty years. Even in the middle of the century several cardinals who sympathised with Jansenism still expected the condemnations to be withdrawn by a future pope.

At first Jansenists used the same language and concepts as other Catholic spiritual writers but as a result of persecution and pressure they became increasingly sectarian and exclusive. Some of them went to such extremes as claiming the power to work miracles, to prophesy or to speak with tongues. When the grave of a devout and charitable Jansenist deacon, François de Paris, became the scene of 'miraculous' cures and prophecies, dances and frenzies, convulsions and even sadism, the government closed the cemetery. These and similar exaggerations, coupled with extravagant claims like the justification of illicit sexual relations performed under the influence of 'divine inspiration', eventually helped to discredit the Jansenists in France.

Of course Jansenism can simply be seen as an ecclesiology supporting the rights of bishops, especially over religious orders, and defending those rights against the interference of pope or king. Some would claim that Jansenism was deliberately confused with ecclesiastical and political Gallicanism and it is true that there was an obvious temptation for Jansenists to seek the support of Gallicans while both parties were sometimes used to disguise political and ecclesiastical ambitions. However the two bishops who appealed to the pope against the extension of the *régale* were both Jansenists. Jansenism was also associated with the presbyterianism of Edmond Richer.

The point was that Jansenism was not a homogeneous movement, while advocates of ecclesiastical reform included descendants of the Counter-Reformation such as Alphonsus Liguori or Leonard of Port-Maurice and moderate advocates of the Enlightenment as well as Jansenists and Gallicans. Jansenism itself could not be identified exclusively with the ideas of the nuns of Port-Royal, and the attitudes of Saint-Cyran were not even the same as those of Quesnel. Archbishop Malvin de Montazet of Lyons and Bishop Bazins de Bezons of Carcassone were Gallican opponents of moral laxity. Bishops Asensio Salas and José Climent of Barcelona were open to the new ideas of the Enlightenment, opposed to the laxity associated with the Jesuits and advocates of a simplified and reformed liturgy; these policies were also supported by Eusebius Amort in Germany. Italian 'Jansenist' reformers included one of the Vatican librarians, a secretary of the Congregation of Propaganda, and Ludovico Antonio Muratori who was archivist to the Duke of Modena and rector of the seminary of Pistoia.

Eventually Jansenism became a temper of mind opposed to the exercise of absolute authority either in religion or politics and to the increasing centralisation of power in Church and State: as such it became increasingly irrelevant in the light of future developments. But as moral reformers the Jansenists did much to improve standards and the respect in which religion was held. They questioned superstitious practices and encouraged the reading of scripture. At the same time their opposition to frequent confession and communion had an adverse effect on the lives of many Catholics and the controversies over Jansenism undoubtedly further weakened the authority of the Church. Furthermore religious controversies as well as actual conflicts, at least indirectly, gave an impetus to the growth of scepticism which was reinforced by the rise of rationalism and scientific developments.

At the time the intellectual inheritance of Catholics and Protestants was common to all educated men. William Harvey had received part of his medical education at Padua, while Luther joined some of his Catholic opponents in condemning Copernicanism. Galileo Galilei argued that in making statements or proposing hypotheses about nature it was necessary to appeal to observation and, if necessary, to ignore the claims of authority. Francis Bacon, who divorced faith and knowledge, reason and revelation, natural and revealed religion, has been seen as another precursor of modern empiricism.

He advocated a scientific method of unbiased investigation of nature and demanded experimental demonstration as the only real form of proof. Giordano Bruno, a former Dominican, went further and accused the Church of being the enemy of scientific progress; a claim which seemed to be justified by the condemnation of Galileo and the death of Bruno who was burnt at the stake as a heretic. However secular and religious politics, as well as theological and biblical claims, played a significant part in the fates of both men. In any case at the beginning of the seventeenth century there were few atheists, sceptics or unbelievers, though there would soon be a rapid increase in the number of unorthodox thinkers, English Deists and French Libertines, as English rationalism quickly spread into continental Europe.

The universe was seen by rationalists as an orderly system guided by a purpose which man could understand. Reason, not revelation, was the justification of knowledge and the real truths of Christianity were available to all men of calm and dispassionate judgement. Thomas Hobbes, however, whose *Leviathan* was censured as atheistic, rejected scripture and revelation, and developed the notion of a secular state based on a social contract with civil law as the sole basis of morality. For Isaac Newton, on the other hand, faith and knowledge were closely related and the order and beauty of nature was one of the strongest proofs of God's existence. John Locke also argued in favour of the existence of God in his *Essay Concerning Human Understanding* but belief was the consequence of rational proof as he showed in his treatise on *The Reasonableness of Christianity*. According to Locke even revelation confirmed the essential reasonableness of Christianity. Christian dogmas were few, simple and intelligible to ordinary people.

Other thinkers, however, questioned whether belief in Christianity was in fact compatible with a rationalist approach. Lord Edward Herbert of Cherbury summarised the fundamental truths of Deism as belief in the existence of a God who must be worshipped by the practice of virtue, sinners must repent, while the just would be rewarded and the reprobate punished in a future life. In general Deists adopted a reasonable or natural religion and only accepted those doctrines which were available to unaided reason; the sole purpose of religion being the practice of natural virtue. In 1696, the year after the publication of *The Reasonableness of Christianity* John Toland produced *Christianity Not Mysterious* which claimed that religion should be reasonable and intelligible, and that those were the very characteristics of Christianity. Anthony Collins's powerful defence of the rights of free inquiry into religion, *Discourse*

of Free-Thinking, appeared in 1713. In 1730 Matthew Tindal produced *Christianity as Old as the Creation* in which he argued that
God's work was perfect, revealing Him perfectly, and interpreted the
Gospel as a representation of natural religion. The Deists also challenged the traditional Christian evidences – miracles and prophecy –
in favour of revelation and had little or no sense of history. Subsequent controversies, therefore, gave rise to such literary curiosities as
Bishop Thomas Sherlock's *Trial of the Witnesses of the Resurrection*, but the really effective response to Deism came from writers like
William Law, Bishop George Berkeley and especially Bishop Joseph
Butler who showed that the issues were far more complicated than
the Deists had ever supposed.

According to Berkeley, nothing existed except the creative process
of spirits, divine and human, and their content or modification, that
is, human experience – memory, imagination, thoughts, dreams,
feelings, sensations – the combinations and procession of which are
the external world. Butler pointed to the significance of self-love,
benevolence and conscience against Hobbes and the hedonists of the
age. In *The Analogy of Religion* he tried to establish the conformity
of natural and revealed religion, emphasised the importance of revelation and conscience, and the role of probability as the guide of life.
However the most radical philosophical demonstration of the insufficiency of rationalism came from David Hume, whose psychologi-
cal analysis led to a sceptical destruction of knowledge as well as the
traditional certainties of God and nature, causation and miracles.

Meanwhile continental writers were increasingly being influenced
by the theories of René Descartes who died in 1650. Descartes was a
devout Catholic who took care to avoid criticising the teachings of
the Church but his philosophical system began with universal and
systematic doubt: to doubt is to think, to think is to be. The fact that
the notion of an infinite and perfect Being was available to the
human mind was proof that there was such an extrinsic reality. For
Descartes, the notion of God was not derived from sense or experience, but was an innate idea implanted by God Himself. However
such a God was still a God of philosophy rather than Christianity,
the principle of universal doubt also threatened the authority of
revelation and the Church, while the demand for irrefutable evidence
opposed the notion of revealed or religious mysteries. Descartes'
exalted view of reason soon became the main if not the only means of
attaining belief for many of those who were influenced by him, while
Cartesian scepticism was quickly used to challenge many traditional
beliefs.

In attempting to reconcile faith and philosophy Nicolas Malebranche, an Oratorian, became a thorough Cartesian and rationalist apologist. With Baruch de Spinoza, however, the 'most immoderate' of Cartesians, the notions of Descartes simply tended to result in pantheism and nihilism. Spinoza was in favour of discarding traditional beliefs, and of a radical separation of faith and morals. He denied biblical inspiration, the historical narratives of the Old Testament, the Christian evidences and the fact that Christianity was a revealed religion; the origin and development of Christianity were simply the result of historical causes. Baron Gottfried Wilhelm von Leibniz, who had also fallen under the influence of Descartes and Malebranche, attempted to promote Christian unity and to reconcile Christianity with scientific developments in an idealistic system of theodicy or 'pre-established harmony'. He also subjected faith and revelation to reason.

The Enlightenment, or *Aufklärung*, was a rationalist movement of the thought, hostile to supernatural claims, though many early supporters of the Enlightenment were educated clerics and many of its basic principles – religious freedom and the rights of man – are now usually taken for granted. But on the whole Catholics at the time found it difficult to come to terms with the Enlightenment and contemporary Christian apologists seemed generally less impressive than their opponents. Pascal was one of the few convincing Catholic apologists, most of whom were unimaginative scholastic theologians. He did not share the naive optimism of many of his contemporaries about the reasonableness, good will and perfectibility of humanity and was aware of the need for faith, a gift of God, as well as reason. His *Pensées* first appeared in an incomplete edition in 1670. Pascal wrote:

Men despise religion; they hate it and fear lest it be true. To cure that sickness one must begin by showing that religion is in no way contrary to reason; next one must show that it is worthy of veneration, and win for it respect; and lastly one must render it lovable, and prove that it is true.

After appealing to an enlightened conscience, Pascal argued that only Christianity could explain the fundamental contradiction in man – a redeemed sinner – before going on to use the more traditional arguments from miracles and prophecy in favour of Christianity.

Richard Simon was another representative of a richer and more intellectual tradition within Roman Catholicism but his career also showed that most contemporary Catholic scholars were not sympathetic to such an approach. Simon, one of the first biblical critics, was an Oratorian who saw himself as a Catholic apologist against Protestantism. In 1678 he published his *Critical History of the Old Testament* and fifteen years later his *Critical History of the text of the New Testament*. Simon recognised that belief in biblical inspiration was quite compatible with the mistakes of those human writers used by God and that theologians should not employ the Bible to judge scientific truths. Simon was condemned by Catholics as well as by Protestants and expelled from his congregation. However his findings could not be suppressed or ignored and were later used by Deists and sceptics in their attacks on scripture and revelation.

The 'solutions' proposed by other apologists to biblical problems were often academically disreputable and sometimes unrealistically bizarre. It could be proved that Eve came from the left side of Adam because the left side of the human body was weaker than the right; the heart was also on the left side and it was that organ – as everyone knew – which caused men to love women. Athanasius Kircher, a Jesuit mathematician who died in 1690, was able to date the confusion of tongues at Babel to the year 1984 B.C. He also rejected the notion that the earth moved around the sun. Jean Hardouin maintained that Christ and his apostles preached in Latin, that the ancient classics were written by monks in the thirteenth century and that the Councils preceding Trent were fabrications. Isaac Joseph Berruyer, who in 1738 presented the passion and salvation of Christ in the form of a novel, practically abandoned scripture to the critics by claiming that Christ had only revealed the dogmatic truths of Christianity after his resurrection.

At the same time, although the *Dialogues* of Galileo were still officially prohibited until the middle of the nineteenth century, the works of Nicolas Copernicus were taken off the Index in 1758 and a seminary in Padua was one of the leading Copernican Institutes in Europe at a time when many educated Catholics still believed that the sun went round the earth. Furthermore many of those Jesuits who accepted the rulings of the Church on Copernicus and Galileo were at the same time designing telescopes, discovering new planets, corresponding with members of the Royal Society and even, in the case of Roger Boscovich, helping to pioneer nuclear physics. If the works of Descartes and Newton were banned at the University of Salamanca, the French Jesuit, Jacques Berthier, described them as 'enemies of ignorance, heresy and enthusiasm'. The Benedictine Benito Jeronimo Feijoo y Montenegro, who was professor of philosophy at Oviedo and a disciple of Bacon, Newton and Descartes, promoted the Enlightenment in Spain during the middle of the eighteenth century. According to a contemporary, it was 'thanks to the immortal Feijoo' that 'spirits no longer trouble our houses; witches have fled our towns, the evil eye does not plague the tender child, and an eclipse does not dismay us'.

Meanwhile the monastery of St Maur was becoming a leading centre of historical research. In 1668 Dom Jean Mabillon produced the first volume of his history of the Benedictines and between 1667 and 1701 he published an edition of the writings of Bernard of Clairvaux and collaborated in a critical examination of the lives of Benedictine saints. The Maurists helped to lay the foundations of historical scholarship and to establish the principles of historical criticism and methodology. They collected invaluable historical source material and produced important critical editions of the Fathers. At about the same time the 'Bollandists' were beginning their critical examinations of the traditional lives of the saints. Other significant ecclesiastical historians included the Gallican Claude Fleury and the Dominican Natalis Alexander, Archbishop Giovanni Domenico Mansi of Lucca and the Prince-Abbot Martin Gerbert of Harb.

There were distinguished dogmatic theologians such as Charles René Billuart, who died in 1757, or moralists like Alphonsus Maria Liguori and Eusebius Amort who was also interested in biblical studies and the development of the natural sciences. Famous preachers included Louis Bourdaloue and Leonard Goffine, the author of a popular handbook for preachers which was translated into fifteen languages. Among the best of the spiritual writers were Jean Pierre de Caussade, author of *Instruction spirituelle* and *Abandon à la Providence divine*, first published much later in 1861, and Ambroise de Lombez who wrote *Traité de la Paix intérieure*. However the condemnation of Quietism inevitably stifled much new and original thought. Advocates of a Catholic Enlightenment, who might have proved effective in a more open atmosphere, included Gregorio Mayáns y Siscar in Spain, Luis Antonio Verney in Portugal, Franz Berg in Germany, who later left the Church, and the Frenchmen Jacques André Emery and Gabriel Gauchat. But these individuals were frequently suspected by their fellow Catholics as well as by other Christians and free-thinking opponents. On the whole most Catholic apologists were content to depend on the traditional arguments from miracles or prophecy that were increasingly being discredited, and few of them had the abilities needed to engage effectively in the difficult task of responding to the satires and ridicule of sceptics and atheists.

The ironic sarcasms of satirical minds mocking the absurdities of religion and the Church were often associated with the development of a radical scepticism which ultimately challenged the very bases of faith and morals. The new philosophers played an important part in the abolition of intolerance, superstition and torture, but they also questioned and challenged the foundations of Christianity and Catholicism. In 1697 Pierre Bayle, who adopted a sceptical approach and sharply distinguished faith and knowledge, published his *Dictionnaire historique et critique*, a rationalist critique of religious claims and a sustained attack on error and superstition. The result was an invaluable collection of material for rationalist critics of religion, Christianity and the Church. Denis Diderot's *Encyclopaedia* presented a general picture of the human mind in every field throughout history. He himself had a fanatical hatred of Christianity, while most of his major contributors were deists or atheists. Consequently the result was another source of propaganda discrediting Christianity and Catholicism.

Jean François Marie Arouet de Voltaire (1694–1778) was a deist and a sceptic who believed in the God of nature, not in the God of theologians. For Voltaire, God had nothing to do with human history and he therefore rejected the notion of a divine revelation. Voltaire was an enemy of all religion, he was anti-semitic as well as hostile to Christianity, although he was also convinced of the need for an alliance between Throne and Altar. Nonetheless, and with increasing bitterness, he attacked the Church, scripture and even Christ Himself and sarcastically condemned the 'crimes', real or imaginary, of religion and Christianity. Baron Montesquieu, author of *De l'esprit des lois* (1748), was also bitterly and sarcastically critical of the Church as he judged religion and churches by their political and social utility.

According the Jean-Jacques Rousseau (1712–78), true religion consisted in the three doctrines of God, liberty and immortality; and he put forward a simple religion of reverence for God and love of humanity. Rousseau believed in the natural goodness of men who were free and equal. He was not basically hostile to Christianity and was careful not to attack the Church, nor did he indulge in anticlericalism. In fact he praised the beauty and holiness of the Gospels. However his confident and over-optimistic theories of the future possibilities open to a free and enlightened humanity were not easily reconcilable with belief in original sin, Christ's redemption or Christian revelation.

The development of the Enlightenment was also associated with the growth of Freemasonry. This movement was first organised in London in 1717 and quickly spread to other countries throughout the world. The original constitution, drawn up by the Anglican clergyman James Anderson, was Deist rather than Christian, but the movement was not originally opposed to Christianity and several Catholics, including priests, became members. Catholics continued to belong to the movement even after 1738 when Clement XII condemned Freemasonry in the bull *In Eminenti*. In 1776 Adam Weishaupt, a canon lawyer, established the 'Order of the Illuminati' at the University of Ingolstadt to help to dispel the ignorance of the clergy and the aristocracy. In time, however, French Freemasonry became increasingly anti-clerical and anti-religious so that by the second half of the nineteenth century it would be regarded as one of the forces most hostile to the Church.

The Enlightenment in Germany was usually a movement of reform within the churches rather than an external attack upon them. Of course the scriptures, miracles and prophecy were critically examined by such commentators as Hermann Samuel Reimarus or Gotthold Ephraim Lessing. But the pattern of events in Germany, where incidentally the romantic reaction also first began, showed that the Enlightenment did not always mean the same thing for hostile sceptics or ecclesiastical reformers, biblical critics and speculative theologians. Lessing himself argued that Christianity was greater than the Gospels and could be proved from the way in which it met the needs of human nature, true religion consisting in the love of God and man. However God was to be found in any of the great faiths, all religious played their part in the spiritual development of mankind and no dogmatic creed could ever be regarded as final or absolute.

Immanuel Kant (1724–1804), Professor of Logic at Königsberg University, was also critical of revelation but he was more concerned – in his own terminology – to leave room for faith by claiming that it was the understanding which prescribed to nature her laws and by emphasising the significance of conscience. He deliberately limited knowledge to render it immune to attacks like those of David Hume. Human awareness of unavoidable moral constraints was no less definite and more significant than human understanding of the material world known through the senses. Kant therefore concentrated on attempting to illustrate how this sense of obligation operated. Obligation had no meaning without freedom, but freedom in turn depended on other realities such as the existence of God and the fact of immortality. According to Kant, the existence of God, freedom of the will and immortality of the soul, things in themselves unknowable, were postulates of the practical reason as demanded by man's moral consciousness.

The Enlightenment in the Catholic Church in Germany was led by

Prince-bishops, reforming pastors and devout theologians. During the last three decades of the eighteenth century there was a Catholic revival in Germany associated with names like Gregory Zirkel of Würzburg, Johann Michael Sailer in Dillingen and Munich, Franz von Fürstenberg and Bernard Overberg in Münster. Fürstenburg was, for some fifty years, vicar-general of Münster where the Church was closely integrated with society and where the priests were famous for their intellectual openness as well as their social and pastoral concern. Princess Amalie von Gallitzin had been deeply impressed on a visit to Münster in 1779 and was formally reconciled with the Chruch in 1786. The Princess, daughter of a Prussian Field-Marshal and wife of the cultural attaché at the Russian Embassy in Paris, was a friend of philosophers like Diderot and soon became the centre of the social, intellectual and religious life of Münster. This Münster circle, with its contacts with leading contemporary intellectual figures such as the ecclesiastical historian Theodor Katerkamp or the biblical exegete Bernard Georg Kellermann, played an important part in the conversion of several leading intellectuals like Frederick Leopold Graff zu Stolberg, Friedrich Schlegel and Adam Müller. Overberg, Stolberg and Schlegel all wrote on the history of revelation while Schlegel and Müller later defended the divine origin of monarchical authority and a hierarchical social order as well as attempting to establish the principles of social Catholicism.

But in spite of intellectual controversies, reverses and persecutions, Christianity in the modern age spread more rapidly throughout the world than ever before, although the results of these missionary endeavours were inevitably mixed and did not always seem to justify the efforts that were made. Unfavourable factors which hindered the efforts of Catholic missionaries included rivalries between religious orders and the poor quality of many missionaries, especially those from the secular clergy, who were frequently badly prepared. Missionaries were not helped by some of the decisions of Roman authorities, the competition of Protestants and the suppression of the Jesuits; it has been estimated that between 1650 and 1700 some five hundred Jesuit missionaries had died from sickness or violence. Furthermore missionaries not only failed to eradicate pagan practices but they also failed to respect native cultures or to adapt Christianity to indigenous civilizations.

The most famous attempts to adapt Christianity to local cultures were those associated with the names of Matteo Ricci in China and Roberto de Nobili in India. The Jesuits won the confidence of Chinese rulers and the respect of the educated classes by their knowledge of science. The mathematician and astronomer Ferdinand Verbiest, who died in 1688, translated Aquinas into Chinese, while his colleague Johann Adam Schall von Bell had earlier reformed the Chinese calendar. Jesuit missionaries appreciated that, if Christianity was to spread in China, there must be some accommodation to Chinese customs and language, particularly the customs of paying reverence to Confucius and to ancestors which, the Jesuits argued, were social rather than religious customs and were no more incompatible with Christianity than the European custom of praying for the dead. The Franciscans and Dominicans, however, were highly critical of 'compromises' with paganism and delated the Jesuits to the Inquisition.

In 1659 the Congregation for the Propagation of the Faith had itself encouraged the formation of a native clergy and the gradual substitution of Christian for heathen customs:

> Do not demand of those peoples that they change their ceremonies, customs, and habits if these do not quite obviously contradict religion and decency . . . the faith is what you shall bring to them, which neither rejects nor fights against any peoples' customs and traditions.

On 1 August 1688 the first Chinese bishop ordained the first Chinese priests in China. However the Roman authorities were a long way from China and only received insufficient information as Protestants accused the Church of tolerating idolatry in China and Jansenists accused the Jesuits of sanctioning superstition. In 1704 Clement XI condemned the Chinese rites of offering sacrifices to Confucius and personal ancestors. The Emperor responded to the papal 'insults' by expelling the legate and other missionaries, withdrawing concessions and prohibiting Christian evangelisation. Confirmations of the Roman decrees over the next few years further divided missionaries, alienated converts and provoked the Chinese authorities so that the young Church in China had to struggle to survive.

The controversy over rites and customs was only one reason for the slow growth of Christianity in China. Christians and Muslims were both considered to be potential allies of opponents of the imperial regime, while the Jesuits were also subjects of a foreign superior. Furthermore the increasing identification of Christianity with the ordinary people, however few converts these were, alienated jealous mandarins and the educated elite. Meanwhile in India Roberto de Nobili had become a Brahmin among Brahmins in an effort to reconcile Christianity and Indian civilization and in 1623

Gregory XV had approved of his activities. However the controversy over Chinese rites again raised the question whether Nobili's methods were justified and in due course the Roman authorities also refused to tolerate the Malabar rites. At the same time, however, Oratorians, Theatines and Carmelites continued to establish institutions for the training of native Indian priests.

Missionary activities were frequently hindered by the economic and political as well as the ecclesiastical policies of secular governments, Catholic and non-Catholic alike. The Congregation for the Propagation of the Faith, established in 1627, was restricted by Catholic colonial powers in its efforts to establish a native clergy or to appoint 'foreign' missionaries. Propaganda was eventually forced to appoint apostolic vicars of episcopal rank in an effort to circumvent Spanish, Portuguese and French rights of patronage over the appointment of missionary bishops. In spite of bitter protests and the opposition of religious orders as well as secular governments, appointments of vicars-apostolic were widely accepted by the end of the seventeenth century. The Jesuit missions in Paraguay meanwhile were destroyed as a result of the influence of slave traders and other economic pressure-groups which opposed the establishment of religious settlements or 'reductions' where the social and economic as well as religious interests of the Indians could be protected. After the British conquest of Canada, Protestant immigrants moved into the country and French missionaries were strictly controlled, though the Quebec Act of 1774 guaranteed the religious freedom of French Canadians who had already established bishoprics, seminaries and colleges, and where Jesuits and Sulpicians, Recollects, Hospitallers and Ursulines were working among the Indians and the colonists.

The spread of Catholicism in the new world was mainly in Canada and South America, though there were Catholic settlements in Maryland and Louisiana, and the Caribbean became Christian, at least in name, between 1500 and 1800. The Church in Brazil, largely evangelised by the Jesuits, was Portuguese in origin and character, whereas Spanish influence tended to dominate the rest of South America and Mexico. Colleges for the Propagation of the Faith were set up in Peru, Mexico, Chile and Colombia. The Dominicans were the first missionaries in Peru from where they spread to the rest of South America. Mexico was evangelised by Franciscans and Dominicans, Augustinians and Jesuits. The Jesuits moved into California as did Dominicans and Franciscans who established missions in Texas, Arizona and New Mexico. Father Junipero Serra, a member of the mission college of San Fernando in Mexico, established a chain of missionary stations all the way to San Francisco. Augustinians and

Dominicans, Franciscans and Jesuits could also be found in the Philippines. Dominicans, Jesuits and Capuchins rivalled each other in the Antilles, while Capuchins and Carmelites worked in the Turkish Empire. In spite of the efforts of several religious orders – 400 Capuchins lost their lives in the Congo – missionary activities in Africa were not at all successful until the nineteenth century and were impeded by the attitudes of Christians towards the slave trade. Nevertheless Lazarists, Franciscans and Trinitarians could be found in North Africa and a few coastal areas were evangelised for a time.

During the seventeenth century Christianity also took root in Indo-China. Alexandre de Rhodes claimed, somewhat optimistically perhaps, that there were 300,000 Christians in Tonking in 1649, while Pierre Lambert de La Motte estimated that there were 60,000 Christians in Cochin China by 1679. La Motte established a seminary at Bangkok for the training of foreign missionaries and native priests who were largely responsible for the survival and spread of Christianity in Indo-China in spite of later persecutions. De Rhodes himself worked in China. He was convinced of the need to establish a native clergy and to adapt Christianity to local cultures. He recruited volunteers from the Jesuits and the secular clergy, and established the Society of the Foreign Missions. De Rhodes also recommended the appointment of vicars-apostolic in missionary territories because these could be directly controlled by the Holy See rather than be subject to the influence of European secular governments.

In France in particular, the clergy and religious, royalty, nobility and middle classes gave material and financial support to the work of missionaries. The Sisters of St Paul, Franciscans and Ursulines were among several female congregations and religious orders which sent missionaries from France and lay people also volunteered to work on the missions. In 1663 the College for Foreign Missions was set up in Paris and at the beginning of the eighteenth century Claude Poullard des Places established the Seminary of the Holy Spirit for poor seminarians who would later work as priests in the foreign missions or in the home missions of the poorer parishes in France. Already it would seem that a few enlightened churchmen were beginning to realise that the task of Christian evangelisation was also necessary at home in Europe, within traditional 'Catholic' countries, as it was in the missionary fields abroad.

It is, of course, impossible for historians to assess the internal spiritual lives of Christians in the past and to determine whether religious vitality at any particular time was stronger or weaker than before, or whether the ecclesiastical authorities promoted the continuing work of reform sufficiently strongly. There were, during the sixteenth and seventeenth centuries, enough examples of intense spirituality to justify the claim that it was a 'century of saints', but at the same time signs of a subsequent decline in religious fervour have been interpreted as evidence of a crisis of conscience or a process of dechristianization. On the whole it would seem to be wrong to exaggerate either the moral superiority or inferiority of one generation over another. Catholics in the seventeenth and eighteenth centuries were guilty of religious formalism, engaging in immoral business dealings, indulging in the pleasures of this world. inflicting physical harm on their neighbours, to as great an extent as their forefathers or their descendants. Examples of scepticism as well as moral deficiencies were not isolated during the seventeenth century, although there was a rapid increase later in the number of those who publicly questioned or denied the biblical, theological and moral claims of Christianity.

In the meantime Catholic missionaries continued to fight against relics of paganism or superstitious practices, while exorcisms of devils or executions of witches continued in both Protestant and Catholic countries. In Austria as late as 1739 those guilty of witchcraft, eating with the devil under the gallows or causing storms and thunder, hail and plagues of vermin were threatened with the death penalty. A missionary travelling through Normandy in 1672 complained that the only things he heard about were 'knotted shoe-laces' which were used by witches to make men impotent or sterile. In 1686 peasants in the Diocese of Autun sacrificed a heifer to the Blessed Virgin in order to secure protection for their cattle against the plague. The authorities of the same diocese in 1689 tried to end a superstition practised by pregnant women who prayed before a statue of Our Lady and then opened the belly of the statue to gaze on an image of the Child Jesus. Curative springs were centres of pilgrimage and devotion as they had been before the advent of Christianity and episcopal pastorals show that pilgrimages as well as fairs provided opportunities for excessive drinking and physical fighting. Corpses of suicides were not allowed to cross the doors of the houses in which they had died in case they found their way back. They were thrown from windows or carried through holes dug beneath the threshold before being imprisoned, tried and hanged.

Christ, Our Lady and the Saints were popularly held to be responsible for both favours and misfortunes. The Blessed Sacrament, or relics of the Saints, were carried in procession to protect crops or to end droughts and in one French archdiocese alone between 1729 and 1762 there were at least 120 requests for formulas of exorcism against insects and rodents. In the diocese of Bamberg in 1773 there was a ritual blessing 'against disease in animals' as well as against flood and fire 'thought to be beyond human control'; the priest in surplice and stole was to carry the Blessed Sacrament in procession and then sing or read the opening of the four gospels to the four points of the compass. Epileptic fits were widely regarded as signs of demonic possession and natural calamities were seen as divine punishments to be followed by acts of reparation. In 1703, after a series of earthquakes, Pope Clement XI urged the cardinals to mortify themselves, cancelled the carnival, ordered women to dress modestly and the faithful to fulfill their Sunday obligations and to fast; papal troops paraded to church as the faithful walked in procession, barefooted and in sackcloth, carrying crosses with ashes sprinkled on their heads.

There was at the time a dramatic increase in the number of retreats and missions. The extreme Marian devotions associated with St Louis-Marie Grignion de Montfort cannot detract from his remarkable success as a missionary preacher in France where Jacques Bridaine and Pierre Humbert also worked. St Francis Régis and St Leonard of Port Maurice were other famous missionary preachers. Christian Brez worked in Germany, the two Paolo Segneri and St Domenico Pirrotti were active in Italy, while Spanish missionaries included Jerónimo López and Pedro de Catalayud who established the Confraternity of the Sacred Heart. Missions might be methodical, lengthy and instructive, popular or merely emotional spectacles which failed to have any lasting effect. Some were clearly successful. The taverns were deserted for ten years after a mission at Sarno and it was still possible in Naples to point to those who had been converted during one of Liguori's missions even after forty years. Usually, however, a solid parochial framework was needed to sustain conversions effected by missionaries as well as to promote attendance at Sunday Mass or the practice of making Easter 'duties' to encourage greater reverence for the sacraments and religious devotions. It was therefore necessary to improve the quality of the secular clergy and to reorganise the uneven distribution of priests and religious. In 1647, for example, 77 of the 105 parishes in the diocese of Mainz were vacant and in Hungary Charles Esterhazy established over one hundred new parishes.

In spite of the reforms of the Council of Trent, the Church continued to suffer from 'traditional' clerical abuses such as conflicts of interest between seculars and regulars, involuntary or ridiculously immature 'vocations', secularized or titular benefices, pluralities and non-residence, worldliness and secularism, ignorance and poverty, concubinage and occasional scandals. At the beginning of the seventeenth century an Augustinian superior was executed as an accessory in the murder of the husband of his mistress. A Cistercian abbess, who had twelve children by twelve different fathers, was eventually evicted by the police. Evidence of clerical abuses can be found in episcopal instructions ordering priests, under pain of excommunication, to wear their cassocks and to reside in their parishes, to hear confessions and teach the catechism, to refrain from hunting and from visiting taverns. In 1643 the Archdeacon of Bourges had discovered that many priests did not even know Latin or the words of absolution, and could not validly administer the sacraments. However the reformation of clergy progressed as the reforms of the Council of Trent were put into effect by such determined ecclesiastics as Cardinal François de la Rochefoucauld who died in 1645. And the eventual improvement in the quality of the clergy cannot be exaggerated. Alexis de Tocqueville was later to comment in his *L'Ancien Régime* (1856): I embarked on this study of society in the past full of prejudices against the clergy; I have finished it full of respect'.

The increased awareness of the need for evangelisation was therefore accompanied with more effective and frequent episcopal visitations and improvements in clerical education. In 1612 Adrien Bourdoise established a society for seminarians in Paris and similar institutions appeared in other French towns but the education was practical rather than intellectual. The first diocesan seminary was only established in Paris in 1696 and the situation was similar in Rouen and Nantes, Bordeaux and Angers. But the third superior general of Saint-Sulpice, Louis Tronson, had resigned as a royal chaplain and even declined a bishopric in order to dedicate his life to the training of priests. Antoine de Calvet opened the seminary of St Charles and Jean Bonnet founded several seminaries in Italy and Poland as well as in France. Later Jacques André Emery would reform the great seminary of Saint-Sulpice. Girolamo Andreucci and Giovanni Battista dei Rossi helped to improve the quality of the Italian clergy and the Spanish Bishops Lorenzo Irigoyen of Pampeluna and Juan Diaz la Guerra of Siguezza contributed to the reformation of seminary education. New seminaries were also opened in Germany and Switzerland. However few seminaries enjoyed financial security, and the character as well as the distribution of seminaries was very uneven; the word was used to describe a distinguished college of Turin University as well as a school at Muro where little boys could simply learn Latin.

Lay organisations and confraternities, as well as religious institutions and establishments, increased rapidly during the Catholic revival which took place in the second half of the seventeenth and the first half of the eighteenth century. Several old orders were reformed or adopted new rules and many new congregations were founded. In 1638 Armand-Jean Le Bouthillier de Rancé, then only twelve years old, was already a canon of Paris, abbot of three abbeys and holder of another forty benefices. However in 1664 he devoted himself to the task of reforming the Cistercian Order at the abbey of La Trappe in Normany. The Benedictines and Capuchins, Canons Regular and Recollects were also reformed by removing abuses and restoring their traditional disciplines and practices. Similarly Antonin Cloche and Sebastian Michaelis promoted the reform of the Dominicans. Vincent de Paul founded his Congregation of Priests, Jean-Jacques Olier the Priests of Saint-Sulpice, and John Eudes the Congregation of Jesus and Mary. Bartholomew Holzhauser established the Bartholomites, Francesco Oliveri the Baptistines, and Louis Marie Baudouin the Fathers of Chavagnes. In 1731 Alphonsus Liguori set up a new congregation of nuns followed by the Redemptorists in the following year. The Passionists, founded by St Paul of the Cross, received canonical approval in 1746. Of course there were also setbacks. In 1669 the French Government had prohibited the establishment of further religious congregations and, following the later suppression of the Jesuits, adopted measures which resulted in the closure of 400 monasteries and the disappearance of orders like the Servites and the Brigittines from France. But although the situation of many religious orders was very insecure on the eve of the French Revolution, the establishment and reformation of so many religious organisations was evidence of religious vitality before that time.

Religious orders were also responsible for much of the pastoral and social work of the Church at the time, and the pattern of canonizations during the eighteenth century illustrated how the Church had come to recognise that works of charity as well as mystical contemplation or martyrdom were also signs of holiness. Vincent de Paul and his colleague Louise de Marillac became symbols of Christian charity. Religious houses provided pensions and alms, homes, asylums and guesthouses, employment, education and medical treatment. But again religious houses varied enormously in size and wealth. The Jesuit house in Apulia had an extensive farm with a large stock of animals and some 300 servants, while the Redemptorists at Illiceto could not afford to repair the leaking roof or to install glass windows.

The Capuchins and the Brothers of St John of God were particularly famous for their care of the poor, the sick and the dying. At Naples in 1657, 96 of the one hundred Camillians ministering to the sick died of the plague. Religious orders and congregations supported the dramatic extension of education among girls as well as boys, the poor as well as the wealthy. In 1684 Jean Baptiste de la Salle founded the Brothers of the Christian Schools who now joined in the task of educating the young with Dominicans, Jesuits and Oratorians, the Sisters of Charity and Daughters of Wisdom, the Ursulines and Canonesses of Saint Augustine, the Order of the Visitation and the Congregation of Notre Dame. The Bavarian congregation of the Benedictines helped to promote the education as well as the religious lives of Catholics in the south of Germany.

The laity became increasingly, if gradually, involved in the charitable and devotional life of the Church and this was reflected in the increasing number of brotherhoods and third orders, confraternities and institutes of devout laity. Although bishops and priests could be members, it was the laity who directed the Company of the Blessed Sacrament, a reform movement involved in practically all types of Catholic activity. Efforts were made, especially in Germany, to increase the participation of the laity in the liturgy. It has been said that the practice of frequent communion had never been more general than it was in the eighteenth century and there was an increased awareness of the Mass as the centre of religious life as well as the emergence of new devotions such as the Forty Hours Adoration. These developments were accompanied with an increased sense of sin and recognition of the significance of confession. At the same time there was a remarkable increase in religious publications and spiritual reading which was only partly the result of the Jansenist controversies. These included original works of apologetics and catechetics, sermons, lives of the saints and spiritual devotion, liturgical texts including translations, as well as biblical, patristic and historical works, new editions of the Bible, *The Imitation of Christ* and *Spiritual Exercises*. The works of German, Spanish and Italian mystical writers were widely available as well as contemporary Christological, Mariological and Platonic spiritual writers. Treatises on the duties of daily life appeared along with works of meditation. Louis Tronson's *Examens particuliers* was constantly reprinted until the present day while St Francis de Sales' *Introduction to a Devout Life* became a spiritual classic and was at one stage reprinted almost every year.

Devotion to the Blessed Sacrament and the Sacred Heart was encouraged by saints like Margaret Mary Alacoque, Leonard of Port Maurice and John Eudes. Many devotions in honour of Our Lady originated in Italy at the end of the seventeenth century and spread rapidly into France, Germany and Spain. Preachers and missionaries encouraged the laity as well as the clergy to live devout lives and instant conversions were not unusual. The French governor of the castle of Ischia became a hermit and there were estimated to be over 1200 hermits in the diocese of Pamplona in 1734. Madame de Maintenon has been described as a 'strong religious prude' and Madame de Montespan lived a life of devotion after her conversion. Louis XIV carefully practised his devotions and religious duties and died in an exemplary way as did many other leading figures at the time. One of the daughters of Louis XV entered a convent noted for its austerity. The development of religious art and music, the popularity of relics, pilgrimages and indulgences, the controversies over Jansenism or Quietism, and even the superstitions and exaggerations of the credulous, all provide evidence of real concern about the spiritual life.

Although the undoubted heroism and romanticism of many saints captured the imagination of their contemporaries, it is not always easy to sympathise with or even to understand some of the religious and social attitudes adopted by saints at the time. Benedict Joseph Labre happily abandoned himself, not to a life of poverty under obedience, but to the degradation of life as a beggar. Vincent de Paul, one of the most attractive saints of the time, felt positively relieved by God of his sense of love and affection for his parents. Jane Frances de Chantal deserted her fourteen-year-old son in order to establish the Visitation nuns. Again the mortifications of the flesh that many saints were prepared to endure or to inflict on themselves could only be parallelled by the tortures to which foreign missionaries, especially in North America, were subjected. The sacrifices were genuine and real but it is not easy to reconcile them with later interpretations of a life of Christian perfection.

Already there was emerging that increasing division between those who practised a religion of conformity and those for whom religion was a matter of personal commitment: a 'quantitative adherence' as opposed to a 'qualitative religion'; 'the christianization of the minority, the dechristianization of the majority'. As far as the great bulk of the population was concerned, dechristianization was simply a refusal to conform to civil, social and religious pressures. It was not so much the result of industrialization, urbanization and proletarianization, though the decline in religious practice was more obvious in urban areas than in the countryside. The point was that, at the beginning of the nineteenth century when political, economic and social revolutions were about to sweep through Europe, the process of christianization was far from complete in spite of the considerable efforts that had been made. The people of Europe were still largely theologically ignorant or illiterate and unduly influenced by doctrines and practices that were something less than 'Christian'.

Nevertheless eighteenth-century society was officially based on a religious foundation. The establishment of the churches was taken for granted even by non-believers. Philosophers were agreed that the State could not function without religion and that in France, for example, religion could only mean Roman Catholicism; some of them, however, might have preferred a civic religion and a few revolutionary idealists were later inclined to support the establishment of the new cults. But they were also convinced that the State was not made for religion but religion for the State, and therefore it had the right to judge and control its teachings and its precepts.

On the eve of the Revolution the French Church enjoyed the moral leadership of the nation, the protection of the government, and it played a crucial part in the lives of all Frenchmen from cradle to grave. The Church controlled education, marriage and the care of the sick. The Church had its own courts, its clergy had a privileged position and only Catholics had rights of citizenship. By the second half of the eighteenth century Protestants were no longer actively persecuted and in 1776 one of them was a minister in all but name, but it was only in 1787 that Frenchmen were allowed to register as Protestants and to practise their religion in private. The French Church was also exempt from taxation and had become extremely wealthy.

By 1789, as a result of bequests and legacies, the industry of monks and financial skills of clerics, the Church was the largest owner of land in France. The annual income of the Church has been estimated to be about 180 million francs and its expenditure at 150 million. However rumour and gossip exaggerated the Church's wealth and underestimated its financial contributions to society through money spent on charity and education. In 1789 the Church supported over 2,000 hospitals and there were fewer pupils in secondary schools by the middle of the nineteenth century than there had been in 1789. Furthermore several bishops in the second half of the eighteenth century improved the economic life of their people by digging canals, draining marshes and organizing associations of peasants as well as by providing charity for the poor.

The monarch had appointed French bishops and abbots since the sixteenth century and during the eighteenth century 850 of the 1100 abbeys in France were held as benefices, many of them by members of the royal family. By the middle of the eighteenth century almost all of the positions of wealth, honour and authority in the French Church were in the hands of aristocrats. Younger sons in aristocratic families frequently moved into their episcopal palaces before the age of thirty and it was incidentally, during the eighteenth century that the custom spread of addressing bishops as 'My Lord' and 'Your Grace' – titles previously reserved for secular princes. Although most appointments were made conscientiously, the very way in which particular bishops had been appointed or promoted could not be ignored or forgotten whatever subsequent zeal or abilities they might display. The fact remained that episcopal appointments were decided on social, economic and political as well as on religious grounds and, since birth was considered more important than faith or merit, there were the inevitable, if occasional, scandals.

Bishop Beaumanoir de Lavardin of Mans in 1684 was generally believed to be an atheist, while a later bishop of Mans preferred the company of rather dubious women to that of his priests and chose to hunt on Sundays rather than officiate in his cathedral. Cardinal de Polignac died in 1741 without ever having visited the diocese of Auch of which he had been bishop for the last twenty years. The notorious Prince Cardinal Armand-Gaston-Maximilian de Rohan could lodge 700 visitors in his palace and kept 180 horses in his stables. There were examples of episcopal as well as papal nepotism. Four members of the Gondi family – one of whom described himself as 'possibly the least ecclesiastical soul in the universe' – had held the see of Paris for almost a century between 1569 and 1662. The Rohans were prince-bishops of Strasbourg from 1704 to 1803. For a century the Wittelsbachs controlled the prince-bishoprics of Cologne, Freising and Regensburg, and in 1730 the two Wittelsbach families included two archbishops and nine bishops. During 1731 the Archbishop of Cologne was also the Bishop of Münster, Osnabrück, Hildesheim and Paderborn. Prince Clement Wenceslaus was Bishop of Freising and Regensburg at the age of 22, Coadjutor of Augsburg at 24, and Archbishop of Trier in 1768 at 28. For three generations the Schönborns and their relatives controlled the ecclesiastical territories on the Rhine and the Main and during the eighteenth century the Schönborn family held three archbishoprics and nine bishoprics.

On the other hand, suffragan bishops, especially in the empire, frequently came from a middle-class background and proved to be effective pastoral reformers. The quality of episcopal nominations generally and continuously improved during the seventeenth and eighteenth centuries and later French bishops were usually more pious, worthy and theologically better educated than their prede-cessors. Archbishops Christophe de Beaumont of Paris gave almost all his wealth to the poor. Bishop Fogasse de La Bastie of Saint-Malo gave away two-thirds of his income to charity. There were reforming bishops like Sebastien Zamet of Langres or those, like Étienne Le Camus of Grenoble, who sympathised with Port-Royal. Jean-Baptiste Gault of Marseilles was influenced by Oratorian ideals, while the Sulpicians influenced Louis de Lascaris d'Urfé of Limoges who wore himself out in the service of his people.

By 1789 most of the French bishops were neither particularly scandalous nor particularly edifying, usually more concerned with political than religious issues, and as attracted by the blessings of this world as those of the next. There were only about five or six scandalous bishops, though the public were naturally more interested in them than in a bishop who lunched on bread dipped in watered wine or another bishop who frequently spent whole nights in prayer before the Blessed Sacrament. In any case, the ordinary people were usually less concerned and less informed about episcopal scandals than the situation in the local parish or religious house. French abbeys, for example, were notoriously wealthy; Citeaux had an annual income of 122,000 francs, while Cluny received almost 100,000 francs for the monks and twice as much again for the abbot. Furthermore the great majority of abbeys were held as sinecures by tonsured aristocrats who were free from ecclesiastical obligations.

Some orders, like the Carthusians or Capuchins, and especially teaching and charitable orders of nuns, kept their rules strictly. But older orders and the monastic orders in particular were often lukewarm. Scandals and depravities were rare but so were poverty and obedience, and the wealth of the monks did not seem to be redeemed by social utility. The numbers of vocations had also declined and there were on average only about ten monks in each house; several Cistercian houses had as few as two or three monks and in some cases only one. The devotion of Trappists or Carmelites, and the heroism of Trinitaires ransoming the captives of pirates, were forgotten or ignored as attention centred on the hunting parties of aristocratic Benedictine abbesses, noble canonesses with temporary vows waiting for handsome suitors and even the scholars of St Maur who indulged in hearty eating and heavy drinking.

But if the higher clergy and religious were often extremely wealthy, the inferior clergy were usually desperately poor because the wealth of the Church was unevenly distributed. Canons, parish priests and even curates in larger towns might well enjoy an enviable standard of living, but the same was not true of priests in the country who were frequently very poor indeed. The tithe owners of almost half the parishes in France were monasteries or chapters who hardly paid the curés enough on which to live. But if the country clergy were poor, they usually lived good, moral lives and had as respected a position within the local community as temporal and spiritual leaders, minor civil servants and ministers of the sacraments. It is clear from the *cahiers* or lists of grievances submitted to the Estates-General that many Frenchmen respected their parochial clergy, despised the idle monks and canons, and hoped to secure for their priests a fairer share in the wealth of the Church.

It would therefore seem that the forces of irreligion did not play any direct part of the collapse of the Gallican Church which was an immediate consequence of the destruction of the *ancien régime*. France at the time was almost universally seen as a Catholic country and it has been argued that, with the usual exceptions of actors and prostitutes, publicans and old soldiers, religious practice was more general between 1650 and 1789 than it had been before. Of course there were regional and social variations as well as different degrees of commitment. In Paris and Bordeaux less than half the population made their Easter duties, whereas ninety per cent did so in the dioceses of Auxerre and Châlons. The irregular distribution of religious practice in France, as elsewhere, can only be explained by a combination of historical and political, social and economic, intellectual and moral, ethnic and geographical factors. There is also evidence that members of the upper classes were neglecting their religious duties and although many middle-class families, especially in the provinces, remained faithful, the intellectual development of the younger generation was undoubtedly influenced by the new philosophers who dominated middle-class circles as well as the *salons* of the upper classes. But however diverse the religious situation in France might be, the events of the Revolution would finally divide those who practised their religion out of a sense of Christian conviction from those who were simply responding to the various political, social and economic pressures of the day.

CHAPTER 6

The Church, Revolution, and Reaction, 1789–1914

The nineteenth century was a period of social, economic and political revolution. The publication of Adam Smith's *Wealth of Nations* coincided with the American Declaration of Independence in 1776. The Roman Catholic Church suffered more immediately and directly than other Christian Churches because a Catholic country was to be one of the leading centres of the political revolution, while some of its most violent repercussions were felt in the Catholic parts of Europe and particularly in Rome itself. The social, economic and political revolutions inevitably brought about fundamental changes within the Church – in the ecclesiastical position of the pope and his relations with other bishops, in relations between Church and State as well as in relations between the Church and society at large.

At first the American Revolution had little effect on the attitudes and opinions of European ecclesiastics, although the career of John Carroll, the first Catholic bishop in the United States, illustrated that Roman Catholicism and democratic republicanism were not incompatible and that it might still be possible for a local Catholic Church to avoid being dominated by the Roman authorities. The American Constitution of 1787 included only one statement on the subject of religion: 'no religious test shall ever be required as a qualification to any office or public trust under the United States'. Fears that the Federal Government might later try to impose an established Church led to the First Amendment: 'Congress shall make no law respecting an establishment of religion, or prohibiting the free exercise thereof'. Relations between Church and State in Europe were more directly transformed following the Revolution in France where the pattern of events illustrates how the rationalism of the Enlightenment gave way to romantic reaction and how Gallicanism and erastianism were replaced by a self-interested union of Church and State.

The American Revolution, however, did have an impact on secular opinion in Europe and proved to be a powerful stimulus towards political reform. The Americans had appealed to natural law and the rights of man in declarations of universal principles and had succeeded in establishing an independent republic in the name of a sovereign people. Furthermore, and partly as a result of the help given to the Americans during the war, the French treasury was almost bankrupt. Charles Alexandre de Calonne therefore introduced a comprehensive plan of reform and, in order to secure its acceptance, called into existence an Assembly of Notables of the two privileged orders, the clergy and nobility. This brought about the first revolt, the revolt of the aristocracy, because the Assembly refused to accept reforms which included attacks on their traditional rights and privileges. An attempt by Archbishop Étienne Charles de Loménie de Brienne to secure financial reform in spite of the judicial aristocracies of the Parlements also failed. The aristocracy resisted, sometimes violently, and demanded a meeting of the Estates-General as the only representative body able to agree to new taxation.

However the meeting of the Estates-General brought to the surface the conflict between the Third Estate and the other two orders over the middle-class attack on privilege and despotism, the bourgeois demand for a just and rational society based on equality of opportunity. The *ancien régime* was a political and social system founded on privilege justified by service, whereas the middle class wanted to establish a system founded on equality. The Gallican Church was not only a stronghold of privilege as an essential pillar of the *ancien régime*, it also suffered from internal divisions between its privileged and its less privileged members. On the whole, therefore, the parochial clergy welcomed the calling of the Estates-General and supported the aims of the middle classes, while the rules governing the elections to the Estates-General enabled parish priests to dominate the electoral assemblies of the clergy who were able to vote individually; canons and monks could only vote through representatives. Consequently the divisions among the clergy and the strength of the lower clergy were reflected in the numbers of clerical representatives – there were 208 parish priests and only 47 bishops among the 296 clerics elected.

After the opening of the Estates-General, the Third Estate attempted to change the traditional system of voting by separate estates in favour of a united chamber where their greater numbers would be more effective. On 13 June three parish priests joined the Third Estate and their example was followed by others. The deputies of the Third Estate then declared themselves to be the National Assembly, a revolutionary break with the old French constitution, and the clergy voted to join them. Although not all the priests were in favour of this move nor all the bishops opposed to it, the clergy's decision was a direct result of their suspicions of the aristocratic bishops and, at least in the opinion of some contemporaries, effectively 'made' the Revolution. The National Assembly defied the king's command to disperse, he was forced to give way and order the other two estates to join the third, but not before the appearance of the first signs of mob rule which was directed in part against the clergy.

In July the king dismissed a popular minister, appointed a reactionary one and summoned royal mercenaries to Versailles. These decisions, coupled with high food prices and widespread unemployment, whipped up the popular fury which resulted in the attack on the Bastille and forced the royal family to return to Paris. Members of the Assembly followed and both King and Assembly were prisoners of the Parisian mob which increasingly became independent of government and a major determining factor in the development of the Revolution. The prisoners who poured out of the dungeons of the Bastille consisted of four forgers, two lunatics and a dissipated young nobleman, but the destruction of the Bastille symbolised the destruction of privilege and the old regime. In an effort to pacify the mob, the Assembly abolished feudalism on the enthusiastic and emotional night of the 4 August. Bishops joined with nobles in renouncing feudal dues, tithes and privileges. The feudal system was destroyed, the task of financial and ecclesiastical reform was about to begin and the way was prepared for that declaration of rights proclaiming liberty, equality and national sovereignty which effectively marked the end of the *ancien régime*.

Originally, then, the French Church was neither inevitably nor necessarily opposed to reform, while the Estates-General was not hostile to the Church in spite of the presence of a few anti-clerical deputies. Many members of the Constituent Assembly were sincere believers who regularly practised their religion. Others were Catholics if only out of a sense of conformity. Comparatively few were irreligious or hostile and even they believed that religion was necessary and that the social and educational responsibilities of the Catholic Church should be preserved; after all the Assembly needed local agents such as parish priests to explain its decrees and instruct the ignorant in their political duties. At the beginning of November, in an effort to solve the financial crisis, all ecclesiastical property was placed 'at the disposal of the nation, which would make itself responsible for defraying the reasonable expenses of worship, the sustenance of ministers and the relief of the poor'. This nationalization of Church property inevitably involved the reorganization of ecclesiastical administration since the State was now responsible for the financial support of the Church, education and the care of the sick and the poor.

The Civil Constitution of the Clergy certainly provided many necessary reforms. Dioceses were reorganised to coincide with civil departments and superfluous dioceses were suppressed, parishes were also organised more logically, while chapters and benefices without the cure of souls were abolished. Curates were to be appointed by parish priests but bishops and pastors were to be elected; episcopal and clerical incomes were graded according to responsibilities and these pastoral responsibilities were clearly laid down. Bishops had to reside in their dioceses and priests could be dispossessed if they were away for more than a fortnight or took employment which interfered with their pastoral duties. Bishops could not act independently of their episcopal vicars and were to be advised by councils whose decisions were binding. Appeals from bishops were to be heard by metropolitans or their councils, not by the Roman authorities. New bishops were to enter into communion with the pope, but without asking for papal confirmation. In short the Civil Constitution put into effect some of the more extreme principles of Gallicanism and Richerism and was imposed by the civil authorities on the grounds that it dealt with the discipline and organisation but not with the dogmatic or doctrinal teaching of the Church. The Constitution recognised papal primacy of honour, not of authority or jurisdiction, but 'without prejudice to the unity of faith and the communion which will be maintained with the visible head of the universal Church'.

Most of the bishops and clergy were in favour of finding ways to make the Constitution acceptable, though there were obvious difficulties. Some clerical incomes were reduced and many urban parishes abolished. The electoral system meant that ecclesiastical appointments might be in the hands of voters who did not include a single cleric or episcopal representative but did include atheists and heretics, anti-clericals and public sinners. The French clergy, indifferent to the fate of religious orders or the privileges of Roman authorities, did not intend to sacrifice their own religious liberties to the State while bishops did not welcome new restrictions imposed on them. Gallican bishops, formerly suspicious of Rome, began to appreciate the value of its support against the dangers of State control as the Assembly attempted to impose changes without consulting the Church. In May 1790 Archbishop J. de Dieu R. de Cucé de Boisgelin of Aix-en-Provence warned of the necessity of referring the question either to an episcopal synod or national council, or alternatively to the pope. But members of the Assembly would not allow a meeting of a synod or council which might provide a platform for counter-revolutionary propaganda, and did not wish to seem more concerned about papal opinions than had Gallican rulers in the past.

In October Boisgelin issued the *Exposition des Principes sur la Constitution Civile* which simply claimed that it was neither permissible nor constitutional to reform the Church without consultation and merely requested that the pope should give his approval to remove any canonical difficulties before the decree was enforced. Several historians would now argue that in substance the first Ultramontane act in modern ecclesiastical history occurred when this *Exposition* was sent to Pius VI (1775–99) with the request that he would dispense from any canonical objections to the Constitution. Meanwhile, however, the people of Avignon rebelled against the pope and requested to be incorporated into France. Tension within France increased as sales of ecclesiastical property drew near. Dioceses and parishes were being left vacant, ecclesiastical elections ignored, and violent clashes were breaking out between Catholic and Protestants. The Assembly therefore passed a decree imposing an oath accepting the Civil Constitution on all clergy holding office and depriving of their parishes those who refused to take the oath.

The imposition of the oath in November 1790 marked the end of national unity and the beginning of civil war; an official religion of the Revolution had been created which would be rejected by the Catholic faithful. When Catholics found themselves persecuted, they inevitably looked for support from others who were also being persecuted and Roman Catholicism became the religion of the counter-revolution. Only two bishops in the Assembly were prepared to take the oath and hardly a third of the clergy in the Assembly followed their example. Of the five bishops outside the Assembly who took the oath, one was depraved, one was hopelessly in debt and another was highly eccentric if not actually mad. Yet about half the clergy in the country, including many devout priests, were willing to take the oath because of the genuine reforms in the Constitution, because the king had sanctioned the decree while the pope had remained silent. The oath was neither anti-Christian nor anti-Catholic and those who took the oath as well as those who refused it were subjected to religious and pastoral as well as political, social or personal pressures. The number of 'jurors' varied at different times in different places; many swore with reservations and many later retracted following the papal condemnation.

Attitudes towards the constitutional clergy also largely depended on local conditions and sympathies in favour of either the Church or the Revolution. Many non-juring clergy could not be replaced, while many of the constitutional clergy proved to be excellent parish priests and many of the constitutional bishops, some of whom tried to protect the non-jurors, were undoubtedly worthy men. However other constitutional clergy complained against non-jurors and constitutional bishops occasionally bitterly attacked them. The Assembly, for its part, used a new oath in favour of the Civil Constitution as a test of patriotism and those priests refusing to take it were suspected of being rebels or traitors to the Revolution. In 1791 a new and more anti-clerical Legislative Assembly came to power and adopted measures which effectively ended the liberty of the non-juring clergy and suppressed the freedom of Catholic worship.

When the French declared war on Austria in April 1792, the non-jurors were widely regarded as a fifth column in league with the *émigrés* and the invading forces, and this association was actively encouraged by some of the *émigrés* as well as by Roman authorities. The pope had by then condemned the 'Declaration of the Rights of Man', the principles of the Revolution and the Civil Constitution of the Clergy. Furthermore the pope gave moral support to the plans of the Austro-Prussian alliance to rescue the French king and queen from the Revolution and he sent an envoy to rulers in Germany in an effort to rally support for the counter-revolution in France. The attitude of the pope was in fact one of the reasons which eventually prompted the French monarch to break with the Revolution and make his attempt to join his allies at Varennes in June. This flight marked the beginning of the persecution of the non-juring clergy and subsequently led to the king's own execution in January 1793. The military successes of foreign enemies, rebellion and civil war in the Vendée, aggravated by an economic and financial crisis, simply intensified the persecution of the non-juring clergy and religious.

Priests and nuns unwilling to identify themselves with the Revolution either went 'underground' or faced the prospect of exile or imprisonment, while the success of the invading forces in 1792 caused that panic in Paris which resulted in the Prison massacres. Almost 1,400 victims were judicially murdered including political prisoners and aristocrats, ordinary criminals and prostitutes, three bishops, some 220 priests and even children. After the surrender of Toulon in September 1793, the Convention ordered the policy of terror which continued until the fall of Maximilien Robespierre in the following year. The actual horrors of the persecution varied according to local circumstances; it was intense in some areas and almost non-existent in others. It would seem that between two thousand and five thousand priests as well as many nuns were executed while many more priests were imprisoned throughout the country. More than 30,000 French priests fled abroad to a life of menial employment and poverty though many others continued to act in hiding, ministering to their people in secret, or, disguising their identities, adopted different professions. Similarly former nuns established catechetical groups. The Daughters of the Heart of Mary, for example, were founded in 1791; they continued to live at home, engaged in secular work and wore ordinary clothes.

Anti-clerical hostility then began to extend to the constitutional clergy who were unable to defend themselves or their Church from the demands of the State. The Legislative Assembly confiscated ecclesiastical property and abolished clerical fees, secularised the registration of births, marriages and deaths, and legalised divorce. The Assembly also resticted the wearing of ecclesiastical dress, encouraged the rejection of celibacy and defended married priests. French towns or villages were allowed to close churches within their boundaries. This movement, divorcing the State from the Constitutional Church, was associated with attempts to replace Catholicism with a new revolutionary religion, a national philanthropic deism, an optimistic and humanitarian natural religion, theophilanthropy, and occasionally with vandalism or sacrilege, the public apostacies of religious and 'de-Christianization'. The ultimate failure of these various movements reminded men of the old argument that religion was the best guarantee of popular morality, while unsuccessful attempts to replace Catholicism provided the strongest social and political argument in favour of its restoration. It was becoming increasingly clear that Catholicism could survive both the destruction of the French Church and the creation of rival forms of worship; but the actual restoration of Catholicism would prove to be spasmodic and subject to violent reversals.

By 1796 the internal and external enemies of the Revolution were either defeated or increasingly controlled. The French forces had taken the offensive and were about to descend into Italy under the youngest of their new generals, Napoleon Bonaparte. Pathetic efforts were made to raise an effective papal army but the security of the Papal States completely depended on the Austrians in the north. The pope was forced to pay a considerable ransom, surrender many works of art and make territorial concessions to the French who then occupied Rome and established a Roman Republic. The French and their supporters attempted to eradicate religion from the lives of the people. They confiscated ecclesiastical treasures, including chalices and works of art, dissolved colleges, convents and monasteries, restricted the number of candidates for ordination and prohibited further recruitment into religious orders. The octogenarian pope was ordered to leave Rome and Pius VI died at Valence in 1799.

The impact of the Revolution and the spread of persecution to Spain, Germany and Belgium helped to turn faithful Catholics into supporters of the counter-revolution but the initial reaction of the Italian clergy, for example, was more mixed and some of them, even some bishops with Gallican or Jansenist sympathies, at first welcomed the republicans. However the spread of persecution ended the possibility of compromise and with the outbreak of guerrilla warfare, local priests were forced to take command. The archpriest of Conntanello was one of the most terrifying guerrilla leaders in central Italy. Cardinal Fabricio Denis Ruffo was a Neapolitan general who commanded a force of 17,000 peasants which included bandits and mercenaries, looters and assassins as well as devout Catholics and churchmen. The leaders of the Belgian resistance to French occupation and the suppression of Catholicism included a canon of Louvain and the abbot of Gembloux. A Spanish Franciscan, whose father had been shot by the French, became one of the cruellest guerrilla leaders in the country while a parish priest led the guerrillas operating around Burgos. Several bishops were members of the different juntas established throughout the country and the Duke of Wellington himself later declared that it was the Spanish clergy who 'kept the people right against the French'.

Napoleon was a great administrator and statesman, and as such was determined to end resistance to the Revolution, the schism in the French Church and ultimately the threat to his own authority. He believed that religion was an agent of law like money, honours or punishments; religious peace and the social utility of religion were both maxims of his policies. 'Society cannot exist without inequality of wealth, and inequality of wealth cannot exist without religion.' In August 1801 Pius VII (1800–23) signed a concordat with Napoleon in which Roman Catholicism was recognised as 'the religion of the great majority of the French people'. The Catholic liturgy was restored, the revolutionary cults were abandoned and papal rights over the canonical institution of bishops were recognised. In an effort to unite constitutional and 'Roman' Catholics, all bishops were to resign and if any refused, the pope would declare their sees to be vacant. Napoleon would then nominate a new hierarchy including a fair proportion of constitutional bishops. Cathedrals and churches were returned to the clergy who were also to be paid a suitable salary, but the church renounced its claims to confiscated ecclesiastical

property. The public practice of the Catholic religion was freely
allowed as long as it conformed to government regulations necessary
for public order.

This last provision became effective immediately because Napoleon coupled publication of the concordat with a series of 'Organic
Articles' which were Gallican and erastian in spirit and intention.
Roman documents or decrees could not be received in France and no
Roman representative could exercise jurisdiction within the country
without the government's permission. Seminaries could not be established without the approval of Napoleon, now First Consul, who
also had to approve of their regulations, one of which was that
professors must teach the Gallican Articles. The civil contract was
given precedence over the religious in marriage, clerics could appeal
from ecclesiastical to civil courts, Protestantism was put on the same
level as Catholicism, government approval was required for all
synods, catechisms and religious feasts except Sundays, public
prayers were to be offered for the consuls and the Republic.

Nevertheless in spite of Napoleon's cynical erastianism, it is
impossible to overestimate the significance of this concordat in the
history of the Church, and it became a model for other treaties
defining relations between Church and State. Although originally
neither side really liked the concordat, it did in fact considerably
strengthen the position of the Holy See. In the first place the concordat allowed the Church in France to exist and so contributed to
the religious revival which was by then beginning to take place in the
country. Secondly, although the immediate administrative effect of
the concordat was to centralize authority in the hands of bishops and
the secular Government, ultimately authority would fall into the
hands of the pope who was also given the power of deposing bishops,
something that would never have been tolerated before the Revolution. The fact that the concordat was an extreme example of Gallican
principles, drawn up in the interests of a thoroughly erastian sovereign who had no claim at all to the divine right of kings, helped to
discredit Gallicanism and strengthen Ultramontanism within the
French Church. It is significant that, in 1816, five exiled prelates who
had opposed the concordat renounced their opposition at the request
of the new government and, in the name of the Gallican Church,
promised to obey whatever decisions the pope made for the welfare
of religion in France.

In 1804 Napoleon was proclaimed Emperor of the French and he
invited the pope to come and anoint him. Both pope and emperor
were anxious about the implications or significance of the ceremony,
while Pius VII was conscious of the further danger of alienating other

European rulers as well as his Catholic supporters. The pope first tried to secure modifications of the Organic Articles but was forced to leave for Paris with nothing more than promises. The studied discourtesy of Napoleon's treatment of Pius VII began with an 'accidental' meeting which enabled the emperor to avoid providing a more public and deferential welcome. At the actual ceremony, Napoleon kept the pope waiting for almost two hours before putting the crown on his own head. Pius had simply been invited to sanction and strengthen the claims of Napoleon's succession. However if Napoleon's erastianism was reminiscent of Joseph II, his invitation was hardly typical of the Hapsburgs or in keeping with the claims of Gallicanism. Furthermore, during the journey the pope had received popular demonstrations of support from the French people, the first signs of a new attitude towards the papacy: the development of a new spirit of Ultramontanism and a rejection of constitutional churches, de-Christianization and the political persecution of Pius VI.

In 1806 Napoleon demanded that the pope oppose the enemies of France, banish them from his territories and exclude their ships from his harbours. Pius VII formally rejected these demands on the grounds that he would then forfeit his political independence and neutrality. Two years later Napoleon ordered the occupation of Rome and decreed that the Papal States should become part of the empire, whereupon he was excommunicated. This excommunication reinforced the national and Catholic resistance which was developing throughout Europe, though significantly, when a group of devout Catholics of the French nobility formed the Knights of the Faith to defend the Church, they associated this cause with that of the legitimate Bourbon king. The pope was then taken to France where for almost five years he was isolated in an effort to break him.

Pius VII retaliated by refusing to institute the bishops nominated by Napoleon and the number of vacant sees increased all over the continent. After several unsuccessful attempts to circumvent this problem, three devout bishops pleaded that the Metropolitan of the Province should be allowed to institute nominated bishops, while ten cardinals, two archbishops and seven bishops also pleaded with the pope to make all possible sacrifices for the sake of the Church. Pius orally and provisionally agreed, but quickly appreciated that, deprived of counsellors, abducted and imprisoned, spied on and reduced to impotence, he had surrendered a crucial part of traditional papal authority. He therefore repudiated what he had done. The pope was then moved to Fontainebleau where Napoleon hoped to force his submission when he himself returned from Russia. Care was taken to avoid any popular demonstrations by moving the pope quickly, at night and in disguise. At one stage the pope fell seriously ill and received the last sacraments.

Napoleon returned from Russia in 1813 determined to reach a settlement with the pope who was unaware of the real situation following the defeat of the *Grande Armée*. Pius was also ignorant of the increasing Ultramontane support for himself and the opposition to Bonaparte who had revoked concessions and financial subsidies previously given to the Church, imprisoned intransigent bishops and conscripted seminarians, purged seminary professors and closed Saint-Sulpice. In this isolated situation Pius VII horrified his Ultramontane supporters by implicitly surrendering papal authority over episcopal investiture. However the pope had only signed confidential and provisional proposals and he considered that Napoleon had again betrayed him when these were published as the 'Concordat of Fontainebleau'. When papal advisers were allowed to return, they published a letter in the pope's own hand in which he declared that his conscience revolted against proposals which he had only signed out of human weakness. Bonaparte once more tried to isolate the pope but, following his defeat at the Battle of the Nations at Leipzig, he offered to restore the temporal power of the pope. However Pius refused to negotiate until he had returned to Rome and enjoyed his complete freedom. The pope's return to Rome was accompanied by those triumphant demonstrations which marked the rise of Ultramontanism, while Napoleon himself was on his way to Elba.

The romantic reaction against the Enlightenment and the political reaction against the French Revolution had begun before 1815 while the development of Ultramontanism was already an established feature of Roman Catholicism; but the fall of Napoleon gave added impetus to the spread of both reaction and Ultramontanism. Francois-Auguste Vicomte de Chateaubriand in France, Count Friedrich Leopold zu Stolberg in Germany, Friedrich von Schlegel in Austria and Alessandro Manzoni in Italy all lauded the emotional satisfaction and cultural inspiration which they found in Christianity and Catholicism, while two other converts, the Swiss Karl Ludwig von Haller and the Dane Nikolaus von Eckstein, also proved to be able Catholic apologists. Louis Gabriel Ambroise Vicomte de Bonald emphasised the need for a religious basis of society and contrasted that necessity with the insufficiency of philosophy as an adequate social foundation. Like Joseph Marie Comte de Maistre, de Bonald insisted on the unity of power or sovereignty and the divine origin of authority; sovereignty must be one and independent, absolute and lasting. On the other hand de Bonald was a Gallican who did not give to the pope the pre-eminence given by de Maistre. De Maistre invoked tradition as a defence against reason and respect for society against individualism. The only true basis of society lay in authority which came from God: a spiritual authority vested in the papacy and a temporal authority committed to monarchs. Other Catholic writers in Europe increasingly identified the Church with the political forces of the right. In 1818 Bishop Rafael de Vélez of Ceuta published his *Apology for Altar and Throne*. In 1820 Adam Müller produced his work *Of the Necessity of a Theological Foundation for the Idea of the State* and in 1825 Prince Capece Minutolo of Canossa completed a book *On the utility of the Roman Catholic Christian religion for the tranquillity of peoples and the security of thrones*. However other Catholics saw things differently, especially in Germany where the Revolution proved to be cultural, social and intellectual rather than simply political.

The forces of the Revolution destroyed political structures in Germany but without dividing people politically nor violently interrupting their political development. German Catholics, therefore, did not fight to restore the past and accepted the abolition of prince-bishoprics, archdioceses and dioceses, universities, abbeys and cathedral chapters, and the secularization of monastic and ecclesiastical properties. Furthermore, with the possible exceptions of Austria and Bavaria, German kings in the nineteenth century tended to be predominantly Protestant, so Catholics were not tempted to identify the interests of Throne and Altar as they attempted to cope with the problems of evangelisation and to bring about a spiritual and intellectual revival within the Church itself. The work of reconstruction within the Catholic Church in German was also accompanied with a greater appreciation of the Church as the vehicle of Catholic life, tradition and doctrine.

It has been said that the study of ecclesiology in the nineteenth century first began when Johann Michael Sailer revived the Pauline notion of the Church as the mystical Body of Christ, a community of grace, embracing heaven and earth. Sailer, one of the first Catholic Romantics, linked the Enlightenment and the Romantic movement. He interpreted the growth and development of the Church in organic terms and it was largely due to him that nineteenth-century theologians were able to rediscover a more spiritual conception of the Church as opposed to the legal notions of the Church which tended to dominate the controversies after the Reformation and during the Enlightenment. Sailer also opposed the centralising policies of the Roman authorities and showed little sympathy for those Catholics like Clemens Maria Hofbauer who wanted closer administrative ties with the Holy See. As a result, Sailer was suspected by German Jesuits and Roman officials, his first book was put on the Index, and he was only elected bishop in 1830.

Johann Joseph von Görres, a layman, had been an enthusiastic supporter of the French Revolution before becoming disillusioned. He then campaigned for the establishment of German democracy and founded *Die Rheinische Merkur* which won the admiration and then incurred the displeasure of Napoleon as well as of reactionary German rulers; it was suppressed in 1816. Görres sympathised with the persecuted Pope Pius VI and fought for the rights of the Church in the new German states. After fleeing from Germany in order to avoid arrest, he became increasingly disenchanted with German politics and concluded that the Catholic Church was the only institution which could survive the forces of Revolution. In 1824 he was formally reconciled with the Church and in 1827 became a professor at Munich University and leader of a group of Catholic scholars including Johann Joseph Ignaz von Döllinger and Franz von Baader. Görres and Döllinger defended the Church against the attacks of Protestants, liberals and rationalists, while attempting to provide a more effective Catholic apologetic and to reconcile traditional Catholic teaching with the conclusions of contemporary research.

Members of the famous Tübingen School, founded by Johann Sebastian Drey and associated with Johann Adam Möhler, also came to a greater appreciation of the historical aspects of Catholic doctrine and teaching. Möhler's early work on the *Unity of the Church*, published in 1825, was clearly influenced by Frederick Ernest Daniel Schleiermacher's understanding of the Church as the external expression of spiritual Christianity, but the book also revealed for the first time the influence of patristic sources on Catholic thought during the Romantic period. Möhler became preoccupied with the importance of tradition and helped to revive the long-forgotten tradition of the Church as Christ living on in history; tradition was dynamic and organic, 'the word of God living eternally in the body of the faithful'. Möhler's most famous work *Symbolism* was an exposition of the doctrinal differences between Christians but it was not written in that spirit of extreme polemic which so often marred apologetic theology. Möhler argued that Christ established a visible society, the Church, which corresponded to human needs and aspirations. The Church must have a head, instituted by Christ, the successor of Saint Peter, in order to preserve its unity. But the pope enjoyed permanent and unchanging 'essential' rights to be distinguished from his 'accidental' powers which varied from time to time and might even become outdated. Döllinger later claimed that, for a whole generation of Catholics, Möhler rediscovered the spiritual or mystical Church behind the legal and institutional structures; he also received Saint Cyprian's ecclesiological formula 'the church in the bishop'. Consequently it is hardly surprising that some German Catholics were able to appreciate the religious and theological dimensions of hierarchical and ecclesiastical government; they could respect episcopacy without accepting the erastian implications of Gallicanism or recognise the position of the pope as the centre of unity without becoming dominated by Ultramontanism.

It was partly as a result of the revival of Catholicism in Germany and France that Nicholas Patrick Stephen Wiseman was prompted to hope for a similar revival in England. There the comparatively small community of 'Old Catholics', politically emancipated in 1829, was about to be transformed by the arrival of thousands of Irish immigrants and to a lesser extent by the conversions of significant members of the Oxford Movement in the Church of England and in particular by the conversions of John Henry Newman and Henry Edward Manning. Wiseman, a flamboyant and enthusiastic churchman, did much to encourage the spread of Ultramontanism within English Catholicism and he was largely responsible for securing the restoration of the hierarchy in 1850. Newman was one of the greatest Christian theologians of the nineteenth century and his writings on the nature of faith, revelation and the Church, justification and doctrinal development, papal infallibility and biblical inspiration, the role of the laity and the significance of conscience had a formative influence on many later theologians. Manning, who later became Archbishop of Westminster, was chiefly concerned with providing for the material as well as the pastoral needs of a rapidly growing community but he was also to play a leading part in securing the definition of papal infallibility at the First Vatican Council. The increasing divisions between Liberal and Ultramontane Catholics were reflected in the careers of Döllinger's pupil, Sir John Acton, and Richard Simpson whose efforts to represent the views of liberal catholicism would be superseded and overwhelmed by the rapid development of Ultramontanism within the Church in England.

Two important factors contributed to the spread of Ultramontanism in Germany. The disruption of secularization and the work of reorganisation had forced German bishops to apply for dispensations to the pope on the basis of his 'universal episcopate', while German secular governments frequently preferred to deal with distant Roman authorities rather than with the leaders of a strong local church. But it is significant that the writings of French Ultramontanes were most influential in an area like Mainz where Catholics had shared the experiences and reactions of their French coreligionists. Bishop Johann Ludwig Colmar had refused to sign the Civil Constitution of the Clergy and during the Terror had lived in hiding, ministering to his flock. Colmar, who was appointed bishop by Napoleon, organised his famous diocesan seminary according to the regulations of the Council of Trent and appointed Franz Leopold Liebermann as superior. Like Colmar, Bishop Andreas Räss of Strasbourg had suffered persecution during the Revolution. Räss, a former teacher in the seminary, founded *Der Katholik* in 1820 and through its pages introduced German Catholics to the theories of writers like Louis Veuillot and the controversies of French Catholics. Räss was also notorious for denouncing what he considered to be the 'errors' of his fellow Catholics.

Mainz was also the first centre in Germany to support the revival of scholasticism. The Romantic movement had removed many earlier prejudices against scholasticism even before the impact of Italian neo-scholasticism. The neo-scholastics were first successful in Piacenza where Vincenzo Buzzetti taught Taparelli d'Azeglio, later Jesuit Provincial at Naples where the scholastics were to win the support of *Civiltà Cattolica*, the influential Jesuit periodical. Matteo Liberatore's *Institutiones Philosophicae* was one of the first modern syntheses of Thomist philosophy, but it was largely through Joseph Kleutgen, a Jesuit professor at the Gregorian University and author of *Theology of the past* and *Philosophy of the past*, that neo-scholasticism began to influence the German theologians. The development of scholasticism and Ultramontanism were also helped by ecclesiastical condemnations. The publication of David Friedrich Strauss' *Life of Jesus* in 1835 reinforced the fears of those who were already suspicious of contemporary intellectual trends and in the same year the Brief *Dum acerbissimus* condemned Georg Hermes who had attempted to reconcile Catholic doctrines with Kantian philosophy. Hermes claimed to prove the fundamental truths of Christianity as postulates of the practical reason with absolute certainty and was accused of overestimating the powers of reason and misinterpreting the role of revelation. In 1857 the works of Anton Günther, who attempted to interpret Catholic sacramentalism in terms of contemporary idealism, were put on the Index. Günther was also accused of overestimating the significance of reason in matters of faith. He was said to have ascribed to reason the power of understanding mysteries and using philosophy as the test of theology. However Günther's critical attacks on neo-scholasticism probably contributed to his condemnation which was the first occasion on which official papal approval was given to scholasticism. Encouraged by their success, the scholastics then secured the appointment of Heinrich Joseph Denzinger to the chair of dogmatics at Würzburg. His *Enchiridion Symbolorum definitionum et declarationum* was intended to inform theologians of the definitive interpretations of the *Magisterium Petri*.

During the nineteenth century German rulers attempted to subject the Church to their control, and these attempts were often associated with efforts to spread Protestantism, especially when Protestantism became explicitly linked with German nationalism. These erastian and proselytising tendencies also reinforced German Ultramontanism. The support of the papacy might prevent the subjection or exploitation of the German Church while the bishops increasingly associated their authority with that of the pope as their own local influence declined. The government of Württemberg, for example, appointed parish priests, cancelled holidays, forbad the exposition of relics and even modified confessional practice. The authorities in Baden would not allow the Archbishop of Freiburg to publish pastoral letters without permission and appointed sixty of the eighty parish priests in his diocese. However this erastian and 'Protestant' campaign was waged systematically and energetically in Prussia where the conflict came to a head over the question of mixed marriages.

In 1825 King Friedrich Wilhelm III extended the application of an earlier decree whereby children were to be educated in their fathers' religion; a move which favoured Protestants since more Protestant men married Catholic women than *vice versa*. Catholics accused the king of breaking a royal promise made in 1815 to protect the Catholic religion and they began to apply the rules on mixed marriages more strictly. In 1830 the pope declared that priests should only attend weddings without giving their blessing in those cases where the promises to safeguard the Catholic education of the children had not been given. The Prussian government refused to allow this Brief to be published and forced the bishops into an agreement which effectively annulled its provisions: parish priests were not obliged to demand the promises and must only refuse the blessing if they knew that arrangements had actually been made to educate children outside the Church. The Roman authorities, anxious to avoid a quarrel, quietly accepted the 'explanations' subsequently offered by the Prussian ambassador in Rome.

In 1835 the Prussian government requested that Archbishop Clemens August Freiherr Droste zu Vischering should be elected to the see of Cologne. The new archbishop directed his clergy to enforce the papal brief and in 1837 he was imprisoned, as was Archbishop Martin von Dunin of Gnesen-Posen. The Roman authorities issued a vigorous protest, European public opinion was scandalized, and Lamennais, the former leader of Ultramontanes and Liberal Catholics, who had just left the Church, joined with Montalembert, Döllinger and Görres in strongly protesting.* Peace was restored when Friedrich Wilhelm IV came to the throne in 1840. He allowed bishops to deal with mixed marriages and established a Catholic Department at the Ministry of Culture. The Constitution of 1848 guaranteed freedom of Catholic worship, complete autonomy in ecclesiastical appointments, freedom to communicate with Rome, the right of association and the right to open schools. However during the next decade German bishops continued to fight for the recognition of their episcopal rights and in particular their rights to educate and appoint priests, to build schools and supervise religious education, to establish religious houses and administer ecclesiastical property. On one occasion the elderly Archbishop Hermann von Vicari of Freiburg was placed under police surveillance and even subjected to house arrest for eight days. In 1852 Catholic deputies in the Prussian Chamber suspected that attempts were again being made to restore Protestant supremacy and so they formed that Catholic group which in 1858 became the 'Centre Party'.

The imprisonment of the Archbishop of Cologne proved to be a turning point in the career of a Prussian civil servant, Wilhelm Emmanuel von Ketteler who, from then on, devoted himself to the service of the Church and identified himself with the needs of the working classes. Several German Catholics, priests and laymen, had already opposed the economic notions of liberal capitalism, criticised industrial abuses and demanded protective legislation. Ketteler himself was impressed with Father Adolph Kolping's attempts to organise workers along Christian lines and used Kolping's organisations to circulate his own ideas on the Church's attitude towards work and labour. During the 1840s Kolping had organised the *Gesellenverein*, societies consisting of master workmen and young journeymen directed by a chaplain who tried to assist the moral and intellectual development as well as to improve the economic conditions of their members. By leaving the initiative to the members rather than to their chaplain, Kolping avoided the paternalism and clericalism of so many Catholic societies. In 1855 there were 12,000 members in 104 branches, and when the founder died in 1865 there were more than 100,000 members. The movement eventually had its

*See also pages 231–7 below.

own periodicals, libraries and infirmaries, and a membership of over half a million people by 1901.

During 1848 and 1849 Bishop Ketteler delivered a series of addresses in his cathedral at Mainz on 'The Great Social Questions of our Age' in which he demanded social justice and condemned economic liberalism as well as socialism. Ketteler supported demands for higher wages, better holidays and trades unions; he advocated legislation to improve the working conditions of men and to control the work of women and children; he insisted on the need for government inspection and protection of wives and mothers who did not go out to work. Through his seminary and various periodicals, he encouraged the formation of priests who were socially concerned. Ketteler initiated the national conferences of German bishops and formulated an episcopal statement on social questions. He also drew a programme for German Catholics which formed the basis of the social policies of the Centre Party. In 1869 Karl Marx referred to Ketteler among others when he wrote to Friedrich Engels 'we have to combat the clerics vigorously, especially in the Catholic areas ... The scoundrels are flirting with the workers' question whenever it seems appropriate'.

Consequently during the nineteenth century the Church in Germany came to be seen as a real Christian social order because of the social and pastoral concern shown by German Catholics, while congresses and organisations led by laymen helped to identify the laity more closely with the Church and the clergy. The first meeting of a national assembly of German Catholics took place in Mainz during 1848. It was arranged by the *Piusverein* which had been founded in the same year by a priest, Adam Lennig, to promote religious liberty and defend the interests of the Church. This congress explicitly opposed the claims of Josephinism, while demanding freedom 'to implant Catholic principles in life as a whole and to work for a solution to the social problem'. German Catholics were becoming more conscious of their rights and their strength, and more Ultramontane but not necessarily more clerical. The *Katholikentag*, which eventually met annually, provided an obvious forum for the discussion of social issues and this emphasis on social problems was further stimulated by the formation of *Volksverein* or meetings of Catholic workers.

Meanwhile in France, on the other hand, the political attitudes of the restored Bourbon King Louis XVIII and his advisers were similar to those leading the aristocratic revolt of 1789, while most of the new French hierarchy were still monarchists, aristocrats and Gallicans. The majority of the French clergy, as well as their bishops, believed that neither the Throne nor the Altar could survive without the other and they exhorted their people to act as good royalists and good Christians. Unfortunately the men of the Restoration showed a complete lack of understanding of the contemporary social and political situation. They were demonstrative and even theatrical in their political and religious claims and attitudes which inevitably provoked first a suspicious and then a hostile reaction. Roman Catholicism was again recognised as the official religion of France in spite of the indifference or hostility of many Frenchmen. The Napoleonic Concordat was retained, since attempts to restore the Concordat of 1516 or to negotiate a new one had to be abandoned in view of the opposition of the Roman authorities to Gallicanism and their determination to base future concordats on the pattern of that agreed with Napoleon. The Organic Articles were also retained and the Gallican Articles were still taught in seminaries. The first administration of the Duc de Richelieu, which ultimately proved too royalist even for the king, removed divorce from the Civil Code, deprived married priests of their pensions and attempted to return civil registers to the clergy. The remains of Voltaire and Rousseau were removed from the Pantheon, which was given over to the Church, control of education was surrendered to the bishops and completely unrealistic legal sanctions were introduced against sacrilege and attacks on religion.

This religious extremism and the consequent political threat to the Church hid the real revival in the Church and the extent to which its character was changing. The French Church had been deprived of educational as well as financial resources and the supply of new priests dramatically declined. In 1806 at least one sixth of French parishes were without a priest and a quarter of the incumbents were aged over sixty. In 1816 a third of the parishes were vacant and by 1820 this would mean about 20,000 parishes. Yet most of these vacancies had been filled by 1830. Furthermore many of these new priests came from the ranks of ordinary people and they were men with a genuine sense of vocation since there was now little prospect of desirable promotion or financial gain. In 1789 only five bishops out of 134 could be regarded as men of humble origins but by the end of the century there were only four nobles out of 90 bishops.

Furthermore the restoration of the Jesuits was followed by the revival of the old monastic orders and the friars, and the spread of new congregations of men and women such as the Institute of Charity and the Oblates of Mary Immaculate, the Marianists and the Picpus Society, the Marist Brothers, the Brothers of Charity and the Brothers of Christian Instruction, the Daughters of Charity and

Sisters of St Vincent de Paul, the Sisters of Mercy and the Sisters of Notre Dame. Most of these new congregations were involved in teaching, missionary activity or corporal works of mercy and many of their recruits came from the ranks of the ordinary people. Although clergy and religious inevitably played the leading part in the Catholic revival and ecclesiastical restoration, there was also an increased awareness of the need for lay participation. The 'Central Office of Catholic Action' was established as early as 1801. Members of the Society of Good Works, founded in 1816, visited the sick and the imprisoned and educated young workers. The Association for the Defence of the Catholic Religion, set up in 1828, also established the newspaper *Le Correspondant*.

The French Revolution had not directly prevented missionary activity though the French occupation of Rome, and the virtual destruction of the Congregation for the Propagation of the Faith meant that there was an urgent need for reconstruction after 1815. At the same time the decline of eighteenth-century rationalism and deism, the revival of the Jesuits and the establishment of new orders, like the Priests of Mercy or the Society of the Holy Ghost, did help to stimulate further missionary developments. In 1822 Marie-Pauline Jaricot established the Association for the Spreading of the Faith which quickly developed throughout Europe and America. The *Annales de la Propagation de la Foi* began to appear regularly in 1824. During the 1830s the Zaveriusverein, the Bonifatiusverein and Ludwig-Missionsverein were set up in Germany, as was the Leopoldine Foundation in Austria. Under Gregory XVI, a former Prefect of Propaganda, the papacy assumed the leadership of the Catholic missionary movement; Pius IX simply continued and amplified the missionary policies of his predecessor. Rome became the centre of Catholic missionary endeavour and vicars apostolic, rather than bishops, were henceforth regularly appointed to missionary sees. In spite of occasional persecutions and political complications during the nineteenth century new foundations such as the Salesians or Verona Fathers, the White Fathers and the Mill Hill Fathers, would later be found working alongside older orders in established missionary fields as well as in new territories only recently accessible with the expansion of colonialism. In 1870 missionary bishops would be present at the First Vatican Council although the Fathers at that time were unable and unprepared to deal adequately with even the most urgent of missionary problems.

In 1824 Charles X, an extreme reactionary and fanatical Catholic, ascended the French throne. He was anointed with the 'newly discovered' oil of St Louis before prostrating himself like an ordinand in the sanctuary of Rheims. Ignorant peasants as well as middle-class sceptics were astonished or amused by these medieval rites and ridiculed their significance. Charles' reign reinforced the alliance between Catholicism and the aristocracy of the *ancien régime* which alienated the educated liberal middle classes who inevitably became anti-clerical. In 1830 a political movement, which began as an attempt to force the king to dismiss an unpopular minister, turned into the July Revolution which was directed as much against the Altar as the Throne. Catholicism was politically discredited and once again became simply the religion of the majority of French people. There was no religious ceremony at the coronation that year of Louis-Philippe and although the new King of the French attended Mass with his family, the monarchy was no longer officially Catholic. The legal restrictions imposed on the Church – a reduced ecclesiastical budget, the expulsion of religious orders, the abolition of military chaplains – were only intended to irritate and further weaken an already moribund organization. Nevertheless in spite of the former union between Throne and Altar, Pius VIII (1829–30) ignored the advice of his nuncio in Paris, Gallican bishops and aristocratic *émigrés* who were all opposed to recognizing the new regime. The pope told the French clergy to obey the established rather than the legitimate ruler and decided, with Louis-Philippe, to maintain the Napoleonic Concordat as the basis of relations between Church and State just at the time when some French Catholics were about to propose a radical alternative.

Hugues-Félicité Robert de La Mennais, or Lamennais (1782–1854), insisted on the social necessity of religion but rejected the theory that religion was merely socially or politically useful for keeping the people in order; Christianity was true as well as socially useful and was socially useful precisely because it was true. According to Lamennais, papal authority was both absolute and infallible, 'The infallible organ of the testimony of the human race to the one true religion'. The pope must therefore regain his right to intervene in the affairs of this world so that he might give effect to the principles of the Gospel. He alone could safeguard the freedom of the children of God against erastian interference, just as he alone could establish that fraternal order between the nations of which a secular agreement like the Holy Alliance was such a mockery. Lamennais hoped to substitute Ultramontanism for Gallicanism; national churches might too easily be controlled or dominated by the State, whereas the universal Church or the union of all Catholics under the pope could not.

Lamennais also argued in favour of an alliance between the

Church and democratic freedom to replace the alliance between Throne and Altar. He prophesied the fall of the Bourbons and feared that the French Church might also fall unless it broke with the monarchy. In time Lamennais defended freedom of conscience as well as freedom for the Catholic Church, a free society with free speech, press and education, separation of Church and State, and an assembly elected by universal suffrage. His reputation was enormously enhanced when the Bourbon Charles X fell in 1830 and with the success of the Revolution, Lamennais urged his fellow Catholics to break with the past and with all forms of legitimism, royalism and absolutism. In collaboration with Jean-Baptiste Henri Lacordaire and Charles René Forbes Comte de Montalembert, Lamennais advocated his views in the newspaper *L'Avenir* which had as its motto, '*Dieu et la liberté*'. The 'pilgrims of God and of liberty' supported freedom of conscience and separation of Church and State, democratic republicanism and national self-determination, social and economic reform, general disarmament and European unity.

Lamennais partly influenced and was himself influenced by the union between Catholics and liberals in Belgium where Catholics had already begun to demand and defend their rights on the basis of constitutional freedom and freedom of conscience. Belgian Catholics began to recognise the advantages of the separation of Church and State as they supported the end of the union with the Netherlands in 1830. The new Belgian constitution guaranteed the freedom as well as support for the Church from the State and four years later the bishops were able to reopen the University of Louvain which became a centre of Catholic liberalism and employed several of Lamennais' disciples. Incidentally, the bishops consciously ignored the desire of the Roman authorities to turn it into a papal institution. Lamennais also influenced the journalist J.G. Le Sage ten Broek and his newspaper *De Ultramontaan*. In the Netherlands, Catholics continued to suffer under various disabilities imposed by their Protestant rulers. However in 1842 two seminary professors, F.J. Van Vree and C. Broere, who had also been influenced by Lamennais, established *De Katholiek*, while J. Smits founded the daily newspaper *De Tijd*. Dutch Catholics used these publications as well as their political influence to defend Catholic interests, remove legal disabilities and promote a Catholic revival which reached a watershed with the restoration of the Dutch hierarchy in 1856.

For several months *L'Avenir* had a daily circulation of about 2,000 subscribers, cleric and lay. Two numbers had been seized by the police within the first five weeks and the editors were prosecuted for attacking the government but acquitted. The *Ami du clergé*, a Gallican publication, joined with legitimist periodicals in attacking Lamennais, while Gallican and monarchist bishops issued pastorals denouncing Lamennais and his friends. *L'Avenir* was forced to cease publication after only a year because of the declining number of subscribers. Liberals as well as Catholics were prejudiced against the 'unnatural' union proposed, while the editors did not try to win support tactfully, but by their over-enthusiastic haste simply shocked their readers into hostility. Nevertheless the questions raised remained to be resolved and Lamennais, Lacordaire and Montalembert decided to go to Rome to seek the support of the pope for their points of view.

In 1815 the papacy had emerged from the recent struggles with a new prestige which was reflected in the decisions taken at the Congress of Vienna. The Congress, it was said, had resulted in 'nothing but restorations' and agreements between the Great Powers of little value for the future balance and preservation of the peace of Europe. However papal nuncios were recognised as doyens of the diplomatic corps and in the number of accredited diplomats in Rome increased from eight in 1816 to sixteen in 1823, including nine representatives of non-Catholic Powers. The political reaction against the horrors of the French Revolution, coupled with the fact that, of all the continental powers, the papacy had been Napoleon's most consistent opponent provided the opportunity for the triumph of the Holy See. The prestige of the papacy was also greatly increased by the character of the reigning pontiff Pius VII and the abilities of his Secretary of State, Ercole Consalvi. This conservative reformer supported the counter-revolution but was willing to accept the irreversible. He defended papal sovereignty on earth, while distinguishing between the temporal and spiritual interests of the Church. However the restoration of almost all the papal states at the Congress of Vienna, including the enclaves in northern Italy, was ultimately to prove the most disastrous event in the history of the papacy during the nineteenth century.

Papal governments tried to adopt two incompatible policies: defeating the new revolutionary movements, while maintaining the absolute neutrality of the Papal States. But isolation was ultimately impossible because papal independence could only be maintained if France and Austria were finely balanced, otherwise the Holy See was subject to the influence of the predominant power. Furthermore the popes proved unable to resist revolutionary movements within the Papal States without external support, while their temporal power was completely dependent on what was happening outside their territories. Between 1831 and 1870 the popes were only able to survive for a few years without the protection of foreign troops and their temporal power came to an end as soon as these were withdrawn. Of course, to have joined a system of political alliances might have involved the popes in foreign wars which were clearly incompatible with their religious position, but this dilemma was an inevitable consequence of the existence of the temporal power. In short, political absolutism, territorial integrity and political neutrality were mutually inconsistent aims.

The situation within the Papal States was made worse by the reactionary policies adopted after the Restoration when a clerical and absolutist regime was, sometimes ruthlessly, reimposed. Those officials who had collaborated too closely with the French were dismissed, while those involved in the arrest of the pope were sent to the galleys. Legal reforms of civil and criminal procedure were cancelled and secularised property restored to ecclesiastical owners. The re-establishment of feudal justice and the Inquisition, however restricted, and the return of the Jews to the ghetto simply seemed obscurantist and vindictive. Such factors as clerical monopoly of political life or lack of public control over finances, the failure to adopt contemporary constitutional and political, judicial and economic reforms gave the Papal States an unenviable reputation. The Roman authorities did make some incidental and isolated attempts at reform, however inadequate; there were improvements in consultation and administration, planning, servicing and taxation. But the concern of the papal government for matters spiritual, coupled with its failure to promote the material welfare of the pope's secular subjects, meant that it seemed increasingly irrelevant or inefficient when it was not positively harmful.

Discontent was widespread throughout the papal territories but especially in the north where *Sanfedisti* and 'Centurians' attempted to fight the political opposition which was developing in the lodges of secret societies. The *Cabonari*, or 'charcoal burners', who included many priests and religious, were nationalist revolutionaries opposed to the Austrian and papal governments, while members of the *Sanfedisti* organised themselves into a type of secret police who adopted the deplorable if common practice of using spies. At Ravenna in 1825 the Cardinal Legate, acting on information provided by the *Sanfedisti* and using emergency powers conferred on him by the pope, sentenced 7 men to death, 54 to forced labour, 6 to life imprisonment, 53 to imprisonment, 2 to exile and 286 to police supervision. An attempt to assassinate the Legate was followed by a number of arrests, summary trials and executions; the bodies were left hanging on the gallows as an example to others. Later reactions could be equally harsh. In 1843 a conspiracy to kidnap three important ecclesiastics, including the future Pius IX, and hold them as hostages was taken too seriously and resulted in 7 executions, the condemnation of more than 50 individuals to the galleys, and the imposition of martial law.

Popes and their officials felt committed by history, principle and prestige to the theocratic government of the Papal States. They refused or failed to see that geography, politics and the general climate of opinion would inevitably destroy this independent theocracy in the middle of the Italian peninsula. Political principles were being adopted which made any appeal to 'legitimate' or legal rights anachronistic and with which no theocracy, however enlightened, could come to terms. At the same time there was no necessary reason why a Church which had so often come into conflict with secular powers should support the principles of legitimacy or even less of absolutism. But the existence of the Papal States also influenced or even dominated many of the decisions and attitudes of the popes who made confused judgements about the ethics of political questions. Leo XII, Gregory XVI and Pius IX denounced democratic liberties precisely because the extension of such liberties to the Papal States was incompatible with theocratic government and it was thought impossible to distinguish the spiritual power of the pope from his temporal authority. Of course many other rulers also failed to solve the political and social problems of the time, but the popes governed religious as well as secular objects and they universally condemned movements in the world at large which seemed similar to those causing difficulties within their own dominions. Furthermore these practical considerations were inevitably reinforced by the ideological alliance between Throne and Altar as well as by the actual experience of revolution.

Thus the Church authorities supported 'legitimate' monarchs even when these were opposed to Catholic interests. Irish Catholics were ordered to submit episcopal nominations to the veto of their Protestant king. Belgian Catholics were expected to remain loyal to their Dutch Protestant ruler. Polish Catholics were ordered to obey the Orthodox Tsar who was persecuting them. In Spain and Portugal clergy and faithful tended to support the forces of absolutism against 'liberals' and 'freemasons' and both sides eagerly anticipated the prospect of power in order to take revenge on their opponents. Churchmen in South America usually allied themselves with the large landowners rather than with the new legislators who were not only 'enlightened' but frequently erastian. During the revolutions ecclesiastical property was confiscated, Catholics were divided, and ecclesiastical authorities only reluctantly accepted the new political situation or rejected the episcopal patronage, for example, which the colonial powers had formerly exercised. Meanwhile the identification of the Church in Italy with the forces of reaction alienated those Catholics who were familiar with Jansenist or Josephist traditions, reinforced anti-clericalism and widened divisions between Catholics and supporters of the Risorgimento.

When Lamennais, Lacordaire and Montalembert arrived in Rome in December 1831 the Austrians had already been asked to suppress a revolt against the pope in the Romagna. Gregory XVI (1831–46) did not need to be reminded – as he was by French, Austrian and Russian politicians as well as by ecclesiastics – of the need to support law and order, and of the danger of adding to the flames of revolution. The pope was faced with unenviable alternatives of seeming to undermine his own position by condemning Lamennais' Ultramontanism or of fomenting revolution if he gave his approval. And Gregory was well aware that the Revolution had despoiled the Church and secularised education, closed convents and monasteries, persecuted priests and nuns, abducted two of his predecessors and proclaimed the worship of the goddess of reason on the high altar of Notre Dame.

The three 'pilgrims' were first asked to explain their position in a memorandum, to be studied later, and were then informed that they could return home. There was a regular consultation on the issues in question, with written reports from a number of theologians. The original examiners were not particularly reactionary and included friends of Lamennais, Gioacchino Ventura as well as Cardinal Luigi Lambruschini. All of them concluded that the work of Lamennais did in fact include errors and the *consensus* of opinion what that the papal pronouncement should be along the lines actually followed in *Mirari vos*. This was the pope's first encyclical and much of it was taken up with the usual conventional material of introduction and exhortation. Lamennais himself as well as *L'Avenir* were neither mentioned nor named, but both were implicitly censured in passages which described freedom of publication as abominable or detestable and condemned universal liberty of conscience as sheer madness and the result of indifferentism; the pope also disapproved of the separation of Church and State.

Lamennais, Lacordaire and Montalembert immediately submitted but the three men were already drawing apart even before Lamennais made his final break with the Church. In 1833 Lamennais published *Paroles d'un Croyant*, a subversive and anarchic combina-

tion of prayer and polemic. Christ was seen to condemn pope and
ecclesiastical hierarchy 'because power is the child of hell and priests
are only the lackeys of kings'. Lacordaire publicly broke with
Lamennais and issued his own *Considérations* on Lamennais' philosophical system. It was later claimed that Lacordaire's criticisms
provoked the second papal condemnation which was said to reflect
his language. However the encyclical *Singulari nos* was once again
influenced by the representations of Austrian, Russian and Prussian
diplomats whose opinions carried far more weight with the Roman
authorities than the writings of Lacordaire.

But in spite of the loss of Lamennais, the Ultramontane and
Liberal Catholic movements previously associated with him continued to make progress. Antoine Frédéric Ozanam provided
Lacordaire with a pulpit from which he delivered the first of his great
conferences and in 1835 Lacordaire was appointed to the pulpit of
Notre Dame. In these sermons Lacordaire began with the fact of the
Church, its necessity, its constitution and authority, and its relations
with the temporal order. He argued in favour of ecclesiastical infallibility and papal primacy and his audiences responded to his elo-
quence, his sincere honesty and the appeal of his personality. The
conferences went from strength to strength in spite of, or perhaps
because of, the inevitable accusations of heresy, and Lacordaire's
sermons had a profound impact on the religious development of
thousands of young men at the time. But although this religious
revival in France was both genuine and real, there were limitations.
The revival was most evident among the upper and middle classes,
workers and peasants seemed hardly affected, while rationalists and
sceptics, anti-clericals and sinners had not disappeared. Furthermore
those who found themselves attracted by Liberal Catholicism were
not necessarily prepared to endure clerical or ecclesiastical obscur-
antism and it yet remained to be seen whether the Liberal and
Ultramontane Catholics would be able to remain united in the years
to come.

1848 was the 'Year of Revolutions' and with the success of revolutionary movements, Italian rulers, including the new Pope Pius IX
(1846–78), were forced to grant constitutions. Furthermore, when
Prince Metternich, the Austrian Chancellor, was compelled to fly
from Vienna, it seemed that the time had come to drive the Austrians
out of Italy. But those Catholics who, like Vincenzo Gioberti, felt
that the secular role of the papacy was compatible with a united Italy
were opposed by intransigents who simply identified and condemned liberal Catholics, heretics, freemasons and Jews. Liberal Catholics included Niccolo Tommaseo author of *Dell, Italia* (1835) and

Alessandro Manzoni, the novelist, but there were also spiritual descendants of Jansenists and Josephists who appreciated the need to reconcile the Church with contemporary developments as well as independent ecclesiastical reformers such as Antonio Rosmini, the author of *The Five Wounds of the Holy Church*. However the pope himself believed that he could not identify the Church with republican revolutionaries or risk the danger of schism in Austria and so he repudiated the movement in favour of Italian unity, the Risorgimento, and refused to declare war on Austria in the interests of Italian nationalism.

The defeat of the Italians by the Austrians at Custozza in 1848 was followed by the return of disillusioned troops to Rome where a revolution broke out following the assassination of Count Pellegrino L.A. Rossi, the moderate and pragmatic premier of the Papal States. The pope refused to accept democratic demands which would have effectively ended the Papal States and became a prisoner of the revolution before escaping into exile. Meanwhile republicans from all over Italy flocked into Rome where, in February 1849, the Assembly voted to end the temporal power of the pope and to establish a democratic Roman Republic. In contrast the revolution in France seemed to be positively favourable to the Church. The clergy were treated with great respect and Catholics were promised the complete freedom which they had been demanding, though many of them would probably have preferred a restoration of the Bourbons. But for the moment even the Ultramontane and conservative Louis Veuillot was prepared to condemn the divine right of kings as Gallican and claim that Catholic theology supported the divine right of peoples.

The point was that French Catholics were ill-equipped to deal with the emerging crises. From the beginning of the century they had needed to reconstruct the Church and deal with the political issues associated with relations between Church and State. At the beginning of the Second Republic these tasks had hardly begun when a third problem, the social problem, emerged dramatically from the background. The development of Social Catholicism was an attempt to deal with the massive problems created by industrialisation – urbanization, pauperism and the new stratification of classes. Social Catholics believed in the possibility and indeed the moral necessity of improving social conditions and Social Catholicism was a reaction against *laissez-faire*, the belief that government intervention would obstruct the automatic and beneficent operation of economic laws and free competition.

Right-wing conservatives and left-wing Catholics both played their part in the origin and development of Social Catholicism. Some legitimists, looking to the past for solutions to contemporary problems, argued from the conditions of the workers against modern regimes, whereas left-wing Catholics looked forward towards new democratic or even socialist orders. The Liberal Catholic Frédéric Ozanam founded the influential Society of St Vincent de Paul to care for the poor and for children, to train apprentices and domestic servants. Ozanam and Lacordaire also helped to establish the republican and democratic *Ere Nouvelle* which supported measures of social and economic reform and openly referred to a 'Christian economy' and 'Christian socialism'. In the 1840s the Bishop of Annecy denounced the abuses of capitalism and demanded legislation to defend the working classes. The Archbishop of Cambrai also issued a pastoral letter on the 'Law of Labour' which manifested a real awareness of social problems.

However the Social Catholics were not typical of Catholics as a whole or of the ecclesiastical authorities. Furthermore the revolution of 1848 was political rather than social. The revolution had made an already bad economic situation even worse and originally the government embarked on a series of public works to moderate increasing unemployment. This seemed to produce an army of men ready for another revolution and so the government cancelled the public works and conscripted men under twenty-five into the army. There followed three days of mob violence as a proletarian insurrection broke out in Paris. Archbishop Denis Auguste Affre of Paris attempted to mediate but was shot in the back by a stray bullet. The insurgents were unfairly held to be responsible and were ruthlessly suppressed. Conservatives throughout the country were horrified at the threat to property, law and order, and even many non-Catholics and anti-clericals looked to the Church as the institution which could best secure the obedience of the people. Most Catholics were willing to co-operate with the forces of law and order since they belonged to those sections of society – nobility, bourgeoisie and peasantry – which most feared the redistribution of wealth and knew least about the problems of industrialization.

When Louis-Napoleon stood for the presidency in 1848, there were two issues in particular which concerned most French Catholics – the freedom of education and the restoration of the pope to Rome. Napoleon promised satisfaction on both points and a French expeditionary force suppressed the Roman republic and restored the papal monarchy. With the establishment of the Second Empire in 1852 and Louis-Napoleon himself as Napoleon III, French Catholics in general identified with the forces of the right, or order and of authority. Meanwhile before returning to Rome in April 1850 the pope rejected any restrictions on his restored political authority and condemned the revolution as well as the idea that the Church might actually benefit from the loss of the temporal power. From then on Pius IX simply refused to distinguish between his spiritual and temporal power but used the former to defend the latter; the Papal States were the Patrimony of St Peter, the material means given by God to safeguard the spiritual independence of the pope.

Pio Nono himself was a pious and attractive man who, for example, industriously worked for the missionary expansion of the Church. However he was also concerned to save the temporal power, to preserve doctrinal 'orthodoxy' and to impose his own disciplinary authority. The pope and the Roman authorities were widely believed to favour 'everything that was old, from dress to opinions, from labels to theology'. Those Catholics who revealed their sympathies for new ideas usually found themselves condemned; Gioberti's writings and Rosmini's *Five Wounds* were put on the Index. At the same time the pope positively encouraged his own supporters like Carlo Maria Curci who founded *Civiltà Cattolica* which was to play an important part in the success of Ultramontanism. The Ultramontanes came to believe that there was an absolute dichotomy between Catholicism and the contemporary world while the pope himself 'took up the position that Christendom had apostatized. The appropriate action of Catholics was intense loyalty to the central power, unity among themselves and separation from the outside world'. This attitude was publicised by such laymen as Louis Veuillot in France, Juan Donoso Cortés in Spain and William George Ward in England.

Catholics throughout the world began to show an increasing sense of dependence on the Holy See and not simply in matters of faith and morals. They developed a strong personal loyalty to the Holy Father, seeking his guidance and direction in practically every area of human activity. New associations and publications supported the movement and in 1860 the pope himself helped to establish the *Osservatore Romano* in order that Catholics everywhere might be informed of his opinions, attitudes and intentions. The dramatic improvement in communications enabled the Roman authorities to exercise greater control over the Church than ever before and increased the number of bishops and pilgrims able to go to Rome as well as the number of priests and seminarians at Roman colleges. Support for Roman policies was encouraged by the appointment of nuncios, cardinals and bishops as well as the distribution of Roman honours such as 'monsignori'. Pius IX created more monsignors in thirty years than his predecessors had done in almost two thousand years and by the end of his pontificate in 1878 almost every bishop in the world had been appointed during his reign. Attempts were even made to redefine the authority of Uniate Patriarchs who, as early as 1837, were expected to ask the pope to confirm their elections and invest them with their palliums, and to ensure that their disciplinary decrees did not deviate from those approved in Rome. Catholicism was transformed within a generation as administration and discipline, devotion and theology were determined by the authorities in Rome.

The definition of the Immaculate Conception in 1854 exemplified the increasing influence of Ultramontanism. Gallicans had previously argued that only general councils could ratify definitions of ecclesiastical dogmas but the Pope alone defined the Immaculate Conception after 'consulting' bishops and theologians, while the only Council held during the nineteenth century defined papal infallibility. The suggestion that the bishops might join the pope in proclaiming the definition of the Immaculate Conception was rejected precisely on the grounds that if the pope alone pronounced a definition which the faithful spontaneously accepted, this would be a practical demonstration of his sovereign doctrinal authority in the Church and of that infallibility with which Christ had invested him.

In 1863 the Liberal Catholics organised an international congress at Malines where Montalembert delivered two addresses criticising those Catholics still devoted to the *ancien régime* and urging them to accept political and religious liberty. Deliberately, but tactlessly, he adopted the formula of Camillo Cavour, the Prime Minister of Sardinia/Piedmont, 'a free Church in a free State', 'which, though snatched from us and put into circulation by a very guilty man remains . . . the symbol of our convictions and our hopes'. Montalembert also quoted Bishop Felix Antoine Philibert Dupanloup: 'We accept, we invoke, the principles and the liberties proclaimed in '89 . . . You made the revolution of 1789 without us and against us, but *for us*, God wishing it so in spite of you'. The subsequent condemnation of Montalembert, which Dupanloup desperately tried to prevent, was courteous, confidential and friendly, but still a condemnation of the political aspirations of the Liberal Catholics.

In the same year another congress was held in Munich on the need for academic freedom, relations between science, history and theology, and the rights of ecclesiastical authorities. A Papal Brief to the Archbishop of Munich did not actually condemn Döllinger himself but implicitly condemned his attitude towards academic freedom by insisting that scholarly research should be conducted with full deference to the ecclesiastical authorities. Catholic thought was to be guided by the ordinary *magisterium* of the Church, the decisions of Roman congregations, including the Index, the teaching of theologians as well as the dogmatic definitions of the Church. The following year saw the publication of the *Syllabus of Errors* and the encyclical *Quanta Cura*, a deliberate act which had been planned over the last thirteen years.

The *Syllabus* was an index of some eighty errors, arranged in ten sections, referring to the relevant papal documents dealing with them. The condemnations of heretical ideas or threats to Church and Society were sometimes justified; it was not surprising that the pope denounced claims that biblical miracles were poetic fictions and Christ himself was a myth. But the *Syllabus* also denied that man was free to profess the religion he believed to be true guided by the light of reason, that those who were not at all in the true Church could hope for eternal salvation, that it was possible to achieve salvation in the practice of any religion, that Catholics might question the compatibility of the pope's temporal and spiritual authority, that the Church could not use force or temporal power, that Church should be separated from State, that it was no longer necessary to hold the Catholic religion as the exclusive religion of the State, that the pope could and should reconcile himself to and agree with progress, liberalism and modern civilization.

By 1864 Pio Nono was totally preoccupied with the Italian nationalist threat to the Papal States and the *Syllabus* was a *cri-de-coeur* against the anti-clerical and anti-papal religious and political policies of the government of Piedmont. The apparent condemnation of progress and liberalism, for example, was taken from an encyclical denouncing the extension of the secularist laws of Piedmont to territories recently occupied by the growing Kingdom of Italy. Unfortunately, however, not all Catholics were Italians and they failed to see the 'errors' in terms of the dissolution of monasteries or the imposition of secular education. Instead the condemnation of modern civilization seemed to them to refer to the telegraph, railways and street lighting!

It was Bishop Dupanloup who distinguished between the thesis and the hypothesis, between the ideal rule of the Church and the conditions of an imperfect world. The *Syllabus*, he argued, was not an outline of practical politics and Protestants or atheists, for example, were to be tolerated without being approved. The pope had no need to reconcile himself with what was good in modern civilization since he had never ceased to promote it! Montalembert described Dupanloup's pamphlet as a 'first-class verbal vanishing trick' but it was still welcomed by Catholics throughout the world with a profound sense of relief.

From 1864 until 1870 Catholics debated the dogmatic significance of the *Syllabus* and although it was not in fact an infallible statement, Ultramontanes still hoped to identify the necessity of the temporal power with dogmatic truth. However the ultimate point at issue was not relations between Church and State but the nature of the Church, and ecclesiological questions were to dominate the First Vatican Council. The doctrine of papal infallibility was already tacitly accepted by most theologians and had been defended by Dupanloup, for example, as his doctoral thesis in 1842. But the 'inopportunists' opposed the definition of papal infallibility since this would strengthen Ultramontanism within the Church, alienate secular governments and other Christian churches. The aspirations of the Ultramontanes were equally clear. On the feast of the Immaculate Conception 1866 the pope invited Catholic bishops to Rome to celebrate the eighteenth centenary of the martyrdoms of Saints Peter and Paul on 29 June 1867 when he announced his intention of calling a General Council which formally opened on the feast of the Immaculate Conception 1869.

Originally the *schema* on the Church only dealt with papal primacy, not infallibility, but opponents of the definition had been deliberately excluded from the deputation which received proposed amendments. The Fathers also debated papal jurisdiction as well as papal infallibility and declared that the pope possessed 'the full plenitude' of jurisdiction, whereas traditionally the authority and ordinary jurisdiction of bishops was said to come directly from God, not through the pope. This centralising act was the logical result of many Roman decisions during the nineteenth century which had overruled local bishops, sometimes as a result of provisions in concordats which had limited episcopal authority in return for direct agreements between pope and secular governments. The Fathers were then ordered by the pope, responding to appeals from the Ultramontanes, to consider forthwith 'the Question' of papal infallibility.

Just over one thousand churchmen were entitled to take part in the Council, but only 700 were present at the opening session and never more than 800 attended. Some eighty per cent of the Fathers were Italians and the deputations were almost entirely composed of supporters of the definition which was finally passed by 533 votes to 2, with about 80 bishops absenting themselves. Just over half the eligible membership actually voted in favour. However it is an indication of the triumph of Ultramontanism that none of the bishops refused to accept the definition once made and that the decisions of the approving Fathers undoubtedly reflected the opinions of the great majority of Catholics throughout the world.

The definition of papal infallibility coincided with the outbreak of the Franco-Prussian War in 1870. Napoleon III withdrew his troops from Rome, leaving the city at the mercy of the Italian forces. The Council, which had discussed only six out of 51 *schema*, was postponed, the Italians occupied Rome and the infallible pope became the prisoner of the Vatican. The internal life of the Church seemed unnaturally calm after the Council; the Church appeared to be committed to the obscurantist policies of Pius IX and failed to adopt any new or vigorous ones. The pope was able to rejoice in the enthusiasm and success of Ultramontanism, he enjoyed a personal popularity without parallel in the history of the modern papacy and was consoled by the missionary expansion of Catholicism. But he had shown little understanding of political realities, social and economic trends, and the intellectual developments of the age. Furthermore the proclamation of papal infallibility and the apparent weakness of the Church at the time coincided with several conflicts between the Church and secular governments.

Secularist and anti-clerical policies were widely adopted even in supposedly Catholic areas from Bavaria, Baden or Wurtemberg in south Germany to the new republics of Argentina, Chile, Colombia, Guatemala, Mexico and Venezuela in Latin America. In 1868 the Austrian government cancelled provisions in the Concordat of 1855 dealing with marriage and education, and when Bishop Franz Joseph Rudigier of Linz protested, he was arrested and imprisoned, though immediately pardoned by the emperor. In 1869 Catholic schools and junior seminaries were subjected to State control and in the following year the emperor protested against the definition of papal infallibility. He refused to allow the dogma to be proclaimed within his empire and declared the concordat null and void. In 1874 the government introduced further laws strengthening the authority of the State over the Church. The Austrian authorities also recognised the Kingdom of Italy and gave help to the schismatic Old Catholic movement which rejected papal infallibility and was also receiving substantial support from the German government.

Prussian victories over Austria in 1866 and over France in 1870 had brought about the unification of Germany and given a great impetus to German nationalism which was also associated with Protestantism. Furthermore many Catholics within Germany joined the Chancellor Bismarck's political opponents, while the Catholic powers of France and Austria were prominent among the external

enemies of Germany. Many European politicians were also suspicious of the 'Vatican Decrees' and Bismarck therefore used the
pretext of the Council to justify his attack on the Church, an attack
known as the *Kulturkampf*. The Catholic department in the Prussian
Ministry of Religion was abolished on the grounds that it had
interfered in Polish affairs. Bismarck then gave legal support to the
'Old Catholics' who refused to accept papal infallibility and threatened any cleric who criticised the new Germany or its constitution
with heavy fines or imprisonment. After the breakdown of diplomatic relations between Berlin and the Vatican, a press campaign in
Germany united Protestants, Liberals and Socialists in a concerted
attack on Catholicism.

In February 1872 Adalbert Falk attempted to subject education to
the direct control of the State and religious congregations were
forbidden to teach or to give religious instruction. In July the Jesuits
and other 'affiliated' bodies such as Lazarists and Redemptorists
were expelled from the country. The state then assumed control over
the education, administration and appointment of the clergy;
seminaries could be closed by government inspectors. Episcopal
appointments had to be submitted to the civil authorities who could
veto them and only Germans could hold positions of ecclesiastical
authority within Germany. The civil courts had the final say in all
appeals from church courts or from the German bishops. The
bishops were also expected to take an oath of unconditional
obedience, ecclesiastical property was handed over to lay
committees, civil marriage was introduced and Church schools
closed. In May 1875 all orders and congregations, except nursing
orders, were expelled from Prussia and in the following month the
provisions safeguarding the position of the Church were removed
from the Prussian constitution.

However the German bishops, priests and people simply ignored
the legislation. Bishops and priests were fined, imprisoned, deposed
and exiled. During 1874 and 1875 five of the eleven Prussian bishops
spent several months in prison, and six bishops dismissed from office
went into exile. Seminaries were closed, sees and parishes remained
vacant as Catholics, deprived of the sacraments, refused to submit.
As a final indignity the few Old Catholics were given priority in the
use of churches and the government established a bishopric for them.
In response liberal and conservative Catholics, French Catholics,
Germans and Poles united under the political leadership of Ludwig
Windthorst in supporting the Centre Party. And through that party,
German Catholics – unlike their French or Italian co-religionists –
were able to play a significant and constructive part in the growth of

parliamentary democracy.

The Centre Party almost doubled its representation in the Prussian Diet and the German Reichstag in spite of the persecution and in time Bismarck came to need the political support of Catholic deputies. In 1878 the new Pope Leo XIII (1878–1903) began a friendly correspondence with the Emperor William I and Bismarck opened negotiations with the Belgian nuncio in Bavaria. Falk resigned in 1879 and two years later Germany re-established diplomatic relations with the Holy See. The process of moderating the anti-Catholic legislation began in 1880 and continued over the next few years. In 1885 Bismarck asked the pope to mediate between Germany and Spain in a dispute over the Caroline Islands and Leo awarded the chancellor the Order of Christ. By 1887 the pope was able to claim that the *Kulturkampf* had been brought to an end.

It is sometimes said that Leo XIII adopted pragmatic policies in his dealings with the contemporary world and that the success of his policies can be seen in the defeat of Bismarck's *Kulturkampf* and the Swiss *Kulturkampf*, in the restoration of diplomatic relations with Brazil, Colombia and Russia, and the withdrawal of anti-clerical legislation in Chile, Mexico and Spain. Several governments invited the pope to arbitrate in their disputes and important Heads of State visited him in the Vatican. However Leo's vision of the papacy was also that of the leader of a reunited Christian world in the City of St Peter. The reunion of separated Christians – Orthodox and Protestant – was one of his main objectives and the subject of several encyclicals and addresses. His efforts were supported by other Catholics, such as Vladimir Soloviev and Etienne Fernard Portal, and promoted by institutions, periodicals and congresses several of which he himself had established or supported.

Meanwhile the Roman question and the issue of the temporal power bedevilled relations between the Vatican and the Kingdom of Italy. After 1870 the papacy, at least in theory, felt at the mercy of the Italian government and open to the charge that it had lost its moral independence. The Holy See therefore refused to recognise the new Italy in case other governments claimed that the pope was subject to Italian influences and so ignored him when dealing with the Church within their own countries. Leo's unwillingness to come to terms with Italian nationalism was probably the greatest failure of his pontificate and contributed to the growing strength of anti-clericalism and anti-Catholicism within Italy. In an effort to undermine the new State, the ecclesiastical authorities had refused to allow Catholics to take part in the political life of the nation. But this policy of *non possumus* simply divided Catholics and hindered the develop-

ment of Social Catholicism, strengthened the forces of the left and
identified the Church with those of the right.

Italian governments at the time were able to enact hostile legislation, give support to Protestants and schismatics, and refuse to
confirm the appointment of bishops. Ecclesiastical property was
confiscated, convents and colleges expropriated, and religious communities dispersed. After the election in 1876 the left-wing anti-
clericals abolished the catechism from primary schools, banned
religious processions, suppressed religious orders, conscripted
priests into the army, dissolved Catholic congresses and threatened
to punish priests who dared 'to make a public attack on State
institutions or governmental decisions'. The secularist laws of Piedmont on education and marriage were later extended throughout
Italy.

The pope's ambiguities or ambivalences were also evident in his
attitude towards scholarship. Leo XIII was well aware of the need for
an intellectual revival within Catholicism. He approved of the establishment of pontifical universities in Europe and America, and provided the Vatican Observatory with modern instruments. In the
encyclical *Aeterni patris*, he instructed seminary teachers to use
Thomism as the basis of clerical education, but although this was an
improvement on previous philosophical eclecticism, the methods
and motives of some supporters of Thomism must be suspected. Leo
was much more open in his attitude towards history and opened the
Vatican archives to competent students; 'one of the most liberal acts
in an illiberal century'. His encyclical on biblical studies, on the other
hand, was more restricted. *Providentissimus Deus* encouraged
modern biblical methodology, but its definition of inspiration
seemed unnecessarily narrow. Leo also appointed a biblical commission of comparatively liberal members but such a commission was
both unsuitable and incapable of acting as a sort of supreme tribunal
to preserve the faith and decide disputed questions, to promote
scholarship and guide scholars.

Leo XIII was much less ambiguous in approaching social and
economic problems. He had been nuncio in Belgium where Social
Catholicism was more influential than in other countries and where
Catholic Governments had supported legislation regulating wages
and the working conditions of women and children, introduced
old-age pensions, promoted technical education, subsidised mutual
aid societies, savings banks and building societies. Leo had also
experienced agricultural poverty as a bishop in Italy – where Social
Catholics included Bishop Geremia Bonomelli of Cremona, the
author of a famous pastoral on 'Property and Socialism', Alessandro

Rossi, who transformed his factory into a Christian corporation, and Giuseppe Toniolo, descendant of Joseph de Maistre and professor of political economy.

Leon Harmel encouraged his workers to share in an industrial partnership and transformed the community into a model Christian town. He wanted to establish a Catholic industrial democracy in practice and a pattern of social relations which could be adopted anywhere. Every worker had his own house and garden, there were family allowances, free medical services and assistance for the elderly, and elected representatives met every fortnight to consider every aspect of the business. Harmel tried to persuade other employers to follow his example and took a group of industrialists to Rome to win the support of the pope who was obviously impressed; this was followed by larger pilgrimages of workers and employers. The Fribourg Union, a group of Social Catholics whose deliberations were sent to the pope, also influenced Leo XIII. They proposed international agreements which included the recognition of a man's right to work and a worker's right to a living wage as well as the insurance of workers against sickness, accident or unemployment. In 1888 the pope discussed their proposals with some of the members and asked for a memorandum which seems to have served as the basis for his own encyclical *Rerum novarum*, published in 1891.

The pope strongly condemned unrestricted capitalism, individualistic liberalism and revolutionary socialism. Private property was the right of all men and the family, not the State, the primary social unit. The pope approved of government intervention to safeguard the spiritual and material interests of the workers who should be paid a family living wage, not a wage dictated by economic pressures. Workers had the right to form associations and Catholics were encouraged to form Catholic unions and organisations. *Rerum Novarum* was a condemnation of extremes, recommending reform rather than radical change, but at the same time it was a landmark and a watershed in the history of Social Catholicism.

On the other hand Leo's limitations in his approach to the contemporary world were revealed in his attitudes towards the Church in the United States. Bishop John Carroll's original attempt to unite rural Anglo-American Catholics in support of the liberal principles of democratic republicanism had been superseded by waves of immigrants who transformed American Catholics into a largely urban and 'foreign' community. In 1844 Isaac Thomas Hecker was received into the Church and became a Redemptorist. Dissatisfied with the Order's failure to adapt to the American way of life, he established the Society of Missionary Priests of St Paul the Apostle or the Paulists. Hecker's intention of Americanizing Catholicism and attracting Protestants was not successful at the time but it did coincide with and influence a third and perhaps the most significant attempt to solve the dilemma of being an American Catholic.

'Americanism' was a Liberal Catholic reform movement which helped to fill the void left by the decline of European liberal catholicism. America became the religious and Catholic as well as the political hope of the future; the Church would find one of its finest historical expressions in the United States. The Americanists advocated separation of Church and State, the recognition of common law, the introduction of democratic procedures and contemporary reforms into ecclesiastical administration. The controversy over Americanism inevitably involved issues already dividing liberal and conservative bishops, and rival ethnic minorities. For example the more conservative American bishops supported their liberal colleagues in opposing German Catholics appealing for ecclesiastical independence and autonomy, and the Roman authorities came out on the side of the American hierarchy. However the more positive policies of the liberal bishops, which involved adapting Catholicism to American society, were opposed by more conservative members of the hierarchy, non-German and German alike. German Catholics, influenced by the *Kulturkampf* at home, claimed that immigrants were losing the faith because of the lack of Catholic organisations for the working classes and Catholic parochial schools, whereas the liberal bishops defended the right of Catholics to belong to the Knights of Labour and supported the public schools.

Several Catholics reached prominent positions within the Knights of Labour, an organisation which defended the rights and supported the claims of the workers. Other Catholics, including some bishops, condemned it as a secret society. Bishop John J. Keane and Archbishop John Ireland wrote a defence, submitted to Rome by Cardinal James Gibbons, which emphasised the need for the Church to be allied with the people rather than with kings or princes, and in 1888 the Holy Office decided that the Knights could be 'tolerated'. The issue of education had already been raised in 1884 when the third plenary Council of Baltimore decreed that each parish should establish its own Catholic school. This policy was supported by Archbishop Michael Corrigan of New York and Bishop Bernard McQuaid of Rochester, by the Jesuits, and by the German and Irish clergy. Liberal Catholics argued that the financial and educational costs were too great and concentrated on safeguarding the religious education of Catholic children attending the public schools. In 1892 the Congregation of Propaganda supported the legislation adopted at Baltimore, while 'tolerating' the situation which existed in Ireland's diocese.

The Americanists also tried to improve relations between Catholics and other religions. At the World Parliament of Religions, held in Chicago in 1892, Cardinal Gibbons participated with the Chief Moderator of the Presbyterian Church in an exhibition illustrating the basic unity of man's religious belief shared by all the great religions of the world. However Leo XIII condemned moves to hold a similar Parliament at the Paris Exhibition of 1900 and one of those supporting the idea, who became an anti-clerical Protestant, described 'Americanism' as a sort of neo-Protestantism. This accusation reinforced the suspicions of those conservative Catholics in Europe and America who were beginning to ask whether the policies of the liberal American bishops should not be identified with the liberalism condemned in the *Syllabus of Errors*. As a result of the various tensions within the American Church, the Roman authorities decided to appoint an apostolic delegate, a move long resisted by bishops sensitive to accusations of foreign domination. Furthermore the attitudes of Archbishop Francis Satolli, like the attitudes increasingly adopted by Roman officials, were more in line with those of the conservative bishops in the United States.

In the encyclical *Longinqua Oceani* Leo praised the American Church but criticised secret societies and warned against the notion that separation of Church and State might be suitable for the rest of the world. Denis J. O'Connell, agent of the American bishops in Rome, was then asked to resign as Rector of the American College largely because his support for the liberal bishops had alienated their conservative colleagues as well as Jesuits, German Catholics and conservative officials in Rome. Gibbons retaliated by appointing O'Connell as vicar of his titular Church. Satolli came out strongly in favour of the German Catholics and successfully asked the pope to condemn the Parliaments of Religion. Keane was asked by the pope to resign as Rector of the Catholic University as he and his colleagues were increasingly and vocally accused of liberalism, disloyalty and heresy.

The liberal bishops responded by trying to broaden the basis of their support and expounding their policies both in Europe and America. In 1891 the publication of Walter Elliott's *Life of Father Hecker* aroused little attention and no controversy. However the Abbé Félix Klein of the Institut Catholique was asked to adapt a translation to the situation in France and in 1898 he described Hecker as the ideal new priest who could reconcile the Church with contemporary developments. Hecker's spirituality was in conformity with modern trends towards independence and freedom, and was based on the interior direction of the Holy Spirit responding to the active virtues of the new saints of the market place, rather than the more passive virtues of monks and hermits. Klein's remarks immediately occasioned a controversy over Hecker's alleged 'Americanism'.

O'Connell himself had taken up the theme of 'Americanism' in an address on Hecker in which he had advocated 'political American-ism' based on the Declaration of Independence and the Anglo-Saxon tradition of common law. He also recommended 'ecclesiastical Americanism' and using Dupanloup's 'thesis' and 'hypothesis' defended the separation of Church and State. Charles Maignen, a French monarchist opposed to Leo's attempt to 'rally' French Cath-olics to the republic, immediately associated O'Connell's address with Montalembert's famous speech at Malines and claimed that 'Americanism' had been condemned in the *Syllabus of Errors*.

The encyclical *Testem Benevolentiae* in 1899 distinguished between religious and political Americanism and condemned the notion of adapting the doctrines, though not the practices, of the Church to the needs of modern society. The extent of individual liberty was strictly defined and the claim that external spiritual guidance had been superseded by more abundant graces of the Spirit was also condemned. Leo criticised those Catholics who claimed to prefer 'active' to 'passive' virtues and who emphasised natural virtues and an active external life at the expense of supernatural virtues and an internal life; such a way of life, the pope maintained, would lead to secularism and indifferentism.

Some of the conservative American bishops thanked the pope for saving their people from heresy, whereas the liberal bishops accepted the encyclical while denying that they or indeed any educated American had ever advocated the doctrines condemned. The pope himself never stated that any particular individual held the condem-ned doctrines and made it clear that the condemnation was not intended to refer to the characteristic qualities of the American people. Leo is also said to have admitted that the controversy had been necessary to clarify French rather than American Catholic opinion.

After the fall of Napoleon III in 1871 France once again became a republic but a republic dominated by conservatives; monarchist deputies, most of whom were Catholics, greatly outnumbered the genuine republicans who tended to be sceptical free thinkers. How-ever in Paris the authority of the government was challenged by a revolutionary Commune which was dominated by the lower middle classes who were largely hostile to both Church and monarchy. The conflict was bitter and extensive and both sides were guilty of atrocities. The *communards* responded to government executions by shooting 74 hostages, including 24 priests and Archbishop Georges Darboy of Paris, who was wearing the cross of Archbishop Affre who had died at the barricades in 1848 and the ring of Archbishop Sibour who had been murdered in 1857.

After the suppression of the Commune there was a superficial religious revival in France and the basilica of the Sacred Heart was built on Montmartre in atonement for the sins of the nation. The government passed legislation favourable to the Church which in turn identified itself with the forces of reaction. However it proved impossible to restore the monarchy, partly because of the existence of rival candidates and Catholic divisions, and the fact of the Third Republic was slowly but inevitably established. In 1876 genuine republicans gained a clear majority in the Chamber of Deputies and in the following year the pope appealed to Catholics throughout the world to press their governments to secure his independence as Head of the Church. Left-wing forces seized this opportunity to attack the Church and Léon Gambetta, leader of the Radical party and briefly French premier, concluded with his famous denunciation of clericalism. In 1879 the republicans won control of the senate and the Catholic president resigned. The new government withdrew privileges granted to the Church by excluding churchmen from councils supervising schools, restricting the right to confer degrees to public institutions and depriving non-authorized religious congregations of the right to teach. By 1887 the republicans had laicized education, re-introduced divorce, removed religion from civil ceremonies, allowed for secular funerals, restricted religious processions, permitted work on Sundays, abolished hospital and military chaplains, extended conscription to seminarians and reduced clerical stipends.

Leo XIII wished to unite French Catholics in defence of their rights by first accepting the fact of the Republic. In November 1890 Cardinal Charles-Martial Allemand Lavigerie gave a speech to government officials in Algiers in which he called on his fellow Catholics to 'rally' to the Republic and provoked a storm of protest from Catholic royalists. The immediate effect of the 'ralliement' simply divided French Catholics further and encouraged some to adopt even more extreme positions. Consequently as a political manoeuvre the 'ralliement' failed; only thirty of its supporters and none of its leaders were elected to the Chamber of Deputies in 1893 and only 76 in 1897. However the pope's desire that French Catholics accept the Republic coupled with his encouragement of Social Catholicism and an intellectual revival helped to foster a new spirit within the French Church. Furthermore the real success of the 'ralliement' came during the First World War when French Catholics died in defence of the Republic and came to play their part in the political life of the nation. Meanwhile one of the crucial reasons for the initial failure was the infamous **Dreyfus affair** which starkly revealed the extent to which so many French Catholics were identified with the anti-semitic forces of the right and thoroughly discredited the Assumptionists in particular.

The government retaliated by passing the Law of Associations which required religious orders to be authorized by the civil authorities. Assumptionists, Jesuits and Carmelites dispersed or went into exile and handed over their schools to the secular clergy. Contemplative, medical and missionary orders were allowed to continue. But Justin Louis-Émile Combes also intended to destroy Church schools, and in 1904 authorized congregations were ordered to close their schools and to abandon all teachings within the next ten years. Combes himself boasted that he had closed well over a half of the Catholic schools in France and a third of the schools run by religious congregations were shut down.

The possibility of abrogating the Concordat and separating Church and State was first raised when the pope refused to accept unsuitable candidates for the episcopacy nominated by Combes. The new Pope Pius X (1903–14) and his Secretary of State, Raphael Merry del Val, proved to be more intransigent than Leo XIII and when, in April 1904, President Émile Loubet defied Catholic protocol by paying a state visit to King Victor Emmanuel in Rome, Merry del Val issued a provocative protest which offended public opinion throughout France. However the formal break took place when Merry del Val demanded the resignation of two bishops who were the subjects of scandalous gossip among conservative Catholics in their dioceses and who were suspected of disclosing ecclesiastical secrets to the civil authorities. In 1905 the French government annulled the Concordat and then decided to separate Church and State. These moves were condemned by the pope in his encyclical *Vehementer* published in 1906. Furthermore as a result of the refusal of the Roman authorities to compromise, the government confiscated most of the wealth and property of the French Church.

If Leo XIII helped to create the modern papacy by improving its international prestige, Pius X became one of the founders of the modern papacy through his internal reforms of the Church and sense of pastoral concern. However Pius' reforms were restricted to the institutional Church itself, for he did not share Leo's interest in

Social Catholicism or the intellectual revival of Catholicism. Pius X prepared for the liturgical revival by promoting frequent communion, reforming the breviary and restoring Gregorian chant. He encouraged Catholic Action and the lay apostolate. He brought about improvements in clerical formation and urged priests to be obedient, assiduous in prayer and devoted to good reading, especially reading the Bible. He also tried to enhance the authority of the Holy See and tighten ecclesiastical discipline by reforming papal administration, the curia, and controlling bishops throughout the world. The reformed code of canon law, for example, emphasised the position of the Roman authorities in the choice and supervision of bishops. Furthermore Pius X checked the least move towards disobedience or doctrinal error. He therefore condemned the 'Modernists' and at least tolerated the activities of conservative and integrist Catholics.

The only common attitudes adopted by the so-called Modernists seem to have been an undue confidence in contemporary developments and a rejection of that unconditional obedience which the Roman authorities had come to expect. Some of the Modernists were concerned with the implications of biblical or historical criticism and these included the devout Baron Friedrich von Hügel, the great link between many Modernists, as well as Alfred Loisy who eventually rejected the sacred character of the Bible and the unique, eternal truthfulness of biblical revelation. The speculative theologians involved included opponents of scholasticism as well as George Tyrrell and Ernesto Buoniauti who interpreted ecclesiastical tradition as the collective spiritual experience of Christianity rather than cold dogmatic formulas or legal definitions and who believed that Christianity must adapt to contemporary realities. Political Modernists rejected political and social conservatism in attempting to reconcile Catholicism with democracy and socialism. Romolo Murri, one of the founders of Christian Democracy, had actually welcomed the election of Pius X, approved of the condemnation of Loisy and was scholastically orthodox, but was still excommunicated as Modernists. Critics of the institutional Church included Antonio Fogazzaro, Albert Ehrhard and Hermann Schell who advocated ecclesiastical reform, the election of bishops, the abolition of compulsory celibacy and improvements in clerical education.

Some Modernists were unduly influenced by evolutionary, immanentist or pragmatic fashions of thought and adopted ideas which it would be difficult, if not impossible, to reconcile with historic Christianity. Emphasis on the Divine Immanence, for example, the omnipresence of God in the World, without the parallel doctrine of Divine transcendence, is practically indistinguishable from pantheism. Some were guilty of historical scepticism or at least biblical or historical positivism and a scientific or historical approach which excluded the supernatural. Some appeared to advocate historical or theological relativism, to over-emphasise critical rationalism or accept a philosophical immanentism which rejected the metaphysical and the transcendent, and in its extreme form reduce religion to ethical considerations. But the point was that the ecclesiastical authorities became so concerned about some of the conclusions of the Modernists and the subsequent controversies that they failed to recognise the seriousness of the very real problems with which the Modernists were attempting to deal. The Roman authorities were particularly incompetent in their dealings with the personalities and issues involved; their training and traditions had left them almost incapable of dealing with Modernism.

Both the papal encyclical *Pascendi* and the Decree of the Holy Office concerning Modernism, *Lamentabili*, were published in 1907 and can be seen in the tradition of such documents as *Mirare vos* and *Quanta cura*; *Lamentabili* was modelled on the *Syllabus* though restricted to the understanding of dogma and biblical interpretation, listing Modernist errors in sixty-five theses mostly taken from Loisy. However many of them were taken out of context and sometimes sentences were added to reinforce the original sense, to point to the logical conclusion or even to take it to extremes. Some of the condemnations seemed to imply that Catholics must reject even moderately conservative biblical criticism. *Pascendi* attempted to describe the typical Modernist as apologist and reformer, theologian and philosopher, historian and scripture scholar. The 'doctrines' and 'heresies' of the Modernists were synthesised and their theology, philosophy and historiography were found to contradict the doctrines of the Church and to lead to agnosticism and phenomenalism, immanentism and symbolism and so to pantheism or atheism. In this sense, *Pascendi* gave form to a heresy which as outlined did not exist and assembled as a whole what no single individual had ever held.

The curia apparently believed that there was a widespread Modernist conspiracy attempting to destroy the faith of the Church, and bishops were ordered to supervise teachers in seminaries and universities and to examine the beliefs of their clergy. The anti-Modernist oath was imposed on professors, pastoral priests and candidates for ordination. Conservative scholars were appointed to the Biblical Commission which refused to allow Catholics to question the Mosaic authorship of the Pentateuch or the unity of Isaiah, the priority of Matthew or the Pauline authorship of Hebrews. Furthermore devout and loyal Catholics in several countries were forced to endure an integrist witch hunt which was at least tolerated by the highest Roman authorities including the pope and the Secretary of State. Monsignor Umberto Benigni established a secret society, the *Sodalitium Pianum*, in the fight against Modernism. Members used codes and aliases – the pope was 'Lady Micheline' or 'Michel' and Merry del Val 'Miss Romey' or 'George' – as they passed information and established contacts, with local agencies and publications.

The integrists poured out a stream of personal attacks and calumnies which divided Catholics and provided ammunition for their enemies. Respectable journals of theology were forced to cease publication and even unjustified accusations of Modernism left innocent men under suspicion, barring them from higher office or restricting their teaching careers. Those who tried to defend themselves were usually ignored by the authorities and when the integrists themselves came under attack, they accused the Church authorities of weakening under the attacks of their enemies. The integrists denounced practically all the leading Catholic scholars of the day and almost all the prominent workers in social and political reform including the future Pope John XXIII for an article which he wrote in 1911.

In September 1914 Pope Benedict XV (1914–22) found an unopened letter to his predecessor in the papal office. It was a denunciation of himself as a Modernist by an extremely conservative Italian bishop and Benedict immediately dispensed with Benigni's services. Merry del Val was replaced by Cardinal Domenico Ferrata who had also been denounced by the integrists. The responsibilities of the Congregation of the Index were transferred to the Holy Office and a new Congregation of Seminaries and Universities under Cardinal Désiré Mercier became more positive in its approach to education and research. Benedict also condemned the activities of the integrists in his first encyclical *Ad Beatissimi*, although this was chiefly concerned with the oubreak of war. If the pontificate of Pius X had seemed to show that the Catholic Church had rejected the theological and biblical scholarship, the social, economic and political developments, the institutional and ecclesiastical reforms advocated during the nineteenth century, the pontificate of Benedict XV dramatically illustrated that Catholicism was not permanently committed to such a reaction and the new pope himself would show that the Church was not totally unprepared to meet the problems and the challenges of the new age.

CHAPTER 7

The Church and the modern world, 1914–1978

Two days after his coronation in 1914 Pope Benedict XV publicly declared that he intended to intervene in every possible way in an effort to bring hostilities in the First World War to an end. But his intentions at the time were misinterpreted and misunderstood by combatants dominated by the passions of militarism and nationalism, and he was denounced by opposing sides as Maledetto XV, the 'Boche pope' and the *Franzosenpapst*. Benedict was also determined to help the victims of war, the wounded, the imprisoned and the deported at whatever cost to himself or to the Church. He spent his own personal fortune as well as the ordinary revenue of the Holy See, and it is estimated that the Vatican spent about 82 million gold lire to relieve the sufferings caused by the war. In collaboration with the International Red Cross, the Vatican became a clearing-house for tracing missing persons, exchanging prisoners and re-establishing family contacts, caring for sick and wounded or even occasionally returning the remains of those killed in action. He was also successful in securing the mitigation of death sentences and the releases of hostages. Although the pope condemned the confiscation of ecclesiastical buildings for military use, he willingly allowed the civil authorities to use Catholic hospitals, colleges and seminaries to assist the afflicted.

Benedict felt 'supremely bound in conscience to counsel, suggest, inculcate nothing else but peace' and to support the cause of mankind rather than men. He described the recourse to arms as 'the darkest tragedy of human hatred and human madness' and referred to the 'suicide of civilized Europe'. He also took practical steps to promote peace negotiations especially in his famous letter to 'the leaders of the belligerent peoples' published on 1 August 1917. This proposed the restoration of the rule of law, suspension of fighting, simultaneous and reciprocal reduction of armaments, and the estab-lishment of international arbitration. At the same time occupied territories were to be restored, and the remaining territorial disputes settled according to the aspirations of the peoples concerned and the general welfare of mankind. The free movement of peoples and common rights over the seas must also be recognised, and demands for reparations or indemnities should be renounced. But the reac-tions of the various governments were cautious, evasive or bluntly hostile and the papal proposals were quickly superseded by events.

But in spite of widespread opposition to the pope's work for peace, his efforts on behalf of the victims of war did much to enhance the international prestige of the papacy; and by the time of his death in 1922 twenty-five states, including almost every major country, had established regular diplomatic representation at the Holy See. In 1870 there had been only 15 papal representatives throughout the world but by 1939 there were 38 nunciatures and 23 apostolic delegations. Although the Holy See was not a member of the League of Nations, Benedict originally gave the organisation his approval and blessing. However his own demands for international co-operation and security went much further. In any case the American government refused to join the League which was associated with the unjust provisions of the Treaty of Versailles and, by the begin-ning of the 1920s, the provisions of the peace settlement were already being challenged. Consequently in May 1920 the pope warned,

> if in most places peace of some sort is established and treaties signed, the germs of former enmities remain; and you well know . . . there can be no stable peace or lasting treaties . . . unless there be a return of mutual charity to appease hate and banish enmity.

Two years later Benedict's successor deplored 'the spirit of bitterness and vengeance' which had been 'increased and almost given official status' by 'an artificial peace established on paper'.

The charitable work of the Holy See had continued after the war as acute social and economic problems of unemployment, famine and disease spread, especially in central Europe and the Far East, and one of Benedict's last acts was an urgent appeal for the relief of famine in Communist Russia. Theoretically the Russian Revolution had put the Catholic Church in the same legal position as the Orthodox Church and so initially this seemed to allow for possibilities of evangelisation. Consequently Benedict XV and Pius XI (1922–39) encouraged the training of suitable missionaries. The Communist authorities and the Holy See were both interested in establishing diplomatic relations; the former as a means of securing international recognition and the latter in the interests of its missionary activities. The end of the Russian civil war coincided with a failure of the harvest and widespread famine, and the pope immediately offered to send a relief mission with food and clothing. This mission was eventually accepted but its members were not allowed to engage in apostolic activities. For six months thousands of people were fed daily but as conditions improved the Communist authorities became increasingly difficult to deal with and the mission was forced to leave. The Vatican still tried to come to terms with Moscow in spite of the fact that the Communists continuously increased their demands until attempts at reconciliation were superseded by Pius XI's accommodation in 1929 with Benito Mussolini, the Fascist Prime Minister and Dictator of Italy, and Joseph Stalin's tightening control over a Russia increasingly recognised by the international community.

Nevertheless Benedict XV successfully initiated a radical reorganisation of missionary activities which was vigorously promoted later by Pius XI. *Maximum illud*, published in 1919, was an eloquent and authoritative plea for the creation of an indigenous clergy and the establishment of native hierarchies. The pope outlined a new programme which marked a turning point in the history of the Church as he demanded that Catholic missionaries renounce the spirit of nationalism and recognise the value and significance of native cultures. Benedict also established the Missionary Union of the Clergy and reorganised the societies for Propagation of the Faith and for Native Clergy. Pius XI urged bishops and religious orders to increase their missionary activities, he opened a new College of Propaganda and established a new Missionary Institute. But most significant of all he supported the autonomy of missionary churches by consecrating native bishops; in 1923 he appointed the first non-European bishop of the Latin rite in India and instituted a native hierarchy for the Malabar Uniates. When Pius XI died in 1939 forty-eight missionary territories were in the charge of native bishops. At the same time the number of bishops or vicars apostolic in the Americas was slightly less than the number of European bishops who numbered just over one-third of the Catholic bishops throughout the world. The Roman authorities also seemed more willing than ever before to leave decisions about local customs and adaptations to the local churches themselves.

Missionary experiences, revolution in communications and totalitarian persecutions were some of the factors influencing the early development of the ecumenical movement. It was originally led by

Protestants, but Catholic authorities were more concerned about the difficulties of the Orthodox Church in the East than 'reunion' with the heretics and schismatics of the West. The collapse of the Turkish Empire, the Russian Revolution and the rise of Arab nationalism seemed to threaten the future of the Orthodox Churches. However Catholic concern, though genuine, was apologetic rather than ecumenical. Benedict himself concentrated on attempting to safeguard the position of Uniates within the Church by providing them with established institutions within the Roman curia and an official place within the constitutional framework of Roman Catholicism. The Church of Jesus Christ, he proclaimed, 'is neither Latin nor Greek nor Slav but Catholic'. Unfortunately it cannot be said that the later history of the Congregation of the Eastern Church always succeeded in putting this high ideal into practice.

Earlier popes had approved of the Week of Prayer for Christian Unity and in 1916 Benedict ordered that a novena of prayers should be recited throughout the Church for the reunion of Christendom. But invitations to take part in early ecumenical meetings were courteously declined and the Holy Office reminded Catholics that they were forbidden to take part in organisations promoting Christian unity. In 1928 Pius XI published *Mortalium Animos* in which the ecumenical movement, as it then existed, was associated with theological relativism and indifferentism in ecclesiology, and seemed to imply that the Catholic Church was not in fact the true Church of God. The encyclical condemned the attempt to establish a 'Pan-Christianity' without basic agreement in faith: 'the unity of Christians can come about only by furthering the return to the one true Church of Christ of those who are separated from it'.

The development of Catholic ecumenism increasingly came to depend on such ecumenical theologians as Paul Courturier, Yves Congar and Max Josef Metzger. Several unofficial Catholic observers had been allowed to attend ecumenical meetings in Lausanne, Oxford and Edinburgh, while Metzger himself established the Society of Christ the King and the Una Sancta movement to promote Christian unity. However his ecumenism and pacifism attracted the attention of the Nazis who arrested him several times and finally executed him as a traitor in 1944. The eventual fate of Metzger illustrates how the major issues with which the Church had to deal were changing after the death of Benedict and the election of Pius XI. The Italian Government had fallen on the opening day of the conclave and from the beginning of his reign Pius XI was determined to improve relations with Italy. He therefore broke with the precedent of his immediate predecessors by giving his first blessing as pope from the outer portico of St. Peter's.

Following the loss of the Papal States and the end of the temporal power the Church authorities had prevented Italian Catholics from taking part in the political life of the nation. However during the First World War Italian Catholics had proved their loyalty, a factor which had moderated the suspicions of 'liberal' anti-clericals, and in December 1918 Don Luigi Sturzo had been given permission to establish the Italian Popular Party independent of the Church. Twelve months later Benedict lifted the *non expedit* and the Party won over a hundred seats in the new Parliament. But the nation was weak and divided, crippled by strikes and conflicts, and threatened either by Communism or by Fascism which seemed to many to be the lesser of the two evils.

Church authorities had been critical of Fascist attacks on Catholicism and in 1922 *Civiltà Cattolica* accused Fascism of imitating and even surpassing 'the violent spirit' of Socialism; Fascism and Socialism were both opposed to 'the most elemental principles' of Christianity. Mussolini for his part was originally anti-religious and anti-Christian as well as anti-clerical, but he came to appreciate the strength and possible utility of 'the religion of the Italians'. He therefore suggested giving financial support to the Church and promised to find a solution to the Roman Question; proposals which had never been made by 'liberal' anti-clericals or supporters of the Popular Party. Mussolini then began both to threaten and to tempt the Church, but consistently made it clear that Sturzo's supporters were among his leading opponents.

Following the March on Rome – which contrary to many reports was not supported by Catholic churchmen – Mussolini was invited to form a government in October 1922. But few Catholics had consistently opposed Fascism and many of those who had endured the petty persecutions of anti-clerical officials welcomed the apparent respect which Fascists showed to the Church and the various measures – social and economic, legal and political – which Mussolini adopted in favour of Catholics. Although several of them, including the pope himself, were still occasionally critical of Fascist activities, most were lulled into a false sense of security and complacency by the promise to solve the Roman Question, by the apparent peace and unity of the nation, by the concessions made in their favour and the restrictions imposed on Freemasons and Socialists, and by international recognition of the new regime. For the moment Fascist harassment of Catholics and ecclesiastical institutions, and the murders of the priest Don Giovanni Minzoni and the socialist deputy Giacomo Matteotti were ignored.

The Church authorities made the first great concession to Mussolini and opened the way to the eventual signing of the Concordat by destroying the Popular Party. The first official announcement of this agreement between Church and State was given to the diplomatic corps at the Holy See in February 1929 following an invitation similar to that issued on the fateful morning of 20 September 1870. The news was greeted with enthusiasm both within Italy and by Catholics throughout the world as a subsequent state visit by the King and Queen of Italy ended the bitter divisions and quarrels between Church and State that had followed the unification of Italy. The pope first recognised the Kingdom of Italy and surrendered his territorial claims in return for a sovereign and independent Vatican City State. In return he was guaranteed financial compensation and a Concordat between Church and State defined the rights and liberties of the Church within Italy and restricted the interference of the secular Government in ecclesiastical affairs.

The territorial base of the Vatican City guaranteed the autonomous and legislative authority of the papacy and permitted it to have its own police force and civil services, postage, coinage and flag, public services, radio and railway station. The treaty also guaranteed the immunity of representatives to the Holy See 'even if their States are not in diplomatic relations with Italy'. Papal churches, palaces and buildings outside the Vatican were given extra-territorial status and papal colleges were exempted from taxation or expropriation. The Vatican also received a considerable financial indemnity from the Italian Government but this was explicitly recognised to be much less than what had been due to the Holy See under the Law of Guarantees, and the use of these funds was strictly controlled. The Concordat declared that Catholicism was the sole and official religion of Italy. It guaranteed freedom of communication between the pope and bishops throughout the world, papal freedom in appointing Italian bishops subject to the political objections of the State, and payment of bishops and priests by the State. Religious congregations were given legal recognition and the freedom and promotion of the non-political activities of Catholic Action were assured. Catholic education became compulsory and the Government recognised Church schools and universities. Holidays of obligation became public holidays.

However even before the treaty had been ratified Mussolini spoke of a regime 'which tomorrow will be more totalitarian than yesterday' and declared that the Church was neither sovereign nor free but subordinate to the general laws of the State. In particular, he announced, 'Education must belong to us'; 'in the sphere of educa-

tion we remain intractable. Youth shall be ours!' The pope responded by opposing the Fascist doctrine of 'educating for conquest' and
declared that although he was prepared to 'treat' with the Devil, he
would prove to be 'intransigent'; truth and right were 'irrefutable,
indestructible, and irresistible'. It is therefore hardly surprising that
relations between Church and State from the signing of the Lateran
Treaty until the spring of 1940 were marked by occasional bitter
conflicts as well as efforts to co-operate and compromise. The Fascists happily extended the provisions of the Concordat in the
Church's favour as long as Catholic aspirations did not conflict with
Fascist interests, and bishops lauded Mussolini in their pastorals and
addresses to Fascist conferences. However few committed representatives on either side really trusted the other.

Any suggestion of unorthodoxy was immediately repudiated by
the pope himself or authoritative Catholic sources. In 1932 for
example all the writings of Giovanni Gentile, the 'philosopher of
Fascism', were put on the Index. Pius XI consistently opposed totalitarianism from the moment that Mussolini first expounded the
notion of the ethical state. In 1926 the Pope deplored the emergence
of 'a theory of the State which is directly repugnant to Catholic
doctrine, namely that the State is its own final end, that the citizen
only exists for the State'. In a public letter significantly addressed to
Cardinal Alfredo Ildefonso Schuster, a prominent supporter of the
regime, the pope declared that an 'objective totalitarianism' which
subordinated the citizen's whole life, 'individual, domestic, spiritual
and supernatural', to the State 'is a manifest absurdity in the theor-
etical order and would be a monstrosity were its realization to be
attempted in practice'. In his encyclical on the Christian education of
youth, *Divini illius Magistri*, he denounced the attempts of the State
to monopolize the training of the young and uncompromisingly
reasserted the primary claims of the family and the Church.

The Lateran Treaty had been in force for less than two years when
conflict broke out over Fascist attacks on Catholic Action and Catholic Youth organisations. Pius XI often expressed the hope that he
would be remembered primarily as 'the Pope of Catholic Action' and
although he himself did not actually begin 'the apostolate of the
laity', he extended and enhanced its activities beyond all recognition.
This ideological and physical attack was deliberately organized and
directed by the Fascist authorities who accused Catholic Action of
being a political relic of the Popular Party. Those periodicals which
published protests against the violence directed against individuals
and institutions were suppressed, while papal and episcopal protests
produced assurances of regret but little action. In April 1931 the

pope sent a memorandum to Cardinal Schuster demanding the protection guaranteed by the Concordat: 'Fascism declares itself to be Catholic. Well, there is one way and one way only to be Catholic – Catholics in fact and not merely in name, true Catholics and not sham Catholics'.

On the feast of Saints Peter and Paul in 1931 the pope prayed at the tomb of the Apostles before signing his encyclical *Non abbiamo bisogno* which, significantly, was written in Italian and first published abroad. Although the Pope did not directly condemn either Fascism or the regime, he warned Catholics against Fascist ideology and condemned Fascist attitudes and actions. He also spoke of 'a real pagan worship of the State' which was 'opposed to the rights of the Church of Jesus Christ and of souls'. The Fascists, infuriated by the international support which the pope received, denounced him, but both sides were anxious to avoid a final break and the public controversy was allowed to die down. Some Italian Catholics were later alienated by the alliance with Hitler, the murder of Engelbert Dollfuss and destruction of the Austrian Republic or the passing of the racial laws, while others supported the crusade against Communism, the armies of General Francisco Franco or 'the high colonizing mission of Italy'.

Even without the Lateran Treaty, the Vatican would probably have remained neutral during the Second Abyssinian War as it had during the First which had been waged by one of its most bitter opponents. However the Pope was effectively 'silenced' in the face of Mussolini's aggression by one of the provisions of the Concordat. But this was not true of other Italian bishops. Cardinal Schuster declared that 'on the plains of Ethiopia, the Italian standard carries forward in triumph the Cross of Christ, smashes the chains of slavery, and opens the way for the missionaries of the gospel.' Another bishop publicly praised 'Italy, our great Duce, and the soldiers who are about to win a victory for truth and righteousness'. The Apostolic Visitor to Addis Ababa 'saluted all the heroic soldiers of the Italian army which the world admires, but at which Heaven has no need to marvel since it is their ally'. Protestant missionaries were expelled, the Head of the Coptic Church was beheaded and Church authorities tried to bring the Ethiopian Church into full communion with that of Rome. The Holy See recognised the King of Italy as Emperor of Ethiopia and Mussolini himself expressed his satisfaction with the attitude of the Vatican during the war.

Some Catholic churchmen also gave their support to Fascist attempts to 'Italianize' the German and Slav speaking Catholics in the north but proved less willing to be associated with later racialist and anti-semitic legislation. Originally the Fascist regime enjoyed the enthusiastic support of most Italian Jews, several of whom described it as a model of tolerance and enlightenment. However Adolf Hitler's visit to Italy in May 1938 marked the formation of the Rome-Berlin Axis and closer collaboration between the two dictators in their domestic and foreign policies. A few bishops protested including Cardinal Schuster who attacked the 'heresy born in Germany and now insinuating itself almost everywhere' which 'by materializing in human blood the spiritual concepts of individual, nation and father-land, refuses to humanity all spiritual values'. He declared that there was no room for racial divisions within Christianity because 'Christ cannot be divided into fragments'. On the other hand, Agostino Gemelli, Franciscan Rector of the University of the Sacred Heart, referred to the 'deicide people' who 'because of their blood and religion, cannot form part of this magnificent country'.

As early as 1928 the Holy Office had condemned 'hatred of the people once chosen by God, the hatred that commonly goes by the name of anti-Semitism'. In May 1938 the Congregation of Semin-aries and Universities instructed Catholic professors to refute those 'pernicious' doctrines of racialism which 'under the false disguise of science, are spread for the perversion of minds and the extirpation of true religion'. But the most famous protest came from the pope himself when he declared that anti-semitism was incompatible with the claim in the Mass that 'Abraham is our Patriarch and forefather'; 'Through Christ and in Christ we are the spiritual progeny of Abra-ham. Spiritually, we are all Semites'. But the pope's work for peace was not only threatened by the rise of nationalistic racialism and political totalitarianism but by an economic situation which gave rise to what he himself called, an economic nationalism.

Quadragesimo Anno was published forty years after *Rerum Novarum* and expanded and developed the social teachings of Leo XIII. Criticisms of socialism were accompanied with warnings against the excesses of capitalism and for the first time a pope recommended the redistribution of national production, profit-sharing and the co-partnership of workers in industry. Pius XI was more willing than his predecessor to contemplate fundamental changes in the social and economic order, to dissociate himself from economic liberalism and to denounce contemporary abuses, particu-larly the unfair distribution of wealth and the exploitation of labour, the increasing concentration of power and the economic domination of the few. Concentration of power led to internal conflicts as well as conflicts between nations, to 'economic nationalism or even econ-omic imperialism'. As he wrote in another context, 'if selfishness abuses this love of country and exaggerates this sentiment of nationalism, and insinuates itself into the relations between one people and another, there is no excess which will not seem to be justified'.

It is sometimes said that Pius XI's three years (1918–21) in Poland had a decisive influence on his later pontificate. It was in Poland that the future Pope first encountered a modern dictator in the person of Marshal Josef Pilsudski, the romantic, idealistic and socialist leader of Poland. Achille Ratti had been sent to Warsaw to help to rebuild the Polish Church and to negotiate a Concordat, but he was also concerned to secure information about the many thousands of Polish and Lithuanian Catholics who had been deported by the Russians to Siberia. In the summer of 1920 the Red Armies laid seige to Warsaw and the papal nuncio, with the American ambassador, were the only members of the diplomatic corps to remain in the city. Ratti had seen with his own eyes the Russian armies which might yet sweep into Europe and he would not quickly forget that after the armistice some three-and-a-half million Latin Catholics were left to the mercy of the Russians. But if the Church under Pius XI was concernèd to resist the growing influence of Communism, it also attempted to resist the new fanatical nationalism spreading throughout Europe. It was no coincidence that the encyclicals *Mit brennender Sorge* and *Divini Redemptoris* should have appeared almost within days of each other.

The condemnation of atheistic Communism has often been contrasted with the attack on Nazism on the grounds that *Divini Redemptoris* was an absolute condemnation whereas *Mit brennender Sorge* was a diplomatic protest. But such criticism ignores the fact that the pope had already condemned the right-wing, anti-semitic, French nationalist movement known as Action Française which opposed his attempts to promote a new 'ralliement' as well as his moves in favour of peace and reconciliation throughout the world. Furthermore the criticism fails to do justice to the force of *Mit brennender Sorge* and seriously underestimates the significance of the attacks on totalitarianism in *Divini Redemptoris*. The juxtaposition of the two encyclicals surely emphasised the pope's increasing hostility to totalitarianism, the growing similarities between the two regimes and the common threat which they posed to Christianity and the Church.

Between 1918 and 1923 the Bolsheviks indulged in a crude and largely unsuccessful campaign to destroy religion. Thousands of priests, monks and nuns, laymen and women were sentenced to death or to starvation in Siberia, imprisoned or sent to concentration camps. Meanwhile the 'Union of Militant Godless' indulged in crude and offensive anti-religious propaganda and ecclesiastical property was confiscated or destroyed. During the period of the 'New Economic Policy' the Soviet government avoided open persecution which might alienate foreign governments and attempted to create its own Church. Priests were not entitled to a ration card because they were not members of a trades union and churches were closed on the grounds that there were insufficient worshippers to justify keeping them open. The 'scientific' attack on religion began about 1928.

At the same time as the Revolution broke out in Russia Mexican Catholics were being persecuted by another Marxist or Communist regime. A new constitution, published in 1917, subordinated Church to State, confiscated ecclesiastical property, suppressed religious orders and expelled foreign priests. After 1924 a deliberate attempt was made to destroy Catholicism, clergy and laity were expelled or executed, and priests forced to minister to their people in secret. The government forces eventually succeeded in winning a bloody civil war and subjected believers to further repression. It was only after the hold of the Church over the Mexican people had been broken that physical persecution eventually ceased. It was therefore hardly surprising that Pius XI should have explicitly associated Communism with persecution and instanced their behaviour in Russia and Mexico as well as Spain.

In 1931 the new Republican government in Spain abrogated the Concordat and separated Church and State, confiscated ecclesiastical property and expelled the Jesuits, secularised education and introduced divorce, abolished clerical privileges and prohibited religious processions. 'With these measures,' declared the Prime Minister, 'Spain ceases to be Catholic'. But the anti-clerical measures were not immediately enforced and the Catholic Church did not at once oppose the establishment of the Republic. However anarchists began to destroy and plunder ecclesiastical institutions throughout Spain and opinion began to polarise. A disputed election in 1936 was followed by an outbreak of violent anti-clericalism which resulted in murders and arson. The troops mutinied and General Franco raised the standard of the Falange against the government.

Although the Holy See adopted a cautious line diplomatically, there was little doubt where the pope's sympathies lay and he could hardly have remained passive in the light of the actual conduct of the war that followed. A dozen bishops, thousands of priests and monks, hundreds of nuns and novices were killed, sometimes brutally. Catholic opinion throughout the world was divided, but most Spanish

Catholics increasingly identified with the Nationalists whose regime would later restore the privileged position of the Church within the Spanish State. Only a few Spanish Catholics were prepared to criticise the exaggerated nationalism and totalitarianism of the Falange, the influence of Nazis and Fascists, and the introduction of racial laws.

After the First World War German Catholics had played a prominent part in the political as well as the cultural life of the nation and no government could survive without the support or at least the neutrality of the influential Centre Party. National Socialism, or Nazism, also conflicted with the ideology as well as the political interests or the Catholic Church, a fact that was generally recognised by German bishops. In 1920 Bishop Clemens August von Galen declared that the Nazi programme included ideas 'which no Catholic could accept without denying his faith'. The German bishops warned Catholics against the Nazis on five occasions between 1920 and 1927. In 1929 the Bishop of Mainz declared that 'a Catholic cannot be a member of the National Socialist Party' and in the following year Cardinal Adolf Bertram of Breslau also expressed his opposition to National Socialism. In 1931 the Bavarian bishops condemned Nazism as heretical. Adolf Hitler, the Nazi leader, for his part hated Christianity and intended to deal with it as he was prepared to deal with Judaism but he disguised his hostility until he had achieved power.

After coming to power in January 1933 Hitler continued to reassure Catholics and Christians but the Catholic bishops still supported the Centre Party even during the elections held to ratify Hitler's *fait accompli*. However within a matter of weeks the bishops withdrew their earlier censures forbidding Catholics to join the Nazi Party and the Centre Party was allowed to vote in Hitler's favour, giving him the majority he needed to assume full authority. This dramatic change seems to have been the result of pressure from some Roman authorities apparently reassured by Hitler's promises. However the bishops had not withdrawn their earlier ideological condemnations and in this ambiguous context the Concordat was signed. By signing this Concordat Hitler secured the recognition of the Holy See, gained international prestige at a time when major Powers were suspicious and reserved, and effectively ended the political opposition of the Centre Party and German Catholics.

Leading Vatican officials, on the other hand, had few illusions but probably hoped to establish a legal basis on which to defend the liberty of German Catholics and on paper the provisions of the Concordat were very favourable to the Church. At the same time the

Secretary of State told the British *chargé d'affaires* that he had to choose within a week between accepting the concessions offered or witnessing the virtual elimination of the Church in Germany. Furthermore the legislation needed to implement the Concordat was never passed and its provisions were constantly ignored. Only five days after the Concordat was signed the Nazis published a law of sterilization which the pope condemned as contrary to Christian morals and within months Vatican officials were protesting against the repeated and frequent violations of the Concordat. Catholic Deputies were arrested and civil servants dismissed, priests and religious were imprisoned or exiled, ecclesiastical correspondence was opened and confiscated, Catholic organisations and periodicals suppressed, Catholic property was confiscated, episcopal palaces were sacked and meetings banned, religious education was restricted and Catholic schools closed. In June 1934 Erich Klausener, a President of Catholic Action, was shot. Adalbert Probst was summoned to Berlin and a few days later his ashes were returned to his widow. Friedrich Beck of Munich University was killed 'accidentally' and Fritz Gerlich, editor of the largest Catholic newspaper in Germany, was found dead in prison.

The German bishops repeatedly protested against those Nazi policies incompatible with Christian teaching as well as against violations of the Concordat. The Archbishop of Munich, Cardinal Michael Faulhaber, consistently denounced the theories of so-called 'German Christians' who were willing to accomodate their religion to Nazism and the persecution of the Jews. In 1934 Cardinal Karl Josef Schulte of Cologne personally protested to Hitler against Alfred Rosenberg's *Myth of the Twentieth Century* which he described as contrary to Christianity. Hitler pretended to disavow Rosenberg but the Cardinal commented, 'Hitler is a sphinx, a sinister man. We shall yet receive a terrible treatment by him'. Meanwhile the Holy See continued to protest against violations of the Concordat, to denounce the violence and ideology of Nazism, and to condemn several of its leading exponents. In 1936 Pius XI described Nazism and Communism as 'enemies of all truth and of all justice' and later accused 'the self-styled champions of civilization against Bolshevism' of using 'the very means employed by their adversaries'.

In August 1936 the German bishops petitioned for a papal encyclical on the problems facing the Church in Germany and a group of them met with the Secretary of State Eugenio Pacelli. Faulhaber prepared the draft, Pacelli added an historical introduction and made a few modifications, the pope himself added the final touches. *Mit brennender Sorge* was secretly distributed throughout the country by an army of motor cyclists and read from every Catholic pulpit on Palm Sunday before it had been seen by any member of the Nazi Party. The bishops themselves read it in their own cathedrals. This encyclical was one of the strongest condemnations of a national regime ever published by the Holy See and not only condemned the persecution of the Church but the neopaganism of Nazi theories and even by implication Hitler, the Führer, himself: he was a mad prophet possessed of repulsive arrogance who would place any mortal however great on the same level as Christ. *Mit brennender Sorge* had an immediate effect on public opinion, especially in the United States, and the German government retaliated by censorship at home and intensifying propaganda abroad. Copies of the encyclical were seized and the presses which had printed it were closed, publications which had published it were suspended and those individuals convicted of distributing it were arrested. But Hitler did not want to go too far. Apart from military considerations, the 'Anschluss' (or joining) of Austria, and the later occupations of Czech and Polish territories, was to mean that the percentage of Catholics in the Third Reich would equal if it did not exceed that of Protestants.

In 1922 Ignaz Seipel, a Catholic priest and leader of the Christian Socialists, became Chancellor of Austria. He was succeeded by Dollfuss, who was murdered by the Austrian Nazis in 1934, and was succeeded in turn by Kurt von Schuschnigg who made the fatal appeal for a plebiscite in favour of Austrian independence in 1938. The Austrian constitution, outlined by Seipel and developed by Dollfuss, was very similar to Pius XI's notion of a Catholic corporate State and a Concordat signed in 1933 was one of the most satisfactory so far made from the point of view of the Church. The Holy See demonstrated its suspicions of the Nazis by nominating as Austrian bishops churchmen who were known to be opposed to the 'Anschluss' and some historians have argued that the real change in the Vatican's attitude to Germany came in 1938, when the German government refused to answer a note from Pacelli about the continued validity of the Austrian Concordat, a refusal which was a direct consequence of the pope's hostility to Hitler on his visit to Rome in 1937.

When Pius XI was asked to receive Hitler in audience, the pope had stipulated that they must discuss the persecution of the Church in Germany. In the event Hitler ignored the pope who left for Castel Gandolfo three days before the Führer's arrival and two months before he usually did. Papal museums and galleries were closed to the public and the *Osservatore Romano*, the Vatican newspaper, studiously ignored Hitler's visit. On the morning after Hitler had arrived the pope publicly deplored the fact that 'it is not found either out of place or out of season to hoist in Rome, on this the feast of the Holy Cross, the symbol of another cross which is not that of Christ'. Only two months before his death Pius XI reminded the cardinals that 'in Germany today a full religious persecution is in progress' and in one of his last public audiences he compared Hitler with the Emperor Nero and Julian the Apostate who had attempted to make Christians responsible for the persecutions unleashed against them.

Eugenio Pacelli was elected Pope as Pius XII (1939–58) at the shortest conclave since 1623; the cardinals elected the first Secretary of State since 1775 and the first native of Rome since 1721. During the six months between his election in March and the outbreak of the Second World War in September 1939 he did everything he could to preserve the peace of Europe. As he wrote in his first encyclical *Summi Pontificatus*, published in October 1939, 'We left no stone unturned, no avenue unexplored, to prevent, in any way which our apostolic office or other means at our disposal made possible, a recourse to arms'. At the same time Pius XII clearly, if not explicitly, condemned the political and religious policies of the German and Russian governments, though his condemnations of war and totalitarianism seemed to lack the force and urgency of Benedict XV or even Pius XI.

The new pope also restated the five 'peace points' proposed by Benedict in 1917: the freedom and independence of nations, progressive disarmament, effective international institutions of arbitration, peaceful and fair revision of outdated treaties and recognition of just national demands, general acceptance of Christian principles and a renewed spirit of goodwill and love, responsibility and justice. The invasions in 1940 of Denmark and Norway, Holland, Belgium and Luxembourg violated every one of the conditions laid down by the two popes and when Pius XII was asked to condemn them, he responded by calling for the 're-establishment of justice and liberty' in Holland, the 'complete liberty and independence' of Belgium, and the 'liberty and independence' of the people of Luxembourg. Incidentally, it was also at about this time in the United States of America that President Franklin D. Roosevelt expressed the desire of working with the pope for the restoration of peace and the solution of post-war problems, whereupon Myron C. Taylor was sent to be the president's personal representative residing at the Vatican.

The danger that Italy might enter the struggle inevitably increased with the military successes of the German armies and the pope redoubled his efforts to preserve Italian neutrality. But following

Italy's declaration of war in 1940, it seemed to some that the Roman authorities became dominated by 'an anxious neutrality' and that the new pope was unwilling – unlike his predecessor – to act as the moral conscience of the world. In fact the neutral and moderate tone of the Holy See at the time would appear to suggest that the ecclesiastical authorities did not believe that the Allies could defeat or even resist the forces of Nazism and that the Holy See must therefore learn to live in a Europe dominated by Nazism and Fascism. The pope shared the opinion of most commentators outside Britain that Hitler's regime could now only be overthrown from inside Germany itself.

However Pius XII had to struggle hard to maintain this 'neutrality' and his determination to do so was the result of several factors. He believed, at least initially, that the very continuance of the war was a greater evil than an immediate peace and still hoped to play a role as mediator. He was well aware of the limited effect that protests had on totalitarian regimes and wished to safeguard the position of Catholics, particularly in Germany where the future of the Church might be threatened either by persecution or by the establishment of a National Church. Finally the pope was alarmed by the increasing threat of Communism especially in eastern Europe. At the same time the pope told American Catholics that statements in *Divini Redemptoris* could not be used to condemn Roosevelt's policy of supplying arms to Russia and he said that it was quite legitimate to resist German aggression even with the help of Russian Communists. Vatican officials consistently told German and Italian diplomats and prelates that if the Holy See was to condemn the religious policies of the Russian Government, it would also have to condemn the religious policies of the German Government.

However the attitudes of Vatican authorities dramatically changed when the pope was informed officially that the American government would not engage in peace negotiations until Nazism had been destroyed. In September 1942 Myron C. Taylor told Pius XII that the United States would continue the struggle until the Allies had achieved total victory and that they would regard any 'Axis-inspired proposals of "peace" ' as 'nothing less than a blow aimed at us'. The pope replied, 'We have read your Memorandum very carefully . . . of the definite, determined stand of the United States government it leaves no shadow of doubt'. The terms of 'Unconditional Surrender' were publicly announced at Casablanca in 1943. The pope already knew that Nazism and Fascism would be destroyed but that as an incidental result the political influence of Russia and of Communism would expand after the War.

The pope's condemnation of modern 'Statolatry' in his Christmas message of 1942 was clearly directed against totalitarian regimes and his reassertion of the primacy of the family over the State obviously contradicted Fascist and Nazi claims. He also referred to the Jews – though the Allies did not believe that he had been explicit enough – when he spoke of 'the hundreds of thousands who, through no fault of their own, and solely because of their nation or race, have been condemned to death or progressive extinction'. The German ambassador was ordered to warn the pope that the Nazis did not lack means of retaliation if the Holy See abandoned its neutral stand. This the ambassador did, although he also told his superiors that 'Pacelli is no more sensible to threats than we are'.

German Catholics were inevitably torn by divided loyalties during the war and Christian resistance to National Socialism was often reluctant and disorganised. Even opponents of Nazism were sometimes prepared to express their loyalty to the German State or the Führer and to support the war effort while actual resistance to the Nazis was frequently first a matter of self-defence. Similarly, although some individual Germans were immediately prepared to help the Jews, most of them protested against the persecution of fellow Christians before condemning the persecution of Jews. Furthermore many of the 'successes' of protesting churchmen were often due to divisions among the Nazis rather than to their own defence of Christian principles. Nevertheless, with all their limitations, the Christian Churches showed greater resistance to the demands of the Nazis than any of the other great German institutions such as the judiciary or the universities, while the German trade unions, the largest and best organised in the world, were eliminated by threats and promises. The real 'successes', like the real 'failures' of Christians against National Socialism, were perhaps inevitably on the individual rather than the institutional level. As one contemporary commentator later put it, for prophets to recall the Church to a higher loyalty and behaviour is sure to bring about the reaction of priests against prophets, of people against their origins.

If Catholics were humiliated by the behaviour of ecclesiastics like the Benedictine Abbot Alban Schachleiter, they could take pride in the courage of many others. The Pallotine Franz Reinisch was beheaded for refusing to take the military oath of allegiance. Bernhard Lichtenberg was denounced for praying for Jews and prisoners in concentration camps. When asked how he felt towards the Führer he replied, 'I have only one Führer, Jesus Christ'. Monsignor Lichtenberg died on his way to Dachau. Father Alfons Maria Wachsmann was executed for 'undermining the morale of the armed forces'. Father Josef Müller was executed for being 'politically unreliable'. Three priests were executed simply because, as one of their judges admitted, 'it was their tragedy that they were Catholic priests'. The Jesuit Alfred Delp was hanged because he was indirectly associated with Count Klaus von Stauffenberg who made the attempt on Hitler's life in 1944. And there were many, many more priests, nuns and layfolk who laid down their lives.

On the outbreak of war the German bishops called on Catholic soldiers to do their duty 'full of the spirit of self-sacrifice' and on all Catholics to pray for 'a victorious conclusion, with a peace beneficial for *Volk und Vaterland*'. However Bishop von Galen declared, 'We will do our duty out of love for our German Fatherland. Our soldiers will fight and die for Germany – but not for those men who bring shame upon the German name before God'. Von Galen was perhaps the most outspoken bishop in condemning euthanasia and sterilization, concentration camps and imprisonment without trial. The pope's letters to the German bishops at the time show that he could do little more than offer encouragement and sympathy. But they also show that originally he supported the bishops who tended to adopt an accommodating line with the Nazi authorities. Later, however, following Cardinal Konrad von Preysing's advice, the pope excluded as episcopal candidates those regarded as too weak in their attitudes to the regime.

Like Benedict XV during the First World War, Pius XII tried to unite Catholics throughout the world in a crusade of prayer for peace – using Benedict's own prayer for peace – and he called on them to provide money, food and clothing to relieve the sufferings of the victims of war. On the outbreak of war, Pius XII established the Pontifical Relief Commission and sent appeals for help to every Catholic diocese in the world. Relief agencies were set up in Norway and Denmark, France, Belgium and the Netherlands, Greece and Yugoslavia. When Italy entered the war, an office was established in Lisbon for the purchase and distribution of supplies from the United States. As the war came to an end the pope set up the International Committee of Catholic Charities with headquarters in Paris to coordinate local and national efforts to assist the victims of war.

Papal representatives throughout the world provided social and pastoral care for prisoners of war, helping them to communicate with their families. A Vatican Information Service was established with sections dealing with prisoners of war, displaced and missing persons, the sick and orphaned, the provision of relief, food, clothing and medical supplies. Appeals for help came from all over the world and the Vatican Radio broadcast thousands of messages every month giving information about soldiers and civilians to families and friends. Meanwhile parcels and medical supplies were being dispatched to prisoners and victims of war in countries as far away as Finland and Greece, Ethiopia and Malaya.

The pope and the Holy See were often asked to act as mediators during the War. In 1941 the English bishops asked the pope to try to save the lives of twenty-five Belgian hostages sentenced to death. The British government asked the Holy See to use its good offices to secure an agreement with Italy for the exchange of sick or wounded prisoners of war. In 1942 the British government again asked the Holy See to try to win the release of Poles interned in Spain and of Allied prisoners threatened with deportation to territories occupied by the Germans and the Apostolic Nuncio in Madrid made repeated representations on their behalf.

Pius XII was particularly concerned that the Church should provide shelter and protection for refugees from the war and victims of persecution. Ecclesiastical buildings in Rome, which were outside the Vatican City State but which enjoyed extra-territorial protection, were used to shelter political and Jewish refugees. Priests and religious were encouraged to shelter Jews in spite of the risks to themselves. There were some 5000 Jews in 155 Roman ecclesiastical establishments including several dozen in the Vatican itself. The Capuchin, Father Pierre Peteul Marie-Benoit, took care of 400 Polish Jews who arrived in Rome in September 1943 and then issued another 500 Jews from France with permits to stay in Rome. But after the end of the war the question was raised whether Pius XII had done enough on behalf of the Jewish victims of Nazi persecution.

In September 1943 the Chief of Police in Rome threatened to send some 200 Jews to the Russian front unless they produced, within thirty-six hours, fifty kilogramms of gold or the equivalent in dollars or sterling. The Chief Rabbi approached the Vatican which immediately placed fifteen kilograms at his disposal and made the money available. In the event the Jews succeeded in raising the money themselves. Nevertheless one of the main accusations against Pius XII is that he did nothing for the Jews of Rome when more than one thousand of them were arrested in October 1943. However it is impossible to appreciate the case for or against the pope without understanding the situation in Rome at the time and in particular the role of Baron Ernst von Weizsäcker, German ambassador to the Holy See.

The Baron hoped to protect the pope by representing him to the German authorities in the most favourable light that he could and by persuading his superiors that the pope was sympathetic to the German 'crusade' against Communism. At the same time Weizsäcker tried to persuade the Vatican authorities to do as little as possible in order to avoid irritating the Nazis. The ambassador preferred to make his own representations to Berlin rather than forward those from the Holy See, partly to protect the pope but also because he felt that he himself had more chance of succeeding with his superiors. Weizsäcker also became convinced that the Nazis intended to kidnap the pope before the Allies reached Rome and therefore sent what his lieutenant, Albrecht von Kessel, later called 'tactical lies' to protect the pope by persuading the Nazis that Pius would not do anything to injure the German cause.

The deportation of 8,000 Jews living in Rome began in October. The pope immediately contacted the Secretary of State who at once invited Weizsäcker to the Vatican. Cardinal Luigi Maglione asked the ambassador to intervene and threatened that the Holy See would issue an official protest if the arrests continued, but Weizsäcker effectively silenced such a protest by promising to do what he could. It was then that Weizsäcker sent the telegram to Berlin which so injured the pope's reputation but which might be interpreted very differently in view of Weizsäcker's private attitudes towards the Vatican and Berlin:

> The curia is particularly shocked that the action took place, so to speak, under the pope's windows. The reaction would be perhaps softened if the Jews could be used for military work in Italy. The groups in Rome hostile to us, exploit the action to force the Vatican out of its reserve. They say that in French towns where similar things happened, bishops took a clear position, and the pope, as head of the Church, could not do less. People are beginning to contrast this pope with his much more fiery predecessor Pius XI. Enemy propaganda abroad will certainly seize the occasion to provoke tension between the curia and ourselves.

Yet by that time more than half the Jews in Rome, it has been estimated, were being sheltered in ecclesiastical buildings opened to them on the instructions of the pope himself. Another 3000 Jews were in hiding elsewhere in Rome but the last one thousand were deported and exterminated. Weizsäcker clearly knew what was happening, that many Jews had escaped with Vatican credentials and that he himself had even been approached by the Secretariat to secure the release or the safety of individual Jews. Jewish delegations, such as the American Jewish Welfare Board, thanked the pope for his efforts on behalf of the Jews. At the end of the war the World Jewish Congress expressed its gratitude and gave twenty million lire to

Vatican charities. When the Chief Rabbi of Rome was received into the Church in 1945, he took the name 'Eugenio'. A former Israeli consul in Italy claimed that,

> The Catholic Church saved more Jewish lives during the war than all the other Churches, religious institutions and rescue organisations put together. Its record stands in startling contrast to the achievements of the International Red Cross and the Western Democracies . . . The Holy See, the Nuncios and the entire Catholic Church saved some 400,000 Jews from certain death.

The massacre of hundreds of thousands of Serbs during the war was only surpassed in horror and violence by the exterminations of Jews and gypsies. The Croatian government – with the help of some Catholic priests – attempted to identify two million Orthodox Serbs with the state of Croatia by forcing them to join the Catholic Church. The Orthodox were subjected to monstrous cruelties and suffered one of the bitterest persecutions in their history. Although Archbishop Ludwig Stepinac of Zagreb had publicly thanked God for the Ustachi government, he also protested against the deportation of the Jews and the policy of forced conversions. On three occasions between 1943 and 1945 Anton Pavelić requested that Stepinac should be replaced but on each occasion the Holy See refused. However, when the Communist partisans gained power in Yugoslavia, all members of the Church became victims of a new persecution and Stepinac himself was arrested.

Hungary had joined the Axis 'crusade' against Communism but Archbishop Jusztinian Seredi, the Prince Primate, was uncompromising in his opposition to Nazi policies. On New Year's Day 1943 he declared in St Stephen's Cathedral

> There is no such thing on earth as a *Herrenvolk* – only those who serve God, and those who serve the Devil. No nation is inferior to another . . . Murder is murder, and he who, for political reasons, orders mass executions will not receive the rites and consolations of the Church. Nor will the Church grant the sacraments to those who, on ideological grounds, abduct human beings for forced labour.

When protesting against anti-semitic legislation, Seredi reminded the Senate of the warning of St Bernard: 'Do not touch the Jews for they are the apple of God's eye'. The pope and the Secretary of State both condemned and protested against the deportation of Jews from Slovakia. When the pope learnt of the exterminations of Jews in the labour camps, he sent a telegram to Admiral Miklos Horthy appealing on their behalf. The papal nuncio provided protection and material help to Hungarian Jews while the Vatican informed other countries about conditions in Hungary which was then subjected to mounting protests from many neutral as well as allied powers.

In Western Europe the pope formally protested to Marshal Philippe Pétain, head of the Vichy government in France, against the persecution of the Jews, instructed the papal nuncio and the Vichy regime to issue another protest and recommended religious communities to provide refuge for Jews. The primate of France, Cardinal Pierre Marie Gerlier, had originally welcomed the establishment of the Vichy regime but his protest against the deportation of Jews was read from every pulpit of his diocese of Lyons and broadcast throughout the nation. Gerlier declared that the French State and Church were divided and refused to bless military volunteers or to say Mass for those who died in the fighting. Other French bishops, such as Archbishop Jules Gerard Saliège of Toulouse, also denounced the deportations and all of them issued a more general protest to Pétain himself.

As early as 1934 the Dutch bishops had warned Catholics against the dangers of National Socialism and in 1936 Dutch Catholics were ordered, under pain of excommunication, not to support Fascist organizations. During the occupation the bishops condemned Nazism and prohibited Catholics from cooperating with the Germans. In 1942 Christian churchmen in Holland agreed to issue a public protest against the deportation of Dutch Jews. The Germans responded by promising to make an exception of those Jews who had been baptised if the churchmen remained silent. The leaders of the Reformed Church agreed but the Catholic bishops issued a pastoral letter condemning the deportation of the Jews. The Germans continued to spare Protestant Jews but immediately began to arrest and deport Catholic Jews.

It is hardly surprising, therefore, that Pius XII should have been anxious to avoid provoking other reprisals especially in Germany and Poland, and so he was largely content to leave the responsibility for making public denunciations to the local hierarchies. Early in 1943 the Holy See was informed about the deportations and executions of the Jews by the papal nuncio and von Preysing and it was also clear by then that a similar persecution was taking place in Poland. The correspondence and documents of the Holy See during this time reveal an ever-increasing sense of frustration and helplessness in trying to respond to the persecution of the Jews in Germany and Poland. When the papal nuncio, acting on instructions from Rome, once raised the issue with the Führer himself, Hitler simply picked up a glass of water and with a motion of disdain flung it to the ground.

In spite of the co-operation – selective though it may have been – between Catholic and Fascists in Italy, the outburst of anti-clericalism which some had predicted and others feared did not take place following the fall of Mussolini. In fact Catholics co-operated extensively with left-wing forces who were anxious to avoid the anti-clericalism of the past if only because of the help given to victims of persecution and members of the Resistance by priests and religious during the war. At the same time a group of Catholic politicians emerged who sought freedom for the Church rather than ecclesiastical privilege or domination and who seemed to embrace the political principles associated with the Popular Party. The Italian people meanwhile were more concerned with the need for reconstruction and reconciliation than with relations between Church and State. Consequently the demonstration of gratitude to Pius XII, following the liberation of Rome, was attended by socialists and communists as well as Catholics. Furthermore the socialists, communists and liberals never proposed adopting any measures which might seem hostile to the Church. The only point at issue was whether the Lateran Treaties should be included in the constitution and in the event they were given constitutional status.

Although Pius XII did not specifically approve of any particular party, his demand that Catholics should support only those parties which were fighting against the enemies of Christ, coupled with the Church's opposition to Communism, undoubtedly contributed to the early successes of the Christian Democrats. However the Party included differing factions that could not easily be reconciled and made it more difficult for Alcide de Gasperi, formerly a leading member of the old Popular party and now leader of the Christian Democratic party and Prime Minister, to safeguard the independence of the Party from the Church. Of course the pope could not ignore the persecution of the Church in Russia, China and the countries of Eastern Europe nor the danger that the Communists might come to power in Italy, France or Greece. In 1949 Catholics were forbidden to join or support the Communist Party, to publish or distribute, read or write Communist literature, and those Catholics who professed, defended or propagated Communist teachings were excommunicated.

In Poland the Communists attempted to establish a schismatic Church, abrogated the Concordat and confiscated ecclesiastical property. Catholic schools were closed and religious publications suppressed. Clergy and laity were convicted as 'spies' and Cardinal

Stefan Wyszynski was confined to a monastery until he was freed following the riots of 1956. Czechoslovakia broke off diplomatic relations with the Holy See following the arrest of Archbishop Josef Beran. Religious houses were closed and the religious themselves imprisoned or deported. In Hungary ecclesiastical properties, including most Church schools, were confiscated, Catholic organisations were suppressed and publications strictly controlled. Cardinal Jozsef Mindszenty was arrested, religious orders were dissolved and those bishops and priests who were allowed to continue to exercise their ministries were closely supervised by the State. Meanwhile in China the Communists adopted the programme of 'Triple Autonomy' for self-support, self-evangelisation and self-government. This was followed by the liquidation of 'counter-revolutionaries', the arrest and expulsion of bishops and hundreds of missionaries, and the eventual establishment of the Patriotic Association of Chinese Catholics.

However Pius XII's references to Communism were on the whole moderate and restrained until the Russian invasion of Hungary in 1956 – when he issued three encyclicals within ten days. Furthermore he was also careful to avoid giving the impression of criticising the Russian people and he condemned the evils of Capitalism and the tyrannies of the Right as well as the Left. The pope was deeply attracted by the ideal of a world community and attempts to establish an international agency to preserve peace. He frequently referred to what he called the 'law of human solidarity and charity' and the fact that the earth was an inheritance of all men as a natural right.

The most significant development during the pontificate of Pius XII was the spread of nuclear weapons and in his Christmas message for 1946 he spoke of the urgent need for disarmament in view of the terrible means of destruction now available. Two speeches in 1953 and 1954 would even seem to suggest that although the pope was not willing to question the established principles of traditional moral theology, he was finding it increasingly difficult to adapt them to the new appalling situation which was now facing the world. He continued to maintain the right of defence, even apparently with the use of nuclear weapons, but he also made it clear that if it became obvious that there was in fact no legitimate defensive use of such weapons, he would draw the logical conclusions.

'The law of human solidarity' dominated the political, social and economic thinking of Pius XII and he showed particular concern for such issues as world poverty, imperialism and widening urbanisation as well as the tragic results of war. Although he did not publish an encyclical on social or economic problems, he outlined 'the social teaching of the Church' in addresses and allocutions, in public and private audiences. Pius condemned both totalitarianism and individualism which both denied the dignity of the human person. He extended social justice to cover relations between industry and agriculture, and to the rights of each nation to share in the markets of the world. Christians were obliged to work to improve the conditions of the working classes and to reform the complex structure of contemporary society. He reminded colonial powers of their obligations and responsibilities, and he himself recognised peoples' rights to self-determination. At the same time the pope opposed class warfare, was unsympathetic to socialism or nationalism and favoured evolution rather than revolution. He advocated a community of interest and action, defending the right to private property as essential to human dignity.

During the 1940s French Catholics in particular had become increasingly aware of the 'de-Christianization' of the urban proletariat and the need to adopt more radical methods of evangelisation, such as the introduction of worker-priests. An Apostolic Exhortation on the priestly life, published in 1950, reflected the pope's reservations and suspicions of the worker-priests whose activities were increasingly restricted over the next few years. But the controversy over the worker-priests illustrated that the problem of 'adaptation' and 'response' were no longer simply of concern in the 'foreign' missions; they were equally pressing in the 'missionary' territories of post-war Europe. During the twentieth century the Roman authorities proved increasingly willing to recognise the significance of local cultures, to extend the authority of local bishops and to encourage the ordination of native bishops and priests. The pope himself held only two consistories in seventeen years, though on both occasions he increased the international representation in the College of Cardinals so that it might become 'a living image of the Church's universality'. However attempts to deal with the problems of evangelisation throughout the world also had an immediate effect on the development of pastoral theology, the liturgical movement and the growth of ecumenism.

In his very first encyclical, Pius XII promised to follow the example of his predecessor in adapting local customs and cultures for use in the Catholic liturgy. In two great encyclicals, *Mystici Corporis Christi* and *Mediator Dei* published respectively in 1942 and 1947, he gave his official approval to the Liturgical movement, while warning against deviations and exaggerations. The pope was determined to safeguard the significance of the ordained priesthood, episcopal authority and private devotions. He defended the use of black vestments, disapproved of 'table' altars and condemned the unauthorised use of the vernacular. The Easter Vigil was restored in 1951 and this was followed by the reform of the Holy Week liturgy. In 1953 evening Masses were approved for the Church throughout the world and the Eucharistic fast was drastically eased. Over the next few years the rules on fasting were further modified and the rubrics simplified, concelebration was re-introduced and vernacular hymns were permitted during Mass. But the pope remained cautious. In 1956 he warned against novel eucharistic opinions, defended traditional eucharistic devotions and 'the unconditional obligation of the use of Latin for the celebrant'. In 1958 the Holy Office reasserted the authority of the Holy See and the bishops over liturgical developments. The development of the liturgical movement and growth of Catholic Action were part cause and part effect of an increased awareness of the role of the laity and appreciation of the Church as the Mystical Body of Christ and community of the faithful. Pius' *Mystici corporis Christi* had marked a crucial stage in the Church's understanding of the role of the laity, although it was not entirely free from those clerical and authoritarian views which were typical of the pope.

The liturgical and ecumenical movements, forms of Catholic Action like the Young Christian Workers, all contributed towards a growing appreciation of the scriptures. In *Spiritus Paraclitus* Benedict XV had already modified some of the more conservative positions adopted by Leo XIII in *Providentissimus Deus*. But it was Pius XII who first encouraged the use of critical methods and by implication gave his approval to the development of biblical theology and the use of form criticism. His encyclical on biblical studies, *Divino Afflante Spiritu*, has been described as 'probably the greatest single achievement' of his reign and 'one of his assured titles to a place in history'. Pius XII also promoted a new translation of the psalter in an effort to further liturgical as well as biblical reforms, and the Biblical Commission publicly adopted a more positive attitude towards such long-standing issues as the dating of the Pentateuch and the interpretation of Genesis.

Later, however, the pope and the ecclesiastical authorities succeeded in inhibiting theological and biblical, pastoral and liturgical developments which had sometimes begun even before the War and were felt to be long over-due. In particular the publication of *Humani Generis* in 1950 revoked some of the concessions made in the field of biblical studies and marked the return to a more intransigent approach which was made even worse by the over-enthusiastic and intemperate way in which this encyclical was sometimes applied on the local level. The pope published *Humani Generis* during the same month that he announced his intention of defining the Assumption of the Blessed Virgin. Pius XII had a particular devotion to the Virgin Mary. In 1942 he consecrated the human race to the Immaculate Heart of Mary, in 1950 he defined the dogma of the Assumption, and in 1953 he proclaimed a special Marian year to commemorate the centenary of the definition of the Immaculate Conception.

Pius XII tended to concentrate authority into his own hands and during his later years as pope found it impossible to carry the burdens which he had imposed on himself. His style of government was triumphalist as well as authoritarian and his spiritual supremacy was reinforced by claims of supernatural experiences and reports that he had seen visions. He especially liked to give his audiences the impression that he was well informed in their particular fields of work or interest and the result was that his speeches on a multiplicity of subjects were occasionally simple to the point of being banal. His best allocutions were in the field of moral theology and although he was hardly revolutionary in his attitude to sexual morality or the theology of marriage, he was unusually frank and open in his discussions of medical ethics. But in spite of these limitations, when Pius XII died in Ocrober 1958 many non-Catholics as well as Catholics believed that his death marked the end of an epoch; they were right, though hardly in the way that they imagined. For when the Cardinals arrived in Rome, they could not ignore the limitations of a pontificate that had previously been concealed only by the prestige and personality of the dead pope himself and it was not without significance that in his speech to the electing Cardinals on choosing a pope, Monsignor Antonio Bacci should have emphasised the need for the pope to be a 'pastor of souls'.

In electing Angelo Roncalli, the cardinals were choosing one of the most experienced diplomats among them. He was well liked and had had pastoral experience as Archbishop of Venice. Finally he had not been associated too closely with his predecessor and was old enough to be considered as a 'transitional' pope. His background was both traditional and sufficiently different to that of Pius XII to suggest that he might adopt a different approach. John XXIII, as Roncalli called himself, had been born in the north and served as a chaplain in the Italian army. He had been secretary and biographer of the liberal Bishop G.M. Radini Tedeschi of Bergamo, one of the leading Italian disciples of Leo XIII. Roncalli's experiences as Apostolic Visitor to Bulgaria, Apostolic Delegate in Greece and Turkey, and nuncio in France would obviously play their part in the formation of his policies as pope. Yet Roncalli had also proved to be a devoted and loyal servant of Pope and Church. He genuinely admired and respected Pius XII and constantly quoted from him. As Patriarch of Venice he had fully supported the political boycott of socialists and communists, though he had also warmly welcomed a Socialist Party Congress and received delegates from a communist women's organisation.

In fact John XXIII first made an impact on public opinion throughout the world by showing himself to be a common Father and pastor. He paid a Christmas visit to children in hospital and received little boys and cripples at the Vatican. He visited the Regina Coeli prison and parishes in the diocese of Rome. But the early moves of the new pope did not foreshadow the later dramatic developments. In 1959 the Holy Office endorsed the earlier political ban on Communists and the pope accepted the decision to end the worker-priests in France. Pope John appointed the rather conservative Cardinal Domenico Tardini as Secretary of State and, although he created more cardinals than ever before, he also increased the percentage of Italians in the Sacred College. In the Apostolic Constitution, *Veterum Sapientia*, the pope insisted on the use of Latin in the liturgy and in sacred studies.

Consequently few contemporaries were expecting any very revolutionary announcement when the pope went to celebrate vespers in the Basilica of St Paul's Without the Walls to conclude the octave of prayer for Christian unity. It was there that Pope John announced his intention of calling an ecumenical council, with the promotion of Christian unity as one of its aims, of holding a Synod for the diocese of Rome and of reforming the Code of Canon Law. This programme has not unnaturally been compared with that of his predecessor, who declared that the three main aims of his pontificate were a new translation of the Psalter, the definition of the Assumption, and the excavation of the tomb of St Peter. The Roman synod was completed within a week without achieving anything of great movement and a commission of thirty cardinals was appointed to revise the Code. But with the opening of the Second Vatican Council, the pope revealed his determination to associate bishops throughout the world with the authority and responsibilities of the Bishop of Rome, to promote the pastoral reform or *aggiornamento* of the Catholic Church and to work for the restoration of Christian unity.

The events of the Second World War, coupled with the spread of Communism, materialism and scepticism, had given a great stimulus to the development of ecumenism although the official attitude of the Catholic Church remained one of suspicious reserve and reluctance to recognise the ecclesial status of other Christian Churches. However non-Catholics were increasingly attracted by the personality of Pope John, his openness and charity, humility and rejection of triumphalism, his trust and confidence in divine providence. Patriarch Athenagoras described him as 'a man sent from God' and Archbishop Geoffrey Fisher of Canterbury called on the pope in December 1960. The pope for his part invited non-Catholics to attend the Council as observers and established the Secretariat for Promoting Christian Unity under Cardinal Augustin Bea in order to further ecumenical relations and to guide the Fathers in Council.

The Council officially opened on 11 October 1962 with 2500 Fathers from almost every part of the world. When the Council ended there were 93 observers representing 29 Churches who, by then, were both consulted and able to comment on proceedings. Four sessions were held during the autumn of every year from 1962 to 1965, though some of the most critical moments occurred when the bishops were away as members of the curia attempted to regain control of a situation which they felt they were in danger of losing. It soon became clear that the Fathers had been able to assert the autonomy of the Council against the curia and that a substantial 'majority' had emerged in favour of *aggiornamento* who were able to define their aims and partly establish the means of achieving them. In general the 'majority' were more ecumenical, pastoral and willing to adapt to the modern world than the 'minority' who were concerned to safeguard the faith and stability, tradition and authority of the Church. The first vote, on the renewal of the liturgy, showed that 46 Fathers were opposed by 2162. In the debate on the sources of Revelation the Fathers voted by 1368 to 822 to remit the rather conservative and narrow document which had been submitted to them. A hasty examination of *schemata* on the Mass Media and the Eastern Churches was followed by a debate on the *schema* on the Church in which the approach adopted by curial officials was again rejected by the Fathers.

Pope John also caught the imagination of the world through his encyclicals, though his first one, *Ad Petri Cathedram*, was an extremely cautious document which passed without comment. John seemed as uncompromising as his predecessors, though his appeal for Christian unity was much warmer and more friendly than theirs. His encyclical on missions was also widely ignored, but it was a worthy successor to *Maximum Illud* which it was intended to commemorate. However the publication in 1961 of *Mater et Magistra*, on social justice and international relations, created a sensation. This encyclical was published on the anniversaries of *Rerum Novarum* and *Quadragesimo Anno* and did not radically depart from the support for moderate reform which had characterised Catholic social teaching since Leo XIII. John's defence of the dignity of labour and support for the wider distribution of property, though developed in contemporary terms, were taken from the teachings of his predecessors. but the pope's obvious concern for social and material welfare, peace and international reconciliation, human and political rights as well as Christian unity, evoked a wide response and not simply from Roman Catholics. The pope seemed to be more sympathetic to modern man than many of his predecessors had been as he adopted a more positive approach to contemporary political, social and economic reforms.

In some ways *Pacem in Terris*, published in April 1963, was also a very traditional document. Pius XII was quoted frequently and the new encyclical covered much the same ground as *Mater et Magistra*: social and economic problems, colonialism and development, the United Nations and international peace. The first section dealt with order between men; the second with relations between the State and its subjects; the third with relations between different States; the fourth with the world community; the fifth and final section consisted of Pastoral Exhortations. However *Mater et Magistra* had been addressed to the Catholic faithful, whereas *Pacem in Terris* was addressed to 'all men of good will' as John XXIII reasserted the pope's responsibility to promote political, economic and social harmony throughout the world. The pope gave his support to the promotion of peace and the work of the United Nations, he defended the rights of all peoples to freedom and political independence, condemned economic and cultural as well as political imperialism, manifested his personal concern for the interests of the developing nations and called on wealthier countries to assist the development of the less fortunate while respecting their political freedoms and local cultures. In short, Pope John condemned the abuses of authority either by oppression or by neglecting to promote the welfare of men and women throughout the world. Communism was never explicitly mentioned.

When the peace of the world was threatened by the building of the Berlin Wall in 1961, the pope issued an appeal for peace which Nikita Khruschev, the Soviet leader, described as 'a good sign'. In spite of this crude attempt to take advantage of the propaganda value of the pope's appeal, a point of contact had been established between the Vatican and the Kremlin. John XXIII made another appeal for peace during the Cuban missile crisis in October 1963. The pope's obviously sincere concern for the preservation of world peace was an important factor in the improvement of relations and the cautious interest which the Russian press began to show in the progress of the Council. Two observers from the Russian Orthodox Church were allowed to attend and the leader of the Ukrainian Church, Archbishop Josef Slipyi of Lwow who had been imprisoned since 1945, was allowed to go to Rome. Khruschev himself sent a message of appreciation when the pope was nominated for the Balzan Peace Prize and John XXIII received the votes of all four Soviet representatives. Khruschev's daughter and son-in-law, the editor of *Izvestia*, were received in audience by the pope. And the last occasion on which Pope John left the Vatican was when he went to receive the Balzan Peace Prize in May 1963. John XXIII died less than two months after the publication of *Pacem in Terris*, but he had already given his last message to the world: the Church, renewed by the Council, must strive – with the help of other Christians and of all men of good will – to establish the unity and peace of all mankind.

Cardinal Giovanni Battista Montini was widely regarded as the one most likely to pursue the polices of John XXIII and Montini's election became so predictable that it was reported in the newspapers two hours before the announcement was actually made. It was typical of him that within days of his election as Pope Paul VI he had reconvened the Council which met shortly after the date originally fixed by his predecessor. Paul himself described the objectives of the Council as:

the self-awareness of the Church
its renewal
the bringing together of all Christians in unity
the dialogue of the Church with the contemporary world.

The new pope quickly showed that he was prepared to allow the deliberations of the Fathers to produce decrees that would scarcely have been imagined when the Council first opened and which paved the way for irreversible change in the attitudes and practices of Catholics throughout the world.

The Second Session was dominated by the debate on the *schema* on the Church. There were long and sometimes fierce discussions on such issues as the permanent diaconate and episcopal collegiality. In fact the opposition to the chapter on religious liberty and the declaration on anti-Semitism was so strong that they had to be revised and resubmitted at the next session, while some observers even feared that they might be suppressed altogether. In December 1963 the *schema* on the liturgy was approved almost unanimously. This was the first real achievement of the Council and revealed the extent of the progress that had been made. Latin was no longer the only or chief language of worship in the Catholic Church and the Council officially recognised the rights of local episcopal conferences in the implementation of liturgical reform. The pope later authorised the most complete and fundamental revision of the sacramental rites and the *Roman Missal* since the Council of Trent.

The Decree of Ecumenism, published in 1964, attempted to lay down the practice and principles governing the Catholic approach to ecumenism without jeopardising in any way the traditional claims of of the Church. The pope had committed himself to promoting Christian unity at the beginning of the Second Session and established Secretariats for Non-Believers as well as Non-Christians. In this first encyclical he had expressed his sorrow 'That We, who promote this reconciliation, should be regarded by many of Our separated brothers as an obstacle to it'. Paul was particularly concerned to heal the breaches with the Orthodox and Anglican Churches. Pope and Patriarch met in the Holy Land in 1963 and, two years later, solemnly lifted the mutual anathemas and excommunications. Paul personally visited Athenagoras in 1967 when the two leaders recognised their Churches as sister-Churches and the Patriarch's return visit to Rome in the same year was followed by a series of visits from leading Orthodox Patriarchs. In 1966 the pope received Archbishop Michael Ramsey of Canterbury and embraced him as a brother. The success of this meeting led to the establishment of the Anglican Roman Catholic International Commission which subsequently produced the 'agreed statements' on Eucharist, Ministry and Authority. A body to study contacts between Catholics and Lutherans had already been established in July 1965.

Meanwhile the Conciliar Decree on Ecumenism and the Constitutions on the Church and Revelation were completed without further difficulty during the Third Session in 1964. The last weeks of the Council in 1965 were rushed as the bishops passed decrees on Bishops, Religious and Seminaries, declarations on Christian Education and Non-Christian Religions, decrees on Divine Revelation and on the Laity, Mission and Priesthood, the declaration on Religious Liberty and the constitution on the Church and the World. In December 1965, at a farewell service for the observers, a pope for the first time joined in worship with non-Catholics. The closing ceremonies took place in the presence of delegations from 81 governments and nine international bodies; no secular government had been represented at the First Vatican Council.

In July 1968 the pope published *Humanae Vitae* in which he condemned abortion, direct sterilization as a means of contraception as well as every action which proposed as an end or a means to render procreation impossible. Although the encyclical had positive aspects – which were too often ignored at the time and can now be seen in a different perspective from that prevailing in the summer of 1968 – its publication undoubtedly occasioned the gravest crisis in Paul VI's pontificate and dramatically raised the crucial and significant issues of ecclesiastical infallibility, the rights of conscience and the responsibilities of Christian love in marriage. The fact that *Humanae Vitae* was published in a year which fell between two episcopal synods inevitably raised the question whether or not the pope should have first consulted the bishops and at the subsequent synod the pope himself appealed for unity. He accepted that collegiality was co-responsibility but emphasised that the pope's duty to respect episcopal rights must be balanced by their duty to recognise papal supremacy.

The establishment of Synods of Bishops had seemed one of the most promising reforms of the Council, and Paul himself was genuinely concerned to give tangible expression to the doctrine of episcopal collegiality as he was also determined to make the curia and the College of Cardinals more representative of the Church throughout the world. The synods first met every two years, and then every three years, to discuss a variety of subjects such as canon law, doctrine and liturgy, marriage, seminaries and priesthood, and the promotion of the work of the Pontifical Justice and Peace Commission. Early agendas were too crowded and unworkable and so the bishops began to concentrate on specific themes such as evangelisation and catechesis. Perhaps as a reaction against other developments in the Church, Paul VI firmly kept the synods under his own control and, although the sense of crisis over *Humanae Vitae* quickly passed, the inevitable tension and possibility of conflict between papal claims and episcopal demands, papal supremacy and episcopal collegiality remained to be resolved.

The New Dutch Catechism for Adults, which was first published in 1964, attempted to present contemporary theological scholarship in a popular way and was an immediate success. The authors consciously adopted a liberal, ecumenical approach in presenting the Christian teaching on creation, miracles and original sin or Catholic beliefs on the Mass and the Real Presence. They were, however, challenged by more conservative Catholics and defended by the Dutch bishops; appeals therefore were made to Rome. The bishops defended their right to explain the faith to the Dutch people and insisted on the necessity of finding new formulations for an unchangeable faith. The Roman authorities emphasised the role of the pope and questioned the validity of the language used by the Dutch theologians.

In 1969 the National Council of the Dutch Church voted in favour of the abolition of compulsory celibacy at a time when many priests and religious throughout the world were publicly rejecting celibacy and confidently expecting a relaxation of the canonical rules. The number who left the active ministry between 1960 and 1970 has no parallel since the sixteenth century. The pope's public defences of celibacy, including his sixth encyclical *Sacerdotalis Caelibatus* published in 1967, failed to satisfy the opposition in spite of support for the pope's stand from bishops throughout the world. In 1971 the National Federation of Priests' Council in the United States voted in favour of the abolition of compulsory celibacy, the Congolese bishops as well as priests meeting in Geneva supported the ordination of married men, and the Latin American Bishops' Council also voted for abolition.

A third major issue, which seemed for a time to threaten the union of the Holy See and the Church in the Netherlands, was the appointment of two bishops who were well-known for their opposition to some of the recent developments in Holland and for their devoted loyalty to Rome. On the other hand the appointment of Cardinal Johannes Willebrands, President of the Secretariat for Promoting Christian Unity, to succeed Cardinal Bernard Alfrink was universally welcomed on all sides. Willebrands was a moderate progressive who followed his predecessor's policy of being a bishop above parties. At the same time the controversies within the Dutch Church undoubtedly helped to weaken the cohesion and strength of Dutch Catholics.

The growing identification of the Church with the nations of the Third World reflected the fact that the number of Catholics in developing countries will soon and even substantially exceed the number of Catholics in North America and Europe. However Pope Paul also expressed genuine hopes and fears when he warned that, if the legitimate expectations of the developing nations were denied, this would have fatal consequences for the causes of international progress, peace and the very future of mankind. In *Populorum Progressio*, published in 1967, the pope denounced the inequitable distribution of wealth and power, and declared that the surplus wealth of the rich must be used for the benefit of the poor and dispossessed. Governments that supported or tolerated political economic or social exploitation were simply unjust and Paul's episcopal appointments were usually distinctly 'progressive'. He also consistently condemned the use of torture or official forms of repression by secular governments as well as all types of terrorism.

The pope's double concern for justice and peace found its focus in the United Nations whose Secretary-General, U Thant, he welcomed to Rome and whose Assembly he addressed on the feast of St Francis in 1965. U Thant himself recorded that he had been deeply moved by the papal address which 'was of historic importance and left a lasting impression on all the diplomats present, to whatever religion they belonged'. Paul VI was the first pope to travel outside Italy since the captive Pius VII in 1809. At the end of a journey to the Far East in 1970 Paul had travelled almost 70,000 miles, more than all his predecessors combined. All these journeys were designed to enable the papacy to play a vital role in contemporary politics by urging conciliation and agreement on the nations. As he himself once said, he was prepared to go anywhere in the cause of peace.

For Pope Paul, the diplomatic machinery of the Vatican was a means of presenting the claims of conscience and morality in the world at a time when the claims of power politics normally prevailed. His almost frenzied activities in support of justice and peace would seem to show that he was determined to avoid the accusation that the Holy See was 'silent', the accusation from which he defended the memory of Pius XII. While maintaining a strictly diplomatic neutrality, Pope Paul made many public appeals and used all diplomatic means at his disposal to end conflicts and establish justice and peace. He worked tirelessly to end the fighting in Vietnam, pleaded repeatedly for peace in the Middle East and Northern Ireland, offered to mediate in the conflict between India and Pakistan, publicly sympathised with the victims of terrorism such as the Israeli athletes at the Munich Olympics, offered himself in exchange for hostages held at Mogadishu airport and for Aldo Moro, the former Italian Premier and long-time friend who had been kidnapped.

In 1964 Pope Paul signed a *modus vivendi* with Tunisia, the first agreement between the Holy See and a nation which recognised Islam as the official state religion. By the tenth anniversary of his election some seventy nations had established diplomatic relations with the Vatican, the number having almost doubled since 1963. At the same time the Holy See was kept informed of developments throughout the world by 36 nuncios, 36 pro-nuncios, 16 apostolic delegates and a *chargé d'affaires*. Similarly the number of State Visits to the pope dramatically increased: there had been ten during the pontificate of Pius XI, 26 during that of Pius XII, 34 during the reign of Pope John and over ninety during Pope Paul's, whose visitors included Presidents Podgorny of Russia and Tito of Yugoslavia as well as Johnson, Nixon and Ford of the United States. In an effort to improve the conditions of Catholics living under Communist governments, Paul VI engaged in negotiations and sometimes secured agreements with Hungary, Czechoslovakia, Yugoslavia, Rumania, Poland and even Russia.

Nevertheless it is not difficult to paint a bleak picture of Catholicism during the pontificate of Paul VI. In the United States alone some ten million Catholics ceased attending Sunday Mass regularly and there was a more marked decline among those young Catholics who had received a complete Catholic education. Meanwhile the number of Catholics educated in Catholic schools there fell by two million, the number of baptisms by almost half a million and the number of converts by about 50,000. According to a survey conducted in 1976, three out of four Catholics approved of sexual intercourse for engaged couples, eight out of ten approved of contraception, seven out of ten of legalised abortion, while four out of ten did not believe that the pope was infallible. But it was not simply that the gap between practising and non-practising Catholics was continuing to widen. Roman Catholics formed a smaller proportion of mankind in the second half than they had at the beginning of the twentieth century, as a result of the population explosion in the East and political, social and economic developments in the West where industrialisation and the abuse of resources, militarism and Communism, secularism and scepticism, indifference and materialism threatened the very future of religion.

However practising Catholics in the modern age were probably more active and devoted than most of their predecessors, while new movements and organisations helped them to meet the problems and challenges of the times. The renewed appreciation of scripture, the liturgical movement, pastoral and catechetical initiatives, spiritual and devotional developments, were all signs of a deeper and richer Christian life. Pope Paul's greatest achievement was to ensure the continuation of his predecessor's revolution and the implementation of the decrees and constitutions of the Vatican Council particularly those on liturgy, collegiality and ecumenism. Furthermore the papacy itself was stronger and more influential during the second half of the twentieth century than it had been at the beginning as the popes increasingly promoted their spiritual and moral influence, not just within the Church but throughout the world. The extent of Paul's contribution to this development can be gauged from the attendance at his funeral in 1978.

Metropolitan Nikodim of Leningrad celebrated a short liturgy for the dead before the body of the pope in St Peter's. Paul was buried in a simple wooden coffin beside which was a single candle, a symbol of

Christ the light of the world. The funeral rites were broadcast live to some 48 nations. There were official delegations present from 95 nations, including representatives from Poland, Hungary and Eastern Germany. Kurt Waldheim, Secretary-General of the United Nations, was also present. There were delegates from thirteen other Christian Churches including the Greek and Russian Orthodox, Rumanian and Bulgarian Orthodox, the Archbishop of Cyprus, Coptic Patriarch of Alexandria, the Old Catholic Union of Utrecht as well as the retired Archbishop of Canterbury, Michael Ramsey, who wore the ring the Pope had given to him in 1966. Pope Paul had emphasised not the political or even the ecclesiastical dignity of the papacy but his role as the 'Servant of the servants of God'. And the chief form of papal service anticipated by Pope John and developed by Pope Paul may well be to stand not only for the unity of Catholics, or even of Christians, but of all men; the pope's function being to increase unity throughout the world so that all men may be one in Christ.

Since he died of a heart attack after only 34 days, commentators have come to very different conclusions about the sort of pope that John Paul I might have been. He issued no major statements, made no great changes in the curia and never even celebrated Mass as Pope on the high altar of St Peter's. At the same time 'the smiling Pope' captivated his audiences and especially children by his humility, modesty and joyful confidence; qualities which also endeared him to people through the world. He refused to wear the tiara, symbol of secular as well as religious authority, and described his first papal Mass as the inauguration of his ministry as supreme pastor rather than a coronation. He rejected the use of such titles as 'Head of the Church' or 'Vicar of Christ' in favour of 'Pope' or 'Bishop of Rome', and he also avoided the use of the majestic plural. Pope John Paul I showed that he was determined to continue the work of his two immediate predecessors. He was committed to implementing the decrees of the Second Vatican Council, promoting ecumenism 'without hesitation', reforming Canon Law, accepting the implications of collegiality, working for development and progress, justice and peace, and the evangelisation of the world. It is difficult to see how without such a programme Catholic Christians can hope to deal with the problems facing Christianity and the Church during the last two decades of the twentieth century; and it is surely not without significance that the first non-Italian pope since 1523, and the first Polish pope in the history of the Church, should have taken the name John Paul II.

Table of major events in Church history

1864   Publication of the *Syllabus of Errors*

1869   Opening of the First Vatican Council

1879   Publication of *Aeterni Patris*

1891   Publication of *Rerum novarum*

1899   Publication of *Testem benevolentiae*

1905   Separation of Church and State in France

1907   Publication of *Lamentabili* and *Pascendi*

1917   Papal letter to the leaders of the belligerent nations

1922   Papal mission to Russia

1926   Condemnation of *Action Française*

1929   Lateran Treaty

1931   Publication of *Non abbiamo bisogno*

1936   Publication of *Mit brennender Sorge, Divini Redemptoris* and *Nos es muy*

1939   U.S. mission to the Vatican

1943   Publication of *Divino Afflante Spiritu*

1962   Opening of the Second Vatican Council

1968   Publication of *Populorum Progressio*; papal visits to Africa and South America, and to the Far East and Australia in 1970

List of popes and their reigns

St. Peter, 29–67
St. Linus, 67–78
St. Cletus, 78–90
St. Clement I, 90–100
St. Anacletus, 100–112*
St. Evaristus, 112–121
St. Alexander I, 121–132
St. Sixtus I, 132–142
St. Telesphorus, 142–154
St. Hyginus, 154–158
St. Pius I, 158–167
St. Anicetus, 167–175
St. Soter, 175–182
St. Eleutherius, 182–189
St. Victor I, 189–98
St. Zephyrinus, 199–217
St. Callistus I, 221–227
St. Urban I, 227–233
St. Pontian, 233–238
St. Anteros, 238–239
St. Fabian, 240–250
St. Cornelius, 251–253
St. Lucius I, 253–254
St. Stephen I, 254–257
St. Sixtus II, 257–258
St. Denis, 259–268
St. Felix I, 269–274
St. Eutychian, 275–283
St. Caius, 283–296
St. Marcellinus, 296–304
St. Marcellus I, 308–309
St. Eusebius, 309–310
St. Melchiades, 311–314
St. Silvester I, 314–335
St. Mark, 336
St. Julius I, 337–352
St. Liberius, 352–366
St. Damasus I, 366–384[1]
St. Siricius, 384–399
St. Anastasius I, 399–401
St. Innocent I, 402–417
St. Zozimus, 417–418

St. Boniface I, 418–422
St. Celestine I, 422–432
St. Sixtus III, 432–440
St. Leo I, 440–461

St. Hilary, 461–468
St. Simplicius, 468–483
St. Felix III,[1] 483–492
St. Gelasius I, 492–496
St. Anastasius II, 496–498
St. Symmachus, 498–514
St. Hormisdas, 514–523
St. John I, 523–526
St. Felix IV, 526–530
Boniface II, 530–532
John II, 532–535
St. Agapitus I, 535–536
St. Silverius, 536–537
Vigilius, 537–555
Pelagius I, 555–561
John III, 561–574
Benedict I, 575–578
Pelagius II, 578–590
St. Gregory I, 590–604
Sabinian, 604–606
Boniface III, 607
St. Boniface IV, 608–615
St. Deusdedit I, 615–619
Boniface V, 619–625
Honorius I, 625–638
Severinus, 638–640
John IV, 640–642
Theodore I, 642–649
St. Martin I, 649–655
St. Eugene I, 654–657
St. Vitalian, 657–672
Deusdedit II, 672–676
Donus I, 676–678
St. Agatho, 678–681
St. Leo II, 682–683
St. Benedict II, 684–685
John V, 685–686

Conon, 686–687
St. Sergius I, 687–701
John VI, 701–705
John VII, 705–707
Sisinnius, 708
Constantine, 708–715
St. Gregory II, 715–731
St. Gregory III, 731–741
St. Zachary, 741–752
Stephen II, 752[2]
St. Stephen III, 752–757
St. Paul I, 757–767
Stephen IV, 768–772
Hadrian (or
Adrian) I, 772–796
St. Leo III, 796–816
St. Stephen V, 816–817
St Pascal I, 817–824
Eugene II, 824–827
Valentine, 827
Gregory IV, 827–844
Sergius II, 844–847
St. Leo IV, 847–855
Benedict III, 855–858
St. Nicholas I, 858–867
John VIII, 872–882
Marinus I, 882–884
Adrian III, 884–885
Stephen VI, 885–891
Formosus, 891–896
Boniface VI, 896*
Stephen VII, 896–897
Remanus, 897–898
Theodore II, 898
John IX, 898–900
Benedict IV, 900–903
Leo V, 903
Christopher, 903–904*
Sergius III, 904–911
Anastasius III, 911–913
Lando, 913–914
John X, 914–928

*Popes marked with an asterisk are not included in all lists.
[1]Some lists include a Felix II, pope from 355. No general agreement is possible on the dates of the popes in the first three centuries.
[2]This pope died before being consecrated. He is not included in some lists and his successor is then counted as Stephen II.

Leo VI, 928–929
Stephen VIII, 929–931
John XI, 931–935
Leo VII, 936–939
Stephen IX, 939–942
Martin III,[3] 942–946
Agapetus II, 946–955
John XII, 955–964
Benedict V, 964–965
John XII, 965–972
Benedict VI, 972–973
Donus II, 974*
Benedict VII, 974–984
John XIV, 984–985
John XV, 985–996[4]
Gregory V, 996–999[5]
Silvester II, 999–1003
John SVII, 1003
John XVIII, 1003–1009
Sergius IV, 1009–1012
Benedict VIII, 1012–1024
John XIX, 1024–1033
Benedict IX, 1033–1044
Gregory VI, 1044–1046[6]
St. Clement II, 1046–7
Damascus II, 1048
St. Leo IX, 1049–1054[7]
Victor II, 1055–1057
Stephen X, 1057–1058
Nicholas II, 1059–1061
Alexander II, 1061–1073
St. Gregory VII, 1073–1085
B. Victor III, 1086–1087
B. Urban II, 1088–1099
Pascal II, 1099–1118
Gelasius II, 1118–1119
Calixtus II, 1119–1124
Honorius II, 1124–1130
Innocent II, 1130–1143
Celestine II, 1143–1144

Lucius II, 1144–1145
B. Eugene III, 1145–1153
Anastasius IV, 1153–1154
Adrian IV, 1154–1159[8]
Alexander III, 1159–1181
Lucius III, 1181–1185
Urban III, 1184–1187
Gregory VIII, 1187
Clement III, 1187–1191
Celestine III, 1191–1198

Innocent III, 1198–1216
Honorius III, 1216–1227
Gregory IX, 1227–1241
Celestine IV, 1241
Innocent IV, 1243–1254
Alexander IV, 1254–1261
Urban IV, 1261–1264
Clement IV, 1265–1268
B. Gregory X, 1271–1276
B. Innocent V, 1276
Adrian V, 1276
John XXI, 1276–1277
Nicholas III, 1277–1280
Martin IV, 1281–1285
Honorius IV, 1285–1287
Nicholas IV, 1288–1292
St. Celestine V, 1294
Boniface VIII, 1294–1303[9]
B. Benedict XI, 1303–1304[9]
Clement V, 1305–1314
John XXII, 1316–1334
Benedict XII, 1334–1342
Clement VI, 1342–1352
Innocent VI, 1352–1362
B. Urban V, 1362–1370
Gregory XI, 1370–1378
Urban VI, 1378–1389

Boniface IX, 1389–1404
Innocent VII, 1404–1406
Gregory XII, 1406–1415
Alexander V, 1409–1410
Alexander V, 1409–1410[10]
John XXIII, 1410–1415[10]
'Clement VII,' 1378–1394[11]
'Benedict XIII,' 1394–1423[11]
Martin V, 1417–1431 (Colonna)
Eugene IV, 1431–1447 (Condulmare)
Nicholas V, 1447–1455 (Parentucelli)

Calixtus III, 1455–1458 (Borgia)
Pius II, 1458–1464 (Piccolomini)
Paul II, 1464–1471 (Barbo)
Sixtus IV, 1471–1484 (Della Rovere)
Innocent VIII, 1484–1492 (Cibo)
Alexander VI, 1492–1503 (Borgia)
Pius III, 1503 (Piccolomini)
Julius II, 1503–1513 (della Rovere)
Leo X, 1513–1521 (Medici)
Adrian VI, 1522–1523 (Boyens)
Clement VII, 1523–1534 (Medici)
Paul III, 1534–1549 (Farnese)

[3]In some lists Martin III is styled Marinus II, and Marinus I as Martin II.
[4]Some lists insert as John XV, pope for a few weeks in 985 and then reckon this pope John XV as John XVI.
[5]Some lists include a John XVII as pope 997–8; he was in fact an anti-pope.
[6]Some lists insert a Sylvester III, 1045 before Gregory VI.
[7]Leo VIII, 963–5, was not the lawful pope.
[8]The English pope, Nicholas Breakspear.
[9]Boniface VII, 984, was an anti-pope as was Benedict X, 1058
[10]These two popes elected by the Council of Pisa.
[11]The French anti-popes of the Great Schism.

Julius III, 1550–1555
(del Monte)
Marcellus II, 1555
(Cervini)
Paul IV, 1555–1559
(Carafa)
Pius IV, 1559–1565
(Medici)
St. Pius V, 1566–1572
(Ghislieri)
Gregory XIII, 1572–1585
(Buoncompagni)
Sixtus V, 1585–1590
(Peretti)
Urban VII, 1590
(Castagna)
Gregory XIV, 1590–1591
(Sfondrati)
Innocent IX, 1591
(Fachinetti)
Clement VIII, 1592–1605
(Aldobrandini)
Leo XI, 1605
(Medici)
Paul V, 1605–1621
(Borghese)
Gregory XV, 1621–1623
(Ludovisi)
Urban VIII, 1623–1644
(Barberini)
Innocent X, 1644–1655
(Pamfili)

Alexander VII,
1655–1667
(Chigi)
Clement IX, 1667–1669
(Rospigliosi)
Clement X, 1670–1676
(Altieri)
Ven. Innocent XI,
(Odescalchi)
1676–1689
Alexander VIII,
1689–1691
(Ottobuoni)
Innocent XII, 1691–1700
(Pignatelli)
Clement XI, 1700–1721
(Albani)
Innocent XIII, 1721–1724
(Conti)
Benedict XIII, 1724–1730
(Orsini)
Clement XII, 1730–1740
(Corsini)
Benedict XIV, 1740–1758
(Lambertini)
Clement XIII, 1758–1769
(Rezzonico)
Clement XIV, 1769–1774
(Ganganelli)
Pius VI, 1775–1799
(Braschi)

Pius VII, 1800–1823
(Chiaramonti)
Leo XII, 1823–1829
(della Genga)
Pius VIII, 1829–1830
(Castiglioni)
Gregory XVI, 1831–1846
(Cappellari)
Pius IX, 1846–1878
(Mastai-Ferretti)
Leo XIII, 1878–1903
(Pecci)
Pius X, 1903–1914
(Sarto)

Benedict XV, 1914–1922
(della Chiesa)
Pius XI, 1922–1939
(Ratti)
Pius XII, 1939–1958
(Pacelli)
John XXIII, 1958–1963
(Roncalli)
Paul VI, 1963–1978
(Montini)
John Paul I, 1978
(Luciani)
John Paul II, 1978
(Woytyla)

Notes on further reading

To prepare an adequate bibliography of Church history, even if it were to be restricted to works written in English, would almost be to produce another book. However, it is possible, first, to recommend several general histories of the Church for readers who would like to go into more detail.

GENERAL WORKS
SPCK study notes:
John Foster: *The First Advance*, AD 29–500 and *Setback and Recovery*, AD 500–1500
Alan Thomson: *New Movements*, AD 1500–1800.

The Pelican History of the Church:
Henry Chadwick: *The Early Church*
R.W. Southern: *Western Society and the Church in the Middle Ages*.
Owen Chadwick: *The Reformation*.
G.R. Cragg: *The Church and the Age of Reason, 1648–1789*.
Alec R. Vidler: *The Church in the Age of Revolution*.
Stephen Neill: *The History of the Christian Missions*.

The Christian Centuries Series edited by L.J. Rogier, R. Aubert and M.D. Knowles:
Jean Daniélou and Henri Marrou, *The First Six Hundred Years*.
David Knowles and Dimitri Obolensky, *The Middle Ages*.
Roger Aubert and Others, *The Church in a Secularised Society*.

A *History of the Christian Church* which will ultimately provide, in some twenty volumes, a full survey of Christianity within Europe and beyond:
Owen Chadwick: *The Popes and the European Revolution*.
Robert T. Hardy: *A History of the Churches in the United States and Canada*.

The most complete series at present available is *History of the Church* in ten volumes edited by Hubert Jedin, with contributions from many contemporary historians. These volumes are detailed with footnotes, sources and guides to further reading.
Volume 1 – From Apostolic Community to Constantine the Great.
Volume 2 – The Imperial Church after Constantine the Great.
Volume 3 – The Church in the Age of Feudalism.
Volume 4 – From the High Middle Ages to the Eve of Reformation.
Volume 5 – Reformation and Counter-Reformation.
Volume 6 – The Church in the Age of Absolutism and Enlightenment.
Volume 7 – The Church between the Revolution and Restoration.

Volume 8 – The Church in the Age of Liberalism.
Volume 9 – The Church in the Industrial Age.
Volume 10 – The Church in the Twentieth Century.
Other general surveys, available in paperback, are:
J.W.C. Wand; *A History of the Early Church to* AD *500* and *A History of the Modern Church from 1500 to the Present Day.*
Margaret Deansley: *A History of the Medieval Church* AD *590–1500.*

Following this list of general histories, we are giving recommendations of further more specific studies which we have found useful. They are listed below, under the chapter divisions of this book.

Chapter 1 – *The Early Church to 461 (pages 11–44)*

Among the books that can be recommended to give an overall picture of the world into which Christianity first emerged are P. Brown *The World of Late Antiquity* (1971); R.M. Grant *Augustus to Constantine* (1971) and *Early Christianity and Society* (1978); and R.A. Markus *Christianity in the Roman World* (1974). General histories include H. Conzleman *History of Primitive Christianity* (1973); W.H.C. Frend *The Early Church* (1965); J.G. Davies *The Early Christian Church* (1965) while A.H.M. Jones *The Decline of the Ancient World* (1975) offers useful background reading. Two valuable earlier works are T.G. Jalland *The Church and the Papacy* (1944) and *The Life and Times of St Leo the Great* (1941).

There are now available in paperback several collections of primary source material including two volumes edited by J.S. Stevenson *A New Eusebius, documents to 337* and *Creeds, Councils and Controversies, 337–461* (1966). H. Bettenson had translated and edited two very helpful collections of writings called *The Early Christian Fathers* and *The Later Christian Fathers* (1970). Good, short introductions to the lives and teachings of some of the major figures in this period are given by H. von Campenhausen in *The Fathers of the Latin Church* (1964) and *The Fathers of the Greek Church* (1963). The history of the growth of the creeds and of doctrine is covered extremely well by J.N.D. Kelly in his *Early Christian Creeds*, now available in paperback (1981), and *Early Christian Doctrines* (1958). A smaller and very helpful book is R. Barr *Main Currents in Early Christian Thought* (1965). E. Schillebeeckx in *Ministry* (1980) devotes the opening chapter to discussing the question of the development of the Threefold Ministry, and A. Kee *Constantine versus Christ* (1981) invites the reader to reassess the contribution of Constantine to the growth of Christianity.

Chapter 2 – *The development of the Western Church and its final separation from the East, 461–1198 (pages 45–80)*

General histories covering the whole of the medieval period, and therefore applicable to this and the following chapters, include N. Cantor *Medieval History* (1965); B. Tierney and S. Painter *Western Europe in the Middle Ages*

300–1475 (1970);G. Barraclough (Ed) *Eastern and Western Europe in the Middle Ages* (1970).

Works more applicable to this early period of medieval history include E.K. Rand *Founders of the Middle Ages* (1928); C. Dawson *The Making of Europe* (1932); R.W. Southern *The Making of the Middle Ages* (1953); and H. Trevor-Roper *The Rise of Christian Europe* (1964). J.M. Wallace Hadrill *The Barbarian West 400–1000* traces the break-up of the Old Roman Empire and the repopulation and new balance of power in the West, while the general history of the Papal States is given in P. Partner *The Lands of St Peter* (1972). The best known biography of Gregory the Great is probably still F.H. Dudden *Gregory the Great* (2 volumes, 1905) but J. Richards *The Consul of God* (1980) replaces it in part; and the same author has also written *The Popes and the Papacy in the Early Middle Ages* (1979), a subject also covered in P. Llewellyn *Rome in the Dark Ages* (1971).

Of special interest to the Church in the British Isles are Bede's *Ecclesiastical History* and *The Anglo-Saxon Chronicle*. The first is a history written by St Bede, who died in 735, and the second selected documents to 1154. L. Hardinge *The Celtic Church in Britain* (1972) and D.J.V. Fisher *The Anglo-Saxon Church* (1973) are both readable and informative, while W. Levison *England and the Continent in the Eighth Century* (1946) still has its value. C.H. Talbot has edited *The Anglo-Saxon Missionaries in Germany*, now available in paperback, which gives lives and other writings and details of Willibrord, Boniface and others. D. Knowles *Christian Monasticism* (1959) is an authoritative short history of monasticism from its origins through to the twentieth century. Of all the Western monks of this period Benedict is of great importance and the *Rule of Benedict* is available in paperback in several editions, among them a translation and edition by J. McCann (1970). D. Farmer *Benedict's Disciples* (1980) is a collection of essays on Benedict and others.

Finally there are two source books edited by B. Tierney *The Middle Ages (Volume 1): Sources of Medieval History* and *The Middle Ages (Volume 2): Readings in Medieval History* which provide primary source material to be taken in conjunction with his more general history. Another source book, H.R. Loyn and J. Percival *Documents of Medieval History, Volume 2: The Reign of Charlemagne* (1975), provides valuable information on the life and reign of this important medieval figure.

Chapter 3 – *Papalism and Conciliarism, 1198–1455 (pages 81–117)*

The history of the papacy throughout the Middle Ages is a subject of crucial importance and W. Ullmann *A Short History of the Papacy in the Middle Ages* (1972) is a full and tightly argued work on it. The reader who wants to go further into the development of the papacy as an institution should consult W. Ullmann *The Growth of Papal Government in the Middle Ages* (1959), and F. Oakley *The Western Church in the Later Middle Ages* (1979). Another less detailed work on the papacy is G. Barraclough *The Medieval Papacy* (1968). B. Tierney *Crisis of Church and State* (1964), G. Mollat *The*

Popes at Avignon (1963) and W. Ullmann *The Origins of the Great Schism* (1948) all discuss particular incidents in papal history. Monasticism and the Religious Orders are described and discussed in D. Knowles *The Religious Orders in England*, 3 Volumes (1948) which remains a classic. S. Tugwell in his edition of *Early Dominicans, A Selection of their writings* (1983) gives an introduction to the life and work of Dominic. The material on Francis of Assisi is vast but J.R.H. Moorman *Saint Francis of Assisi* (1976) is a useful introduction and the complete writings of Francis and Clare have recently been translated and edited by R.J. Armstrong and I. Brady *Francis and Clare, The Complete Works* (1983).

D. Knowles *The Evolution of Medieval Thought* and G. Leff *Medieval Thought* (1958) are two short works which introduce the reader to the history of ideas and philosophy in this period, as does M. Lambert *Medieval Heresy* (1977). R.I. Moore *The Birth of Popular Heresy* (1975) and C.M.D. Crowder *Unity, Heresy and Reform 1378–1460* (1977) are volumes 1 and 3 of the series *Documents of Medieval History* and provide selections from primary source material. S. Runciman *History of the Crusades* remains the fullest and most readable account of the Crusading ideal and movement. J.R.H. Moorman *A History of the Church in England* (1976) and D.L. Edwards *Christian England (Volume 1): Its story to the Reformation* (1981) are both informative works.

The reader will find a general atlas helpful in giving a geographical picture to the historical story. The Penguin *Atlas of World History (Vol. 1)* (1974) and Nelson *An Atlas of World History* edited by S. De Vries, T. Luykx and W.O. Henderson (1965) are both useful, although the latter gives larger and more detailed maps.

Chapter 4 – *The Protestant Reformation and the progress of Catholic Reform 1455–1648 (pages 118–172)*

The material on the Reformation and Post-Reformation period is vast and only a limited and readily available selection is suggested here. On the general political and social background J.R. Hale *Renaissance Europe 1480–1520* (1971) and G.R. Elton *Reformation Europe 1517–1559* (1963) are part of the (paperback) Fontana History of Europe series. Two more modern approaches are S. Ozment *The Age of Reform, 1250–1550* (1980) and *The Reformation in the Cities* (1975). Among more specifically religious histories are R. Bainton *The Reformation of the 16th century* (1953); J.M. Todd *The Reformation* (1972); and J. Dolan *History of the Reformation* (1975). G. Rupp *Luther's Progress to the Diet of Worms* (1964) is a short, authoritative treatment of Luther's life. R.H. Bainton *Here I Stand – a Life of Martin Luther* (1959) is a longer biography. G. Rupp *The Righteousness of God* is an exposition of the main points of Luther's theology. G. Ebeling *Luther, An Introduction to his Thought* can also be recommended. F. Wendel *Calvin* (1963) devotes half his book to a biography of John Calvin and the second half to a discussion of his theology. J.T. McNeill *The History and Character of Calvinism* (1967) discusses both Calvin and his successors, concluding with an appraisal of Calvinism today. J. Dillenberger *Martin Luther, A Selection from his writings* (1961) and *John Calvin, A Selection from his Writings* (1971) offer the reader quite extensive selections from the main writings of both men.

A.G. Dickens *The English Reformation* (1964) and G.R. Elton *Reform and Reformation in England 1509–1558* (1977) give accounts of the Reformation in England. P. Hughes *The Reformation in England (3 Volumes)* (1953) is an impressive and detailed work from a Roman Catholic scholar. *Essays on the Scottish Reformation 1513–1625* ed D. McRoberts (1962) is a large compilation of essays which gives fairly specialised information on the reasons for and course of the Scottish Reformation. P. Janelle *The Catholic Reformation* (1963) traces the history of the Catholic response to the Protestant Reformation. H. Jedin *History of The Council of Trent* in two volumes (1957) is a detailed study of this famous council. A smaller work by Jedin is *The Crisis and Closure of the Council of Trent* (1967). Two source books are H.J. Hillerbrand *The Protestant Reformation* (1968) and A.G. Dickens and D. Carr *The Reformation in England to the Accession of Elizabeth – a selection of documents* (1962).

Chapter 5 – The Age of Rationalism and Absolutism, 1648–1789 (pages 173–210)

Useful general histories on this period include E.E.Y. Hales *Revolution and Papacy 1769–1846* (1960) and F. Heyer *The Catholic Church from 1648 to 1870* (1969). J. Delumeau *Catholicism between Luther and Voltaire* (1977) re-evaluates some traditional interpretations. More specialized studies include C.A. Bolton *Church Reform in 18th Century Italy* (1969); B. Groethuysen *The Bourgeois: Catholicism vs. Capitalism in Eighteenth Century France* (1968); and R.R. Palmer *Catholics and Unbelievers in Eighteenth Century France* (1939).

There are several accounts of intellectual developments at the time including the relevant volumes of F. Copleston's *A History of Philosophy* and B. Willey's *Seventeenth-Century Background* and *Eighteenth-Century Background*, all of which have been reprinted several times. Other looks worth mentioning in this context are G.R. Cragg *From Puritanism to the Age of Reason* (1950); P. Gay's anthologies *Deism* (1968) and *The Enlightenment* (1973); and those edited by S. Hampshire *The Age of Reason* and I. Berlin *The Age of Enlightenment*, first published in 1956. The growth of toleration has been fully covered in the two volumes by J. Lecler *Toleration and the Reformation* (1960) and the development of missionary activity exhaustively described in seven volumes by K.S. Latourette, *A History of the Expansion of Christianity* (now available in paperback). L. Cognet *Post-Reformation Spirituality* (1959) can be consulted on the history of spirituality, R.A. Knox *Enthusiasm* (1959) is still useful on Jansenism, while W.V. Bangert *A History of the Society of Jesus* (1972) and D. Mitchell *The Jesuits* (1980) are helpful modern histories of the order.

Chapter 6 – The Church, Revolution, and Reaction, 1789–1914 (pages 211–256)

General histories covering the nineteenth century include K.O. von Aretin *The Papacy and the Modern World* (1970); E.E.Y. Hales *The Catholic Church in the Modern World* (1958); J.D. Holmes *The Triumph of the Holy See* (1978); and K.S. Latourette *Christianity in a Revolutionary Age* in five volumes now available in paperback.

There are several useful studies and histories of the Church in France: A. Dansette *Religious History of Modern France* (1961) in two volumes; M. Larkin *Church and State after the Dreyfus Affair* (1974); J. McManners *Church and State in France 1870–1914* (1972), and *The French Revolution and the Church* (1969); P. Spencer *Politics of Belief in Nineteenth-Century France* (1954); A.R. Vilder *A Century of Social Catholicism 1820–1920* (1964), and *Prophecy and Papacy: A Study of Lamennais, the Church and the Revolution* (1954). A Dru has produced an authoritative short account of the Church in Germany, *The Church in the Nineteenth Century* (1963). J. Hennessey *American Catholics* is now the standard single-volume account of Catholicism in the United States. See also for England J.D. Holmes *More Roman than Rome: English Catholicism in the Nineteenth Century* (1978); for Italy, A.C. Jemolo *Church and State in Italy 1850–1950* (1960), and for a picture of Rome at the time, N. Blakiston (Ed.) *The Roman Question: Extracts from the dispatches of Odo Russell from Rome 1858–1870* (1962). C. Butler *The Vatican Council*, first published in two volumes in 1936 and reprinted in a one-volume edition in 1962, is still one of the better accounts of the Council, while E.E.Y. Hales has painted a sympathetic yet scholarly picture of *Pio Nono: A study in European politics and religion in the nineteenth century* (1956). The best single biography of *John Henry Newman* is that by C.S. Dessain . B. M. G. Reardon *Liberalism and Tradition: Aspects of Catholic thought in Nineteenth-century France* is account of intellectual developments there.

Chapter 7 – The Church and the modern world, 1914–1978 (pages 257–293)

General histories of Church and Papacy in the twentieth century include C. Falconi *The Popes in the Twentieth Century* (1967); J.D. Holmes, *The Papacy in the Modern World* (1981); and F.X. Murphy, *The Papacy Today* (1981). P. Nichols *The Politics of the Vatican* (1968) and *The Pope's Divisions* (1981), and P. Hebblethwaite *The Year of the Three Popes* (1979), are among the better commentaries on the contemporary papacy. Two informed books dealing with recent ecclesiastical developments are J.A. Hardon *Christianity in the Twentieth Century*, and W.A. Purdy *The Church on the Move* (1966). The significance of Pope John XXIII is well described by E.E.Y. Hales, *Pope John and his Revolution* (1965) while the Pope's own *Journal of a Soul* was published in the same year and in paperback. J. Guitton

The Pope Speaks (1968) is almost equally revealing on Pope Paul VI. A. Rhodes *The Vatican in the Age of the Dictators, 1922–1945* (1973) and H. Stehle *Eastern Politics of the Vatican 1917–1979* (1981) are the best discussions of the attitudes within the Vatican to various totalitarian regimes although D.A. Binchy *Church and State in Fascist Italy* (1941) and P.W. Mariaux *The Persecution of the Catholic Church in the Third Reich* (1940) are still worth reading. T. Haecker *Journal in the Night* (1949) and B. Häring *Embattled Witness: Memories of a Time of War* (1977) are moving testimonies of committed Catholic theologians, a layman and a priest, during the war years.

The development of the ecumenical movement is covered by H.E. Fey *The Ecumenical Advance: A History of the Ecumenical Movement, 1948–1968* (1970) and by G.H. Tavard *Two Centuries of Ecumenism* (1960). J.A. Coleman *The Evolution of Dutch Catholicism, 1958–1974* (1978) has carefully analysed events in the Netherlands.

Index